GREENBERG'S® AMERICAN TOY

TRAINS

From 1900 with Current Values!

Gary A. Beimborn
100 Harbor Blvd. #52
Belmont, CA 94002

by

Dallas J. Mallerich III

Wallace-Homestead Book Company

Radnor, Pennsylvania

LIONEL® AND AMERICAN FLYER® ARE THE REGISTERED TRADEMARKS OF THE LIONEL COR-PORATION, New York, New York. Lionel and American Flyer trains are manufactured by Lionel Trains, Inc. of Mount Clemens, Michigan, the licensee of the Lionel Corporation.

Histories, Listings and Values for —
LIONEL • AMERICAN FLYER • MARX • IVES • AND MORE!

Copyright © 1990
Bruce C. Greenberg

Greenberg Publishing Company, Inc.
7566 Main Street
Sykesville, MD 21784
(301) 795-7447

Also published by:
Wallace-Homestead
A Division of Chilton Book Company
Radnor, PA 19089

First Edition

Manufactured in the United States of America

Greenberg Publishing Company, Inc. offers the world's largest selection of Lionel, American Flyer, Marx, Ives, LGB, and other toy train publications as well as a selection of books on model and prototype railroading, dollhouse miniatures, and toys. For a copy of our current catalogue, send a stamped, self-addressed envelope to Greenberg Publishing Company, Inc. at the above address.

Greenberg Shows, Inc. sponsors the world's largest public model railroad, dollhouse, and toy shows. The shows feature extravagant operating model railroads for N, HO, O, Standard, and 1 Gauges as well as a huge marketplace for buying and selling nearly all model railroad equipment. The shows also feature a large selection of dollhouses and dollhouse furnishings. Shows are currently offered in metropolitan Baltimore, Boston, Ft. Lauderdale, Cherry Hill in New Jersey, Long island in New York, Norfolk, Philadelphia, Pittsburgh, and Tampa. To receive our current show listing, please send a self-addressed stamped envelope marked *Train Show Schedule* to the address above.

Library of Congress Cataloging-in-Publication Data

Mallerich, Dallas J.
     Greenberg's American Toy Trains: from 1900 with current values!/
by Dallas J. Mallerich. — 1st ed.
        p. cm.
    ISBN 0-87069-579-7
     1. Railroads — Models. I. Greenberg Publishing Company.
II. Title.
TF 197.M225 1990
625.1'9—dc20
                                        90-38043
                                           CIP

1 2 3 4 5 6 7 8 9 0   9 8 7 6 5 4 3 2 1 0

Acknowledgments

In a work this large, there are many people to thank — from those who have given their encouragement to those who have rolled up their sleeves and put their pens to paper. Over the past fifteen or so years, the quality and depth of Greenberg publications have improved dramatically (from a good beginning!) due to the concern of literally thousands of enthusiasts who have shared their views, concerns, and expertise.

The following individuals actively participated in the review of the historical accounts, listings, and values included in this book:

Bob Burgio, Phil Catalano, Alfred Clarke, Jim Flynn, Joe Grzyboski, Frank Hare, David Hoover, Marty Johnson, Roland Manz, Ron Martin, Dave McEntarfer, Bill Nelson, John Newbraugh, John Parker, James Peterson, Lou Redman, Larry Reed, Pete Riddle, I. D. Smith, Mike Solly, Stan Troski, and **Charles Weber.**

The following individuals have authored, coauthored, or edited the *Greenberg Guides* used as a basis for this handbook (several of these people also helped directly on this edition):

John Bradshaw, Marcy Damon, Donna Dove, Jack Fazenbaker, Cindy Lee Floyd, Bruce Greenberg, Linda Greenberg, John Hubbard, Roland LaVoie, Eric Matzke, Al McDuffie, Harwood Owings, Chris Rohlfing, Alan Schuweiler, and **James Walsh.**

Quite a few of the black and white photographs were taken by our friend **Roger Bartelt.** Several additional photographs were provided by **Larry Archer.** Those not credited were taken by Greenberg staff photographers over the years. For this edition, darkroom preparation of the various photographs was skillfully handled by **Brad Schwab** and **Bill Wantz.**

In addition to outside contributors, there is always the friendly assistance of fellow Greenberg staff members to remember. **Donna Price**, proofreader, patiently reviewed each page for content and style to insure its readability and accuracy for our readers. **Maureen Crum, Samuel Baum**, and the author collectively designed the front and rear covers, with special thanks going to Maureen for her creativity. **Wendy Burgio** lent a helping hand when it came time to enter Donna's many corrections. In addition to helping with the cover, Samuel Baum, production supervisor, reviewed the historical prefaces for each chapter for style and clarity.

The Author

Dallas Mallerich was born in 1964 in Washington, DC. Raised in Ellicott City, Maryland, he attended the University of Maryland and received a BA in Economics with a certificate in Accounting. Although he originally intended to make a career of financial planning, he has resigned himself to his full-time occupation of "professional train enthusiast."

Although Dallas received his first train set at age two, he did not develop a real interest in trains until his teenage years. His interests include building finely-scaled models as well as collecting unusual small-scale toy trains.

Dallas authored his first book, *Greenberg's Guide to N Gauge Trains*, at age 17. In 1987 he finished an ambitious book entitled *Greenberg's Guide to Athearn Trains*, which documented both the history and production of one of the nation's leading HO train manufacturers. He has edited and contributed to numerous Greenberg publications. Additionally, he has written articles for *NTrak Newsletter, N-Thusiast, N-Scale,* and *Railroad Model Craftsman.*

Dallas and his wife Teresa reside in suburban Maryland. Together they actively enjoy many hobbies, including toy and model trains, antique and reproduction dolls, antique automobiles, and Habsburg history.

GREENBERG'S® AMERICAN

Introduction

Color Gallery

Lionel

American Flyer

TOY TRAINS

Marx

Ives

Other Toy Train Makers

Glossary

VARIETY! Brendon Floyd (above) is impressed by the variety of shapes and sizes used by toy train makers. From left to right: (1) a Märklin Z scale model of an experimental German train, (2) an HO model of an old-fashioned steam locomotive, (3) a Lionel O Gauge model of the General — a Civil War locomotive popularized by Disney's movie, (4) an LGB train with "Americanized" headlight and cowcatcher on a German-style train, and 5) a sample of Lionel's big Standard Gauge trains from the early 20th century. Behind Brendon is a sampling of American and European toy trains collected by publisher Bruce Greenberg.

Foreword

I think toy trains are great, and I am very pleased that I have been asked to write a book that would meet the needs of so many people — from the individual who rediscovers the toys of his or her youth in a dusty attic to the antiques and collectibles dealers who wish to be more conversant about these charming examples of Americana.

Over the years, the related hobbies of collecting and operating toy trains have grown so tremendously that entire volumes are dedicated to very specific topics, such as repairing prewar (pre-World War II) Lionel trains or collecting boxed sets sold by Lionel. The challenge for the newcomer or casual collector is that of finding material that is informative, but not overwhelming. I believe that this compact guide will do just that.

Greenberg's American Toy Trains is designed to help you identify and value the most widely-collected and widely-available electric toy trains made in the United States since 1900. These include models by Lionel, American Flyer, Ives, and Marx. I have focused primarily on the Standard Gauge (also called Wide Gauge), O Gauge, and S Gauge models, which are the ones most commonly described as "toy trains." For Lionel, I have also included listings of the company's early 2-7/8" Gauge trains, which you are not likely to stumble upon too often, and the smaller OO Gauge trains that are similar in size to today's popular HO scale models. Collectors of Marx trains are often interested in all of that company's models, so I have also included 3/16" scale Marx trains.

Over the years, scores of companies have produced toy trains and accessories. Many of these names are utterly forgotten, while others are associated with trains eagerly collected by small groups of dedicated specialists. To help you identify a few of the "other" companies, I have provided a brief overview of eighteen firms with representative listings of their products. Although their trains are no longer prevalent in the marketplace, some of these firms were in their time very powerful. Carlisle & Finch, for example, led the American manufacturers of electric toy trains in the late 1890s. Dorfan, at one time, gave Ives, American Flyer, and Lionel very stiff competition in the years between World Wars I and II. Where possible, I have indicated where you can find additional information about these companies.

Sometimes, one will find fairly recent examples of HO scale "starter sets" at swap meets and flea markets. These include the sets made by Bachmann, Life-Like, and Tyco that are sold through chains such as Toys 'R Us and mail-order by companies like Sears. Although these certainly can be enjoyable, they simply have not enjoyed the nostalgic value associated with the stockier O Gauge and Standard Gauge trains of Christmas Past. In order to maintain a reasonably compact guide, we have omitted the trains that fall into the "scale model" category, including HO, N, and Z scale models. Collectors should not be discouraged, however, as the Greenberg catalogue features a number of fine books about these and other specialized topics.

Another recent specialty is collecting LGB trains. Made in Germany, these fine models operate indoors or outdoors (even in the snow!). Their bright colors and sturdy construction appeal to a growing number of families. For more information about LGB trains, consult either *Greenberg's Guide to LGB Trains* for identification and values or *Model Railroading with LGB,* a Greenberg publication, for ideas about building an indoor or outdoor layout.

Now that I have told you what you will find in the listings of this book, I would like to pass on some information about buying and selling toy trains, deciding whether or not to clean them, and a few words of warning about the pitfalls you may encounter. All aboard!

Gathering Information

As you might expect, buying and selling toy trains requires some special effort. After all, you cannot sell them on the side of the road as a vegetable grower might sell his/her wares. Nor can you simply walk into an antique shop and expect a broad variety of toy trains. Although toy trains can be bought and sold through newspaper advertisements and indeed found at antique shops, there exists a highly developed network of clubs, shops, magazines, and meet-style exhibitions through which the greater portion of toy train transactions occur.

Among the clubs, there are national groups, such as the Train Collectors Association (TCA), the Lionel Collectors' Club of America (LCCA), the Lionel Operating Train Society (LOTS), and the Toy Train Operating Society (TTOS), which offer regular publications and sponsor meets for their members. Another place to meet other collectors is your local hobby shop. Check the Yellow Pages (look under "Hobbies" or "Hobby Shops") and look for shops that offer "new and used" equipment, current Lionel trains, or other items of interest to you. Often, the clerks at these shops are hobbyists who can direct you to more information.

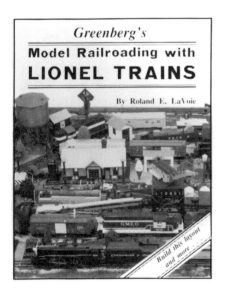

Greenberg's

Model Railroading with

LIONEL TRAINS

By Roland E. LaVoie

Build this layout and more . . .

Train collectors and modelers are fortunate to have a large variety of magazines and books available to them. This excellent guide provides an introduction (or reintroduction) to hobbyists building layouts with Lionel trains.

In addition to the various club publications, you might enjoy periodicals such as *Classic Toy Trains, Model Railroader,* or *Railroad Model Craftsman.* These are generally available at newsstands and book stores that offer a large selection of magazines. You might also check your local library.

Train shows are usually advertised both in the magazines mentioned above and in the current events columns of local newspapers. It is well worth the price of admission to attend one of these shows, even if you only want to look at trains. Basically, train collectors come from all walks of life: doctors, lawyers, accountants, engineers, construction workers, sales people, etc. In public settings, you generally cannot look at a person and tell whether or not he or she likes toy trains. At a train show, however, there is no mistaking them! People come dressed in T-shirts decorated with the logos of famous toy train manufacturers or famous real railroads. They come with decorative railroad belt buckles, engineer's caps, pins, and buttons. Most of all, they come with a great deal of enthusiasm. If you really want to learn about toy trains, one of the best things to do is to go talk to other people who are already established in the hobby.

Before you make any major purchases, be certain that you have an idea of what specialization you might wish to adopt. Will you buy only American Flyer or Lionel trains? Do you wish to have only trains made during the years of your childhood? Would you like to have a collection of trains lettered for the real railroads in your area, regardless of manufacturer? The possibilities may seem endless!

Once you have established a goal, it will be easier to make sensible purchases — be certain to decide on a budget before you go too far!

Buying and Selling Toy Trains

When you attend a train show or review mail-order selling lists, you are likely to note some discrepancy in prices. This occurs for several reasons. First of all, sellers are motivated by different reasons. Some are private collectors who occasionally sell duplicates to fund other additions to their collections. Others are casual dealers; they buy and sell trains fairly actively, but their livelihoods do not depend upon it. Still others are full-time professionals, with overhead expenses such as shop rent, travel expenses, advertising and mailing costs, etc.

The most obvious factors affecting train values are **supply** and **demand**. A 1957 Chevy is hardly "rare," nevertheless it is one of the most sought-after automobiles of the period. In toy trains, there are many analogies. The "baby boomers" enjoyed some of Lionel's most innovative trains — locomotives with smoke, diesels with horns, milk cars with automatic unloading mechanisms, and a variety of animated accessories. Although these were manufactured in relatively large quantities, they are among the most sought-after toy trains of our century. True, the most common cabooses and gondolas (cars found in nearly every train set) bring only $2-3 a piece, but certain locomotives, when found in top condition, easily bring four-figure prices.

Another factor that affects prices is the **relative knowledge** of the buyer and seller. Quite simply, what appears to be a very ordinary train to one person might be viewed as a great rarity by a specialist. Unfortunately, some dealers over-react to this possibility by marking virtually everything in their stock with high prices justified by the words "scarce" and "rare" on the price tags. If you cannot justify the difference between a dealer's price and those found in this or other reliable price guides, seek more information! Ask a knowledgeable friend to look at the item for you. If you are at a show, ask the people who are running it whether they can recommend an expert who will help you make a decision.

The **personalities** of the buyer and seller also affect prices. Some people are very friendly, others are very stubborn. Although prices are not always negotiable, it is seldom offensive if you politely ask. The major exceptions would be larger shops in which em-

A prime showcase for the forces of supply and demand is the auction. In April 1989 the Lionel Boy's Set being displayed here was sold for a record-setting $23,000 before an anxious crowd. Courtesy Greenberg Auctions.

ployees simply would not have the authority to negotiate and other shops, small or large, posting signs that indicate firm prices.

The seller's **desire to sell** and a buyer's **eagerness to buy** affect both the price and the terms of a transaction. At various shows, I have often encountered dealers who say, "I've got to sell this today — make me an offer!" and others who say, "You won't see another one like this — that price is *firm!*" Occasionally, I have accidentally driven up the price that I have paid as a buyer. This happens when you are so excited to find an item that you say, "I'll take it!" before you ask "How much?"

The prices that you find in this guide are based on *obtained* prices, rather than asking prices. Generally, the prices reported here represent a "ready sale," or a price perceived as a fair value by the buyer. They may sometimes appear lower than those seen on trains at meets for two reasons. First, items that sell often sell in the first hour of a train meet, and therefore, are no longer visible. (A good portion of the action at most meets occurs in the first hour — when everyone is rushing around looking for the best deal.) The items that do not sell in the first hour have a higher price tag, and this price, although not representing the sales price, is the price observed. Another source of discrepancy is the willingness of some sellers to bargain over price — a factor that few are likely to note on their price tags!

Prices reported for scarce items and for desirable items in better condition reflect transactions between knowledgeable buyers and sellers.

Still other factors may affect prices. Some dealers go to a great deal of effort to carry a selection of items in a highly-specialized field. Naturally, they go to extra effort in finding these items, and they expect to market them appropriately. Other dealers may go to great pains to clean and service their pieces (these steps should only be done by knowledgeable dealers or collectors!), and thus they may reasonably expect a premium for the extra services provided. Prices also vary by region.

The staff at Greenberg Publishing Company receives many inquiries as to whether or not a particular piece is a "good value." This book will help answer that question; but, there is NO substitute for experience in the marketplace. *We strongly recommend that novices do not make major purchases without the assistance of friends who have experience in buying and selling trains.*

In the case where there is insufficient data upon which to establish a value, I have indicated No Reported Sales (NRS) in the value column. Although some items may be rare or otherwise valuable, NRS alone does not indicate that a piece is a high-value item. In some cases, a new variation might be listed as NRS, simply because the item's scarcity could not be determined immediately.

If you sell your trains to a dealer who is going to resell them, you should expect to receive approximately half of the prices shown here. This is fair considering that the dealer will have to pay for advertising or tables at shows and that he or she is likely to have the trains for some time before they are actually sold. For scarcer and high-dollar items, you can often achieve a much higher price (up to 70% or 80% of the values shown).

Condition

One of the major factors affecting values is an item's condition. I have provided values for each item in "Good" and "Excellent" conditions. The following definitions should help you grade your trains:

FAIR — Well-scratched, chipped, dented, rusted or warped.

GOOD — Scratches, small dents or dings, dirty.

VERY GOOD — Few scratches, exceptionally clean, no dents or rust.

EXCELLENT — Minute scratches or nicks, no dents or rust, all original and virtually unused.

LIKE NEW — Virtually mint, only the faintest signs of handling, such as fingerprints or very minor discoloration.

MINT — Brand new, absolutely unmarred, all original and unused, in original box with any additional items that came with it, such as instruction sheets, and factory inspection slip.

Although items in mint condition generally bring a premium over those in excellent condition, novices are recommended to be wary of dealers using the term loosely. Advanced collectors will remove mint items from their original boxes only with white gloves and only on rare occasions — such as presenting them for photography in a book. New dealers might be well-advised to grade items conservatively; it is one of the best ways to build a business with repeat customers.

To Clean or Not to Clean

DON'T! Many times, individuals who have a single train to sell have asked me whether they should clean it up first. My answer is almost always, "Don't!" Toy trains are manufactured with a variety of finishes — lacquer or enamel paints, lithography, brass plating, etc. — and it requires special knowledge to clean each one correctly. Generally, it is safe to remove dust with a soft cloth, but do not use any household cleaners or even soap and water unless you know exactly what you are doing. Collectors who are interested in buying your trains will not usually be discouraged by dirt or dust on a toy.

The same advice applies to dealers. If you specialize in selling antique watches, do not assume that the same cleaning techniques can be used on trains.

If you feel that you must clean your trains, consult one of the Greenberg how-to books and talk to experienced friends. *Greenberg's Model Railroading with Lionel Trains* by Roland LaVoie provides many easy-to-use suggestions for proper cleaning and light maintenance.

In some cases, items that have been **restored** may look like original items in excellent or better condition. Most clubs require sellers to identify restored trains as such, but buyers must beware anytime they are considering a large purchase. Generally, restored items will bring prices at or slightly above those shown for original items in good condition. Like cleaning, restoring trains is a skill that must be carefully developed.

Storage, Packaging, Shipping

I personally subscribe to the notion that a collection of trains should be displayed properly to provide the most enjoyment. I like wooden cases with sliding glass doors. These allow your house guests to enjoy your trains, while protecting them from dust and fingerprints. By displaying trains, you may discover that some of your friends are budding collectors themselves or that others may have trains that they would be willing to sell to you.

If you cannot display your train collection, you should store the items carefully to protect them from excess heat or moisture. Think twice before putting them in your basement or attic. Will they stay clean and dry?

If you are taking your trains to a dealer or to a show to sell them, you should wrap them in newspaper or bubble-wrap to keep them from bumping each other. Special items or items in top condition deserve special treatment, such as cloth wrappings or other protective packaging.

If you are shipping your trains to a collector whom you have reached by mail, to an auction house, or to a mail-order dealer, be certain to package them very carefully. Allow for plenty of packing material — styrofoam peanuts, crumbled newspaper, or shredded paper — to buffer the items against shock. Keep in mind that couplers and the various protruding details on your trains may be fragile. A few minutes of preparation in packing trains can save hours of frustration if an item is broken.

It is usually a good idea to take advantage of the insurance offered by carriers such as the US Post Office and United Parcel Service; the cost is nominal. Be certain to follow their guidelines for packaging to be certain that your claim will be satisfied should damage occur.

Identification

Many times, I have heard, "I have an old Lionel locomotive and four cars — how much are they worth?" Unfortunately, answering such a question is not easy. Even if we know the specific year, we must know which locomotive. Remember the analogy of a 1957 Chevy? A two-door convertible certainly sells better than a station wagon. Likewise, the top of the line locomotives from a given year usually have greater values than those of the common engines.

The following guidelines should help you as you thumb your way through this guide whether you are looking for the trains you had as a kid or trying to decide how much to pay for a set sitting before you at a flea market. Admittedly, there are many exceptions that must be overlooked to make these generalized guidelines; nevertheless, they should prove very useful on the whole.

LIONEL: This company had the most aggressive marketing department of the major toy train makers. Therefore, it is not surprising that they proudly placed their name on many of their trains. Many Lionel trains are lettered with some variation of the following: "BUILT BY LIONEL", "LIONEL LINES", or the stylized "L" within a circle on this side. Others may be identified with a plate indicating "BUILT BY LIONEL" or something similar on the underside.

The Lionel Corporation identified its trains in many different ways, including lettering on the sides, raised lettering on locomotive castings, brass plates, and identification plates on the undersides of locomotives (as shown here). R. Bartelt photograph.

Most Lionel trains are numbered according to Lionel's catalogue numbers (as opposed to using real train numbers, as scale model makers would). This system makes Lionel trains among the easiest to identify. Simply locate the item number and look it up in the numerical list. In some cases, the number on the side differs from the catalogue number. I have tried to provide appropriate cross references for these items.

Prewar Lionel — Mostly tinplate rolling stock, many with lettering on brass plates; die-cast or tinplate locomotives. Prewar production includes primarily O Gauge and Standard Gauge, which were widely sold and still readily found. You are not very likely to find the earliest 2-7/8" Gauge models often; if you do find them, beware of reproductions. The later prewar OO Gauge models are found occasionally; they are about the same size as HO trains.

Postwar Lionel — Most popular period, covers 1945-1969; mostly plastic rolling stock with metal trucks and frames; locomotives have die-cast or plastic bodies. Lionel introduced a short-lived line of HO trains in 1957. Although they have not been widely popular with Lionel collectors, the HO models constitute an emerging interest field. The HO trains will be covered in an upcoming Greenberg's Guide.

Modern Era Lionel — In 1970 Fundimensions licensed the rights to manufacture and sell Lionel trains. Although Fundimensions began by marketing to the toy market, the company expanded to include collectors by introducing special editions and nostalgic re-issues of classic Lionel pieces. Most models have molded plastic bodies with various metal components. Some steam locomotives have die-cast bodies.

AMERICAN FLYER: Like Lionel, American Flyer typically put its name on the trains, with lettering such as "BUILT BY AMERICAN FLYER" or "AMERICAN FLYER LINES". Unfortunately, the catalogue numbers do not correspond to train numbers quite so neatly. Once you have determined whether the item is prewar Wide Gauge, prewar O Gauge, or postwar S Gauge, you can check for the number in the corresponding section. If that does not lead you directly to the item, then try matching the road name; that is the lettering on the side of the item, such as "CHICAGO AND NORTH WESTERN". Some of the early cast-iron American Flyer locomotives have raised letters "A. F." on the cabs.

At one time, brass plates were the most "fashionable" method for decorating toy trains. Here is an example of a plate with American Flyer markings (prewar). R. Bartelt photograph.

Prewar Wide Gauge — Models made for 2-1/4" Gauge track, same as Lionel's Standard Gauge. Most models have enameled tinplate bodies with brass plates or rubber-stamped lettering. Locomotives have either tinplate or die-cast bodies.

Prewar O Gauge — Either clockwork or electrically-powered locomotives; cast-iron, die-cast metal, or tinplate locomotives; mostly tinplate rolling stock. American Flyer's prewar trains may not have identification marks; look for faint lettering, lettering on undersides of motors, etc. to aid in identification.

Postwar S Gauge — About two thirds the size of O Gauge, these are the classic American Flyer trains remembered by members of the "baby boom" generation; they were marketed in head-to-head competition with Lionel's larger O Gauge models. Distinctive in that they run on two-rail track, these models usually have plastic or die-cast bodies. These trains have distinctive link-type couplers, which are apparent in the photographs used to illustrate the listings in the appropriate section.

Close-up of a Marx/Marlines logo from a stamped-steel coal tender. R. Bartelt photograph.

MARX: Generally speaking, Marx trains dominated the "low end" of the toy train market. The majority of Marx trains are made from either lithographed steel (which was used all the way into the 1970s) or plastic (which was adopted quite early). The round Marx logo features "MAR" superimposed upon a large "X". The round trademark, "MARLINES", "JOY LINE", "LINEMAR", and "MARX-TRONIC" are some of the identifying trademarks that you may spot.

Marx trains were sold in many different outlets, including Montgomery Ward, J. C. Penney, Sears Roebuck, and Western Auto. It is not uncommon to find a Marx set in a box carrying another brand name.

Individual items may or may not have identifying catalogue numbers. Therefore, I have broken down the Marx listings under descriptive headings to make identification somewhat easier. If you have a particularly large collection to evaluate, I would heartily recommend the two-volume *Greenberg's Guide to Marx Trains*, which is profusely illustrated in color.

IVES: Ives produced a variety of O Gauge and Standard Gauge tinplate trains before World War II. The majority were either lithographed or enameled — the latter with either rubber-stamped lettering or brass plates. Most Ives trains have some form of identification, such as "IVES LINES" or "THE IVES RAILWAY LINES" on their sides. Some of the lithographed cars had prototypical (real railroad) markings on the sides; these usually had some form of Ives identification on the ends.

Sometimes it is difficult to identify an Ives piece, because the rubber-stamped lettering has worn off an early enameled piece. In these and similar cases, it is best to study the photographs in this and other guides to lead you to the correct manufacturer. Then scan the listings for similar items, looking for identifiers, such as "boxcar" to identify the car type and colors or markings that will place your car.

Like the other big firms, Ives used a variety of techniques for marking its trains. This boxcar has rubber-stamped lettering on the end. R. Bartelt photograph.

Fakes and Reproductions

In the world of train collecting, you will find that collectors are interested in having more than just one of "each" car produced by a certain manufacturer. They are, in fact, interested in a variety of subtle variations that may be found within a particular item's production. For example, a car made during a five-year production run might be found with different types of trucks or couplers, representing the changing technology during its manufacture. The same car might also be found in different colors, representing either accidental changes by the production department or deliberate changes intended to make an item "more realistic" or "more colorful" to promote sales.

Because of the high prices that legitimate paint or color samples or rare variations bring among collectors, certain unscrupulous (or worse) elements of the hobby have in the past years attempted to "create" paint or color samples by various techniques.

With the help of Charles Weber, a chemist and long-time train collector, and letters from concerned individuals, the Greenberg staff has become aware of a number of items that have resulted from chemical alteration. Among the effects achieved are the change of yellow lettering to white or off-white, the change of yellow or orange bodies to white or off-white without disturbing the normal shade or color of the original black lettering, and the change of paint from silver to gold. There are a number of other techniques that have been used, so collectors — even advanced collectors — are well advised to use extra caution when considering unusual pieces. You might consider asking for a written guarantee of authenticity from the dealer or collector selling an unusual piece, but expert inspection should still be made when possible.

In addition to fakes, collectors and dealers should be aware that there is a substantial market for reproductions of old and/or rare toy trains. This can cause a fair amount of confusion. Selling reproductions is a legitimate way of bringing some truly classic designs within the financial reach of average collectors. Unfortunately, some people try to pass off reproductions as original pieces; some even go to the trouble of artificially aging the models to give them the patina of years past.

Reproductions are *not* all indicated in the listings. In some listings, I have indicated that a reproduction has been made of a certain item. This is intended to help you raise the question when considering a purchase. Reproductions, when sold and marked as such, have an acceptable place in the hobby.

Ready, Set, Go!

Now that you have read through this brief overview, you are ready for the next step. Thumb through the text and study a few listings in each section, look at the photographs and note the characteristics unique to each company's trains, then go to trains shows or flea markets and begin observing them in person.

The hobby of collecting toy trains can provide endless hours of enjoyment for you as it has to thousands of others. *Welcome aboard!*

— Dallas Mallerich

LIONEL PREWAR STANDARD GAUGE: This attractive train is made up of several early Standard Gauge items, including the No. 5 steam locomotive with a four-wheel tender, the 12 Lake Shore gondola, the 14 CM & StP boxcar, and the 17 NYC & HRRR caboose. R. Sullens Collection.

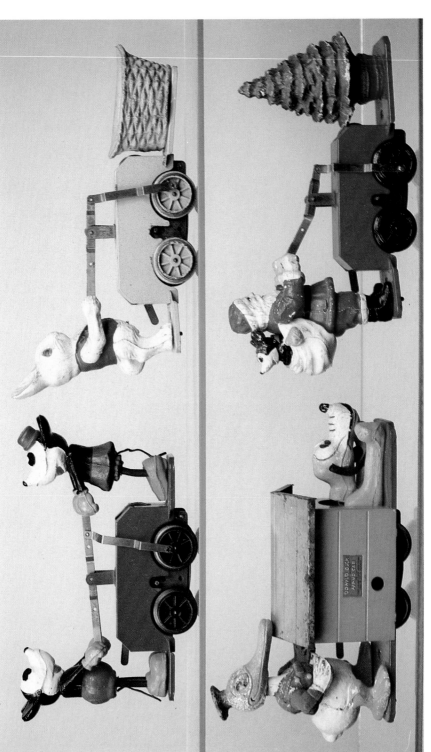

LIONEL PREWAR O GAUGE. *Folklore has it that the Mickey Mouse handcar set saved the Lionel Corporation from the clutches of the Great Depression, but the truth is that Lionel's more realistic trains — such as the streamline Flying Yankee — put Lionel back on its financial feet. Shown here are the 1100 Mickey and Minnie handcar, the 1103 Peter Rabbit handcar, the 1107 Donald Duck handcar, and the 1105 Santa and Mickey handcar. R. Sullens Collection.*

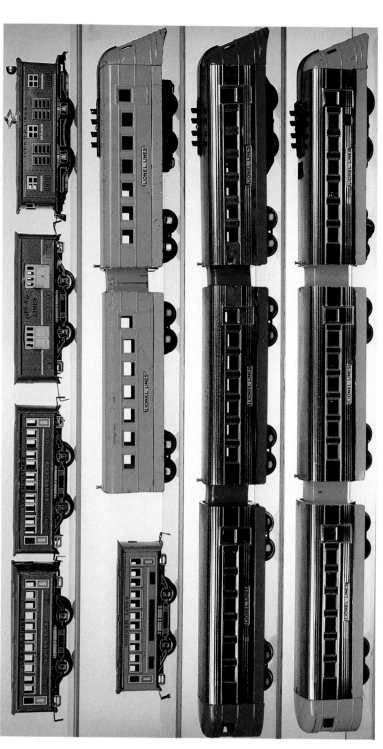

LIONEL PREWAR O GAUGE. After Lionel acquired Ives, it used the Ives trademark for its low price train sets. The set on the top shelf includes an 1810 locomotive, 1813 baggage car, and two 1811 Pullmans. The 1011 Pullman on the second shelf is a Lionel "Winner Lines" car derived from the Ives design. The orange streamline units on the second shelf are the 1700 locomotive and 1701 coach. The chrome and red streamline set is made up of the 1700 locomotive, the 1701 coach, and the 1702 observation. The chrome and orange streamline set on the bottom shelf includes the 1816 locomotive, 1817 coach, and 1818 observation.

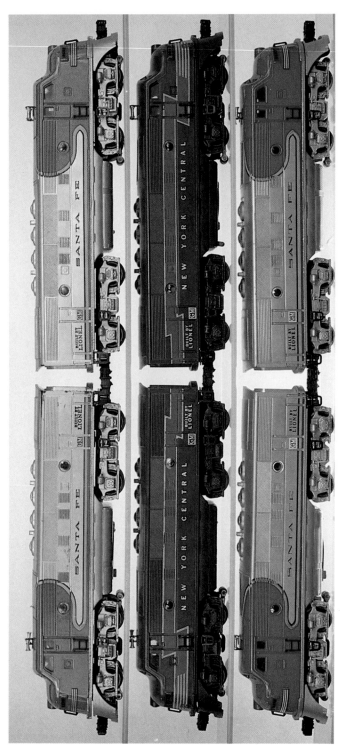

LIONEL POSTWAR O GAUGE. The F-3 series started in 1948 with the 2333 Santa Fe AAs shown on the top shelf and the 2333 New York Central AAs. The 2343 Santa Fe AA on the bottom shelf was introduced in 1950. Advanced collectors place great importance on the subtle difference in the "BUILT BY LIONEL" and "GM" decals that can be found when the two sets of Santa Fe diesels are compared. L. Nuzzaci Collection.

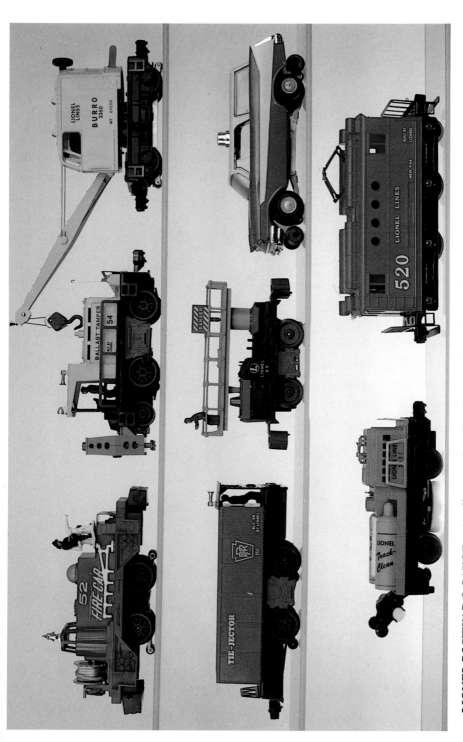

LIONEL POSTWAR O GAUGE. A collection of small, self-powered novelties collectively called "motorized units." From left to right, the 52 Fire Car, 54 Ballast Tamper, and 3360 Burro crane. On the second shelf the 55 Tie-Jector, 69 maintenance car, and 68 executive inspection car. On the bottom shelf, the 3927 track cleaning car and 520 box cab electric. L. Nuzzaci and R. Lord Collections.

LIONEL POSTWAR O GAUGE. *Here is a Lionel train set the way many people remember them, spread out on the living room floor. This is Set 49N9694 sold by Sears in 1961. It features the 746 N & W locomotive, which did not appear in the Lionel catalogue.*

R. Greisbeck Collection.

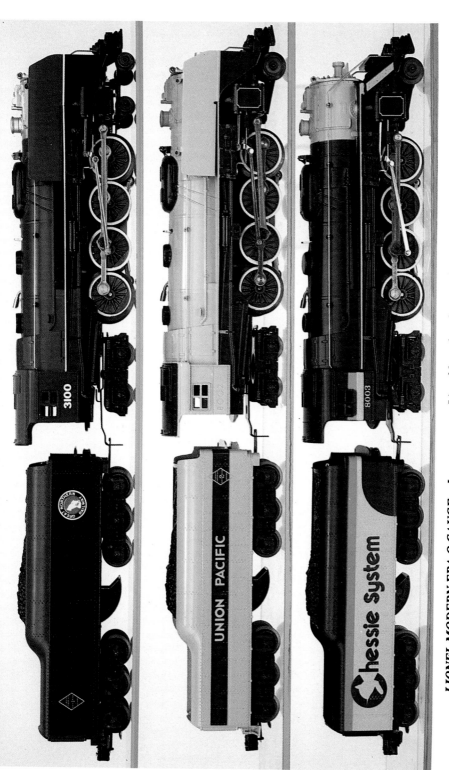

LIONEL MODERN ERA O GAUGE. In recent years Lionel has placed an emphasis on producing colorful steam locomotives, such as the three shown here. Featured: 3100 Great Northern, 8002 Union Pacific, and 8003 Chessie System. A. Rudman, F. Stem, and L. Caponi Collections.

LIONEL MODERN ERA O GAUGE. A colorful assortment of diesel locomotives. On the top shelf, the 1776 Bicentennial locomotive and the special edition 1976 Bicentennial locomotive produced for the Train Collectors Association. On the middle shelf, the 7500 Lionel 75th Anniversary Special locomotive of 1975 and the 8050 Delaware & Hudson U36C of 1980. On the bottom shelf, the 8061 Chessie System and the 8155 Monon. A. Rudman, F. Stern, L. Caponi, and R. LaVoie Collections.

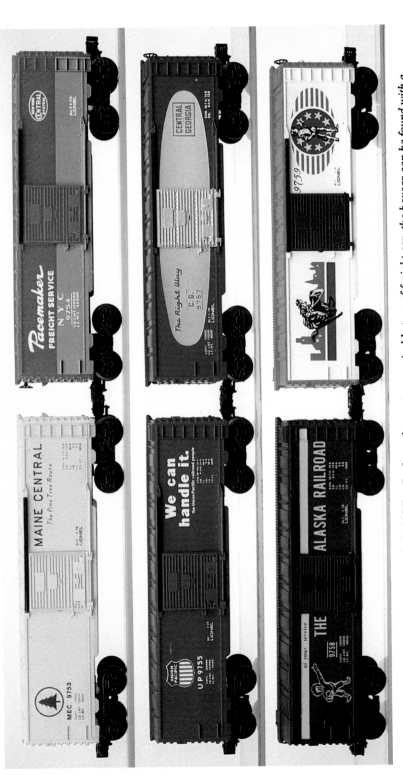

LIONEL MODERN ERA O GAUGE. *Perhaps the most recognizable type of freight car, the boxcar can be found with a variety of decorative heralds and railroad names. On the top shelf, the 9753 Maine Central and the 9754 New York Central Pacemaker. On the middle shelf, the 9755 Union Pacific and the 9757 Central of Georgia. On the bottom shelf, the 9758 Alaska Railroad and the fanciful 9759 Paul Revere boxcar. A. Rudman, L. Caponi, F. Stem, and R. LaVoie Collections.*

AMERICAN FLYER PREWAR WIDE GAUGE. The handsome Lone Scout set features a 4635 electric-outline loco-motive, the 4250 Club Car, 4251 Pullman, and the 4252 observation (shown in two versions on the bottom shelf).

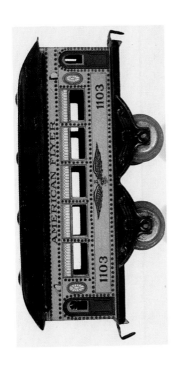

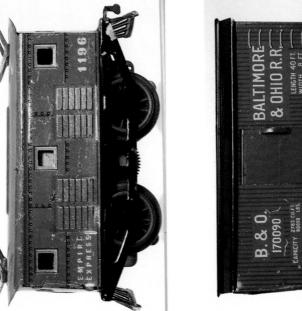

AMERICAN FLYER PREWAR O GAUGE. Shown here are several interesting lithographed cars. From top left, the 1196 Empire Express locomotive, the 1103 American Flyer coach (with the popular winged-locomotive herald), the 1110 B & O boxcar (numbered 170090 on the car), and the 1117 American Flyer caboose.

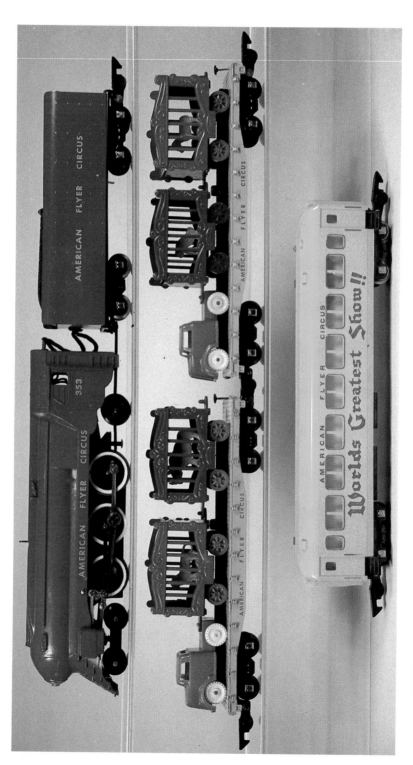

AMERICAN FLYER POSTWAR S GAUGE. *A child's delight, the American Flyer Circus train with a brilliant red 353 streamline locomotive, two flatcars, and a Pullman coach. Of course adults enjoy these a great deal, too! R. Loria Collection.*

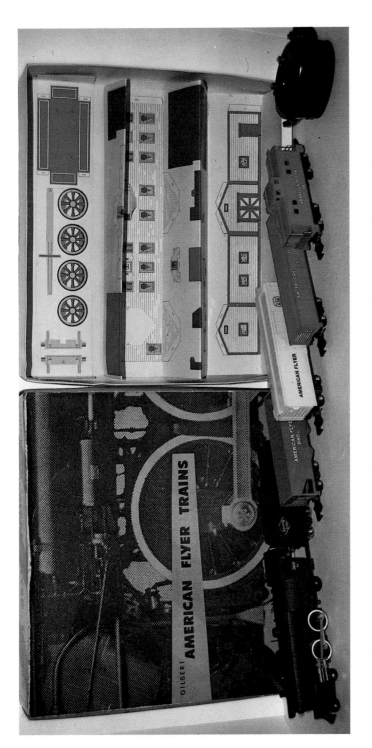

AMERICAN FLYER POSTWAR S GAUGE. In 1950 American Flyer offered this appealing set with a cut-out paper farm set as an accessory. Today the original farm set is very desirable, but reproductions are available for those more budget-minded. Original shown here from the R. Loria Collection.

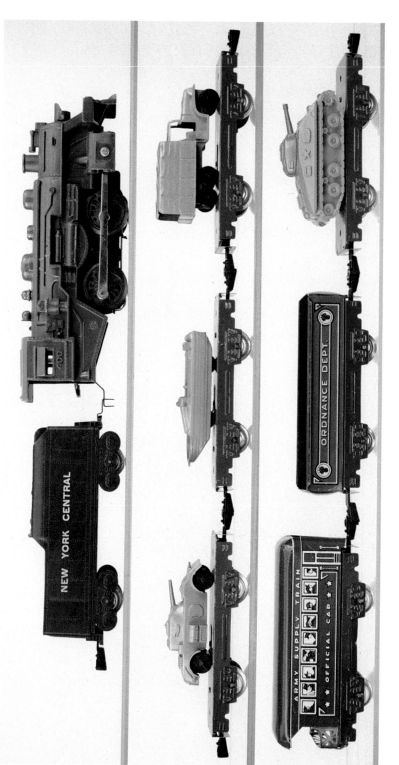

MARX O GAUGE. The Army set with its removable (and often lost) loads gave kids plenty of play action. It is powered by the 400 locomotive with (1951) tender. The cars on the middle shelf are (572M) flatcars with various military vehicles. The cars on the bottom shelf are the (558M) Official Car, the (552M) Ordnance Dept. gondola, and another (572M) flatcar. H. Diehl Collection.

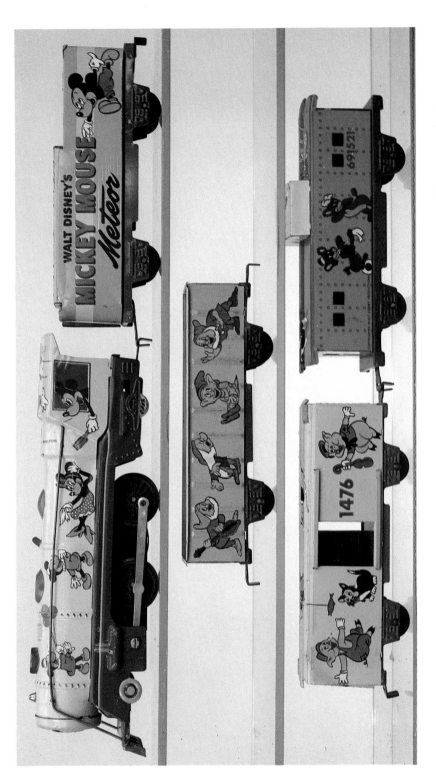

MARX O GAUGE. The Mickey Mouse Meteor train is almost completely covered by colorful illustrations of Disney characters. The opposite side of the train has a different set of characters! H. Diehl Collection.

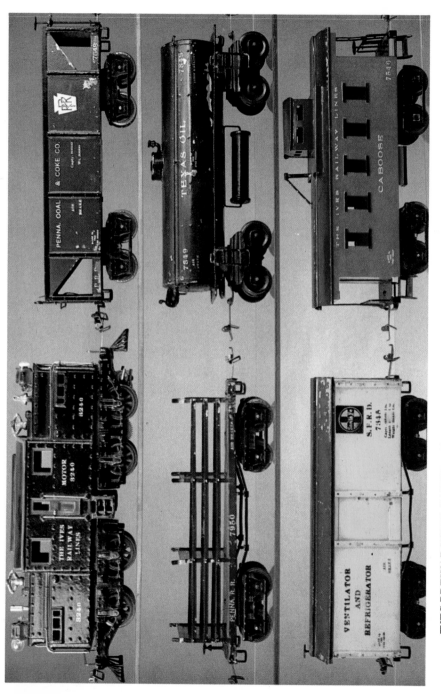

IVES PREWAR WIDE GAUGE. From top left, these elegant trains are the 3240 locomotive, the 7648 Penna. Coal & Coke Co. hopper, the 7950 Penna. flatcar with stakes, the 7849 Texas Oil tank car, the 7345 Santa Fe refrigerator car, and the 7546 caboose.

Highlights of Lionel Prewar History

The history of Lionel trains is one of rapid evolution and, perhaps, revolution (in the sense of a turning wheel). Founded by enterprising Joshua Lionel Cowen, the outfit quickly developed into a successful national manufacturer that would eventually dominate the toy train industry. In this course, the company went from one owner-operated, to one with massive facilities and hundreds of employees, to a subsidiary of another major corporation, and, finally, back to a company under the watchful guidance of a strong-willed individual.

Unlike many immigrants living in New York City before the turn of the century, Cowen's father [the family's name was Cohen; Joshua chose to Americanize his own] came with both a livelihood and the means to pursue it. One of nine children, Joshua Lionel Cowen was born on August 25, 1877. The children were well educated, and Joshua, being a clever and perhaps mischievous child rapidly developed mechanical skills and a keen interest in the newfangled electricity, the potential of which Edison and his contemporaries had only begun to tap.

Although toy trains had been offered much earlier — push-toys and live steam models for some time, and American-made electric models starting in the 1890s — Cowen in a sense rediscovered the wheel when he conceived of electrically-operated trains as window dressings for the merchants in his native New York City. He quickly designed and assembled an electrified open-top car (allowing for small merchandise to ride inside) and demonstrated its features to shopkeepers. He not only received orders from merchants but also from many of the shoppers who saw them and wished to have such toys for their homes.

The original 2-7/8" Gauge line of trains grew to include an interesting variety of models: steam and electric-outline locomotives, trolleys, and freight and passenger cars. In addition to the manufacture of these fine toys (often marketed as "educational" instruments, both by Cowen and others making similar goods), Cowen engaged in other electrical manufacturing, including government contracts.

In 1906 the Lionel Manufacturing Company, as it was then called, introduced a new series of trains with a track gauge of 2-1/8" and its hallmark three-rail track design, which facilitated simple electrical circuits even in the most complex track arrangements. Although 2-1/8" was actually an unusual measurement [European trains with 2" gauge track were already popular], Cowen, in his characteristically immodest fashion, adopted the phrases "Standard of the World" and "Standard Gauge" to describe his trains. Typically his advertisements strongly boasted of not only the quality and durability of his products but also of their superiority over others.

During World War I, Cowen expanded his facilities — now employing several hundred workers — to produce both toy trains and military goods, the latter under government contract. Appealing to boys and their fathers (literally promising that working together on the toy railroad would "weld the bonds" between them), Cowen continued to expand the reaches of his toy train empire. In 1915 Lionel introduced its most-popular line, O Gauge, which allowed an even broader class of Americans to enjoy the trains. Quite simply, the O Gauge trains occupied less floor space and required less of an outlay for purchase.

In 1918 The Lionel Corporation [privately held by Cowen and two colleagues] succeeded the manufacturing company. With the war behind, the new corporation excelled in the Roaring Twenties with extravagant trains, lavish catalogues, and excellent press coverage. The firm advertised its products in national magazines, sponsored radio shows, and held model photo contests with judges from major railroads. In fact, all went extremely well until the crash of October 1929. Just before the crash, the major toy makers were making ridiculously expensive trains: Lionel's "Transcontinental Limited" (State Set) at $110, Ives' expensive "Prosperity Special," and American Flyer's chrome-plated "Mayflower" at $100. One only has to think of parents trying to find $50 train sets at Toys 'R Us today to realize how expensive these premium trains had become, although it should be realized that a broad selection of less-expensive models was also offered.

Racked by depression, the 1930s challenged Cowen as they challenged the rest of the country. The Ives Company, a long-time competitor, had fallen into bankruptcy — its name and tooling sold to Lionel and American Flyer. Lionel came close to a similar fate. In 1934 it went into a brief receivership, during which the company produced one of its most celebrated toys, the Mickey and Minnie Mouse handcar. Although the media credited Lionel's financial turnaround to the outstanding sales of this item, others feel that the company's line of new streamline trains actually did the job. Perhaps the truth is that both combined to rejuvenate the company, as Cowen had thoughtfully included a catalogue of other (more expensive) Lionel items with each of the hundreds of thousands of $1 handcars sold. In 1935 Lionel came out of receivership.

From 1938 through 1942 Lionel had a brief fling with OO Gauge, which was half the size of its O Gauge trains. The move reflected a growing interest among adults in scale model trains. For many of these folks, who sought to make realistic railways with scenery and long trains in limited space, smaller trains were necessary. Lionel's attempt, however, was half-hearted. The company had long expounded the virtues of its three-rail O Gauge system over the more complex two-rail track system, which it now utilized for the OO Gauge line. Production of these trains did not resume after World War II.

In 1939 Lionel discontinued its large Standard Gauge trains, which, perhaps, had run their course. Americans had been humbled by the 1930s, and the more modest O Gauge trains better reflected their new lifestyles.

In 1942 Lionel's production of toy trains, as well as that of other toy makers, ceased for the duration of World War II. The company again engaged in military contracts. By doing so, Lionel gained not only financial resources but also important technological resources — new manufacturing techniques and the means by which to acquire new production equipment.

Although Cowen had achieved remarkable success in forty years of manufacturing trains, it can be seen from a study of early postwar production that he had only begun to hit his stride before the wartime cessation made him pause.

For additional information refer to *Greenberg's Guide to Lionel Trains, 1901-1942*, Volumes I and II.

Reproductions

Many prewar Lionel items have been reproduced. An (*) by a listing indicates that excellent reproductions of that item are available. Additionally, reproduction repair parts are available for many items. Persons considering large purchases of prewar trains should therefore rely on the expertise of friends who have experience with prewar Lionel trains.

Lionel Prewar (1901-1942)

		Gd	Exc
001	Steam, 4-6-4 (OO), black, "5342" on cab window, three- rail operation, 1938-42.	120	225
1	Bild-A-Motor, three-speed reversible, 1928-31.	60	125
1	Trolley, four wheels, open platform, 1906-08 (Standard), 1910.* (Non-powered trailer versions of this item are worth slightly less.)		
	(A) Cream body, orange band and roof.	1300	3000
	(B) White body, blue band and roof.	1200	3000
	(C) Cream body, blue band and roof.	900	2000
	(D) Cream body, blue band and roof, "CURTIS BAY".	1500	3500
	(E) Blue, cream band, blue roof.	1000	2000
002	Steam, 4-6-4 (OO), black, "5342" on cab window, three-rail operation, 1939-42.	100	200
2	Bild-A-Motor, three-speed reversible, 1928-31.	60	125
2	Countershafting structure, 11-1/2" long, 1904-11.		NRS
2	Trolley (Standard), four wheels, six windows, 1906-16. (Non-powered trailer versions of this item are worth slightly less.)		
	(A) Yellow, red band.	900	2000
	(B) Red, yellow band.	900	2000
003	Steam, 4-6-4 (OO), black, "5342" on cab sides, two-rail operation, 1939-42.		
	(A) With 003W whistling tender.	130	275
	(B) With 003T non-whistling tender.	120	250
3	Trolley (Standard), eight wheels, nine windows, 1906-13.		
	(A) Cream, orange band.	1400	3000
	(B) Cream, dark olive green band.	1400	3000
	(C) Orange, dark olive green band.	1400	3000
	(D) Dark green, cream windows.	1400	3000
	(E) Green, cream windows, "BAY SHORE".	1650	3500
004	Steam, 4-6-4 (OO), black, "5342" on cab sides, two-rail operation, 1939-42.		
	(A) With 004W whistling tender.	120	245
	(B) With 004T non-whistling tender.	110	225
4	Trolley (Standard), eight wheels, nine windows, 1906-12.		
	(A) Cream, dark olive green band and roof.	3000	5000
	(B) Green or olive green, cream windows and roof.	3000	5000
4	Electric, 0-4-0 (O), brass trim, 9-1/4" long, 1928-32.		
	(A) Orange, black frame.	450	700
	(B) Gray, apple green stripe, black frame.	475	800
4U	Kit form version of 4 Electric (O), 1928-29. Must be unbuilt, in original box for prices shown.	800	1000
5	Steam, 0-4-0 (Standard), black cab, bluish boiler, 1906-26.		
	(A) "N.Y.C. & H.R.R."	800	1200
	(B) "PENNSYLVANIA".	1100	1900

Gd   **Exc**

The handsome No. 8 is a simple four-wheel locomotive. It is called an "electric-outline" locomotive, because it is patterned after real (prototype) electric locomotives that once operated on real railroads. R. Bartelt photograph.

		Gd	Exc
	(C) "N.Y.C. & H.R.R.R." (three *R*s).	1000	1700
	(D) "B. & O.R.R."	1200	2000
6	Steam, 4-4-0 (Standard), black cab, bluish boiler, red window trim and pilot, gold lettering, 1906-23.	800	1200
7	Steam, 4-4-0 (Standard), brass boiler, nickel cab, red-spoked wheels, brass tender, 1910-23.*	1800	2800
8	Electric, 0-4-0 (Standard), 1925-32.		
	(A) Maroon, brass windows and trim.	80	160
	(B) Olive green or mojave with brass windows and trim.	60	125
	(C) Red, brass or cream windows.	75	150
	(D) Peacock, orange windows.	200	450
8	Trolley (Standard), eight wheels, open trucks, 1908-09.*		
	(A) Cream, orange band and roof.	3000	5000
	(B) Dark green, cream windows.	3000	5000
8E	Electric, 0-4-0 (Standard).		
	(A) Mojave, brass windows and trim.	80	160
	(B) Red, brass or cream windows.	70	140
	(C) Peacock, orange windows.	200	400
	(D) Pea green, cream stripe, red lettering.	250	450
9	Electric, 0-4-0 (Standard), dark green, 1929.*	1200	2000
9	Trolley (Standard), cream, orange band and roof, 1909.	3000	5000
9E	Electric, (Standard), 1928-30.*		
	(A) 0-4-0.	600	1200
	(B) 2-4-2, two-tone green.	750	1500
	(C) 2-4-2, gun-metal gray.	700	1250
9U	Electric, 0-4-0 (Standard), orange, 1928-29.	700	1350
10	Electric, 0-4-0 (Standard), 1925-29.		
	(A) Mojave, brass trim.	75	160
	(B) Gray, brass trim.	75	160
	(C) Peacock, brass inserts.	75	160
	(D) Red, cream stripe.	350	700

		Gd	Exc
10	Interurban (Standard), gold lettering, 1910-12.		
	(A) Maroon.	2000	4000
	(B) Dark olive green.	800	1500
10E	Electric, 0-4-0 (Standard), 1926-36.		
	(A) Olive green, black frame.		NRS
	(B) Peacock, dark green or black frame.	200	375
	(C) State brown, dark green frame.	250	500
	(D) Gray, black frame.	75	165
	(E) Red, cream stripe.	350	700
011	Switches, pair (O), 1933-37.	20	40
11	Flatcar (Standard), various colors, 1906-26.	32	50
012	Switches, pair (O), 1927-33.	12	30
12	Gondola (Standard), various colors, 1906-26.	32	50
013	Pair 012 Switches, 439 panel board.	55	125
13	Cattle car (Standard), various colors, 1906-26.	50	80
0014	Boxcar (OO), 6-7/8" long, 1938-42.		
	(A) Yellow, maroon roofwalk, "LIONEL LINES".	40	80
	(B) Tuscan body and roofwalk, "PENNSYLVANIA".	25	50
14	Boxcar (Standard), various colors, 1906-26.	40	70
0015	Tank car (OO), 5-3/4" long, 1938-42.		
	(A) Silver, "SUN OIL".	25	50
	(B) Black, "SHELL".	25	50
15	Oil car (Standard), various colors, 1906-26.	32	50
0016	Hopper car (OO), "SOUTHERN PACIFIC", 5-1/2" long, 1938-42.		
	(A) Gray.	35	75
	(B) Black.	35	65
16	Ballast dump car (Standard), various colors, 1906-26.	85	175
0017	Caboose (OO), "PENNSYLVANIA" or "NYC", red,1938-42.	25	50
17	Caboose (Standard), various colors, 1906-26.	32	50
18	Pullman (Standard), 1906-27.		
	(A) Dk. olive green, maroon doors, non-removable roof, non-op. doors.	700	1500
	(B) Dark olive green, removable roof.	80	125
	(C) Yellow-orange, cream windows, removable roof.	275	600
	(D) Orange, removable roof.	80	125
	(E) Mojave, removable roof.	275	600
19	Combine (Standard), 1906-26.		
	(A) Dk. olive green, maroon doors, non-removable roof, non-op. doors.	900	1800
	(B) Dark olive green, removable roof.	80	125
	(C) Yellow-orange, cream windows, removable roof.	225	375
	(D) Orange, removable roof.	80	125
	(E) Mojave, removable roof.	275	600
20	Direct current reducer, 1906.		NRS

Gd   Exc

*A handsome 35
New York Central
Pullman.*

		Gd	Exc
020	90° crossover (O), 1915-42.	2	5
020X	45° crossover (O), 1917-42.	3	7
20	90° crossover (Standard).	2	5
20X	45° crossover (Standard), 1928-32.	3	7
021	Switches, pair (O), 1915-37.	8	20
21	Switches, pair (Standard), 1915-25.	10	20
21	90° crossover (Standard), 1906.	7	15
022	Switches, pair, remote (O), 1938-42	15	30
22	Switches, pair (Standard), 1906-25.	10	25
023	Bumper (O), 1915-33.	5	10
23	Bumper (Standard), 1906-23.	5	10
24	Railway station (Standard), 1906.		NRS
0024	Boxcar, P R R (OO), 6-7/8" long, 1939-42.	25	50
25	Open station, 11" x 11", 1906.		NRS
25	Bumper (Standard), 1927-42.	7	15
025	Bumper (O), 1928-42.	5	10
0025	Tank car (OO), 5-3/4" long, 1939-42.		
	(A) Black, "SHELL".	25	50
	(B) Silver, "SUNOCO".	25	50
26	Passenger bridge, 24" long, 1906.		NRS
27	Lighting set for car interiors, 1911-23.	7	15
27	Station (Standard), lithographed, 21" x 9", 1909-12.		NRS
0027	Caboose (OO), red, "N.Y.C.", 4-5/8" long, 1939-42.	25	50
28	Double station with dome, 18-1/2" x 22", 1909-12.		NRS
29	Day coach (Standard), 1909-27.		
	(A) Dark olive green, nine-window body.	1000	2000
	(B) Maroon, ten-window body, non-removable roof.	800	1000
	(C) Dark green, ten-window body, non-removable roof.	2000	3000
	(D) Dark olive green, ten-window body, removable roof.	450	675
	(E) Dark green, ten-window body, removable roof.	375	600
30	Silent track bed (Standard), curved, 1931-37.	2	5

		Gd	Exc
030	Silent track bed (O), curved, 1931-39.	2	5
31	Combine (Standard), 1921-25.		
	(A) Maroon.	60	85
	(B) Orange.	90	150
	(C) Dark olive green.	55	80
	(D) Brown.	60	85
31	Silent track bed (Standard), straight, 1931-37.	3	5
0031	Curved track (OO), two-rail, 1939-42.	10	12
32	Mail car (Standard), 1921-25.		
	(A) Maroon.	60	85
	(B) Orange.	90	150
	(C) Dark olive green.	55	80
	(D) Brown.	60	85
32	Miniature figures, one dozen, 1909-18.	—	75
32	Silent track bed (Standard), 90° crossing, 1931-37.	2	5
0032	Straight track (OO), two-rail, 1939-42.	15	18
33	Electric, 0-6-0, early (Standard), gold lettering, 1912.		
	(A) Dark olive green, "NEW YORK CENTRAL LINES" in oval.	250	600
	(B) Black, "NEW YORK CENTRAL LINES" in oval.	300	750
	(C) Dk. olive green, "NEW YORK CENTRAL LINES" in block letters.	300	750
	(D) "PENNSYLVANIA RAILROAD".	400	975
33	Electric, 0-4-0, later (Standard), 1913-24.		
	(A) Dark olive green or black, lettered "NEW YORK CENTRAL".	60	125
	(B) Black, lettered "C & O".	350	700
	(C) Maroon, red, or peacock.	300	600
33	Silent track bed (Standard), 45° crossing, 1931-37.	2	5
033	Silent track bed (O), 45° crossing, 1931-39.	2	5
34	Electric, 0-6-0 (Standard), dark olive green, red windows, 1912.	450	900
34	Electric, 0-4-0 (Standard), dark olive green, 1913.	175	400
34	Silent track bed for switches (Standard), 1931-37.	2	5
034	Silent track bed for switches (O), 1931-39.	2	5
0034	Connection curved track (OO), two-rail, 1939-42.	15	18
35	Boulevard lamp, 6-1/8" high, 1940-42.	10	25
35	Pullman, first series (Standard), 1912-13.		
	(A) Dark blue.	250	450
	(B) Dark olive green.	80	100
35	Pullman, second series (Standard), 1914-18.		
	(A) Dark olive green, maroon windows.	30	50
	(B) Maroon, green windows.	50	75
	(C) Orange, maroon windows.	75	125
35	Pullman, third series (Standard), 1918-26.		
	(A) Dark olive green, maroon windows.	30	40

		Gd	Exc

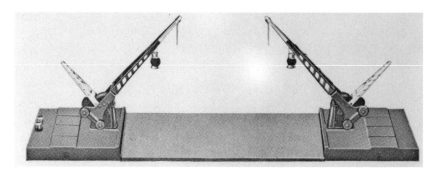

47 automatic illuminated crossing gates.

		Gd	Exc
	(B) Maroon, green windows.	25	35
	(C) Orange, maroon windows.	90	150
	(D) Brown, green windows.	30	40
36	Observation, first series (Standard).		
	(A) Dark blue.	200	450
	(B) Dark olive green.	80	100
36	Observation, second series (Standard).		
	(A) Dark olive green, maroon windows.	30	40
	(B) Maroon, green windows.	25	35
	(C) Orange, maroon windows.	90	150
	(D) Brown, green windows.	30	40
36	Observation, third series (Standard).		
	(A) Dark olive green, maroon windows.	30	40
	(B) Maroon, green windows.	30	40
	(C) Orange, maroon windows.	90	150
	(D) Brown, green windows.	30	40
38	Electric, 0-4-0 (Standard), 1913-24.		
	(A) Black.	70	125
	(B) Red.	350	750
	(C) Mojave or pea green.	300	600
	(D) Dark green.	200	400
	(E) Brown.	200	350
	(F) Red, cream trim.	300	600
	(G) Maroon.	125	300
	(H) Gray.	80	140
41	Accessory contactor, 1937-42.	1	2
042	Switches, pair (O), 1938-42.	15	30
42	Electric, 0-4-4-0, square hood (Standard), dark green, 1912.	900	1500
42	Electric, 0-4-4-0, round hood (Standard), 1913-23.		
	(A) Black or gray.	200	450
	(B) Maroon.	1000	2000

		Gd	Exc
	(C) Dark gray.	300	600
	(D) Dark green or mojave.	400	800
	(E) Peacock.	900	1800
	(F) Olive or dark olive green.	600	1200
43/043	Bild-A-Motor gear set, 1929.		NRS
43	Boat, runabout; red, white, and beige; 17" long, 1933-36, 1939- 41.	200	350
0044	Boxcar (OO), tuscan, 6-7/8" long, 1939-42.	25	50
0044K	Boxcar kit (OO), tuscan, 6-7/8" long, 1939-42.	50	100
44	Boat, speedster, green, white, and brown, 17" long, 1935-36.	200	400
45/045/45N	Automatic gateman, green base, red roof, 1935-42.	15	30
0045	Tank car (OO), 5-3/4" long, 1939-42.		
	(A) Black, "SHELL".	25	50
	(B) Silver, "SUNOCO".	25	50
0045K	Tank car kit (OO), unpainted, 5-3/4" long, 1939-42.	50	100
46	Crossing gate, 1939-42.	30	75
0046	Hopper (OO), "SOUTHERN PACIFIC" or "READING", black, 1939-42.	25	50
0046K	Hopper car kit (OO), black, 1939-42.		
	(A) "SOUTHERN PACIFIC".	40	75
	(B) "READING".		NRS
47	Crossing gate, green base, 1939-42.	35	95
0047	Caboose (OO), unpainted gray, "N.Y.C.", 1939-42.	25	50
0047K	Caboose, kit (OO), 1939-42	50	100
48W	Whistle station, lithographed, 1937-42.	10	20
49	Lionel airport, lithographed cardboard, round, 1937-39.	70	175
50	Airplane, red, with pylon and controls, 1936.	60	150
50	Electric, 0-4-0 (Standard), red window trim and pilots, 1924.		
	(A) Dark green or dark gray.	80	150
	(B) Maroon.	200	400
	(C) Mojave.	100	200
50	Cardboard train, cars, accessories (O), 1943.*	200	300
51	Steam, 0-4-0, 5 late, "N.Y.C. & H.R." or "PENNSYLVANIA" eight-wheel tender (Standard), c. 1912- 23.	750	1000
51	Lionel airport, lithographed cardboard, square, 1936, 1938.	70	175
52	Lamppost, die-cast, 10-1/2" tall, 1933-41.	30	60
0051	Curved track (OO), three-rail, 1939-42.	5	8
53	Electric, 0-4-4-0, early (Standard), maroon, gold ventilators, 1912- 14.	800	1700
53	Electric, 0-4-0, later (Standard), square hood, gold lettering.		
	(A) Maroon.	450	800
	(B) Mojave.	600	1200
	(C) Dark olive green.	500	1000
53	Electric, 0-4-0, latest (Standard), maroon, gold lettering, 1920-21.	150	400
53	Lamppost, die-cast, 8-1/2" or 8-7/8" tall, 1931-42.	20	35

Gd   **Exc**

No. 87 SIGNAL   No. 83 TRAFFIC SIGNAL

The 87 signal has the large "RAILROAD CROSSING" symbol, while the 83 traffic signal simply has colored lights.

		Gd	Exc
0053	Straight track (OO), three-rail, 1939-42.	5	8
54	Electric, 0-4-4-0, early (Standard), brass, red ventilators, 1912.*	2500	3500
54	Electric, 0-4-4-0, late (Standard), brass, red ventilators, 1913-23.	1500	2400
54	Lamppost, 9-1/2" tall, 1929-35.	20	35
0054	Connection curved track (OO), three-rail, 1939-42.	10	12
55	Airplane with stand, red and silver, with pylon and control, 1937-39.	150	350
56	Lamppost, removable lens and cap, 7-3/4" tall, 1924-42.	15	30
57	Lamppost, with street names, 7-1/2" tall, 1922-42.	20	40
58	Lamppost, gooseneck, 7-3/8" high, 1922-42.	10	25
59	Lamppost, cast-iron base, 8-3/4" high, 1920-36.	15	30
60/060	Telegraph post (Standard/O), 6-1/2" or 8-3/4" tall.	2	6
60	Electric, 0-4-0, F. A. O. S. Special (Standard).	—	2000
60	Automatic trip (Standard), 1906-12.	2	5
61	Electric, 0-4-4-0, F. A. O. S. Special (Standard).	—	2400
61	Lamppost, one globe, 12-3/4" tall, 1914-36.	15	30
0061	Curved track (OO), three-rail, 1938.	3	8
62	Electric, 0-4-0, F. A. O. S. Special (Standard).	—	2000
62	Semaphore, olive green, red crossarm, 8-3/4" tall, 1920-32.	10	25
0062	Straight track (OO), three-rail, 1938.	5	8
63	Lamppost, two globes, die-cast, 12-3/4" tall, 1933-42.	100	150
63	Semaphore, black base, orange staff, 14" tall, 1915-21.	10	25
0063	1/2 curved track (OO), three-rail, 1939-42.	10	12
64	Highway lamp post, green, 6-3/4" tall, 1940-42.	10	35
64	Semaphore, black, orange staff, 6-3/4" high, 1915-21.	12	36
0065	1/2 straight track (OO), three-rail, 1939-42.	10	12
65	Semaphore, one-arm, 1915-26.	11	30
65	Whistle controller, black metal box, 1935.	2	3
66	Semaphore, two-arm, black, orange staff, 14" tall, 1915-26.	11	30
66	Whistle controller, black metal box, 1936-39.	2	3
0066	5/6 straight track (OO), three-rail, 1939-42.	10	12
67	Lamppost, cast-iron, 13" tall, 1915-32.	30	60

		Gd	Exc
67	Whistle controller, black metal box, 1936-39.	2	3
68/068	Crossing sign.	1	2
69/069/69N	Electric warning signal, 1921-42.	11	25
70	Outfit: (2) No. 62, (1) No. 59, (1) No. 68; 1921-32.	25	75
0070	90° crossover (OO), three-rail, 1939-42.	18	25
071	(6) 060 Telegraph poles (O), black, orange or green base, 1924-42.	50	100
71	(6) 60 Telegraph poles (Standard)	50	100
0072	Switches, pair (OO), 1938-42.	120	175
0074	Boxcar (OO), tuscan, 6-7/8" long, 1939-42.	25	50
0075	Tank car (OO), "SHELL" or "SUNOCO", 5-3/4" long, 1939-42.	25	50
076/76	Block signal, stamped rectangular base, 1923-28.	15	40
76	Warning bell and shack, pressed steel, 1939-42.	60	150
0077	Caboose (OO), red, "N.Y.C.", 4-5/8" long, 1939-42.	25	50
77/077/77N	Automatic crossing gate, 1923-39.	15	30
78/078	Train signal (Standard), 1924-32.	20	50
79	Flashing signal, 11-1/2" tall, 1928-40.	30	60
80/080/80N	Semaphore (Standard), 1926-42.	25	60
80	Automobile, w/ eight sections of track (36" dia.), driver, and starting post, 1912-16.	600	1100
81	Automobile, w/ eight sections of track (30" dia.), driver, and starting post, 1912-16.	600	1100
81	Controlling rheostat, 1927-33.	1	3
81	Crossing signal, 1927-33.	1	3
82/082/82N	Train control semaphore, 1927-42.	30	65
83	Flashing traffic signal, die-cast, 6-1/4" tall, 1927-42.	35	75
84/084	Semaphore, 1927-32.	30	65
84	(2) Automobiles, with eight sections of track (36" dia.), driver, and starting posts.	1300	2500
85	Telegraph pole (Standard), 9" tall, 1929-42.	4	10
85	(2) Automobiles, with eight sections of track (36" dia.), eight sections of track (30" dia.), eight straight sections, and starting post.	1200	2500
86	(6) Telegraph poles, 9" tall, 1929-42.	45	100
87	Flashing crossing signal, drum-shaped head, 6-3/4" tall, 1927-42.	35	75
88	Battery rheostat, 1915-27.	1	3
88	Rheostat controller, 1933-42.	1	3
89	Flagpole, ivory, 14" tall, 1923-34.	8	20
90	Flagpole, ivory, 14-3/4" tall, 1927-42.	15	35
91	Circuit breaker, 1930-42.	7	15
092	Signal tower, 4-1/8" x 2-13/16", 1923-27.	40	85
92	Floodlight tower, two bulbs, 20-1/2" tall, 1931-42.	70	150
93	Water tower, 8-3/8" tall, 1931-42.	15	30
94	High tension tower, three crossarms with porcelain insulators, 25' of copper wire, 1932-42.*	70	150
95	Controlling rheostat, 1934-42.	1	3

	Gd	Exc

Top shelf: 114 CM & StP boxcar and 117 NYC & HRRR caboose. Bottom shelf: 112 Lake Shore gondola and the original box for the 114 boxcar.

		Gd	Exc
96	Remote-control elevator, hand-operated with buckets, 1938-42.	70	150
097	Telegraph set (O), one crossing sign and six poles.	35	60
97	Coal elevator, motor driven, black base, 1938-42.	70	150
98	Coal bunker, cream structure, black base, 1938-40.	150	300
99/099/99N	Train control, 1932-42.	30	75
100	Electric locomotive (2-7/8"), 10-1/2" long, 1903-05.*	3000	4000
100	Trolley, 5-7/8" long frame, 1910, 1912-15. (Non-powered trailer versions of this model sell for slightly less.)		
	(A) Blue, white windows.	700	1500
	(B) Blue, cream windows.	1000	2000
	(C) Red, cream windows.	700	1500
100	(2) Bridge approaches (Standard), stamped steel, 28" long, 1920-31.	10	20
100	Wooden gondola (2-7/8"), 14-1/2" long, 1901.		NRS
101	Bridge span, (2) approaches (Standard), stamped steel, 42" long, 1920-31.	15	40
101	Summer trolley (Std.), blue and maroon, gold lett., (5) benches, 1910.	800	1800
102	(2) Bridge spans, stamped steel, 2 approaches (Std.), 1920-31.	25	60
103	(3) Bridge spans, 2 approaches (Std.), stamped steel, 70" long, 1920-31.	45	100
104	Bridge span (Standard), stamped steel, 14" long, 1920-31.	10	20
104	Tunnel (Standard), 1909-14.	30	75
105	Bridge (Standard), 6", 1911-14.	10	25
105	(2) Bridge approaches (O), stamped steel, 21" long, 1920-31.	5	10
106	Bridge span (O), (2) approaches, stamped steel, 31-1/2" long, 1920-31.	20	50
106	Rheostat, 1911-14.	3	9
107	Direct current reducer, 110 V, 1923-32.		NRS
108	(2) Bridge spans (O), (2) approaches, stamped steel, 42" long, 1920-31.	20	50
109	(3) Bridge spans (O), (2) approaches, stamped steel, 52" long, 1920-32.	25	60
109	Tunnel (Standard), stamped steel, 1913-14.	17	35
110	Bridge span (O), stamped steel, 10-1/2" long, 1920-31.	5	10
111	Box of 50 bulbs, 1920-31.	—	100
112	Gondola (Standard), various colors, 1910-26.	30	50
112	Station, terra-cotta base, cream sides, 13-3/4" x 9-1/4", 1931-35.	80	175

		Gd	Exc
113	Cattle car (Standard), various colors, 1912-26.	35	55
113	Station, terra-cotta base, cream sides, outside light brackets, 1931-34.	95	200
114	Boxcar (Standard), "CM & ST P", usually orange, 1912-26.	25	45
114	Station, terra-cotta base, cream sides, two light brackets, 1931-34.	450	1000
115	Station, illuminated, 13-3/4" x 9-1/4", 1935-42.	100	200
116	Station, two skylights, 19-1/2" x 9-1/4", 1935-42.*	450	1000
116	Ballast car (Standard), various colors, 1910-26.	40	60
117	Caboose (Standard), "NYC & HRRR"; red, brown, or maroon, 1912-26.	30	50
117	Station, 13-3/4" x 9-1/4", no lights, 1936-42.	75	150
118	Tunnel (O), 8" long, various sizes, 1922-32.	7	15
118L	Tunnel, 8" long, lighted, 1926.	9	20
119	Tunnel, 12" or 16" long, 1920-42.	7	15
119L	Tunnel, 12" long, with hotel, 1927-33.	9	20
120	Tunnel, 17" or 20" long, 1922-27.	18	35
120L	Tunnel, 17" long, lighted, 1927-42.	25	45
121	Station (Standard), 1909-17.		
	(A) 14" x 10" x 9".		NRS
	(B) 13-1/2" x 9" x 13".	80	200
121	Station (Std.), no signs or illum., light gray base, brown walls, 1920-26.	45	100
121X	Station (Standard), illuminated, made by Schoenhut, 1917-19.	80	200
122	Station (Standard), gray base, salmon sides, 1920-30.	45	100
123	Station (Standard), gray base, dull brown walls, 1920-23.	45	100
123	Tunnel, house on side of mountain, 18-1/2" x 16-1/4" (O), 1933-42.	50	100
124	Station, "LIONEL CITY", 1920-36.*		
	(A) Tan or gray base, pea green roof.	45	100
	(B) Pea green base, red roof.	100	200
125	Station, "LIONELVILLE", lithographed, dark mojave base, 1923-25.	50	100
125	Track template, for tracing track plans, 1938.	1	3
126	Station, "LIONELVILLE", lithographed, gray or mojave base, 1923-36.	50	100
127	Station, "LIONEL TOWN", lighted, 8-1/2" x 4-1/4", 1923-36.	35	75
128	Station and terrace; terrace includes flower beds, flag, stairways, and electric lamps, 1928-42.*	500	1100
129	Terrace, with flower beds, flag, stairways, and electric lamps, 1928-42.*	450	900
130	Tunnel, 17" or 26" long, metal, 1920-36.	120	250
130L	Tunnel, 26" long, metal, 1927-33.	120	250
131	Corner display, part of 198 and 199 display units, 1924-28.	70	200
132	Corner grass plot, part of 198 and 199 display units, 1924-28.	70	200
133	Heart-shaped plot, part of 198 and 199 display units, 1924-28.	70	200
134	Oval-shaped plot, part of 198 and 199 display units, 1924-28.	70	200
134	Station, "LIONEL CITY", w/stop, brown, red roof, 1937-42.	140	250
135	Circular plot, part of 199 display unit, 1924-28.	70	200
136	Large elevation, part of large display units, 1924-28.		NRS
136	Station, "LIONELVILLE", w/stop, green base, 1937-42.	60	100

Gd   **Exc**

The 158 platform set is a perfect addition to an O Gauge layout. It can be used alone as a small commuter stop or as part of an elaborate station complex.

		Gd	Exc
137	Station, with stop, ivory walls, 1937-42.	40	100
140L	Tunnel, 37" long, curved, sheet steel, 1927-32.	190	400
150	Electric, 0-4-0 early (O), dark green, red windows, 1917.	65	90
150	Electric, 0-4-0 late (O), black frame, 1918-25.		
	(A) Brown, brown or olive window frames.	70	100
	(B) Maroon, dark olive window frames.	65	90
	(C) Dark green or olive.	70	100
	(D) Mojave.	150	300
	(E) Peacock.	150	300
152	Electric, 0-4-0 (O), 1917-27.		
	(A) Dark green.	40	60
	(B) Gray.	50	70
	(C) Mojave.	150	300
	(D) Peacock.	150	300
152	Crossing gate, double arm, red base, 1940-42.	9	20
153	Block signal, green base, red and green lights, 1940-42.	10	25
153	Electric, 0-4-0 (O), 1924-25.		
	(A) Dark green.	60	90
	(B) Gray.	75	110
	(C) Mojave.	150	300
154	Electric, 0-4-0 (O), dark green, 1917-23.	75	125
154	Highway signal, black base, two red lights, 1940-42.	10	25
155	Freight shed, illuminated, 1930-42.*		
	(A) Yellow base, burnt orange floor, maroon roof.	90	200
	(B) White base, terra-cotta floor, gray roof.	120	250
156	Electric, 4-4-4 (O), 1917-23.		
	(A) Dark green.	375	500
	(B) Maroon.	425	550
	(C) Olive green.	475	650
	(D) Gray.	525	750
156	Electric, 0-4-0 (O), dark green, 1917-23.	350	500

		Gd	Exc
156	Station platform, illuminated, green base, red roof, 1939-42.	20	55
156X	Electric, 0-4-0 (O), 1923-24.		
	(A) Maroon.	325	450
	(B) Olive green.	375	500
	(C) Gray.	450	650
	(D) Brown.	400	550
157	Hand truck, 3-3/4" long, part of 163 accessory set, red, 1930-32.	15	30
158	Electric, 0-4-0 (O), 1923-24.		
	(A) Gray, red windows.	60	100
	(B) Black.	75	125
158	Set: (2) 156 platforms and (1) 136 station; 1940-42.	75	150
159	Block actuator, 1940.	10	25
161	Baggage truck, 4-1/2" long, part of 163 accessory set, green, 1930-32.	20	50
162	Dump truck, 4-1/2" long, part of 163 accessory set, 1930-32.	22	50
163	Set: (2) 157 hand trucks, (1) 162 dump, (1) 160 baggage; 1930- 42.*	90	200
164	Log loader, green, red roof, 1940-42.	70	150
165	Magnetic crane, green, cream cab, 1940-42.	70	150
166	Whistle controller, 1940-42.	2	3
167	Whistle controller, 1940-42.	2	3
167X	Whistle controller (OO), 1940-42.	2	3
169	Controller, "TELEDYNE", 1940-42.	1	3
170	Direct current reducer, 220 volts, 1914-38.	2	4
171	DC to AC inverter, 110 volts, 1936-42.	2	4
172	DC to AC inverter, 229 volts, 1939-42.	2	4
180	Pullman (Standard), gold lettering, dark olive doors, 1911-21.		
	(A) Maroon body and roof.	80	90
	(B) Brown body and roof.	90	130
181	Combine (Standard), gold lettering, 1911-21.		
	(A) Maroon, dark olive doors.	80	100
	(B) Brown, dark olive doors.	80	100
	(C) Yellow-orange, orange doors.	225	275
182	Observation (Standard), gold lettering, 1911-21.		
	(A) Maroon, dark olive doors.	80	100
	(B) Brown, dark olive doors.	80	100
	(C) Yellow-orange, orange doors.	225	275
184	Bungalow, illuminated, lithographed, various colors, 1923-32.	25	40
185	Bungalow, not illuminated, lithographed, various colors, 1923-24.	17	40
186	(5) 185 Bungalows, excellent price requires original box, 1923-32.	140	300
186	Log loader outfit, add $100 for original box, 1940-41.	100	200
187	(5) 185 Bungalows, excellent price requires original box, 1923-24.	140	300
188	Elevator and 3659X dump car, add $100 for orig. box, 1938-41.	90	200
189	Villa, illuminated, lithographed, various colors, 1923-32.	55	125

	Gd	Exc

The charming 191 Villa with its original box.

		Gd	Exc
190	Observation (Standard), 1914-18, 1923-27.		
	(A) Dk. olive green, maroon doors, non-removable roof, non-op. doors.	900	1800
	(B) Dark olive green, removable roof.	80	125
	(C) Yellow-orange, cream windows, removable roof.	225	375
	(D) Orange, removable roof.	80	125
	(E) Mojave, removable roof.	275	600
191	Villa, illuminated, lithographed, various colors, 1923-32.	55	125
192	Illuminated villa set: 189 Villa, (2) 184 Bungalows, 1927-32.		NRS
193	Accessory set, (1 each) 69, 76, 77, 78, 80, 1927-29.	140	300
194	Accessory set, 1927-29.	140	300
195	Terrace, (1) 184, (1) 189, (1) 191, (1) 90, (2) 56, 1927-30.	275	600
196	Accessory set, (1) 127, (6) 60, (1) 62, (1) 68, (2) 58, 1927.	150	300
200	Electric express (2-7/8"), 12-1/4" long, 1903.*	4000	5000
200	Turntable, pea green and red, 17" diameter, 1928-33.*	75	150
200	Wooden gondola (2-7/8"), 14-1/2" long, 1902.		NRS
200	Trailer (Standard), red, yellow bands, 1910-13.	—	3000
201	Steam, 0-6-0 (O), 1940-42.		
	(A) With 2201B tender with bell.	325	600
	(B) With 2201T tender without bell.	300	550
202	Summer trolley, red and yellow, 1910-13.		
	(A) "ELECTRIC RAPID TRANSIT".	800	2400
	(B) "PRESTON ST."	2000	4000
203	0-4-0, armored loco (O), 1917-21.	700	2000
203	Steam, 0-6-0 (O), 1940-42.		
	(A) With 2203B tender with bell.	300	450
	(B) With 2203T tender without bell.	275	425
204	Steam, 2-4-2 (O), with tender, 1940.		
	(A) Black locomotive.	30	65
	(B) Gun-metal gray locomotive.	40	100
205	Merchandise containers (3), green, 3-1/2" x 3" x 4", 1930-38.*	120	250
206	Sack of coal, approximately 1/2 lb., 1938-42.	5	15

		Gd	Exc
208	Tool set: pick, shovel, axe, rake, hoe, and sledge; packed in enameled metal chest with brass handle, 1934-42.*	30	75
209	Wooden barrels (4), 2-1/8" tall, 1934-42.	6	15
0209	Barrels (4), 1-3/8" tall, 1934-42.	4	10
210	Switches, pair (Standard), 1926, 1934-42.	10	25
211	Flatcar (Standard), black, 1926-40.*	60	80
212	Gondola (Standard), 1926-40.*		
	(A) Gray or green.	100	150
	(B) Maroon.	75	100
213	Cattle car (Standard), 1926-40.*		
	(A) Mojave, maroon roof.	175	250
	(B) Terra-cotta, green or maroon roof.	125	175
214	Boxcar (Standard), "LIONEL LINES", 1926-40.*		
	(A) Terra-cotta, green roof.	225	300
	(B) Cream body, orange roof.	150	250
	(C) Yellow, brown roof.	350	500
214R	Refrigerator car (Standard), 1929-40.*		
	(A) Ivory or white, brass plates, peacock roof.	375	550
	(B) White, light blue roof, nickel roof.	500	800
215	Tank car (Standard), 1926-40.*		
	(A) Pea green.	120	150
	(B) Ivory.	175	250
	(C) Silver.	250	500
216	Hopper car (Standard), dark green, 1926-38.*		
	(A) Brass plates.	175	250
	(B) Nickel plates.	400	800
217	Caboose (Standard), 1926-40.*		
	(A) Orange, maroon roof.	250	325
	(B) Red, peacock roof.	120	150
	(C) Red body and roof, white door.	150	200
217	Lighting set, to illuminate (3) passenger cars, 1914-23.		NRS
218	Dump car (Standard), mojave, 1926-38.*	160	200
219	Crane (Standard), 1926-40.*		
	(A) Peacock, red boom.	120	175
	(B) Yellow, light green boom.	250	300
	(C) Ivory, light green boom.	250	325
	(D) Cream, red boom.	120	230
	(E) White, green boom.	275	350
220	Floodlight car (Standard), 1931-40.*		
	(A) Terra-cotta base.	200	275
	(B) Green base.	300	350
220	Switches, pair (Standard), 1926.*	10	25
222	Switches, pair (Standard), 1926-32.	20	40

Gd   **Exc**

The 225E loco-motive, shown here without its tender Note the rugged proportions. R. Bartelt photograph.

		Gd	Exc
223	Switches, pair (Standard), 1932-42.	30	75
224/224E	Steam, 2-6-2 (O), with tender, 1938-42.		
	(A) Black locomotive, die-cast 2224 tender.	80	140
	(B) Black locomotive, plastic 2224 tender.	60	100
	(C) Gun-metal gray locomotive, die-cast 2224 tender.	200	450
	(D) Gun-metal gray locomotive, sheet-metal 2689 tender.	60	100
225	222 switches and 439 panel, 1929-32.	75	150
225/225E	Steam, 2-6-2 (O), 1938-42.		
	(A) Black locomotive, 2235 or 2245 tender.	160	225
	(B) Black locomotive, 2235 plastic tender.	150	200
	(C) Gun-metal locomotive, 2225 or 2265 sheet metal tender.	150	200
	(D) Gun-metal locomotive, die-cast 2235 tender.	225	450
226/226E	Steam, 2-6-4 (O), black, 1938-41.	300	450
227	Steam switcher, "8976" on cab window, black, 0-6-0 (O), 1939-42.		
	(A) With 2227B tender with bell.	600	850
	(B) With 2227T tender without bell.	600	800
228	Steam switcher, 0-6-0 (O), black, 1939-42.		
	(A) With 2228B tender with bell.	600	900
	(B) With 2228T tender without bell.	600	850
229	Steam switcher, 2-4-2 (O), 1939-42.		
	(A) Black or gun-metal with 2689W whistling tender.	45	70
	(B) Black or gun-metal with 2689T non-whistling tender.	35	50
	(C) Black with 2666W whistling tender.	45	70
	(D) Black with 2666T non-whistling tender.	35	50
230	Steam switcher, 0-6-0 (O), black, 1939-42.	900	1500
231	Steam switcher, 0-6-0 (O), black, 1939.	900	1500
232	Steam switcher, 0-6-0 (O), "8976" on cab, black, 1930.	900	1500
233	Steam switcher, 0-6-0 (O), "8976" on cab, black, 1940-42.	900	1500
238/238E	Steam, 4-4-2 (O), gun-metal or black, 1936-38.		
	(A) With 265W or 2225W whistling tender.	175	250
	(B) With 265 or 2225T non-whistling tender.	175	250

		Gd	Exc
248	Electric, 0-4-0 (O), 1926-32.	75	125
249/249E	Steam, 2-4-2 (O), 1936-37.		
	(A) Gun-metal, 265T or 265W tender.	125	175
	(B) Black, 265W tender.	135	185
250E	Steam, Hiawatha, 0-4-0 (O), streamlined; orange, gray, and black; 250W, 250WX, or 2250W tender, 1935-42.*	800	1300
250	Electric, 0-4-0 early (O), usually dark green, 1926.	150	200
250	Electric, 0-4-0 late (O), 1934.		
	(A) Yellow-orange body, terra-cotta frame.	150	200
	(B) Terra-cotta body, maroon frame.	165	225
251	Electric, 0-4-0 (O), 1925-32.		
	(A) Gray body, red windows.	175	250
	(B) Red body, ivory stripe.	200	300
	(C) Red body, without ivory stripe.	185	275
251E	Electric, 0-4-0 (O), 1927-32.		
	(A) Red body, ivory stripe.	200	300
	(B) Red body, without ivory stripe.	185	275
	(C) Gray, red trim.	175	250
252	Electric, 0-4-0 (O), 1926-32.		
	(A) Peacock or olive green.	85	125
	(B) Terra-cotta or yellow-orange.	110	165
252E	Electric, 0-4-0 (O), 1933-35.		
	(A) Terra-cotta.	110	165
	(B) Yellow-orange.	95	135
253	Electric, 0-4-0 (O), 1924-32.		
	(A) Maroon.	150	275
	(B) Dark green.	90	125
	(C) Mojave.	90	150
	(D) Terra-cotta.	150	275
	(E) Peacock.	80	125
	(F) Red.	175	310
253E	Electric, 0-4-0 (O), 1931-36.		
	(A) Green.	75	125
	(B) Terra-cotta.	125	225
254	Electric, 0-4-0 (O), green or mojave, 1924-32.	70	150
254E	Electric, 0-4-0 (O), olive green or pea green, 1927-34.	80	175
255E	Steam, 2-4-2 (O), gun-metal, 263W or 263WX tender, 1935-36.	375	500
256	Electric, 0-4-4-0 (O), 1924-30.*		
	(A) Rubber-stamped lettering with black outline around "LIONEL".	500	900
	(B) Rubber-stamped lettering without outline around "LIONEL".	450	550
	(C) "LIONEL" and "256" on brass plates.	475	750
257	Steam, 0-4-0 (O), black, with/without orange stripe, 1930.		
	(A) Black tender.	90	175

Gd   Exc

Observation cars are named for their open observation platforms, as found on this 312 Lionel Lines observation. R. Bartelt photograph.

		Gd	Exc
	(B) Black crackle-finish tender.	150	250
258	Steam, 2-4-0 early (O), 1930.		
	(A) With four-wheel 257 tender.	80	155
	(B) With eight-wheel 258 tender.	95	175
258	Steam, 2-4-2 late (O), 1941.		
	(A) Black.	35	50
	(B) Gun-metal.	50	75
259	Steam, 2-4-2 (O), black, 1932.	55	80
259E	Steam, 2-4-2 (O), black, four-whl. or eight-whl. tender, 1933-34, 36-38.	45	60
260E	Steam, 2-4-2 (O), 1930-35.*		
	(A) Black, green or black frame.	300	400
	(B) Dark gun-metal body and frame.	400	550
261	Steam, 2-4-2 (O), black, brass/copper trim, 1931.	140	200
261E	Steam, 2-4-2 (O), black, brass/copper trim, 1935.	160	225
262	Steam, 2-4-2 (O), black, 1931-32.	100	165
262E	Steam, 2-4-2 (O), 1933-34.		
	(A) Gloss black, copper and brass trim.	110	175
	(B) Satin black, nickel trim.	135	220
263E	Steam, 2-4-2 (O), 1936-39.*		
	(A) Gun-metal gray.	300	450
	(B) Two-tone blue, from Blue Comet set.	400	700
264E	Steam, 2-4-2 (O), 1935-36.		
	(A) Red, "RED COMET".	110	225
	(B) Black.	165	300
265E	Steam, 2-4-2 (O), 1935-39.		
	(A) Black or gun-metal.	130	195
	(B) Light blue, "BLUE STREAK".	350	475
270	Bridge, 10" long (O), single-span, red or maroon, 1931-42.	12	20
270	Lighting set, two bulbs with 3' of cord and sockets, 1915-23.		NRS
271	Set (O), (2) 270 spans, 1931-33, 1935-40.	25	60
271	Lighting set, two bulbs with 3' of cord and sockets, 1915-23.		NRS

		Gd	Exc
272	Set (O), (3) 270 spans, 1931-33, 1935-40.	25	60
280	Bridge (Standard), 14" long, red, green, or gray, 1931-42.	15	25
281	Set (Standard), (2) bridge spans, 1931-33, 1935-40.	25	50
282	Set (Standard), (3) bridge spans, 1931-33, 1935-40.	40	75
289E	Steam, 2-4-2 (O), black or gun-metal, 1937.	150	225
300	Electric trolley car (2-7/8"), 16-1/2" long, 1903-05.	2000	3000
300	Hell Gate bridge (Standard), 1928-42.*		
	(A) Cream towers, green trusses, orange base.	350	850
	(B) Ivory towers, aluminum trusses, red base.	350	1100
301	Batteries (2-7/8"), 1903-05.		NRS
302	Plunge battery (2-7/8"), 1902.		NRS
303	Carbon cylinders (2-7/8"), 1902.		NRS
303	Summer trolley (Std.), olive green and yellow, (8) benches, 1910-13.	1500	3000
304	Composite zincs (2-7/8"), 1902.		NRS
306	Glass jars (2-7/8"), 1902.		NRS
308	Set (O), (5) signs for trackside detail, 1940-42.	6	15
309	Electric trolley trailer (2-7/8"), 16-1/2" long, 1904-05.	1700	2200
309	Pullman (Standard), 1924-39.		
	(A) Maroon body and roof, mojave windows.	70	150
	(B) Mojave body and roof, maroon windows.	70	150
	(C) Light brown body, dark brown roof, cream windows.	85	175
	(D) Medium blue body, dark blue roof, cream windows.	120	250
	(E) Apple green body, dark green roof, cream windows.	120	250
	(F) Pale blue body, silver roof and windows.	70	150
	(G) Maroon body, terra-cotta roof, cream windows.	90	175
310	Baggage (Standard), 1924-39.		
	(A) Maroon body and roof, mojave windows.	70	150
	(B) Mojave body and roof, maroon windows.	70	150
	(C) Light brown body, dark brown roof, cream windows.	80	175
	(D) Medium blue body, dark blue roof, cream windows.	120	250
	(E) Apple green body, dark green roof, cream windows.	120	250
	(F) Pale blue body, silver roof and windows.	70	150
310	Rails and ties, complete section, (2-7/8"), 1903-05.		NRS
312	Observation (Standard), 1924-39.		
	(A) Maroon body and roof, mojave windows.	70	150
	(B) Mojave body and roof, maroon windows.	70	150
	(C) Light brown body, dark brown roof, cream windows.	85	175
	(D) Medium blue body, dark blue roof, cream windows.	120	250
	(E) Apple green body, dark green roof, cream windows.	120	250
	(F) Pale blue body, silver roof and windows.	70	150
	(G) Maroon body, terra-cotta roof, cream windows.	90	175
313	Bascule bridge (O), green base, building with cream walls, 1940-42.		

		Gd	Exc

A reproduction 381E is hard at work on this Standard Gauge layout.

		Gd	Exc
	(A) Silver bridge.	140	375
	(B) Gray bridge.	185	450
314	Girder bridge (O), 10" long, die-cast sides, silver or gray, 1940-42.	6	15
315	Trestle bridge (O), 24-1/2" long, silver or gray, 1940-42.	20	40
316	Trestle bridge (O), 24" long, silver or gray, 1940-42.	10	30
318	Electric, 0-4-0 (Standard), brass trim, 1924-32.		
	(A) Gray, dark gray, or mojave.	100	225
	(B) Pea green.	150	250
	(C) State brown.	250	400
318E	Electric, 0-4-0 (Standard), 1926-35.		
	(A) Gray, mojave, or pea green.	110	225
	(B) State brown.	200	400
	(C) Black.	400	900
319	Pullman (Standard), maroon, mojave windows, 1924-27.	70	125
320	Baggage (Standard), maroon, mojave windows, 1925-27.	70	125
320	Turnout (2-7/8"), 1903-05.		NRS
322	Observation (Standard), maroon, mojave windows, 1924-27.	70	125
330	Crossing, 90° (2-7/8"), 1903-05.		NRS
332	Baggage (Standard), 1929.		
	(A) Red body and roof, cream doors.	45	75
	(B) Peacock body and roof, orange doors.	45	75
	(C) Gray body and roof, maroon doors.	45	75
	(D) Olive green body and roof, red doors.	50	90
	(E) State brown body, dark brown roof, cream doors.	100	250
	(F) Peacock body, dark green roof, orange doors.	60	100
	(G) Peacock body and roof, red doors.	75	125
	(H) Mojave body, maroon roof and doors.	120	175
337	Pullman (Standard), 1925-32.		
	(A) Red body and roof, cream doors.	45	75
	(B) Mojave body and roof, maroon doors.	45	75
	(C) Olive green body and roof, red doors.	50	90

		Gd	Exc
	(D) Olive green body and roof, maroon doors.	45	75
	(E) Pea green body and roof, cream doors.	100	200
338	Observation (Standard), 1925-32.		
	(A) Red body and roof, cream doors.	45	75
	(B) Mojave body and roof, maroon doors.	45	75
	(C) Olive green body and roof, red doors.	50	90
	(D) Olive green body and roof, maroon doors.	45	75
339	Pullman (Standard), 1925-33.		
	(A) Peacock body and roof, orange doors.	45	75
	(B) Gray body and roof, maroon doors.	45	75
	(C) State brown body, dark brown roof, cream doors.	100	250
	(D) Peacock body, dark green roof, orange doors.	60	100
	(E) Mojave body, maroon roof and doors.	120	175
340	Suspension bridge (2-7/8"), 1903-05.		NRS
341	Observation (Standard), 1925-33.		
	(A) Peacock body and roof, orange doors.	45	75
	(B) Gray body and roof, maroon doors.	45	75
	(C) State brown body, dark brown roof, cream doors.	100	250
	(D) Peacock body, dark green roof, orange doors.	60	100
	(E) Mojave body, maroon roof and doors.	120	175
350	Track bumper (2-7/8"), 1903-05.	20	35
370	Jars and plates (2-7/8"), 1903-05.		NRS
380	Electric, 0-4-0 (Standard), 1923-27.	200	350
380	Elevated pillars (2-7/8"), 1903-05	40	75
380E	Electric, 0-4-0 (Standard), brass trim, 1926-28.		
	(A) Mojave.	300	550
	(B) Maroon.	200	350
	(C) Dark green.	250	400
381	Electric, 4-4-4 (Standard), State green, apple green frame, 1928-29.*	1500	3500
381E	Electric, 4-4-4 (Standard), 1928-36.*		
	(A) State green, apple green sub-frame.	1200	2250
	(B) State green, red sub-frame.	1500	2800
381U	Electric, 4-4-4 (Standard), State green, apple green frame, 1928-29.*	1600	3800
384	Steam, 2-4-0 (Standard), black, brass and copper trim, 1930-32.	300	400
384E	Steam, 2-4-0 (Standard), black, brass and copper trim, 1930-32.	300	410
385E	Steam, 2-4-2 (Standard), black, metal trim, 1933-39.*	450	675
390	Steam, 2-4-2 (Standard), black, with or without orange stripe, 390T tender, 1929.	450	750
390E	Steam, 2-4-2 (Standard), 1929-31.		
	(A) Black, with or without orange stripe.	450	650
	(B) Two-tone blue, cream-orange stripe.	600	1200
	(C) Two-tone green, orange or apple green stripe.	1000	2000
392E	Steam, 4-4-2 (Standard), 1932-39.*		

		Gd	Exc

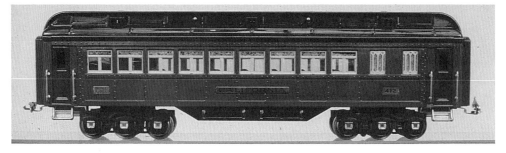

The 412 California Pullman is an example of the prized "State" car series. The originals are quite valuable, so collectors must be conscientious about identifying reproductions, which are worth much less. Additionally, restored examples are worth less than original, unrestored cars.

		Gd	Exc
	(A) Black, 384 tender.	650	1000
	(B) Black, large 12-wheel tender.	1200	1700
	(C) Gun-metal gray.	1000	1500
400	Express Trolley Trailer (2-7/8"), 12-1/4" long, 1903.	2000	3000
400E	Steam, 4-4-4 (Standard), copper and brass trim, 1931-40.*		
	(A) Black or dark gun-metal.	1200	2000
	(B) Medium blue boiler, dark blue frame.	1200	2400
	(C) Crackle black finish (beware of fakes).	2500	6000
402	Electric, 0-4-4-0 (Standard), mojave, 1923-27.	300	450
402E	Electric, 0-4-4-0 (Standard), mojave, 1926-29.	325	450
408E	Electric, 0-4-4-0 (Standard), 1927-36.*		
	(A) Apple green or mojave; red pilots.	600	1200
	(B) Two-tone brown, brown pilots.	1800	2700
	(C) Dark green, red pilots.	1600	3500
412	Pullman, "CALIFORNIA" (Standard), 1929-35.*		
	(A) Light green body, dark green roof, green or yellow windows.	850	1500
	(B) Light brown body, dark brown roof, yellow windows.	900	1800
413	Pullman, "COLORADO" (Standard), 1929-35.*		
	(A) Light green body, dark green roof, green or yellow windows.	850	1500
	(B) Light brown body, dark brown roof, yellow windows.	900	1800
414	Pullman, "ILLINOIS" (Standard), 1929-35.*		
	(A) Light green body, dark green roof, green windows.	975	2100
	(B) Light brown body, dark brown roof, yellow windows.	975	1800
416	Observation, "NEW YORK" (Standard), 1929-35.*		
	(A) Light green body, dark green roof, green windows.	850	1500
	(B) Light brown body, dark brown roof, yellow windows.	900	1800
418	Pullman (Standard), mojave, gold lettering, 1923-32.*	175	250
419	Combination (Standard), mojave, gold lettering, 1923-32.*	175	250
420	Pullman, "FAYE" (Std.), two-tone blue, cream windows, 1930-40.*	525	850
421	Pullman, "WESTPHAL" (Standard), two-tone blue, cream windows, 1930-40.*	525	850

		Gd	Exc
422	Observation, "TEMPEL" (Standard), two-tone blue, cream windows, 1930-40.*	525	850
424	Pullman (Standard), green body, dark green roof, 1931-40.*		
	(A) Brass trim.	325	500
	(B) Nickel trim.	350	600
425	Pullman (Standard), green body, dark green roof, 1931-40.*		
	(A) Brass trim.	325	500
	(B) Nickel trim.	350	600
426	Observation (Standard), green body, dark green roof, 1931-40.*		
	(A) Brass trim.	325	500
	(B) Nickel trim.	350	600
428	Pullman (Standard), 1926-30.*		
	(A) Dark green body and roof, various window colors.	225	300
	(B) Orange body and roof, apple green windows.	350	700
429	Combine (Standard), 1926-30*		
	(A) Dark green body and roof, various window colors.	225	300
	(B) Orange body and roof, apple green windows.	350	700
430	Observation (Standard), 1926-30.*		
	(A) Dark green body and roof, various window colors.	225	300
	(B) Orange body and roof, apple green windows.	350	700
431	Diner (Standard), 1927-32.*		
	(A) Mojave body, screw-mounted roof.	300	450
	(B) Mojave body, hinged roof.	400	600
	(C) Dark green body, orange windows.	350	600
	(D) Orange body, apple green windows.	350	600
	(E) Apple green body, red windows.	350	600
435	Power station, 7-1/2" x 6" base, various colors, 1926-38.*	75	150
436	Power station, 9-1/8" x 7-5/8" base, various colors, 1926-37.*		
	(A) "POWER STATION" plates over doors.	70	140
	(B) "EDISON SERVICE" plate.	200	350
437	Switch tower, mojave base, burnt orange and white/ivory, 1926-37.*	125	250
438	Signal tower, 6" x 4-3/4" x 12" tall, 1927-39.*		
	(A) Mojave base, orange house walls.	140	300
	(B) Gray base, ivory house walls.	210	450
	(C) Black base, white house walls.	210	450
439	Panel board, 8-3/16" x 7-3/16", red, 1928-42.	35	75
440/0440/440N	Signal bridge, 20-1/2" w. x 14" h., red or terra-cotta base, 1932-42.	150	500
440C	Panel board, light red frame, black board, 1932-42.	35	75
441	Weighing station (Standard), green base, cream building, 1932-36.	225	500
442	Landscape diner, illuminated, cream or ivory, 1938-42.	60	150
444	Roundhouse (Standard), 24" wide at rear, terra-cotta sides, 1932-35.*	1100	2500
444-18	Roundhouse clip, 1933.		NRS
450	Electric, 0-4-0 (O), 1930.		

Gd   **Exc**

The boxy 517 caboose and the 516 hopper car.

		Gd	Exc
	(A) Red, black frame.	250	400
	(B) Apple green, dark green frame.	350	500
455	Electric range, green legs, cream oven and stove sides, 1930, 1932-33.	200	500
490	Observation (Standard), mojave, gold lettering, 1923-32.*	175	250
500	Dealer display, pine bushes, 1927-28.		NRS
500	Electric derrick car (2-7/8"), 14-1/2" long, 1903-04.*	3000	4000
501	Dealer display, small pine trees, 1927-28.		NRS
502	Dealer display, medium pine trees, 1927-28.		NRS
503	Dealer display, large pine trees, 1927-28.		NRS
504	Dealer display, rose bushes, 1924-28.		NRS
505	Dealer display, oak trees, 1924-28.		NRS
506	Dealer display, platform with composition board, two sections, 1924-28.		NRS
507	Dealer display, platform with composition board, three sections, 1924-28.		NRS
508	Dealer display, sky background, two composition boards, 1924-28.		NRS
509	Dealer display, mountains on composition board, 1924-28.		NRS
510	Dealer display, canna bushes, 1927-28.		NRS
511	Flatcar (Standard), various shades of green, 1927-40.	35	50
512	Gondola (Standard), 1927-39.		
	(A) Peacock.	40	55
	(B) Green.	55	70
513	Cattle car (Standard), 1927-38.		
	(A) Olive green.	75	125
	(B) Orange.	60	100
	(C) Cream, maroon roof.	200	400
514	Boxcar (Standard), 1929-40.		
	(A) Cream yellow, orange roof.	75	100
	(B) Yellow, brown roof.	100	175
514	Refrigerator car (Standard), 1927-28.		
	(A) White, peacock roof.	250	475
	(B) Cream, peacock roof.	225	300
	(C) Ivory, peacock roof.	300	700

		Gd	Exc
	(D) Cream, green roof.	275	600
514R	Refrigerator car (Std.), 1929-40.		
	(A) Ivory, peacock roof, brass plates.	120	150
	(B) Ivory, light blue roof, nickel plates.	375	500
	(C) White, light blue roof, brass or nickel plates.	120	150
515	Tank car (Standard), 1927-40.		
	(A) Ivory or terra-cotta.	90	125
	(B) Light tan.	120	150
	(C) Silver.	100	150
	(D) Orange, red "SHELL" decal.	375	500
516	Hopper car (Standard), red, 1928-40.	100	150
517	Caboose (Standard), 1927-40.		
	(A) Pea green, red roof.	35	65
	(B) Red body and roof.	75	100
	(C) Red, black roof, orange windows.	250	400
520	Floodlight car (Standard), 1931-40.		
	(A) Terra-cotta base.	75	125
	(B) Green base.	100	175
529	Pullman (O), four wheels, 1926-32.		
	(A) Olive green body and roof.	10	20
	(B) Terra-cotta body and roof.	10	25
530	Observation (O), four wheels, 1926-32.		
	(A) Olive green body and roof.	10	20
	(B) Terra-cotta body and roof.	10	25
550	Miniature figures (Standard), set of six, "J. HILL & CO., ENGLAND" on bases, 1932-36.*	95	150
551	Engineer (Standard), 3" tall, 1932.	10	20
552	Conductor (Standard), 3" tall, 1932.	10	20
553	Porter (Standard), 3" tall, with removable foot stool, 1932.	10	20
554	Male passenger (Standard), 3" tall, 1932.	10	20
555	Female passenger (Standard), 3" tall, 1932.	10	20
556	Red Cap figure (Standard), 3" tall, 1932.	10	25
600	Derrick trailer (2-7/8"), 14-1/2" long, 1903-04.	3500	5000
600	Pullman, early (O), four wheels, 1915-23.		
	(A) Dark green.	20	60
	(B) Maroon or brown.	15	30
600	Pullman, late (O), eight wheels, 1933-42.		
	(A) Light red or gray; red roof.	35	75
	(B) Light blue, aluminum finish roof.	50	100
601	Pullman, early (O), 7" long, dark green, maroon inserts, 1915-23.	15	30
601	Observation, late (O), 1933-42.		
	(A) Light red body and roof.	35	75
	(B) Light gray, red roof.	35	75

		Gd	**Exc**

A pair of 610 Pullman cars from 1926-1930.
These were produced in a variety of attractive colors.

		Gd	Exc
	(C) Light blue body, aluminum finish roof.	50	100
602	Baggage (O), N Y C, dark green, 1915-23.	15	30
602	Baggage (O), 9" long, "LIONEL LINES", 1933-42.		
	(A) Light red or gray; red roof.	40	80
	(B) Light blue body, aluminum finish roof.	60	110
602	Observation, uncatalogued (O), 1922	10	20
603	Pullman, early (O), yellow-orange body and roof, 1922.	30	60
603	Pullman, later (O), 6-1/2" long, orange body and roof, 1920-25.	15	35
603	Pullman, latest, 7-1/2" long, 1931-36.		
	(A) Light red body and roof.	255	50
	(B) Red body, black roof.	20	35
	(C) Stephen Girard green, dark green roof.	20	35
	(D) Maroon body and roof, "MACY SPECIAL".	35	75
604	Observation, later (O), 6-1/4" long, orange, 1920-25.	15	25
604	Observation, latest (O), 7-1/2" long, 1931-36.		
	(A) Light red body and roof.	25	50
	(B) Red body, black roof.	20	35
	(C) Yellow-orange body, terra-cotta roof.	20	35
	(D) Stephen Girard green, dark green roof.	20	35
	(E) Maroon body and roof.	40	90
605	Pullman (O), 10-1/4" long, 1925-32.		
	(A) Gray body and roof, "LIONEL LINES".	50	100
	(B) Gray body and roof, "ILLINOIS CENTRAL".	50	100
	(C) Red body and roof, "LIONEL LINES".	100	150
	(D) Red body and roof, "ILLINOIS CENTRAL".	150	200
	(E) Orange body and roof, "LIONEL LINES".	100	150
	(F) Orange body and roof, "ILLINOIS CENTRAL".	175	250
	(G) Olive green body and roof, "LIONEL LINES".	150	200
606	Observation (O), 10-1/4" long, 1925-32.		
	(A) Gray body and roof, "LIONEL LINES".	50	100
	(B) Gray body and roof, "ILLINOIS CENTRAL".	50	100

		Gd	Exc
	(C) Red body and roof, "LIONEL LINES".	100	150
	(D) Red body and roof, "ILLINOIS CENTRAL".	150	200
	(E) Orange body and roof, "LIONEL LINES".	100	150
	(F) Orange body and roof, "ILLINOIS CENTRAL".	100	150
	(G) Olive green body and roof, "LIONEL LINES".	150	200
607	Pullman (O), 7-1/2", 1926-27.		
	(A) Peacock body and roof, "LIONEL LINES".	20	35
	(B) Peacock body and roof, "ILLINOIS CENTRAL".	30	60
	(C) Two-tone green, "LIONEL LINES".	20	40
	(D) Red body and roof, "LIONEL LINES".	30	55
608	Observation (O), 7-1/2", 1926-37.		
	(A) Peacock body and roof, "LIONEL LINES".	20	35
	(B) Peacock body and roof, "ILLINOIS CENTRAL".	30	60
	(C) Two-tone green, "LIONEL LINES".	20	40
	(D) Red body and roof, "LIONEL LINES".	30	55
609	Pullman (O), blue, aluminum roof, 1937.	30	60
610	Pullman, early (O), 8-1/2" long, 1915-25.		
	(A) Dark green body and roof.	20	50
	(B) Maroon body and roof.	35	75
	(C) Mojave body and roof.	35	75
610	Pullman, late (O), 8-3/4", 1926-30.		
	(A) Olive green body and roof.	25	50
	(B) Mojave body and roof.	25	50
	(C) Terra-cotta body, maroon roof.	50	100
	(D) Pea green body and roof.	35	75
	(E) Light blue body, aluminum finish roof.	65	170
	(F) Light red, aluminum finish roof.	50	100
611	Observation (O), blue body, aluminum finish roof, 1937.	30	60
612	Observation, early (O), 8-1/2" long, 1915-25.		
	(A) Dark green body and roof.	25	50
	(B) Maroon body and roof.	35	75
	(C) Mojave body and roof.	35	75
612	Observation, late (O), 8-3/4" long, 1926-30.		
	(A) Olive green body and roof.	25	50
	(B) Mojave body and roof.	25	50
	(C) Terra-cotta body, maroon roof.	50	100
	(D) Pea green body and roof.	35	75
	(E) Light blue body, aluminum finish roof.	65	170
	(F) Light red, aluminum finish roof.	50	100
613	Pullman (O), 10-1/4" long, 1931-40.*		
	(A) Terra-cotta, maroon and terra-cotta roof.	50	100
	(B) Light red, light red and aluminum roof.	125	250

Gd **Exc**

The gondola is a car with many purposes. It can be loaded with all sorts of bulky loads, as well as sand and other loose commodities. This is the 652 Lionel Lines gondola of 1935-1940. R. Bartelt photograph.

		Gd	Exc
	(C) Blue, two-tone blue roof.	75	150
614	Observation (O), 10-1/8" long, 1931-40.*		
	(A) Terra-cotta, maroon and terra-cotta roof.	50	100
	(B) Light red, light red and aluminum roof.	125	250
	(C) Blue, two-tone blue roof.	75	150
615	Baggage (O), 1933-40*	60	125
	(A) Terra-cotta, maroon and terra-cotta roof.	50	100
	(B) Light red, light red and aluminum roof.	125	250
	(C) Blue, two-tone blue roof.	75	150
616E/616W	Diesel only (O), 1935-41	45	75
616E/616W	Set: 616, 617, 617, and 618.	200	275
617	Coach (O), 1935-41.		
	(A) Blue and white.	75	150
	(B) Chrome, gun-metal skirts.	35	60
	(C) Chrome, chrome skirts.	50	90
	(D) Silver finish.	65	125
618	Observation (O), 1935-41.		
	(A) Blue and white.	75	150
	(B) Chrome, gun-metal skirts.	35	60
	(C) Chrome, chrome skirts.	50	90
	(D) Silver finish.	65	125
619	Combine (O), 1936-38.		
	(A) Blue, white window band.	85	200
	(B) Chrome, chrome skirts.	85	200
620	Floodlight car (O), gray or aluminum finished light housing, 1937-42.	20	25
629	Pullman (O), 6-1/2" long, 1924-32.		
	(A) Dark green body and roof.	15	25
	(B) Orange body and roof.	15	25
	(C) Red body and roof.	10	20
	(D) Light red body and roof.	20	35
630	Observation, 6-1/2" long, 1926-31.		

		Gd	Exc
	(A) Dark green body and roof.	15	25
	(B) Orange body and roof.	15	25
	(C) Red body and roof.	10	20
	(D) Light red body and roof.	20	35
636W	Diesel only (O), yellow and brown, 1936-41.	60	100
636W	Set: 636W, 637, 637, and 638.	200	400
637	Coach (O), yellow, brown roof, 1936-39.	50	100
638	Observation (O), yellow, brown roof, 1936-39.	50	100
651	Flatcar with wood load (O), light green, 1935-40.	10	20
652	Gondola (O), yellow or burnt orange, 1935-40.	12	25
653	Hopper car (O), 1934-40	20	30
654	Tank car (O), 1934-38.		
	(A) Orange or aluminum finish.	12	25
	(B) Gray.	18	40
655	Boxcar (O), 1934-42.		
	(A) Cream, maroon roof.	15	30
	(B) Cream, tuscan roof.	20	40
656	Cattle car (O), 1935-40.		
	(A) Light gray, vermilion roof.	25	40
	(B) Burnt orange, tuscan roof.	50	75
657	Caboose (O), 1934-42.		
	(A) Red body and roof.	10	20
	(B) Red, tuscan roof.	12	25
659	Dump car (O), 1935-42	25	40
700	Electric, 0-4-0 (O), dark green, red window, 1913-16.	250	400
700	Window display (2-7/8"), 1903-05.		NRS
700E	Steam, 4-6-4 scale Hudson, "5344" (O), black, white lett., 1937-42.*	1900	3500
700K	Steam, 4-6-4 unbuilt kit (O), 1938-42.	3500	5000
701	Electric, 0-4-0 (O), dark green, red window trim, 1913-16.	350	500
701	Steam, 0-6-0. (See 708)		
702	Baggage (O), plain gray for armored set, beware of altered cars, 1917-21.	90	200
703	Electric, 4-4-4 (O), dark green, red window trim, 1913-16.	1300	2000
706	Electric, 0-4-0 (O), dark green, red window trim, 1913-16.	300	500
708	Steam, 0-6-0, "8976" on boiler front (O), black, 1939- 42.*	1900	3000
710	Pullman (O), 11-1/2" long, 1924-34.		
	(A) Red, "LIONEL LINES".	100	175
	(B) Orange, "LIONEL LINES".	75	150
	(C) Orange, "NEW YORK CENTRAL".	100	175
	(D) Orange, "ILLINOIS CENTRAL".	150	300
	(E) Two-tone blue, "LIONEL LINES".	150	275
	(F) Orange, "NEW YORK CENTRAL".	100	175
711	Remote control Switches, pair (O72), 1935-42.	75	150

	Gd	**Exc**

The 806 Lionel Lines stock car features an operating door and attractive brass trim.

		Gd	Exc
712	Observation (O), 11-1/2" long, 1924-34.		
	(A) Red, "LIONEL LINES".	100	175
	(B) Orange, "LIONEL LINES".	75	150
	(C) Orange, "NEW YORK CENTRAL".	100	175
	(D) Orange, "ILLINOIS CENTRAL".	150	300
	(E) Two-tone blue, "LIONEL LINES".	150	275
	(F) Orange, "NEW YORK CENTRAL".	100	175
714	Boxcar, scale (O), Bakelite, tuscan, "PENNSYLVANIA", 1940-42.*	300	500
714K	Boxcar, unbuilt kit (O), gray primer, 1940-42.	—	800
715	Shell tank car, scale (O), die-cast, black, 1940-42.*		
	(A) "S.E.P.S. 8124" decal.	275	450
	(B) "S.U.N.X. 715" decal.	350	650
715K	Tank car, unbuilt kit (O), gray primer, 1940-42.	—	650
716	Hopper car, scale (O), die-cast, black, "532000", 1940- 42.*	400	600
716K	Hopper, unbuilt kit (O), gray primer, 1940-42.	—	850
717	Caboose, scale (O), die-cast, tuscan, 1940-42.*	325	450
717K	Caboose, unbuilt kit (O), gray primer, 1940-42.	—	650
720	90° crossing (O72), 1935-42.	7	15
721	Manual switches, pair (O72), 1935-42.	45	100
728	Electric, dark green, "QUAKER", 1916.		NRS
730	90° crossing (O72), 1935-42.	20	35
731	Remote-control switches, pair, T-rail (O72), 1935-42.	85	175
732	Electric, "QUAKER", 1916.		NRS
752E/752W	Streamlined diesel locomotive (O), 1934-41.		
	(A) Yellow and brown.	150	225
	(B) Aluminum finish.	130	200
753	Coach (O), part of articulated set, aluminum finish or yellow/brown, 1936-41.		
		75	150
754	Observation (O), part of articulated set, aluminum finish or yellow/brown, 1936-41.		
		75	150
760	16 piece curved track (O72), 1935-42.	25	50

		Gd	Exc
761	Curved track (O72), 1934-42.	**1**	**2**
762	Straight track (O72), 1934-42.	**1**	**2**
762	Insulated straight track (O72), 1934-42.	**2**	**3**
763E	Steam, 4-6-4 (O), 1937-42.		
	(A) Gun-metal, 263 or 2263W oil tender.	**1000**	**2750**
	(B) Gun-metal, 2226X or 2226WX tender.	**2000**	**5500**
	(C) Black, 2226WX tender.	**1200**	**3000**
771	Curved track, T-rail (O72), 1935-42.	**3**	**6**
772	Straight track, T-rail (O72), 1935-42.	**4**	**10**
773	Fishplate outfit (O72), 1936-42.	**25**	**30**
782	Combine (O) from articulated set; orange, gray, and maroon; 1935- 41.	**185**	**400**
783	Coach (O) from articulated set; orange, gray, and maroon; 1935- 41.	**185**	**400**
784	Observation (O) from articulated set; orange, gray, maroon; 1935-41.	**185**	**400**
792	Combine (O), part of articulated set, maroon and red, 1937-41.	**300**	**800**
793	Coach (O), part of articulated set, maroon and red, 1937-41.	**300**	**800**
794	Observation (O), part of articulated set, maroon and red, 1927-41.	**300**	**800**
800	Boxcar (2-7/8"), 14-1/2" long, 1904-05.*	**2000**	**3000**
800	Boxcar (O), 1915-26.		
	(A) Light orange, brownish-maroon roof, "WABASH / 6399".	**15**	**50**
	(B) Orange body and roof, "PENN RR / 4862".	**10**	**35**
801	Caboose (O), brown or maroon, "WABASH / RR / 4890", 1915-26.	**15**	**35**
802	Stock car (O), green, "UNION / STOCK / LINE", 1915-26.	**20**	**40**
803	Hopper car, early (O), dark green, 1923-28.	**20**	**30**
803	Hopper car, late (O), peacock, 1929-34.	**20**	**25**
804	Tank car (O), early, dark gray, 1923-28.	**20**	**25**
804	Tank car (O), late, aluminum or yellow-orange finish, 1929-34.	**20**	**25**
805	Boxcar (O), 1927-34.		
	(A) Pea green, terra-cotta roof.	**20**	**25**
	(B) Pea green, maroon roof.	**25**	**50**
	(C) Orange, maroon roof.	**25**	**40**
806	Stock car (O), 1927-34.		
	(A) Pea green, terra-cotta roof.	**30**	**45**
	(B) Orange; maroon, orange, or pea green roof.	**20**	**30**
807	Caboose (O), 1927-40.		
	(A) Peacock, dark green roof.	**20**	**25**
	(B) Red, peacock roof.	**20**	**25**
	(C) Light red body and roof.	**23**	**28**
809	Dump car (O), 1930-41.		
	(A) Orange bin.	**20**	**35**
	(B) Green bin.	**20**	**40**
810	Crane (O), 1930-42.		
	(A) Terra-cotta cab, maroon roof, peacock boom.	**50**	**100**

Gd   Exc

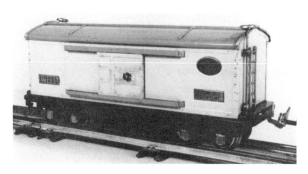

An attractive 814 boxcar with a sliding door and brass details, including nameplates, ladders, and brakewheels R. Bartelt photograph.

		Gd	Exc
	(B) Cream cab, vermilion roof, light green boom.	50	100
811	Flatcar (O), 1926-40.		
	(A) Maroon.	30	55
	(B) Aluminum finish.	35	75
812	Gondola (O), mojave or dark green, 1926-42.	20	40
812T	Tool set (Std.), spade, pick, and shovel in orange and bluebox, 1930-41.	15	30
813	Stock car (O), 1926-42.		
	(A) Orange, pea green roof.	30	65
	(B) Orange, maroon roof.	30	65
	(C) Cream, maroon roof.	60	120
	(D) Tuscan body and roof.	—	1200
814	Boxcar (O), 1926-42.		
	(A) Cream, orange roof.	20	75
	(B) Cream, maroon roof.	50	100
	(C) Yellow, brown roof.	50	80
814R	Refrigerator car (O), 1929-42.		
	(A) Ivory, peacock roof.	50	125
	(B) White, light blue roof.	60	175
	(C) Flat white, brown roof.	300	600
815	Tank car (O), 1926-42.		
	(A) Pea green, maroon frame.	125	250
	(B) Pea green, black frame.	35	75
	(C) Aluminum, black frame.	25	55
	(D) Orange-yellow, black frame.	75	125
816	Hopper car (O), 1927-42.		
	(A) Olive green.	40	90
	(B) Red body.	35	80
	(C) Black body.	200	400
817	Caboose (O), 1926-42.		
	(A) Peacock, dark green roof.	25	60
	(B) Red, peacock roof.	35	75

		Gd	Exc
	(C) Light red body and roof.	35	75
820	Boxcar (O), 1915-26.		
	(A) Orange, "ILLINOIS CENTRAL".	25	40
	(B) Orange, "UNION PACIFIC".	35	50
820	Floodlight car (O), 1931-42.		
	(A) Terra-cotta.	50	125
	(B) Green.	65	150
	(C) Light green.	50	125
821	Stock car (O), green, 1915-16, 1925-26.	45	75
822	Caboose (O), brown or maroon, 1915-26.	35	50
831	Flatcar with lumber load (O), dark green, 1927-34.	15	25
840	Industrial power station, 26" x 21-1/2" x 18"; must include grates, steps, and smokestacks for values shown, cream or white sides, 1928-40.*	1200	3000
900	Ammunition car (O), gray or khaki, 1917-21.	60	125
900	Boxcar trailer (2-7/8"), 14-1/2" long, 1904-05.	2000	3000
901	Gondola (O); brown, maroon, gray, or green, 1917-27.	20	35
902	Gondola (O), 1927-34.	15	25
910	Grove of trees, 16" x 8-3/4" base, 1932-42.*	70	150
911	Country estate w/ house, illum., 16" x 8" base, various colors, 1932-42.	175	350
912	Suburban home, illuminated, 16" x 8" base, various colors.	175	350
913	Landscaped bungalow, illuminated, 16" x 8-3/4" base, 1940-42.	140	275
914	Park landscape, 1932-35.	90	200
915	Tunnel (Std.), molded felt on wooden base, 65" x 28-1/2" x 23-1/2", 1932, 1934-35.	100	250
916	Tunnel (O), 29-1/4" or 37" long, 1935.	70	150
917	Scenic hillside with two houses, 34" x 9-1/2", 1932-36.	90	200
918	Scenic hillside with one house, 30" x 9-1/2", 1932-36.	90	200
919	Park grass, 8 oz. bag, 1932-42.	7	15
920	Village with buildings, two end sections, 57" x 31-1/2", 1932-33.	600	1500
921	Scenic park, three pieces, 85" x 31-1/2", 1932-33.	1000	2500
921C	Park center with buildings, 28" x 31-1/2", 1932-33.	400	1000
922	Terrace, illuminated, 13" x 3-3/4" base, 1932-36.	80	150
923	Tunnel (O), curved, felt on wood base, 40-1/4" long, 1933-42.	70	200
924	Tunnel (O72), felt on wood base, 30" long, 1935-42.	50	125
925	Lubricant, 2 oz., 1935-42.	1	2
927	Flag plot, silk flag, 14-3/4" tall, 1937-42.	60	125
1000	Passenger car (2-7/8"), 14-3/4" long, 1905.*	3500	5000
1000	Trolley trailer (Std.), blue, white windows, 1910-13.		
1010	Trolley trailer, matches 10 Interurban, maroon or dark olive, 1910-14.	600	1400
1010	Electric, 0-4-0 (O), light orange or tan, 1931-32.	45	75
1011	Pullman (O), light or dark orange, 1931-32.	10	30
1012	Station, lithographed building with transformer inside, 1932.	20	35
1013	Curved track, tubular rail (O27), 1932-42.	.10	.25

	Gd	Exc

Two of Lionel's inexpensive, four-wheel passenger cars with lithographed bodies, the 1011 Winner Lines Pullman (left) and the 1811 Ives R.R. Lines (right).

		Gd	Exc
1015	Steam, 0-4-0 (O), black, copper trim, 1931-32.	60	90
1017	Winner station, lithographed building with transformer inside, 1933.	15	40
1017	Transformer in tin station, 1932-33.	15	40
1018	Straight track, tubular rail (O27), 1932-42.	.10	.25
1019	Observation (O), light or dark orange, 1931-32.	25	50
1019	Remote-control track (O27), 1938-42.	1	2
1020	Baggage (O), light or dark orange, 1931-32.	50	100
1021	90° crossover (O27), Winner, 1932-42.	1	2
1022	Tunnel, no building, 18-3/4" long (O), 1935-42.	7	15
1023	Tunnel (O), 19" long, felt composition, 1934-42.	10	15
1024	Switches (O27), pair, 1937-42.	2	5
1025	Bumper (O27), black die-cast body, red bulb, 1940-42.	6	15
1027	Lionel Junior station, lithographed, transformer inside, 1934.	15	40
1028	Transformer, 40 watts, 1939.	2	4
1029	Rheostat, 25 watts, 1935-39.	1	2
1030	Electric, 0-4-0 (O), dark orange, green roof, 1932.	60	90
1030	Rheostat, 40 watts, 1935-38.	2	3
1035	Steam, 0-4-0 (O), black, hooded headlight, 1932.	65	95
1036	Rheostat, 40 watts, c. 1940.	2	3
1037	Rheostat, 40 watts, 1940-42.	1	2
1038	Rheostat, 30 watts, c. 1940.	2	3
1039	Rheostat, 35 watts, 1937-40.	1	2
1040	Rheostat, 60 watts, 1937-39.	5	10
1041	Rheostat, 60 watts, 1939-42.	5	10
1045	Operating watchman, red base, blue man, 1938-42.	10	25
1050	Passenger car trailer (2-7/8"), 14-3/4" long, 1905.	3500	5000
1100	Handcar, Mickey Mouse (O), 1935-37.*		
	(A) Red base.	400	500
	(B) Apple green base, orange shoes, Minnie with green skirt.	500	700
	(C) Orange base.	600	950
1100	Trolley trailer, matches 101 (Standard), blue and maroon, 1910-13.		NRS

		Gd	Exc
1103	Handcar (O), Peter Rabbit, yellow base, 1935-37.	400	850
1105	Handcar (O), Santa Claus w/Mickey in sack, 1935-36.		
	(A) Red base.	575	900
	(B) Green base.	625	1000
1107	Transformer in tin station, 1933.	15	40
1107	Handcar (O), Donald Duck, 1936-37.		
	(A) White dog house with red roof.	450	800
	(B) White dog house with green roof.	425	700
	(C) Orange dog house with green roof.	600	1200
1121	Switches, pair (O27), 1937-42.	15	25
1506L	Steam, 0-4-0 (O), clockwork, black and red, 1933-34.	90	115
1506M	Steam, 0-4-0 (O), clockwork, red, "MICKEY MOUSE" tender, 1935.	225	400
1508	Steam, 0-4-0, Commodore Vanderbilt with Mickey Mouse, clockwork, red, 1935.	275	400
1511	Steam, 0-4-0 (O), black or light red, 1936-37.	100	150
1512	Gondola (O), blue, lithographed, 1931-33, 1936-37.	6	12
1514	Boxcar (O), cream, blue or orange roof, lithographed, 1931-37.	6	12
1515	Tank car (O), aluminum finish, lithographed, 1933-37.	6	12
1517	Caboose (O), red, lithographed, 1931-37.	6	12
1518	Diner (O), 1935.	35	75
1519	Band (O), 1935.	35	75
1520	Animal (O), 1935.	35	75
1550	Switches, pair, clockwork, 1933-37.	2	5
1555	90° crossover, clockwork, 1933-37.	1	2
1560	Station, lithographed, cream walls, red roof, 1933-37.	12	20
1569	Accessory set, (4) telegraph poles, (1) semaphore, (1) railroad sign, (1) gate, (1) clock, 1933-37.	20	45
1588	Steam, 0-4-0 (O), red, brown roof, 1936-37.	100	150
1630	Pullman (O), blue, 1938-42.		
	(A) Aluminum windows.	15	25
	(B) Light gray windows.	20	30
1631	Observation (O), blue, 1938-42.		
	(A) Aluminum windows.	15	25
	(B) Light gray windows.	20	30
1651E	Electric, 0-4-0 (O), 1933.	100	150
1661E	Steam, 2-4-0 (O), gloss black, red frame, 1933.	65	100
1662	Steam, 0-4-0 (O), black, white lettering, 1940-42.	130	200
1663	Steam, 0-4-0 (O), black, white lettering, 1940-42.	160	250
1664/1664E	Steam, 2-4-2 (O), 1938-42.		
	(A) Gun-metal.	45	70
	(B) Black.	45	65
1666/1666E	Steam, 2-6-2 (O), 1938-42.		
	(A) Gun-metal.	55	80

	Gd	Exc

The sleek 1668E Lionel Lines streamlined steam locomotive is a favorite of many collectors. R. Bartelt photograph.

		Gd	Exc
	(B) Black.	45	75
1668/1668E	Steam, 2-6-2 (O), gun-metal or black, 1937-41.	60	100
1673	Coach (O), blue, 1936-37.		
	(A) Aluminum windows.	15	25
	(B) Light gray windows.	20	30
1674	Pullman (O), 1936-37.	20	35
1675	Observation (O), 1936-37.	20	35
1677	Gondola (O), lithographed, 1933-35.		
	(A) "IVES / R.R. LINES", light blue.	20	50
	(B) "LIONEL" on side, blue or red.	10	30
1678	Stock car (O), dark pea green, "IVES" on side, 1931- 35.	225	375
1679	Boxcar (O), lithographed, 1933-42.		
	(A) Cream, "IVES" on side.	15	40
	(B) Cream, "LIONEL" on side.	10	30
	(C) Cream or yellow, "BABY RUTH" logo.	5	15
1680	Tank car (O), lithographed, 1933-42.		
	(A) Aluminum finish, "IVES TANK LINES".	20	40
	(B) Aluminum finish, no "IVES" lettering.	5	15
1681	Steam, 2-4-0 (O), 1934-35.		
	(A) Black, red frame.	30	70
	(B) Red, red frame.	60	90
1681E	Steam, 2-4-0 (O), 1934-35.		
	(A) Black, red frame.	30	70
	(B) Red, red frame.	60	90
1682	Caboose (O), lithographed, 1933-42.		
	(A) Vermilion, "IVES" on side.	10	25
	(B) Red or tuscan, "LIONEL".	5	15
1684	Steam, 2-4-2 (O), black, 1942.	30	50
1685	Coach, uncatalogued (O), 1933-37.		
	(A) Gray, maroon roof.	140	300
	(B) Red, maroon roof.	100	200

		Gd	Exc
	(C) Blue, silver roof.	100	190
1686	Baggage, uncatalogued (O), 1933-37.		
	(A) Gray, maroon roof.	140	300
	(B) Red, maroon roof.	100	200
	(C) Blue, silver roof.	100	190
1687	Observation, uncatalogued (O), 1933-37.		
	(A) Gray, maroon roof.	140	300
	(B) Red, maroon roof.	100	200
	(C) Blue, silver roof.	100	200
1688/1688E	Steam, 2-4-2 (O), gun-metal, 1936.	30	50
1689E	Steam, 2-4-2 (O), 1936-37.		
	(A) Gun-metal.	50	70
	(B) Black.	40	60
1690	Pullman (O), dark red/brown roof or light red body and roof, 1933-39.	8	15
1691	Observation, uncatalogued (O), dark red/brown roof or lt. red body/roof.	8	15
1692	Pullman, uncatalogued (O), greenish-blue, 1939.	15	30
1693	Observation, uncatalogued (O), greenish-blue.	15	30
1700E	Diesel, power unit only (O), 1935-37.	20	40
1700E	Set: 1700, 1701 (2), 1702 (O), 1935-37.		
	(A) Aluminum and light red.	55	200
	(B) Chrome and light red.	55	100
	(C) Orange and gray.	150	300
1701	Coach (O), 1935-37.		
	(A) Chrome sides and roof.	10	25
	(B) Silver sides and roof.	15	30
	(C) Orange and gray.	35	75
1702	Observation (O), 1935.		
	(A) Chrome sides and roof.	10	25
	(B) Silver sides and roof.	15	30
	(C) Orange and gray.	35	75
1703	Front end coach w/hooked coupler, uncatalogued, chrome or silver finish, 1935-37.	35	75
1707	Gondola, lithographed, burnt orange, "IVES", 1932.	15	30
1708	Stock car, lithographed, green, "IVES", 1932.	100	350
1709	Boxcar, lithographed, Stephen Girard green, "IVES", 1932.	20	40
1712	Caboose, lithographed, orange, "IVES", 1932.	20	40
1717	Gondola, uncatalogued (O), lithographed, orange, 1933-40.	10	20
1717X	Gondola, uncatalogued (O), lithographed, orange, 1940.	10	30
1719	Boxcar, uncatalogued (O), lithographed, light blue, 1933-40.	15	25
1719X	Boxcar, uncatalogued (O), lithographed, light blue, 1941-42.	15	25
1722	Caboose, uncatalogued (O), lithographed, red, 1933-42.	15	25
1722X	Caboose, uncatalogued (O), lithographed, red, 1939-40.	8	20
1766	Pullman (Standard), Ives design, 1934-40.*		

Gd   Exc

During the Depression years Lionel offered inexpensive lithographed cars like this 1813 baggage car. R. Bartelt photograph.

		Gd	Exc
	(A) Terra-cotta, maroon roof, brass trim.	300	600
	(B) Red, maroon roof, nickel trim.	300	500
1767	Baggage (Standard), Ives design, 1934-40.*		
	(A) Terra-cotta, maroon roof, brass trim.	300	600
	(B) Red, maroon roof, nickel trim.	300	500
1768	Observation (Standard), Ives design, 1934-40.*		
	(A) Terra-cotta, maroon roof, brass trim.	300	600
	(B) Red, maroon roof, nickel trim.	300	500
1811	Pullman (O), four wheels, various colors, 6" long, 1933-37.	10	30
1812	Observation (O), four wheels, various colors, 6" long, 1933-37.	25	50
1813	Baggage (O), four wheels, peacock or light red, 6" long.	50	100
1816/1816W	Diesel (O), clockwork, silver, 1935-37.	65	200
1817	Coach (O), chrome, orange band, 1935-37.	20	40
1818	Observation (O), chrome, orange band, 1935-37.	20	40
1835E	Steam, 2-4-2 (Standard), black, 1934-39.	450	750
1910	Electric, 0-6-0 early (Standard), dark olive green, red vents, 1910-11.	750	1600
1910	Electric, 0-6-0 late (Std.), dark olive green, red pilots, 1912.	450	1000
1910	Pullman (Std.), dark olive green body and roof, maroon doors, 1909-10.	800	1500
1911	Electric, 0-4-0 early (Std.), maroon or dark olive green, 1910-12.	1000	2000
1911	Electric, 0-4-0 late (Standard), 1913.	700	1200
1911	Electric, 0-4-4-0 (Std.), maroon, gold "1911 SPECIAL", 1911-12.	1000	2000
1912	Electric, 0-4-4-0 (Standard), dark olive green, 1910-12.		
	(A) "New York, New Haven and Hartford".	1800	3200
	(B) "NEW YORK CENTRAL LINES".	1500	2700
1912	Electric, 0-4-4-0 Special (Std.), dark olive green, 1911.*	2000	5000
2200	Trolley trailer, matches 202 (Std.), red and yellow, gold lett., 1910-13.	1100	2500
2600	Pullman (O), red, ivory trim, 1938-42.	45	100
2601	Observation (O), red, ivory trim, 1938-42.	45	100
2602	Baggage (O), red, ivory trim, 1938-42.	65	125
2613	Pullman (O), 1938-42.*		
	(A) Blue, two-tone blue roof.	90	200

		Gd	Exc
	(B) State green, two-tone green roof.	180	325
2614	Observation (O), 1938-42.*		
	(A) Blue, two-tone blue roof.	90	200
	(B) State green, two-tone green roof.	180	325
2615	Baggage (O), 1938-42.*		
	(A) Blue, two-tone blue roof.	115	225
	(B) State green, two-tone green roof.	200	350
2620	Floodlight (O), gray or aluminum finished light housing, 1938-42.	18	45
2623	Pullman (O), Bakelite, tuscan, 1941-42.		
	(A) "IRVINGTON".	100	225
	(B) "MANHATTAN".	90	200
2624	Pullman (O), Bakelite, tuscan, 1941-42.	700	1500
2630	Pullman (O), blue, 1938-42.	15	30
2631	Observation (O), blue, 1938-42.	15	30
2640	Pullman, illuminated (O), 1938-42.		
	(A) Light blue, aluminum finish roof.	20	35
	(B) State green, dark green roof.	20	40
2641	Observation, illuminated (O), 1938-42.		
	(A) Light blue, aluminum finish roof.	20	35
	(B) State green, dark green roof.	20	40
2642	Pullman (O), tuscan, 1941-42.	15	30
2643	Observation (O), tuscan, 1941-42.	15	30
2651	Flatcar (O), light green, 1938-42.	15	35
2652	Gondola (O), yellow or burnt orange, 1938-41.	10	30
2653	Hopper car (O), 1938-42.		
	(A) Stephen Girard green.	20	45
	(B) Black.	35	75
2654	Tank car (O), 1938-42.		
	(A) Aluminum finish, "SUNOCO".	10	35
	(B) Orange, "SHELL".	12	45
	(C) Light gray, "SUNOCO".	20	45
2655	Boxcar (O), 1938-39.		
	(A) Cream, maroon roof.	20	55
	(B) Cream, tuscan roof.	20	60
2656	Stock car (O), 1938-39.		
	(A) Light gray, red roof.	30	60
	(B) Burnt orange, tuscan roof.	50	90
2657	Caboose (O), red, red or tuscan roof, 1940-41.	10	20
2657X	Caboose (O), "X" on box (not car), red, 1940-41.	10	20
2659	Dump car (O), green, black frame, 1938-42.	25	40
2660	Crane (O), cream cab, red roof, green boom, 1938-42.	21	45
2672	Caboose (O), tuscan, "477618", 1942.	10	20

Gd   **Exc**

The 2679 boxcar features a billboard design advertising Baby Ruth candy bars. The body is lithographed. R. Bartlet photograph.

		Gd	Exc
2677	Gondola (O), red, lithographed, 1940-42.	9	18
2679	Boxcar (O), yellow, blue or peacock roof, lithographed, 1938-42.	9	20
2680	Tank car (O), lithographed, 1938-42.		
	(A) Aluminum finish, "SUNOCO".	9	20
	(B) Orange, "SHELL".	9	20
2682	Caboose (O), lithographed, red or brown, 1938-42.	8	20
2682X	Caboose (O), 1938-42	8	20
2717	Gondola (O), uncatalogued, lithographed, burnt orange, 1938-42.	14	30
2719	Boxcar (O), uncatalogued, lithographed, peacock, 1938-42.	15	30
2722	Caboose (O), uncatalogued, litho., orange-red, maroon roof, 1938-42.	14	30
2755	Tank car (O), gray or aluminum finish, "SUNOCO", 1941-42.		
2757	Caboose (O), tuscan, "477618", 1941-42.	20	30
2757X	Caboose (O), 1941-42.	20	30
2758	Automobile boxcar (O), tuscan, "PENNSYLVANIA", 1941-42.	25	35
2810	Crane (O), yellow cab, light red roof, green boom, 1938-42.	60	125
2811	Flatcar (O), aluminum finish, 1938-42.	60	125
2812	Gondola (O), 1938-42.		
	(A) Green.	20	40
	(B) Dark orange.	35	75
2812X	Gondola (O), dark orange, 1941-42.	35	75
2813	Stock car (O), cream or light yellow, maroon roof, 1938-42.	100	175
2814	Boxcar (O), 1938-42.		
	(A) Cream, maroon roof.	60	100
	(B) Orange, brown roof.	300	600
2814R	Refrigerator car (O), 1938-42.		
	(A) White, light blue roof, nickel plates.	150	275
	(B) White, brown roof, no plates.	400	800
2815	Tank car (O), 1938-42.		
	(A) Aluminum finish.	30	65
	(B) Orange.	75	150
2816	Hopper car (O), 1935-42.		

		Gd	Exc

The 3814 Lionel Lines "Merchandise" car features an attractive multicolor logo at upper right. R. Bartelt photograph.

		Gd	Exc
	(A) Red.	40	85
	(B) Black.	85	150
2817	Caboose (O), 1936-42.		
	(A) Light red body and roof.	35	75
	(B) Flat red, tuscan roof.	60	125
2820	Floodlight car (O), green base, 1938-42.		
	(A) Stamped nickel searchlights.	75	150
	(B) Gray die-cast searchlights.	125	225
2952	Gondola (O), orange, "30164", 1940-42.	90	200
2954	Boxcar (O), tuscan, "100800", 1940-42.	200	450
2955	Tank car (O), black, 1940-42.		
	(A) "SHELL" decal.	200	500
	(B) "SUNOCO" decal.	300	700
2956	Hopper car (O), black, "532000", 1940-42.	200	425
2957	Caboose (O), tuscan, 1940-42.	200	425
3300	Trolley trailer, dark olive and yellow, 1910-13.	1400	3000
3651	Operating lumber car (O), black, silver lettering, 1939-42.	10	20
3652	Operating gondola (O), yellow, black frame, 1939-42.	17	40
3659	Operating dump car (O), light red, black frame, 1939-42.	11	20
3811	Operating lumber dump car (O), black, 1939-42.	25	50
3814	Operating merchandise car (O), tuscan, 1929-42.	65	100
3859	Operating dump car (O), red bin, black frame, 1938-42.	20	50
4862	(See 800(B) boxcar)		
4890	(See 801 caboose)		
5342	(See 001, 002, 003, and 004 steam locomotives, OO Gauge)		
6399	(See 800(A) boxcar)		
8124	(See 715(A) tank car)		
8976	(See 227, 228, 229, 230, 706, and 708)		
19400	(See 717 and 2957 cabooses)		
100800	(See 714 and 2954 boxcars)		
477618	(See 2672 and 2757 cabooses)		

		Gd	Exc
532000	(See 716 and 2956 hoppers)		
No number	(Mickey Mouse) "CIRCUS DINING CAR", lithographed, 1935.	35	75
No number	Mickey Mouse Band car, lithographed, 1935.	35	75
No number	Mickey Mouse Circus car, lithographed, 1935.	35	75
A	Miniature motor, 1904.	50	100
A	Transformer, 40 or 60 watts, 1927-37.	1	2
B	New Departure motor, 1906-16.	50	100
B	Transformer, 50 or 75 watts, 1916-38.	1	2
C	New Departure motor, 1906-16.	50	100
D	New Departure motor, 1906-14.	50	100
E	New Departure motor, 1906-14.	50	100
F	New Departure motor, 1906-14.	50	100
G	Battery fan motor, 1906-14.	50	100
K	Power motor, 1904-06.	50	100
K	Transformer, 150 or 200 watts.	2	5
L	Power motor, 1905.	50	100
L	Transformer, 50 or 75 watts.	1	2
M	Battery motor, 1915-20.	30	75
N	Transformer, 50 watts.	1	2
Q	Transformer, 50 watts.	1	2
Q	Transformer, 75 watts.	7	12
R	Battery motor, 1915-20.	30	75
R	Transformer, 100 watts, 1938-42.	10	20
S	Transformer, 50 watts.	1	2
S	Transformer, 80 watts.	7	12
T	Transformer, 75, 100 or 150 watts.	1	3
U	Transformer, Alladin.	1	2
V	Transformer, 150 watts, 1939-42.	25	45
W	Transformer, 75 watts.	1	3
Y	Battery motor, 1915-20.	40	80
Z	Transformer, 250 watts, 1939-42.	35	60
106	Rheostat, 1911-14.	3	9
1029	25 watts, 1936.	1	2
1030	40 watts, 1935-38.	2	3
1031	Rheostat, circa 1938.	2	3
1036	Rheostat, circa 1941.	2	3
1037	40 watts, 1940-42.	1	2
1038	Rheostat, circa 1940.	2	3
1039	35 watts, 1937-40.	1	2
1040	60 watts, 1937-39.	5	10
1041	60 watts, 1939-42.	5	10

Gd   Exc

Track, Lockons, and Contactors

Sometimes newcomers or antique dealers are surprised to learn that antique track has so little value. The truth is that people who operate their trains generally prefer to buy new track, rather than operate with old track that might have kinks or rust. Trains that ran on O27 track before World War II can be run on modern O27 track, etc. So, if you want to sell old track, you generally have to make it appealing by selling at the prices shown here.

	Gd	Exc
O Straight	.20	.50
O Curve	.15	.40
O72 Straight or curve	1	2
O27 Straight	.10	.30
O27 Curve	.10	.20
Standard Gauge straight or curve; per section:	.50	1
O Gauge lockon	.10	.25
Standard Gauge lockon	.25	.50
UTC lockon	.25	.75
145C Contactor	.50	1
153C Contactor	.50	1.50

Highlights of Lionel Postwar History

While the War Production Board had mandated the cessation of toy train manufacture during the war, the creativity of Joshua Lionel Cowen and his superb staff remained unbridled. Many plans were made; many ideas discussed. The postwar Lionel trains would be the best ever — the most action, the greatest selection.

In February 1945 the W. P. B. lifted its restrictive orders and thus initiated the race to resume train production. Lionel won hands-down; Gilbert and Marx did not manage to get their trains back on the shelves until 1946.

Soon, Lionel's engineering and production departments hit their stride again. In 1946 the company introduced what has become perhaps the most memorable of all Lionel train features — the smoke that came from the locomotives when one dropped a small white pill into the heating unit. In the next two years Lionel introduced several of its most popular locomotives, the Pennsylvania Railroad GG-1 electric and the Santa Fe and New York Central F-3 diesels.

For the first time ever a complete family appeared on the cover of Lionel's catalogue in 1949. For the previous 48 years the company had virtually ignored women and girls. Today many women remember their disappointment as their brothers excluded them from the supposedly masculine enjoyment of toy trains. Lionel would continue to ignore the potential interest of girls until the release of their almost laughable pastel-colored "Girl's Set" in 1957.

As the postwar economy boomed, Lionel's sales skyrocketed. Joshua Lionel Cowen had come to stride with his abilities. He captured boys' imaginations with his remarkable advertising; made permanent happy memories for millions; and created what is probably the single most highly-recognized trade name of all toy makers. The company's bold advertising spread the word further and wider — Lionel trains made boys happy, Lionel trains made boys men, and so on.

In the early 1950s children of the postwar "baby boom" reached the ideal age for Lionel trains. This vast market offered Lionel more potential sales than it had ever considered. Furthermore, the parents of these children knew trains. Trains had been a vital part of the war effort (delivering troops and equipment to the ports for shipment overseas); trains still hauled more freight than did highway trucks; trains carried Eisenhower on his campaign tour. Joshua Lionel Cowen understood better than any other the need to give children not only trains and tracks, but also buttons and switches, bells and whistles. The famous Lionel milk car exemplified the aging man's ability to see through a child's eyes.

But there were problems. Joshua Lionel Cowen was indeed an aging man; his energies were no longer unlimited. The company itself had grown tremendously, becoming a large "corporation" with unionized labor and enough middle management to remove the patriarchal flair that Cowen had impressed on so many prewar workers. Owing to its size, the company also felt the need to expand and did so by expanding into markets it did not know (e.g., Airex fishing equipment, the Linex stereo camera). Cowen's son Lawrence, a bright, articulate man, had risen to a position to manage the company, but he lacked the dynamic, purposeful drive of his father.

External factors also played against The Lionel Corporation. Discounters like Two-Guys from Harrison and Korvettes eroded the traditional network of Lionel dealers, which included hardware stores, family-owned toy/hobby shops, and the toy departments in large retail stores.

Lionel fought, but the retail price maintenance that it relied on disappeared. In the faceless environment of discount stores, customers purchased trains without the helpful guidance of knowledgeable salesmen (many of whom were train enthusiasts themselves). Lionel had heavily relied on salesmen and displays to demonstrate the *exciting* and *action-filled* aspects of its trains. Static display would not and could not do this.

The late 1950s also brought several other phenomena that would adversely affect Lionel's sales. First, the Russian launch of Sputnik and the heightening of the Cold War brought with it an increased awareness of rockets and space craft. While these captured the imaginations of the new youth, Lionel's gimmick-laden space and military trains did not. Second, slot cars became a fad-like craze in the toy market. Most children were learning to drive before they rode their first train — cars, not trains, interested them.

Under the management of a team led by Roy Cohn, a young distant relative of Joshua Lionel Cowen, the company attempted in various ways to resurrect its position in the toy market and interest in toy trains. In 1967, for the first time since the wartime hiatus of 1943-1944, Lionel failed to issue a new consumer catalogue.

The Lionel Corporation purchased the American Flyer trademark and tooling from A. C. Gilbert in 1967, two years before it finally ceased production of its own toy trains. In a fortunate coincidence, General Mills was engaged in an aggressive acquisition program of acquiring toy companies. General Mills licensed the right to manufacture Lionel trains, with use of the Lionel trademark and tooling.

Although there have been additional corporate changes in the interim, the overall outlook has turned very positive — so much so that the period of post-1970 production is dubbed "Modern Era" by collectors. Additional details can be found in the "Lionel: 1970-1990" section.

Lionel Postwar (1945-1969)

		Good	Exc
022	Remote-control switches, pair (O), 1945-49.	25	55
022A	Remote-control switches, pair (O).	—	100
30	Water tower, 1947-50.	25	80
35	Boulevard lamp, 1945-49.	8	20
36	Remote-control set (Super O), 1957-60.	1	4
37	Uncoupling track set (Super O), 1957-66.	1	4
38	Water tower, 1946-47.	50	250
38	Accessory adapter track (Super O), 1957-61.	1	4
39	Operating set (Super O), 1957.	1	4
39-25	Operating set (Super O), 1961-66.	1	4
41	US Army, switcher, black, white lettering, 1955-57.	45	95
42	Picatinny Arsenal, switcher, olive drab, white lettering, 1957.	100	200
042/42	Manual switches, pair (O), 1946-59.	10	35
43	Power track, 1959-66.	1.50	3
44-80	Missiles, 1959-60.	3	7
44	US Army, mobile launcher, blue, gray launcher, 1959-62.	60	150

		Gd	Exc

"SAVE TIME — HAVE FARE READY"
as you enter the Lionelville Rapid Transit
trolley. This little charmer has operated
on train layouts, in shop windows, and
under Christmas trees for over 30 years.

No.	Description	Gd	Exc
45	US, mobile launcher switcher, olive drab, gray launcher, 1960- 62.	80	250
45	Automatic gateman, 1946-49.	15	30
45N	Automatic gateman, 1945.	15	30
50	Lionel, gang car, orange, blue or gray bumpers, three men, 1955- 64.	30	55
51	Navy Yard, switcher, light blue, white lettering, 1956-57.	65	150
52	Fire car, red, gray pump and hose reel, white lettering, 1958-61.	100	225
53	Rio Grande, snowplow, 1957-60.		
	(A) "a" in "Rio Grande" backwards.	100	300
	(B) "a" printed correctly.	200	400
54	Ballast tamper, yellow, black lettering, one man, 1958-61, 1966, 1968-69.	100	200
54-6446	Norfolk & Western, quad hopper, 1954.	10	30
54-6446	Norfolk & Western, cement, gray.	10	30
55-150	Ties, 1957-60.	1.50	3
55	Tie-jector, red, white lettering, "5511" on side, 1957-61.	100	175
56	Lamppost, 1946-49.	10	35
56	M & St L, mine transport, red and white, red lettering, 1958.	175	500
57	AEC, switcher, white and red, white lettering, 1959-60.	250	675
58	Lamppost, 1946-60.	8	25
58	Great Northern, snowplow 2-4-2, green and white, green logo, 1959-61.	275	600
59	Minuteman, switcher, white, red and blue lettering, 1962-63.	225	550
60	Lionelville, trolley, yellow, red roof, 1955-58.	100	275
64	Street lamp, 1945-49.	10	35
65	Lionel Lines, handcar, yellow, red pump, two men, 1962-66.	100	325
68	Inspection car, DeSoto wagon, red and cream, no lettering, 1958- 61.	100	250
69	Lionel, maintenance car, dark gray and black, one man, 1960-62.	150	300
70	Yard light, 1949-50.	10	35
71	Lamppost, 1949-59.	2	10
75	Tear drop lamp, 1961-63.	5	15
76	Boulevard street lamp, 1955-56, 1968-69.	2	4
89	Flagpole, 1956-58.	10	30
93	Water tower, 1946-49.	7	25

		Gd	Exc
97	Coal elevator, 1946-50.	50	135
100	Multivolt-DC/AC, transformer, 1958-66.		NRS
109	Trestle set, 1961.		NRS
110	Trestle set, 1955-69.	3	15
111	Trestle set, 1956-69.	3	8
111-100	Trestle piers, 1960-63.	1	3
112	Remote-control switches, pair (Super O), 1957-66.	20	75
114	Newsstand with horn, 1957-59.	20	75
115	Passenger station, 1946-49.	100	200
118	Newsstand with whistle, 1958.	20	75
119	Landscaped tunnel, 1957.	2	5
120	90° crossing (Super O), 1957-66.	1	3
121	Landscaped tunnel, 1959-66.	2	5
122	Landscaped tunnel, 1968.	2	5
123	Lamp assortment, 1955-59.		NRS
123-60	Lamp assortment, 1960-63.		NRS
125	Whistle shack, 1950-55.	7	30
128	Animated newsstand, 1957-60.	50	100
130	60° crossing (Super O), 1957-61.	1	4
131	Curved tunnel, 1959-66.	2	5
132	Passenger station, 1949-55.	11	30
133	Passenger station, 1957-66.	11	25
137	Passenger station, 1946. (See prewar section)		
138	Water tower, 1953-57.	35	70
140	Automatic banjo signal, 1954-66.	10	20
142	Manual switches, pair (Super O), 1957-66.	10	20
145	Automatic gateman, 1950-66.	15	30
148	Dwarf trackside signal, 1957-60.	15	50
150	Telegraph pole set, 1947-50.	5	25
151	Automatic semaphore, 1947-69.	10	25
152	Automatic crossing gate, 1945-48.	10	20
153	Automatic block control, signal, 1945-69.	10	20
154	Automatic highway signal, 1945-69.	7	20
155	Blinking light signal with bell, 1955-57.	10	25
156	Station platform, 1946-51.	15	40
157	Station platform, 1952-59.	6	20
160	Unloading bin, 1952.	.25	1
161	Mail pickup set, 1961-63.	20	75
163	Single target block signal, 1961-69.	7	20
164	Log loader, 1946-50.	65	150
165	Crane, 1946-47.	70	150
167	Whistle controller, 1945-46.	1	3

		Gd	**Exc**

225 Chesapeake & Ohio Alco diesel A unit.

		Gd	Exc
175	Rocket launcher, 1958-60.	50	150
175-50	Extra rocket, 1959-60.	1.50	3
182	Magnetic crane, 1946-49.	70	150
192	Operating control tower, 1959-60.	60	150
193	Industrial water tower, 1953-55.	30	75
195	Floodlight tower, 1957-69.	20	30
195-75	Eight-bulb extension, 1958-60.	6	10
196	(A) Smoke pellets, 1946.	—	20
196	(B) Smoke pellets, 1958-59.	12	50
197	Rotating radar antenna, 1947.	—	20
199	Microwave/relay tower, 1958-59.	18	65
202	UP, Alco A unit, orange, black lettering, 1957.	25	75
204	Santa Fe, Alco AA units, blue, yellow cab roof and lettering, 1957.	50	125
205	Missouri Pacific, Alco AA units, blue, white lettering, 1957- 58.	50	125
206	Artificial coal, large bag, 1946-68.	—	6
207	Artificial coal, small bag.	—	4
208	Santa Fe, Alco AA units, blue yellow cab roof and lettering, 1958-59.	50	150
209	New Haven, Alco AA units, black, orange, and white, 1958.	100	350
209	Wooden barrels, set of four, 1946-50.	—	3
210	Texas Special, Alco AA units, red, white stripe and lettering, 1958.	50	150
211	Texas Special, Alco AA units, red, white stripe and lettering, 1962-66.	60	125
212	US Marine Corps, Alco A, blue, white stripes and lettering, 1958-59.	50	135
212	Santa Fe, Alco AA units, silver and red, yellow and black trim, 1964-66.	50	150
212T	US Marine Corps, dummy locomotive, blue, white stripes and lettering, 1958-59.	175	375
213	Railroad lift bridge, 1950.	Not Manufactured	
213	M & St L, Alco AA units, red, white stripe and lettering, 1964.	50	150
214	Plate girder bridge, 1953-69.	2	5
215	Santa Fe, Alco AB units, silver and red, yellow and black trim, 1965.	50	150
216	(A) Burlington, Alco A unit, silver, red stripes and lettering, 1958.	75	250

		Gd	Exc
216	(B) M & St L, Alco A unit, red, white lettering.	75	150
217	B & M, Alco AB units, black and blue, white stripe and lettering, 1959.	50	150
218	Santa Fe, silver and red, yellow and black trim, 1959-63.		
	(A) Double A units.	60	125
	(B) AB units.	60	125
219	MP, Alco AA units, blue, white lettering, circa 1959.	50	125
220	Santa Fe, Alco A unit, silver and red, yellow and black trim, 1961.	50	125
221	2-6-4, "NEW YORK CENTRAL" 221T/221W tender, 1946-47.		
	(A) Gray die-cast body.	50	115
	(B) Black die-cast body.	40	100
221	Rio Grande, Alco A unit, yellow, black stripes and lettering, 1963-64.	35	75
221	US Marine Corps, Alco A unit, olive drab, white stripes and lettering.	75	225
221	Santa Fe, Alco A unit, olive drab, white stripes and lettering.	75	225
222	Rio Grande, Alco A unit, yellow, black stripes and lettering, 1962.	35	75
223	218C Santa Fe, Alco AB units, 1963.	50	150
224	Steam 2-6-2, die-cast body, 2466T/2466W tender, 1945-46.	60	100
224	US Navy, Alco AB units, blue, white lettering, 1960.	75	175
225	C & O, Alco A unit, dark blue, yellow lettering, 1960.	40	100
226	B & M, Alco AB units, black and blue, white stripe and lettering, 1960.	50	125
227	Canadian National, Alco A unit, green, yellow trim and lettering, 1960.	50	125
228	Canadian National, Alco A unit, green, yellow trim and lettering, 1960.	50	100
229	M & St L, Alco AB units, red, white stripes and lettering, 1961-62.		
	(A) A unit only.	50	100
	(B) A and B units.	75	140
230	C & O, Alco A unit, blue, yellow stripe and lettering, 1961.	50	100
231	Rock Island, Alco A unit, black and red, white lettering, 1961- 63.	50	125
232	New Haven, Alco A unit, orange and black, white lettering, 1962.	50	90
233	Steam 2-4-2, plastic body, 233W tender, 1961-62.	12	25
235	Steam 2-4-2, plastic body, 1130T tender, 1962.	15	30
236	Steam 2-4-2, plastic body, 1961-62.		
	(A) 1050T slope-back tender.	10	25
	(B) 1130T tender.	10	25
237	Steam 2-4-2, plastic body, 1963-66.	10	25
238	Steam 2-4-2, plastic body, 243W tender, 1963-64.	10	35
239	Steam 2-4-2, die-cast body, 1964-66.	10	35
240	Steam 2-4-2, plastic body, 1961.	15	85
241	Steam 2-4-2, die-cast body, 1958.	20	40
242	Steam 2-4-2, plastic body, 1962-66.	15	25
243	Steam 2-4-2, plastic body, 243W tender, 1960.	15	25
244	Steam 2-4-2, plastic body, 244T/1130T tender, 1960-61.	15	25
245	Steam 2-4-2, plastic body, 1959.	15	25
246	Steam 2-4-2, plastic body, 244T/1130T tender, 1959-61.	15	30

		Gd	Exc
247	Steam 2-4-2, plastic body, 247T B & O tender, 1959-61.	20	40
248	Steam 2-4-2, plastic body, 1958.	15	40
249	Steam 2-4-2, plastic body, 250T "PENNSYLVANIA" tender, 1958.	15	40
250	Steam 2-4-2, plastic body, 250T "PENNSYLVANIA" tender, 1957.	15	40
251	Steam 2-4-2, die-cast body.		
	(A) Slope-back tender.	15	30
	(B) 250T-type tender.	15	30
252	Crossing gate, 1950-62.	7	20
253	Block control signal, 1956-59.	10	30
256	Operating freight station, 1950-53.	6	20
257	Freight station with diesel horn, 1956-57.	20	65
260	Bumper, die-cast, 1949-69.	3	10
262	Highway crossing gate, 1962-69.	6	20
264	Operating forklift platform, 1957-60.	50	140
270	Metal bridge (O).	15	30
282	Gantry crane, 1954.	60	150
282R	Gantry crane, 1956.	60	150
299	Code transmitter beacon set, 1961-63.	20	55
308	Railroad sign set, die-cast, 1945-49.	10	25
309	Yard sign set, die-cast, 1950-59.	3	12
310	Billboard, 1950-68.	1	2
311	Billboard, 1969.	1	2
313	Bascule bridge, 1946-49.	150	300
314	Scale model girder bridge, 1945-50.	2	10
315	Trestle bridge, 1946-47.	15	45
316	Trestle bridge, 1949.	10	30
317	Trestle bridge, 1950-56.	5	15
321	Trestle bridge, 1958-64.	5	10
332	Arch-under bridge, 1959-66.	10	30
334	Operating dispatching board, 1957-60.	50	125
342	Culvert loader, 1956-58.	50	125
345	Culvert unloading station, 1958-59.	70	200
346	Culvert unloader, 1965-67.	50	125
347	Cannon firing range set, 1962-64.	75	150
348	Culvert unloader, 1966-69.	50	125
350	Engine transfer table, 1957-60.	65	175
350-50	Transfer table extension, 1957-60.	25	90
352	Ice depot, 1955-57.	50	125
353	Trackside control signal, 1960-61.	5	20
356	Operating freight station, 1952-57.	30	70
362	Barrel loader, 1952-57.	30	60
362-78	Wooden barrels, 1952-57.	2	6

Gd   Exc

The 520 Lionel Lines electric is
described as a "box cab" electric
because of its boxy shape.

		Gd	Exc
364	Conveyor lumber loader, 1948-67.	30	60
364C	On/off switch, 1959-64.	1	2
365	Dispatching station, 1958-59.	35	75
375	Turntable, 1962-64.	50	145
394	Rotary beacon, 1949-53.	8	20
395	Floodlight tower, 1949-56.	8	30
397	Diesel operating coal loader, 1948-57.	30	75
400	Baltimore & Ohio, RDC passenger car, silver, blue lettering, 1956-58.	100	200
404	Baltimore & Ohio, RDC baggage-mail, silver, blue lettering, 1957-58.	150	350
410	Billboard blinker, 1956-58.	10	30
413	Countdown control panel, 1962.	6	12
415	Diesel fueling station, 1955-57.	30	100
419	Heliport control tower, 1962.	75	200
443	Missile launch platform, 1960-62.	15	20
445	Switch tower, lighted, 1952-57.	20	50
448	Missile firing range set, 1961-63.	25	50
450	Signal bridge, two-track, 1952-58.	15	35
452	Signal bridge, single-track, 1961-63.	40	80
455	Operating oil derrick, 1950-54.	50	140
456	Coal ramp/ 3456 hopper, 1950-55.	100	180
460	Piggyback transportation, 1955-67.	20	50
460P	Piggyback platform.	20	40
461	Platform with truck and trailer.	25	70
462	Derrick platform set, 1961-62.	30	90
464	Lumber mill, 1956-60.	30	90
465	Sound dispatching station, 1956-57.	30	60
470	Missile launching platform, 1959-62.	12	25
480-25	Conversion coupler, 1950-60.	.50	1.50
480-32	Conversion. magnetic coupler, 1961-69.	.50	1.50
494	Rotary beacon, 1954-66.	10	30
497	Coaling station, no car, 1953-58.	50	125
520	Lionel Lines, box cab electric, red, white lettering, 1956-57.	35	90

	Gd	**Exc**

The 675 Lionel Lines steam locomotive with a 2-6-2 wheel arrangement.

600	MKT, NW-2 switcher, red, white lettering, 1955.	75	150
601	Seaboard, NW-2 switcher, black and red, red and white trim, 1956.	75	150
602	Seaboard, NW-2 switcher, black and red, red and white trim, 1957-58.	90	175
610	Erie, NW-2 switcher, black, yellow lettering, 1955.	75	150
611	Jersey Central, NW-2, orange and blue, blue and white lettering, 1957-58.	75	150
613	Union Pacific, NW-2 switcher, yellow, gray hood, red lettering, 1958.	75	200
614	Alaska, NW-2 switcher, blue, yellow lettering, 1959-60.		
	(A) Plastic bell on top of body, no dynamic brake unit.	90	160
	(B) No bell, yellow dynamic brake unit and air reservoirs.	100	180
	(C) Similar to (B), but "BUILT BY LIONEL" outlined in yellow.	125	250
616	Santa Fe, NW-2 switcher, black, white stripes and lettering, 1961-62.	75	175
617	Santa Fe, NW-2 switcher, black, white stripes and lettering, 1963.	100	200
621	Jersey Central, NW-2 switcher, blue, orange lettering, 1956- 57.	50	125
622	Santa Fe, NW-2 switcher, black, white lettering, 1949-50.		
	(A) Large "GM" decal on cab.	125	300
	(B) Small "GM" decal on cab.	100	275
623	Santa Fe, NW-2 switcher, black, white lettering, 1952-54.	75	200
624	C & O, NW-2 switcher, blue, yellow stripes and lettering, 1952- 54.	125	250
625	Lehigh Valley, GE 44-ton switcher, red and black, white stripe and lettering, 1957-58.	50	130
626	Baltimore & Ohio, GE 44-ton switcher, blue, yellow lettering, 1959.	75	275
627	Lehigh Valley, GE 44-ton switcher, red, white stripe and lett., 1956-57.	75	125
628	Northern Pacific, GE 44-ton switcher, black, yellow lettering, 1956-57.	75	125
629	Burlington, GE 44-ton, silver, red stripe and lettering, 1956.	75	250
633	Santa Fe, NW-2 switcher, blue, yellow stripes and lettering, 1962.	50	105
634	Santa Fe, NW-2, blue, yellow lettering, 1963, 1965-66.		
	(A) Yellow safety stripes on ends, 1963, 1965.	40	80
	(B) No safety stripes, 1966.	40	80
635	Union Pacific, NW-2 switcher, yellow, red stripes and lettering, 1963.	40	90
637	Steam 2-6-4, die-cast body, 1960.		
	(A) 2046W "LIONEL LINES" tender.	40	85

		Gd	Exc
	(B) 736W "PENNSYLVANIA" tender.	40	85
638-2361	Van Camps Pork & Beans, boxcar, red, white and yellow lettering, 1962.	10	20
645	Union Pacific, NW-2 switcher, yellow, red stripes and lettering, 1969.	40	90
646	Steam 4-6-4, die-cast body, 2046W tender, 1954-58.	75	175
665	Steam 4-6-4, 2046W/6026W tender, 1954-59.	60	135
671	Steam 6-8-6, die-cast body, 671W tender, 1946-49.	50	150
671RR	Steam 6-8-6, "ELECTRONIC CONTROL", 671W tender, 1952.	75	150
675	Steam, die-cast body, 2466W/2466WX/6466WX tender, 1947.		
	(A) 2-6-2, disc drivers.	45	115
	(B) 2-6-4, spoked drivers.	50	125
681	Steam turbine, 6-8-6, 2046W-50/2671W/2671WX "PENNSYLVANIA" tender, 1950-51, 1953.	75	170
682	Steam 6-8-6, 2046W-50 "PENNSYLVANIA" tender, 1954-55.	150	250
685	Steam 4-6-4, die-cast body, 6026W tender, 1953.	75	175
703-10	Special smoke bulb, 1946.	—	3
726	(A) Steam 2-8-4, Berkshire, die-cast body, 1946.	200	375
726	(B) Steam 2-8-4, 1947-49.	250	400
726RR	Steam 2-8-4 Berkshire, die-cast body, 1952.	100	225
736	2-8-4, die-cast body, 2046W/736W/267W, 1950-66.	175	275
746	Streamlined steam 4-8-4, die-cast body, "NORFOLK & WESTERN" tender, 1957.		
	(A) Tender with long, full-length stripe.	500	1450
	(B) Tender with short stripe.	400	1200
760	Curved track, 16 sections (O72), 1954-57.	15	35
773	Steam 4-6-4, die-cast body.		
	(A) 2426W tender with six-wheel trucks, 1950.	650	1850
	(B) "PENNSYLVANIA" tender, 1964.	475	1350
	(C) "NEW YORK CENTRAL" tender, 1965-66.	475	1375
909	Smoke fluid, 1957-58.	—	2
919	Artificial grass, 1946-64.	—	3
920	Scenic display set, 1957-58.	15	60
920-2	Tunnel portals, pair, 1958.	8	20
920-5	Artificial rock, 1958.	.50	2
920-8	Lichen, 1958.	.50	2
925	Lionel lubricant, tube, 1946-69.	.50	2
926	Lionel lubricant, tube, 1955.	.25	1
926-5	Instruction booklet, 1946-48.	.25	1
927	Lubricating kit, 1950-53.	2	7
928	Maintenance and lubricating kit, 1960-63.	2	5
943	Ammo dump, 1959-61.	4	8
950	US railroad map, 1958-66.	3	12
951	Farm set, 1958.	3	20
952	Miniature figure set, 1958.	3	15

Gd   **Exc**

If only it were always so easy to identify a toy train —the Lionel 1002 has a clear identity.

953	Miniature figure set, 1960-62.	2	15
954	Swimming pool and playground set, 1959.	3	15
955	Farm building and animal set, 1958.	3	15
956	Stockyard set, 1959.	3	15
957	Farm building and animal set, 1958.	3	15
958	Vehicle set, 1958.	3	15
959	Barn set, 1958.	3	15
960	Barnyard set, 1959-61.	3	15
961	School set, 1959.	3	15
962	Turnpike set, 1958.	3	18
963	Frontier set, 1959-60.	3	15
964	Factory set, 1959.	3	18
965	Farm set, 1959.	3	15
966	Fire house set, 1958.	3	15
967	Post office set, 1958.	3	15
968	TV transmitter set, 1958.	7	20
969	Construction set, 1960.	10	30
970	Ticket booth, 1958-60.	25	50
971	Lichen package, 1960-64.	2	4
972	Landscape tree assortment, 1961-64.	2	4
973	Complete landscaping set, 1960-64.	3	6
974	Scenery set, 1962-63.	4	8
980	Ranch set, 1960.	3	15
981	Freight yard set, 1960.	3	15
982	Suburban split level set, 1960.	3	15
983	Farm set, 1960-61.	10	35
984	Railroad set, 1961-62.	3	15
985	Freight area set, 1961.	7	18
986	Farm set, 1962.	5	15
987	Town set, 1962.	10	35
988	Railroad structure set, 1962.	6	15

		Gd	Exc
1001	Steam 2-4-2, plastic body, 1001T tender, 1948.	12	25
1002	Lionel, gondola; silver, yellow, or red, 1949.	50	195
1002	Lionel, gondola, 1948-52.		
	(A) Blue, white lettering.	2	5
	(B) Black, white lettering.	2	5
	(C) Silver, black lettering.	50	195
	(D) Red, white lettering.	50	195
1004	Pennsylvania / Baby Ruth boxcar, orange, blue lettering, 1949-51.	2	4
1005	Sunoco, single-dome tank car, gray, 1948-50.	1	3
1007	Lionel Lines, offset-cupola caboose, red, 1948-52.	2	5
1008	Uncoupling unit (O27), 1957.	.50	1
1008-50	Uncoupling track (O27), 1948.	.25	1
1010	Transformer, 35 watts, 1961-66.	3	5
1011	Transformer, 25 watts, 1948-49.	3	5
1012	Transformer, 40 watts, 1950-54.	3	5
1015	Transformer, 45 watts, 1956-60.	5	8
1016	Transformer, 35 watts, 1959-60.	3	5
1019	Remote-control track set (O27).	1.50	5
1020	90° crossing (O27), 1955-69.	1.50	3
1021	90° crossing (O27), 1945-54.	1.50	3
1022	Manual switches, pair (O27), 1953-69.	2	10
1023	45° crossing (O27), 1955-69.	1.50	3
1024	Manual switches, pair (O27), 1946-52.	5	10
1025	Transformer, 45 watts, 1961-69.	3	10
1025	Illuminated bumper (O27), 1946-47.	1	1.50
1026	Transformer, 25 watts, 1963-64.	1	1.50
1032	Transformer, 75 watts, 1948.	9	14
1033	Transformer, 90 watts, 1948-56.	20	30
1034	Transformer, 75 watts, 1948-54.	15	20
1037	Transformer, 40 watts, 1946-47.	1	1.50
1041	Transformer, 60 watts, 1945-46.	5	7
1042	Transformer, 75 watts, 1947-48.	9	14
1043	(A) Transformer, 50 watts, black, 1953-57.	2	3
1043	(B) Transformer, 60 watts, ivory, 1957.	40	50
1044	Transformer, 90 watts, 1957-59.	20	30
1045	Operating watchman, 1946-50.	8	20
1047	Operating switchman, 1959-61.	30	100
1050	Steam 0-4-0, plastic body, 1050 tender (O27), 1959.	12	25
1053	Transformer, 60 watts, 1956-60.	5	8
1055	Texas Special, Alco A unit, red, white lettering, 1959-60.	25	75
1060	Steam 2-4-2, plastic body, 1050T, 1130T tender, 1960-61.	12	25
1061	Steam 0-4-0, plastic body, 1963-64; 2-4-2, 1969.		

Gd   **Exc**

The 1110 steam locomotive is from Lionel's low-priced Scout series.

		Gd	Exc
	(A) Slope-back "LIONEL LINES" tender.	12	25
	(B) 1130T "SOUTHERN PACIFIC" tender.	25	50
1062	Steam, plastic body, 1963-64.		
	(A) 0-4-0 wheel arrangement.	12	25
	(B) 2-4-2 wheel arrangement.	12	25
1063	Transformer, 75 watts, 1960-64.	9	14
1065	Union Pacific, Alco A unit, yellow, red stripe and lettering, 1961.	15	40
1066	Union Pacific, Alco A unit, yellow, red stripe and lettering, 1964.	15	40
1073	Transformer, 60 watts, 1962-66.	3	5
1101	Steam 2-4-2, die-cast body, 1948.	12	25
1101	Transformer, 25 watts, 1948.	1	1.50
1110	Steam 2-4-2, "LIONEL SCOUT" tender, 1949, 1951-52.	12	25
1120	Steam 2-4-2, "LIONEL SCOUT" tender, 1950.	12	25
1121	Remote-control switches, pair (O27), 1946-51.	7	25
1122	Remote-control switches, pair (O27), 1952-53.	10	30
1122-34	Remote-control switches, pair, 1952-53.	10	35
1122-500	Gauge adapter (O27), 1957-66.	.25	1
1122E	Remote-control switches, pair (O27), 1953-69.	10	35
1130	Steam 2-4-2, 1130T or 6066T tender, 1950.		
	(A) Plastic body.	12	25
	(B) Die-cast body.	20	45
1615	Steam 0-4-0, die-cast body, 1615T tender, 1955-57.		
	(A) No grab-irons on steam chest or tender.	55	140
	(B) Grab-irons on front of steam chest and tender.	100	250
1625	Steam 0-4-0, die-cast body, 1625 tender, 1958.	65	200
1640-100	Presidential kit, 1960.	10	25
1654	Steam 2-4-2, die-cast body, 1654T/1654W tender, 1946-47.	15	30
1655	Steam 2-4-2, die-cast body, 6654W tender, 1948-49.	15	35
1656	Steam 0-4-0, die-cast body, 6403 tender, 1948-49.	125	225
1665	Steam 0-4-0, die-cast body, 2403B tender, 1946.	125	275
1666	Steam 2-6-2, die-cast body, 6654W/2466WX, 1946-47.	25	70

		Gd	Exc
1862	General 4-4-0, gray and red, green 1862 tender, 1959-62.		
	(A) Gray smoke stack.	75	175
	(B) Black smoke stack.	75	175
1865	Western & Atlantic, coach, yellow, brown roof, 1959-62.	13	30
1866	Western & Atlantic, baggage, yellow, brown roof, 1959-62.	17	30
1872	General 4-4-0, gray and red, multicolor 1872T/1875W tender, 1959-62.	100	250
1875	Western & Atlantic, coach, yellow, tuscan roof, 1959-62.	40	100
1875W	Western & Atlantic, coach, yellow, tuscan roof, 1959-62.	40	80
1876	Western & Atlantic, baggage, yellow, tuscan roof, 1959-62.	25	60
1877	No number, flatcar, 1960-65.	3	5
(1877)	Flatcar with fence and six horses, brown, 1959-62.	60	125
1882	General 4-4-0, black and orange, 1882T tender, 1959-62.	150	450
1885	Western & Atlantic, coach, blue, brown roof, 1959.	75	250
1887	Flatcar with fences and six horses, brown, yellow lettering, 1959.	60	125
2003	Track "Make-up" kit for "O27 Track", 1963.		NRS
2016	Steam 2-6-4, 6026W tender, 1955-56.	20	60
2018	Steam 2-6-4, 6026W tender, 1955-56.		
	(A) Black body and tender, regular production.	25	65
	(B) Blue body and tender, part of blue "Boy's Set", complete set sold for $23,000 in 1988.		
2020	Steam 6-8-6, die-cast body, 2020W tender, 1946-47.	25	140
2023	Union Pacific, Alco AA units, 1950-51.		
	(A) Yellow, gray roof, red stripes and lettering.	100	250
	(B) Same as (A), but black body shell painted yellow, gray nose.	500	1500
	(C) Silver body and frame, gray roof.	100	250
2024	Chesapeake & Ohio, Alco A, blue, yellow stripe and lettering, 1969.	35	75
2025	Steam 2-6-2, 2-6-4, 2460WX/2466WX/6466WX/6466W tender, 1947-49, 1952.	50	95
2026	Steam 2-6-2, 6466T/6466W/6466WX tender, 1948-49, 1951-53.	40	70
2028	Pennsylvania, GP-7, tuscan, yellow lettering, 1955.	90	250
2029	Steam 2-6-4, 1964-69.		
	(A) 243W "LIONEL LINES" tender.	40	70
	(B) 243W "PENNSYLVANIA" tender.	125	175
	(C) Same as (A), but "Hagerstown, Maryland" manufacturing plate on bottom of locomotive.	50	85
2031	Rock Island, Alco AA, black, red and white trim, 1952-54.	125	400
2032	Erie, Alco AA units, black, yellow stripes and lettering, 1952-54.	100	225
2033	Union Pacific, Alco AA, silver, black lettering, 1952-54.	100	250
2034	Steam 2-4-2, die-cast body, 1952.	20	35
2035	Steam 2-6-4, 2466W tender, 1950-51.	50	75
2036	Steam 2-6-4, 6466W tender, 1950.	40	70
2037	Steam 2-6-4, black engine, 1954-55, 1957-58.	50	85

	Gd	Exc

Popular with railfans and modelers alike, the real GG-1 locomotives had a distinctive body created by famed industrial designer Raymond Loewy. Lionel's models of the GG-1 are among the company's most popular trains.

		Gd	Exc
2037-500	Steam 2-6-4, pink engine, from "Girl's Set", 1957.*	300	500
2041	Rock Island, Alco AA, black, red and white trim, 1969.	50	110
2046	Steam 4-6-4, 2046W tender, 1950-53.	100	175
2055	Steam 4-6-4, die-cast body, 1025W/2046W, 1953-55.	65	140
2056	Steam 4-6-4, die-cast body, 2046W tender, 1952.	90	190
2065	Steam 4-6-4, die-cast body, 2046W/6026W, 1954-57.	80	140
2240	Wabash, F-3 AB units, gray and blue, white and yellow trim, 1956.	300	700
2242	New Haven, F-3 AB units, black; white, silver, and orange, 1958-59.	400	850
2243	Santa Fe, F-3 AB units, silver and red, yellow and black trim, 1955-57.	225	400
2243C	Santa Fe, F-3 B unit, matches 2243, 1955-57.	75	175
2245	Texas Special, F-3 AB, red and white, silver frame, 1954-55.	225	500
2257	Lionel, offset-cupola caboose, 1948.		
	(A) Tuscan or red, not illuminated.	3	6
	(B) Tuscan or red, illuminated, with extra details.	10	20
2321	Lackawanna, Trainmaster, gray, maroon stripe, yellow trim, 1954-56.		
	(A) Gray roof.	200	475
	(B) Maroon roof.	300	700
2322	Virginian, Trainmaster, yellow and blue, 1965-66.	325	575
2328	Burlington, GP-7, silver, black lettering, red frame, 1955-56.	150	375
2329	Virginian, Rectifier, yellow and blue, 1958-59.	250	650
2330	Pennsylvania, GG-1, green, gold stripes, 1950.	275	1250
2331	Virginian, Trainmaster, yellow, 1955-58.		
	(A) Black stripe, gold lettering.	550	1250
	(B) Blue stripe, yellow lettering.	350	750
2332	Pennsylvania, GG-1, gold or silver stripes, 1947-49.		
	(A) Black body.	550	1250
	(B) Brunswick green (very dark, almost black).	175	500
2333	Santa Fe, F-3 AA units, silver and red, yellow and black trim, 1948-49.	225	500
2333	NYC, F-3 AA units, two-tone gray, white trim, 1948-49.	225	500
2337	Wabash, GP-7, blue and gray, white stripes and lettering, 1958.	100	300

		Gd	Exc
2338	Milwaukee Road, GP-7, orange and black, white and/or black lettering, 1955-56.		
	(A) Orange band on body and cab.	750	1750
	(B) Orange band on body only, solid black cab.	100	225
2339	Wabash, GP-7, blue and gray, white stripes and lettering, 1957.	100	250
2340	Pennsylvania, GG-1, five gold stripes, 1955.		
	(A) Tuscan body.	350	1600
	(B) Dark green.	350	1500
2341	Jersey Central, Trainmaster, orange and blue, white lettering, 1956.	800	1950
2343	Santa Fe, F-3 AA units, silver and red, yellow and black trim, 1950-52.	200	650
2343C	Santa Fe, F-3 B unit, silver and red, yellow and black trim, 1950-55.		
	(A) Screen roof vents.	95	235
	(B) Louver roof vents.	65	195
2344	NYC, F-3 AA units, two-tone gray, white trim, 1950-52.	175	575
2344C	NYC, F-3 B unit, two-tone gray, white trim, 1950-52.	100	250
2345	Western Pacific, F-3 AA, silver and orange, black lettering, 1952.*	800	1800
2346	Boston & Maine GP-9, blue and black, white lettering, 1965-67.	100	250
2347	C & O, GP-7, blue, yellow handrails and lettering, 1962.	1250	2750
2348	M & St L, GP-9, red, blue roof, white lettering, 1958-59.	150	425
2349	Northern Pacific, GP-9, black; gold and red striping, 1959-60.	200	375
2350	New Haven, EP-5, black; white and orange trim, 1956-58.	350	750
2351	Milwaukee, EP-5, yellow, black roof, white stripe, 1957-58.	200	500
2352	Pennsylvania, EP-5, tuscan, gold stripe and lettering, 1958-59.	225	525
2353	Santa Fe, F-3 AA units, silver and red, yellow and black trim, 1953-55.	225	600
2354	NYC, F-3 AA units, two-tone gray, white trim, 1953-55.	225	525
2355	Western Pacific, F-3 AA, silver and orange, black trim, 1953.	600	1550
2356	Southern, F-3 AA units, green and gray, yellow trim, 1954-56.	450	1250
2356C	Southern, F-3 B unit, green and gray, yellow trim, 1954-56.	125	325
2357	Lionel, offset-cupola caboose, 1948.	10	20
2358	Great Northern, EP-5, orange and green, yellow stripes and lettering, 1959-60.	300	750
2359	Boston & Maine, GP-9, 1961-62.	100	250
2360	Pennsylvania, GG-1, 1956-58, 1961-63.		
	(A) Tuscan body, five gold stripes.	475	1450
	(B) Dark green body, five gold stripes.	475	1150
	(C) Tuscan, single gold stripe.	350	850
2363	Illinois Central, F-3 AB, brown, orange stripe, yellow trim, 1955-56.		
	(A) Black lettering.	300	1200
	(B) Brown lettering.	350	1350
2365	C & O, GP-7, blue, yellow handrails and lettering, 1962-63.	125	350
2367	Wabash, F-3 AB units, gray and blue, white trim, 1955.	325	1000

		Gd	Exc
2368	Baltimore & Ohio, F-3 AB units, blue, black stripe, 1956.	700	2200
2373	Canadian Pacific, F-3 AA units, gray and maroon, yellow trim, 1957.	700	1800
2378	Milwaukee Road, F-3 AB units, gray and orange, yellow trim, 1956.		
	(A) Yellow stripe along roof line.	1000	2600
	(B) Without yellow stripe.	700	1950
2379	Rio Grande, F-3 AB units, yellow and silver, black and green trim, 1957-58.	400	1100
2383	Santa Fe, F-3 AA units, silver and red, yellow and black trim, 1958-66.	125	225
2400	Maplewood, Pullman, green, gray roof, 1948-49.	25	100
2401	Hillside, observation, green, gray roof, 1948-49.	25	100
2402	Chatham, Pullman, green, gray roof, 1948-49.	25	100
2404	Santa Fe, Vista Dome, aluminum paint, blue lettering, 1964-65.	11	30
2405	Santa Fe, Pullman, aluminum paint, blue lettering, 1964-65.	12	30
2406	Santa Fe, observation, aluminum paint, blue lettering, 1964-65.	12	30
2408	Santa Fe, Vista Dome, aluminum paint, blue lettering, 1964-65.	12	35
2409	Santa Fe, Pullman, aluminum paint, blue lettering, 1964-65.	15	35
2410	Santa Fe, observation, aluminum paint, blue lettering, 1964-65.	15	35
2411	Flatcar with big pipes, die-cast, gray, 1946-48.		
	(A) Three black metal pipes (must be original).	20	100
	(B) Three wood logs.	10	25
2412	Santa Fe, Vista Dome, silver, blue stripe, 1959-63.	12	40
2414	Santa Fe, Pullman, silver, blue stripe, 1959-63.	12	40
2416	Santa Fe, observation, silver, blue stripe, 1959-63.	12	40
2419	DL & W, work caboose, gray, black lettering, 1946-47.	15	30
2420	DL & W, work caboose, with light, gray, 1946-49.	25	80
2421	Maplewood, Pullman, aluminum paint, 1950, 1952-53.		
	(A) Gray roof, black stripe.	25	100
	(B) Aluminum-painted roof, no stripes.	20	40
2422	Chatham, Pullman, 1950, 1952-53.		
	(A) Gray roof, black stripe.	25	100
	(B) Aluminum-painted roof, no stripes.	20	40
2423	Hillside, observation, 1950, 1952-53.		
	(A) Gray roof, black stripe.	25	100
	(B) Aluminum-painted roof, no stripes.	20	40
2429	Livingston, Pullman, 1950, 1952-53.		
	(A) Gray roof.		NRS
	(B) Aluminum-painted roof, no stripes.	20	45
2430	Pullman, metal, blue, silver roof, 1946-47.	12	25
2431	Observation, metal, blue, silver roof, 1946-47.	12	25
2432	Clifton, Vista Dome, aluminum paint, red lettering, 1954-58.	15	35
2434	Newark, Pullman, aluminum paint, red lettering, 1954-58.	15	35
2435	Elizabeth, Pullman, aluminum paint, red lettering, 1954-58.	15	35

Gd　　Exc

Having trouble with derailments? Bring out the "big hook," like the 2460 Bucyrus Erie crane made by Lionel.

		Gd	Exc
2436	Summit, observation, aluminum paint, red lettering, 1954-58.	20	40
2436	Mooseheart, observation, aluminum paint, red lettering, 1957- 58.	30	65
2440	Pullman, metal, two-tone green, 1946-47.	20	40
2441	Observation, metal, two-tone green, 1946-47.	20	40
2442	Pullman, metal, brown, 1946-47.		
	(A) Silver lettering.	20	65
	(B) White lettering.	20	55
2442	Clifton, Vista Dome, aluminum paint, red stripe.	20	55
2443	Observation, metal, brown, 1946-47.		
	(A) Silver lettering.	20	65
	(B) White lettering.	20	55
2444	Newark, Pullman, aluminum paint, red stripe, 1955-56.	20	55
2445	Elizabeth, Pullman, aluminum paint, red stripe, 1955-56.	25	65
2446	Summit, observation, aluminum paint, red stripe, 1955-56.	20	55
2452	Pennsylvania, gondola, black, white lettering, 1945-47.	5	15
2452X	Pennsylvania, gondola, black, white lettering, 1946-47.	4	10
X2454	Pennsylvania, boxcar, orange, 1945-46.		
	(A) Orange doors.	20	110
	(B) Brown doors.	20	100
X2454	Baby Ruth, boxcar, "PRR" logo, orange, 1946.	5	15
2456	Lehigh Valley, short hopper, black, 1948.	5	15
2457	Pennsylvania, caboose, metal, N5, 1946-47.		
	(A) Red, white lettering.	10	25
	(B) Brown, white lettering.	—	150
X2458	Pennsylvania, boxcar, brown, white lettering, 1947.	25	50
2460	Bucyrus Erie, crane, 12-wheel, 1946-50.		
	(A) Gray cab.	60	200
	(B) Black cab.	35	75
2461	Transformer car, die-cast, gray, 1947-48.		
	(A) Black transformer.	30	80
	(B) Red transformer.	40	100

Gd   **Exc**

The 2625 Irvington car comes from the popular "Madison" series of heavyweight passenger cars.

		Gd	Exc
2465	Sunoco, two-dome tank car, silver, blue or black decal lettering, 1946-48.		
	(A) "GAS/SUNOCO/OILS" within diamond.	20	75
	(B) "SUNOCO" only within diamond.	5	15
	(C) "SUNOCO" extends beyond diamond.	5	15
2472	Pennsylvania, caboose, metal, N5, red, white lettering, 1945-47.	8	20
2481	Plainfield, Pullman, yellow, red stripes, 1950.	50	160
2482	Westfield, Pullman, yellow, red stripes, 1950.	50	160
2483	Livingston, observation, yellow, red stripes, 1950.	50	160
2521	President McKinley, observation, aluminum, gold stripe, 1962-66.	40	80
2522	President Harrison, Vista Dome, aluminum, gold stripe, 1962-66.	40	80
2523	President Garfield, Pullman, aluminum, gold stripe, 1962-66.	40	80
2530	Railway Express Agency, baggage, aluminum, 1953-60.		
	(A) Small doors.	50	100
	(B) Large doors, 1954 only.	125	375
2531	Silver Dawn, observation, aluminum, 1952-60.	25	60
2532	Silver Range, Vista Dome, aluminum, 1952-60.	25	60
2533	Silver Cloud, Pullman, aluminum, 1952-60.	25	60
2534	Silver Bluff, Pullman, aluminum, 1952-60.	40	80
2541	Alexander Hamilton, observation, aluminum, maroon stripe, 1955-56.*	70	190
2542	Betsy Ross, Vista Dome, aluminum, maroon stripe, 1955-56.*	70	190
2543	William Penn, Pullman, aluminum, maroon stripe, 1955-56.*	70	190
2544	Molly Pitcher, Pullman, aluminum, maroon stripe, 1955-56.*	70	190
2550	Baltimore & Ohio, RDC combine, silver, blue lettering, 1957-58.	250	550
2551	Banff Park, observation, aluminum, maroon stripe, 1957.*	95	225
2552	Skyline 500, Vista Dome, aluminum, maroon stripe, 1957.*	95	225
2553	Blair Manor, Pullman, aluminum, maroon stripe, 1957.*	150	325
2554	Craig Manor, Pullman, aluminum, maroon stripe, 1957.*	150	325
2555	Sunoco, single-dome tank car, silver, yellow diamond, 1946-48.	12	35
2559	Baltimore & Ohio, RDC, silver, blue lettering, 1957-58.	200	325
2560	Lionel Lines, crane, eight-wheel, 1946-47.		
	(A) Black boom.	20	60

		Gd	Exc
	(B) Brown boom.	20	60
	(C) Green boom.	20	60
2561	Vista Valley, observation, aluminum, red stripe, 1959-61.*	95	225
2562	Regal Pass, Vista Dome, aluminum, red stripe, 1959-61.*	125	300
2563	Indian Falls, Pullman, aluminum, red stripe, 1959-61.*	100	300
2625	Madison, Pullman, tuscan, white lettering, 1946-47.*	75	250
2625	Manhattan, Pullman, tuscan, white lettering, 12-wheel, 1946- 47.*	75	250
2625	Irvington, Pullman, tuscan, white lettering, 12-wheel, 1946- 50.*	75	225
2627	Madison, Pullman, tuscan, white lettering, 12-wheel, 1948- 50.*	75	225
2628	Manhattan, Pullman, tuscan, white lettering, 12-wheel, 1948- 50.*	75	225
2630	Pullman, metal, light blue, gray roof, 1946.		NRS
2631	Observation, metal, light blue, gray roof, 1946.	15	30
2671	TCA, tender, special edition body shell lettered "NATIONAL CONVENTION 1968".	—	75
2755	SUNX, single-dome tank car, silver, black decal lettering, 1945.	40	150
X2758	Pennsylvania, boxcar, brown, white lettering, 1945-46.	10	30
2855	SUNX, single-dome tank car, white decal lettering, 1946.		
	(A) Black tank, "GAS/SUNOCO/OILS" within diamond.	50	150
	(B) Black tank, "GAS/OILS" omitted from diamond.	50	200
	(C) Gray tank, "2855" on underside only.	50	175
X2954	Pennsylvania, boxcar, tuscan, white lettering, postwar trucks on prewar car.	150	300
2955	SUNX, single-dome scale tank, black tank, 1940-42, 1946.	110	275
2956	Baltimore & Ohio, scale hopper car, black, 1946.	150	325
2957	NYC, scale caboose, 1946.	70	250
(3309)	Turbo missile launch car, red car, 1960.	10	35
3330	Flatcar with submarine kit, blue car, 1960-62.	35	120
3330-100	Operating submarine, kit, 1960-61.	10	25
(3349)	Missile launching car, 1960.		
	(A) Red body.	20	50
	(B) Olive drab body.	60	275
3356	Santa Fe Express, green, yellow lettering, 1957-60, 1964-66.	30	40
3356-150	Horse corral car set.	10	25
3357	Hydraulic Maintenance car, cop and hobo chase, blue.	15	45
3359-55	Lionel Lines, two-bin dump, red and black, gray bins, 1955-58.	10	35
3360	Operating Burro crane, yellow, red lettering, 1956-57.	150	300
3361-55	Operating log dump car, gray, four logs, 1955, 1958.	10	25
3362	Flatcar with helium tanks, green, silver tanks, 1961-63.	10	35
3364	Log dump car, 1965-69.	15	45
3366	Circus car and corral set, 1959-62.	90	175
3366	Circus car, white; nine white rubber horses, 1959-62.	45	70
3366-100	(9) White horses, 1959-60.	5	10
3370	Western & Atlantic, car with sheriff and outlaw, green, 1961- 64.	45	65

	Gd	Exc

What's that in the gondola — a hobo? Ah, but there is the policeman chasing him off the car, or at least 'round and 'round. The 3444 Erie operating gondola is one of the clever inventions that insured Lionel's success.

		Gd	Exc
3376	Bronx Zoo, car with bobbing giraffe, 1960-69.		
	(A) Blue, white lettering.	15	40
	(B) Green, yellow lettering.	35	100
	(C) Blue, yellow lettering.	40	110
3376	Giraffe activator unit.	12	25
3386	Bronx Zoo car (O27).	20	60
3409	Helicopter launching car, blue, white lettering, 1961-62.	15	100
3409	Satellite car, blue, white lettering, 1961.	35	100
3410	Helicopter car, blue, white lettering, 1961-62.	20	50
3413	Mercury capsule car, red, gray superstructure and capsule, 1962-64.	40	110
3419	Remote-controlled helicopter car, blue, 1959-65.	25	90
3424-100	Low bridge signal set.	10	20
3424	Wabash, operating boxcar, blue, white lettering, 1956-58.	25	60
3428	U. S. Mail, operating boxcar, red, white, and blue, 1959.	25	75
3429	USMC, helicopter car, olive drab, white lettering, 1960.	45	120
3434	Poultry Dispatch, stock car, brown, 1959-60, 1965-66.	30	90
3435	Traveling Aquarium car, green, "swimming" fish, 1959- 62.	40	85
3444	Erie, operating gondola, red, cop chases hobo around crates, 1957-59.	25	50
3451	Operating log dump car, black, 1946-47.	10	40
3454	Pennsylvania, oper. merchandise car, brown, white lettering, 1946-47.	35	100
3456	Norfolk & Western, operating hopper, black, white lettering, 1951-55.	15	40
3459	Lionel Lines, operating dump car, 1946-48.		
	(A) Aluminum-finished bin, blue lettering.	75	200
	(B) Black bin, white lettering.	20	45
	(C) Green bin, white lettering.	20	55
3460	Flatcar with two trailers, red, dark green trailers lettered "LIONEL TRAINS", 1955.	20	45
3461	Lionel operating log car, three logs, 1949.		
	(A) Black.	10	40
	(B) Green car.	20	45
3462	Automatic milk car, white, black lettering, 1947-48.	30	75
3462P	Milk car platform.	2	5

		Gd	Exc
X3464	AT & SF, operating boxcar, orange, black lettering, 1949-50, 1952.	10	25
X3464	NYC, operating boxcar, tan, white lettering, 1952.	10	25
3469	Lionel Lines, operating dump car, black, 1949-55.	10	35
3470	Target launcher, white superstructure, 1962-64.		
	(A) Dark blue car.	20	60
	(B) Light blue car.	40	125
3472	Automatic milk car, white, black lettering, 1953.	20	40
3474	Western Pacific, boxcar, silver, yellow feather, 1952-53.	15	50
3482	Automatic milk car, white, black lettering, 1954-55.	20	60
3484	Pennsylvania, operating boxcar, tuscan, 1953.		
	(A) White lettering.	15	50
	(B) Gold lettering.	15	50
3484-25	AT & SF, operating boxcar, orange, 1954-57.		
	(A) White lettering.	20	90
	(B) Black lettering.	—	900
3494-1	NYC, Pacemaker boxcar, red and gray, 1955.	20	90
3494-150	Missouri Pacific, operating boxcar, blue and gray, 1956.	45	125
3494-275	State of Maine, operating boxcar; red, white, and blue, 1956.	40	75
3494-550	Monon, operating boxcar, maroon, white lettering, 1957.	100	275
3494-625	SOO, operating boxcar, tuscan, white lettering, 1957.	100	275
3509	Satellite car, green, white lettering, 1961.	15	40
(3510)	Satellite car, no number, red, white lettering, 1961-62.	10	30
3512	Ladder Co. car, red, 1959-61.		
	(A) Black rooftop ladder.	25	70
	(B) Silver rooftop ladder.	35	125
3519	Satellite car, green, white lettering, 1961-64.	15	50
3520	Searchlight car, die-cast, gray frame, orange generator, 1952-53.	20	50
3530	GM Electro Mobile Power, blue, white trim, 1956-58.		
	(A) Orange generator.	40	70
	(B) Gray generator.	40	70
3530	Searchlight car with pole and base.	25	75
3535	AEC Security car, red, gray gun, 1960-61.	20	90
3540	Operating radar car, red, gray superstructure, 1959-60.	40	125
3545	Lionel TV car, blue superstructure, yellow TV camera and base, 1961-62.	40	125
3559	Operating coal dump car, black, red bin, 1946-48.	10	20
3562-1	AT & SF, operating barrel car, 1954.		
	(A) Black body, black barrel trough.	65	150
	(B) Black body, yellow trough.	60	150
	(C) Gray, red lettering.	200	400
3562-25	AT & SF, operating barrel car, 1954.		
	(A) Red lettering.	100	300
	(B) Blue lettering.	15	30

Gd   Exc

Up periscope! The 3820 USMC flatcar carries an interesting load.

		Gd	Exc
3562-50	AT & SF, operating barrel car, yellow, black lettering, 1955-57.	15	40
3562-75	AT & SF, operating barrel car, orange, black lettering, 1958.	20	50
3619	Helicopter car, yellow, red and black lettering, 1962-64.	30	75
3620	Searchlight car, gray, 1954-56.		
	(A) Orange generator, gray searchlight.	25	50
	(B) Orange generator and searchlight.	50	150
3620X	Searchlight car, gray, orange generator, 1955.	25	40
3650	Extension searchlight car, 1956-59.	25	60
3656	Armour, operating cattle car, orange, 1949-55.		
	(A) "ARMOUR" sticker on door, white lettering.	20	50
	(B) Same as (A), but black lettering.	20	60
	(C) No "ARMOUR" sticker, black lettering.	20	40
	(D) Same as (C), but white lettering.	20	40
3656	Stockyard with cattle.	18	50
3662-1	Automatic milk car, white, brown roof, 1955-60, 1964-66.	30	60
3665	Minuteman operating car with missile, white sides, blue roof, 1961-64.	20	45
3666	Minuteman boxcar with cannon, white sides, blue roof.	150	500
3672	Bosco, operating boxcar, yellow, tuscan roof and ends, 1959- 60.	110	425
3820.	Flatcar with submarine, olive drab, gray submarine, 1960-62.	30	180
3830	Flatcar with submarine, blue car, gray submarine, 1960-63.	30	90
3854	Operating merchandise car, tuscan, white lettering, 1946-47.	200	500
3927	Lionel Lines, track cleaning car, orange, black lettering, 1956-60.	60	110
3927	Track cleaning fluid, 1957-69.	.50	2
3927-75	Track cleaning fluid, 1957-69.	.50	2
4357	Pennsylania, N5 caboose, electronic, tuscan, white lettering, 1948-50.	50	150
4452	Pennsylvania, gondola, electronic, black, white lettering, 1946-48.	30	75
4454	Baby Ruth, PRR boxcar, electronic, orange, black lettering, 1946.	50	150
4457	Pennnsylvania, N5 caboose, electronic, red, white lettering, 1946-47.	40	140
4671	Steam 6-8-6, 4671W tender, electronic, 1946-49.	75	150
5159	Maintenance kit, 1964-68.	1	3
5159-50	Maintenance and lubricant kit, 1969.	1	3

		Gd	Exc
5160	Viewing stand.	50	100
5459	Lionel Lines, dump car, electronic, black, 1946.	30	70
5511	(See 55)		
6002	NYC, gondola (O27), 1949.	4	10
X6004	Baby Ruth / PRR, boxcar, orange, blue lettering, (O27) 1951.	2	5
6007	Lionel Lines, offset-cupola caboose (O27), 1950.	2	5
6012	Lionel, gondola, 1955-56.	2	5
6014	Airex, boxcar, red, yellow logo, white lettering, (O27).	50	115
6014	Bosco / PRR, boxcar (O27), 1958.		
	(A) White, black lettering.	18	42
	(B) Orange, brown lettering.	4	9
6014	Campbell Soup, boxcar (O27), 1969.		NRS
6014	Chun King, boxcar, red, white lettering, (O27).	58	115
6014	Frisco, boxcar, red, white lettering, (O27).	4	9
X6014	Baby Ruth / PRR, boxcar, (O27).		
	(A) White.	2	4
	(B) Red.	4	12
6014	Wix, boxcar (O27), white, red lettering, uncatalogued.	50	100
6015	Sunoco, single-dome tank car (O27), yellow, black lettering, 1954-55.	3	6
6017	Lionel Lines, offset-cupola caboose (O27), 1951-61.	3	7
6017-50	USMC, caboose, blue, white lettering, 1958.	20	50
6017-100	B & M, offset-cupola caboose, 1959, 1964-65.		
	(A) Light to medium blue.	10	30
	(B) Purplish blue.	150	450
6017-185	AT & SF, offset-cupola caboose, gray, white lettering, 1959.	10	30
6017-200	US Navy, offset-cupola caboose, blue, white lettering, 1960.	25	80
6017-225	AT & SF, offset-cupola caboose, red.	10	45
6017-235	AT & SF, offset-cupola caboose, red.	20	40
6019	RCS Track Set (O27), 1948-66	1	3
6024	Nabisco Shredded Wheat, boxcar, orange, black lettering, 1957.	10	25
6024	RCA Whirlpool, boxcar (O27), orange, black lettering, 1969.	30	55
6025	Gulf, single-dome tank car (O27), 1956-57.		
	(A) Gray, blue lettering.	3	10
	(B) Orange, blue lettering.	3	10
	(C) Black, red "GULF" emblem.	3	10
6027	Alaska, offset-cupola caboose, blue, yellow lettering, 1959.	25	75
6029	Uncoupling Track (O27), 1955, 1961-63.	.25	1
6032	Lionel, gondola, black (O27), 1952-53.	2	5
X6034	Baby Ruth / PRR, boxcar (O27), 1953.		
	(A) Orange, blue lettering.	5	12
	(B) Red, white lettering.	5	12
	(C) Orange, black lettering.	5	12

Gd   **Exc**

A very ordinary workhorse from the Lionel stables, the 6062 NYC gondola. Packaged in many sets, the gondolas provided a great deal of enjoyment for the train operators, who could load or unload them at will.

		Gd	Exc
6035	Sunoco, single-dome tank car (O27), gray, blue and red lettering, 1952-53.	1	3
6037	Lionel Lines, offset-cupola caboose (O27), brown, white lett., 1952-54.	2	4
6042	Lionel, gondola (O27), blue or black, uncatalogued.	2	5
6042-125	Lionel, gondola (O27), blue, uncatalogued.	2	5
6044	Airex, blue, (O27).		
	(A) White and yellow lettering.	5	12
	(B) White and orange lettering.	40	80
6045	Lionel Lines, two-dome tank car, 1958, 1963.		
	(A) Gray, blue lettering.	3	5
	(B) Orange, black lettering.	3	10
6045	Cities Service, two-dome tank, green, white lettering, uncat., 1960.	6	12
6047	Lionel Lines, offset-cupola caboose, red or tuscan, 1962.	2	4
6050	Lionel Savings Bank, boxcar, white and green, coin slot in roof, 1961.	9	18
6050	Swift, refrigerator, red, white lettering, 1962.	10	20
6050	Libbys Tomato Juice, boxcar, white; red and blue lettering, 1961.		
	(A) Green stems on tomatoes.	12	25
	(B) Green stems missing.	50	100
6057	Lionel Lines, offset-cupola caboose, red or brown, 1959-62.	2	4
6057-50	Lionel Lines, offset-cupola caboose, orange, black lettering, 1962.	5	25
6058	C & O, offset-cupola caboose, yellow, 1961.		
	(A) Blue lettering.	10	45
	(B) Black lettering.	10	50
6059-50	M St L, offset-cupola caboose, red, white lettering, 1961- 63.	3	8
6059-60	M St L, offset-cupola caboose, red, white lettering, 1963-69.	3	8
6062	NYC, gondola, black, white lettering, 1959-64.	3	10
6062-50	NYC, gondola, black, 1968-69.	2	6
6067	Caboose (no letters), offset-cupola, 1962.	2	4
6076	Lehigh Valley, hopper, 1963.		
	(A) Gray body.	4	8
	(B) Black body.	4	8
	(C) Red body.	4	8

		Gd	Exc
	(D) Yellow body.	4	8
6076	ATSF, hopper, gray, black lettering, 1963.	9	20
(6076)	Hopper, no lettering.		
	(A) Olive drab.	10	35
	(B) Gray body.	2	7
6109	Flatcar with logs, gray, 1952	35	45
6110	Steam 2-4-2, die-cast body, 1950-51.	12	25
6111	Flatcar with pipes, red, 1957.	5	12
6111	Flatcar with logs, yellow, 1955.	3	8
6111	Flatcar with unknown load, various colors, 1955-56.	6	15
6112	Lionel, gondola, 1956-58.		
	(A) Black body.	3	8
	(B) Blue body.	2	6
	(C) White body.	4	14
(6112)	Lionel, gondola, 1960.		
	(A) Blue body.	2	5
	(B) Olive drab body.	10	30
6112-1	Lionel, gondola, blue, white lettering.	2	5
6112-135	Lionel, gondola, black, three canisters.	1	3
6119	DL & W, work caboose, red, 1955-56.	10	25
6119-25	DL & W, work caboose, orange, 1957-59.	10	25
6119-50	DL & W, work caboose, brown, 1956.	10	35
6119-75	DL & W, work caboose, gray, 1957.	10	35
6119-100	DL & W, work caboose, red, 1963-66.	10	20
(6119-125)	Work caboose, olive drab, no lettering, circa 1960.	50	225
(6120)	Work caboose, yellow, no lettering, 1962.	7	20
6121	Flatcar with pipes, yellow, 1955.	5	15
6130	AT & SF, work caboose, red, 1965-68.	10	30
6142	Lionel, gondola, black, 1961-66, 1970.	2	5
6142-50	Lionel, gondola, green, 1961-63, 1966.	2	5
6142-75	Lionel, gondola, blue, 1961-63.	2	5
6142-100	Lionel, gondola, green, 1964-65.	2	5
6142-150	Lionel, gondola, blue.	2	5
6142-175	Lionel, gondola.	2	5
6151	Flatcar with patrol truck, 1958.		
	(A) Yellow car.	20	60
	(B) Orange car.	17	50
	(C) Cream car.	20	60
6162	NYC, gondola, blue, three canisters, 1961-69.	2	7
6162-60	Alaska, gondola, yellow, three canisters, 1959.	20	40
6162-110	NYC, gondola, canisters.		
	(A) Blue body.	3	7

Gd   Exc

6346-56 Alcoa Aluminum covered hopper car.

		Gd	Exc
	(B) Red body.	15	30
6167	Lionel Lines, offset-cupola caboose, red, white lettering, 1963.	2	4
(6167-25)	Caboose, red, no letters, offset-cupola.	2	5
(6167-50)	Caboose, yellow, no letters, offset-cupola, 1964.	2	6
6167-85	Union Pacific, offset-cupola caboose, yellow, 1964-69.	6	25
(6167-100)	Caboose, red, no lettering, offset-cupola, 1964.	2	4
(6167-125)	Caboose, red or brown, no lettering, offset-cupola, 1964.	2	4
(6167-150)	Caboose, yellow, no lettering, offset-cupola.	2	4
6175	Flatcar with rocket, 1958-61.		
	(A) Black car.	25	60
	(B) Red car.	25	60
6176	Lehigh Valley, hopper.		
	(A) Yellow.	3	7
	(B) Gray.	3	7
	(C) Black.	3	7
(6176)	Hopper (no lettering), yellow	3	7
6219	C & O, work caboose, blue, yellow lettering, 1960.	20	65
6220	Santa Fe, NW-2 switcher, black, white lettering, 1949-50.		
	(A) Large "GM" decal on cab.	100	275
	(B) Small "GM" decal on cab.	100	275
6250	Seaboard, NW-2 switcher, blue and orange, blue and white lettering, 1954-55.	100	275
6257	Lionel, offset-cupola caboose, red, 1948-56.	2	4
6257-25	Lionel, offset-cupola caboose, red.	2	4
6257-50	Lionel, offset-cupola caboose, red.	2	4
6257-100	Lionel, offset-cupola caboose, red.	5	15
6262	Flatcar with wheels, gray superstructure, 1956-57.		
	(A) Black car.	15	40
	(B) Red car.	50	400
6264	Flatcar with lumber for forklift set, red, white lettering, 1957.	20	45
6311	Flatcar, reddish-brown, three plastic pipes, 1955.	15	40
6315	Gulf, single-dome chemical tank, 1956-59.		

		Gd	Exc
	(A) Burnt orange and black.	20	45
	(B) All-orange.	10	30
6315	Lionel Lines, single-dome tank car, orange, black lettering, 1963-66.	10	30
6342	NYC, gondola, red, black channel, 1956-58.	7	25
6343	Barrel ramp car, red, white lettering, 1961-62.	15	35
6346-56	Alcoa, quad hopper, silver, blue lettering, 1956. (See 6436-110)		
6352-1	PFE reefer from icing set, orange, brown doors, 1955-57.	25	65
6356-1	NYC, two-level stock car, yellow, black lettering, 1954-55.	10	35
6357	Lionel, offset-cupola caboose, red or brownish-red, 1948-57.	6	15
6357-25	Lionel, offset-cupola caboose, maroon.	6	15
6357-50	AT & SF, offset-cupola caboose, red, white lettering.	250	900
6361	Flatcar with timber, green, white lettering, 1960-61, 1964-69.	25	75
6362-55	Truck car with three trucks, orange, black, 1956.	10	30
6376	Lionel Lines, Circus Car, white, red lettering, 1956-57.	20	50
(6401)	Flatcar with van, no lettering, circa 1960.	3	8
(6401-50)	Flatcar, olive drab, no number.	3	7
(6402)	Flatcar, with reels or boat, gray.	4	12
6404	Flatcar with auto, 1960.		
	(A) With red auto.	20	60
	(B) With yellow auto.	—	150
	(C) With brown auto.	—	250
	(D) With green auto.	—	250
6405	Flatcar with trailer, brown, yellow trailer, 1961.	10	35
(6406)	Flatcar with auto, no lettering, 1960.		
	(A) Brown, red auto with windows and gray bumpers.	15	35
	(B) Brown, yellow auto with windows and gray bumpers.	30	120
	(C) Gray, dark brown car with windows and gray bumpers.	—	200
(6407)	Flatcar with rocket, red, gray superstructure, 1963.	75	450
(6409-25)	Flatcar, no numbers, red or gray.	4	10
6411	Flatcar with logs, gray, 1948-50.	10	30
6413	Mercury Project car, two gray Mercury capsules, 1962-63.		
	(A) Powder blue car.	30	150
	(B) Aquamarine car.	40	175
6414	Evans Auto Loader, red, black superstructure, four autos, 1955-57.		
	(A) Premium cars with windows, bumpers, and rubber tires; most are red, yellow, blue, and white.	20	60
	(B) Four cheap cars without trim, two red and two yellow.	—	450
	(C) Four red premium cars with gray bumpers.	50	175
	(D) Four light yellow premium cars with chrome bumpers.	—	450
	(E) Four dark yellow premium cars with gray bumpers.	—	450
	(F) Four dark brown premium cars with chrome bumpers.		NRS
	(G) Four brown premium cars with gray bumpers.	—	1700
	(H) Four medium green cars with chrome bumpers.		NRS

		Gd	Exc
	(I) Four green premium cars with gray bumpers.	—	1700
6415	Sunoco, three-dome tank car, silver, 1953-55, 1964-66, 1969.	5	20
6416	Boat Loader, red, black superstructure, 1961-63.	75	150
6417	Pennsylvania, N5C caboose, tuscan, white lettering, 1953-57.		
	(A) Lettered "NEW YORK ZONE".	10	25
	(B) Without "NEW YORK ZONE".	80	225
6417-25	Lionel Lines, N5C caboose, tuscan, white lettering, 1954.	10	25
6417-50	Lehigh Valley, N5C caboose, 1954.		
	(A) Gray, red lettering.	30	100
	(B) Tuscan, white lettering.	—	1200
6418	Bridge, metal base, plastic sides	1	4
6418	Flatcar with steel girders, gray, 1955-57.	30	65
6419	DL & W, work caboose, light gray, 1949-50, 1953-57.	10	25
6419-57	Norfolk & Western, work caboose, light gray, numbered "576419", 1957.	40	100
6420	DL & W, work caboose, dark gray, 1949-50.	30	85
6424	Flatcar with two autos, black; white, yellow, turquoise, or red autos, 1956-59.	15	35
6425	Gulf, three-dome tank car, silver, orange logo, blue lettering, 1956-58.	10	30
6426	Sunoco, tank car, blue, yellow lettering.	5	20
6427	Esso, tank car, red, white lettering.	5	20
6427	Lionel Lines, N5C caboose, tuscan, white lettering, 1955-60.	10	25
6427-60	Virginian, N5C caboose, dark blue, yellow lettering, 1958.	90	300
6427-500	Pennsylvania, N5C caboose, sky blue, white lettering, lettered "576427", from Girl's Set, 1957-58.*	100	325
6428	U S Mail, boxcar, red, white, and blue, 1960-61.	10	35
6429	DL & W, work caboose, light gray, 1963.	100	300
6430	Flatcar with Cooper-Jarrett vans, red flatcar, 1955-58.		
	(A) Gray vans with aluminum signs.	15	50
	(B) White vans with blackened aluminum signs.	15	50
6431	Flatcar with vans, red, white lettering, 1965.	40	225
6434	Poultry Dispatch, red, white lettering, 1958-59.	30	55
6436-1	Lehigh Valley, quad hopper, black, white lettering, 1955.	10	35
6436-25	Lehigh Valley, quad hopper, maroon, white lettering, 1955.	10	35
6436-110	Lehigh Valley, quad hopper, red, white lettering, 1963-68.	15	35
6436-500	Lehigh Valley, hopper, lilac, "643657", from Girl's Set, 1957-58.*	75	200
6436-1969	TCA, quad hopper, red, white lettering, 1969.	—	125
6437-25	Pennsylvania, N5C caboose, tuscan, white lettering, 1961-68.	10	25
6440	Flatcar with vans, red, two gray vans, 1961-63.	25	75
6440	Pullman, metal, two-tone green, yellow lettering, 1948-49.	20	40
6441	Observation, metal, two-tone green, yellow lettering, 1948-49.	20	40
6442	Pullman, metal, two-tone green, yellow lettering, 1949.	25	60
6443	Observation, metal, two-tone green, yellow lettering, 1949.	25	60
6445	Fort Knox Gold Reserve, silver, clear windows, coin slot, 1961-63.	40	100

		Gd	Exc
6446-1	Norfolk & Western, hopper, "546446", gray, black lettering, 1954-55.	15	45
6446-25	Norfolk & Western, hopper, "546446", 1955-57.		
	(A) Black, white lettering.	15	35
	(B) Gray, black lettering.	15	40
6447	Pennsylvania, N5C caboose, tuscan, white lettering, 1963.	80	275
6448	Target car, 1961-64.		
	(A) Red, white lettering.	10	20
	(B) White, red lettering.	10	20
6452	Pennsylvania, gondola, black.	4	10
6454	Erie, boxcar, 1949-53.	20	50
6454	Baby Ruth / PRR, boxcar, orange, brown doors, 1948.	50	200
6454	Southern Pacific, boxcar, light brown, white lettering, 1950-53.	15	40
6454	Pennsylvania, boxcar, tuscan, white lettering, 1949-53.	20	50
6454	AT & SF, boxcar, orange, brown doors, 1948.	10	30
6454	NYC, boxcar, 1951.		
	(A) Orange, brown doors, white lettering.	40	150
	(B) Brown, white lettering.	20	50
	(C) Tan, white lettering.	10	30
6456	Lehigh Valley, short hopper.		
	(A) Black.	5	9
	(B) Maroon.	5	9
6457	Lionel, offset-cupola caboose, 1949-52.	10	25
6460	Bucyrus Erie, crane, eight-wheel, 1952-54.		
	(A) Black cab.	15	35
	(B) Red cab.	40	80
6460-25	Bucyrus Erie, crane, eight-wheel, with box, red cab, 1952- 54.	40	80
6461	Transformer car, 16-wheel, gray, black transformer, 1949-50.	25	75
6462	Pennsylvania, gondola, black	2	8
6462	NYC, gondola.		
	(A) Black, 1949-54.	2	8
	(B) Red, 1950-52, 1954, 1956-57.	2	8
	(C) Green, 1954-56.	3	9
6462-25	Gondola, green.	4	10
6462-75	NYC, gondola, bright red.	4	10
6462-100	NYC, gondola, red.	3	10
6462-125	NYC, gondola, red.	3	9
6462-500	NYC, gondola, pink, for Girl's Set, "6462", 1957.*	50	150
6463	Rocket Fuel, two-dome tank, white, red lettering, 1962-63.	10	25
6464-1	Western Pacific, boxcar, 1953-54.		
	(A) Silver, blue lettering.	25	75
	(B) Silver, red lettering.	500	1600
	(C) Orange, silver lettering.	500	1600

		Gd	Exc

Fast freight moves in the 6464-125 New York Central Pacemaker boxcar.

		Gd	Exc
6464-25	Great Northern, boxcar, orange, white lettering, 1953-54.	20	50
6464-50	M & St L, boxcar, tuscan, white lettering, 1953-56.	20	50
6464-75	Rock Island, boxcar, green, gold lettering, 1953-54, 1969.	25	75
6464-100	Western Pacific, boxcar, 1954-55.		
	(A) Silver body, yellow feather.	30	100
	(B) Orange body, yellow feather.	30	100
	(C) Orange, blue feather, numbered "1954".	—	2000
	(D) Orange, blue feather, numbered "6464-100".	150	600
6464-125	NYC, boxcar, gray and red, white lettering, 1954-56.	30	100
6464-150	Missouri Pacific, boxcar, blue and gray, 1954-55, 1957.	25	110
6464-175	Rock Island, boxcar, silver, 1954-55.		
	(A) Blue lettering.	25	100
	(B) Black lettering.	300	1000
6464-200	Pennsylvania, boxcar, tuscan, white lettering, 1954-55.	40	125
6464-225	Southern Pacific, boxcar, black; red, white, and yellow lettering, 1954-56.	35	100
6464-250	Western Pacific, boxcar, orange, blue feather, 1966-67.	40	100
6464-275	State of Maine, boxcar; red, white, and blue; black and white lettering, 1955, 1957-59.	20	75
6464-300	Rutland, boxcar, green and yellow, 1955-56.		
	(A) All-yellow door, outlined herald.	20	75
	(B) Green and yellow door, outlined herald.	300	750
	(C) All-yellow door, solid herald.	550	1500
	(D) Green and yellow door, solid herald.	—	2500
6464-325	B & O Sentinel, boxcar, blue and silver, multicolor lettering, 1956.	125	400
6464-350	MKT / Katy, boxcar, tuscan or maroon, white lettering, 1956.	80	200
6464-375	Central of Georgia, boxcar, maroon and silver, red and white lettering, 1956-57, 1966-67.	30	90
6464-400	B & O Timesaver, boxcar; blue, orange, and silver; 1956-57, 1969.		
	(A) Lettered "BLT 5-54".	20	75
	(B) Lettered "BLT 2-56".	60	175
6464-425	New Haven, boxcar, black, orange door, white, 1956-58.	20	40
6460-450	Great Northern, boxcar, green and orange, 1956-57, 1966-67.	30	90

Gd **Exc**

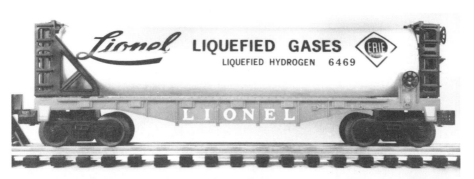

6469 Lionel Liquefied Gases car, a bulkhead flatcar with cylindrical tank added.

		Gd	Exc
6464-475	B & M, boxcar, blue; black and white lettering, 1957-60, 1967-68.	15	35
6464-500	Timken, boxcar, yellow and white, multicolor lettering, 1957-58, 1969.	20	60
6464-510	NYC Pacemaker, boxcar, light green-blue, light yellow door, part of Girl's Set, 1957-58.	150	450
6464-515	MKT, boxcar, light yellow, light green-blue door, 1957- 58.	150	450
6464-525	M & St L, boxcar, 1957-58, 1964-66.		
	(A) Red, white lettering.	20	50
	(B) Maroon, white lettering.	—	750
6464-650	D & RGW, boxcar, yellow and silver, black stripes and lettering, 1957-58, 1966-67.		
	(A) Yellow and silver sides, silver roof, black stripe on door.	22	90
	(B) Same as (A), but no black stripe on door.	75	150
	(C) Yellow and silver sides, yellow roof, no black stripe on door.	300	750
6464-700	Santa Fe, boxcar, red, white lettering, 1961, 1967.	20	100
6464-725	New Haven, boxcar, 1962-68.		
	(A) Orange, black door.	20	50
	(B) Black, orange door.	50	175
6464-825	Alaska, boxcar, blue and yellow, yellow and orange lettering, 1959-60.	100	150
6464-900	NYC / P & LE, boxcar, jade green; red, black, and white lettering, 1960-67.	25	90
6464-1965	TCA Pittsburgh, boxcar, blue, gray door, white lettering, 1965.	—	250
6465	Sunoco, two-dome tank car, silver, blue or black lettering, 1948-50.	3	10
6465	Cities Service, two-dome tank car, green, white lettering, 1960-62.	6	15
6465	Gulf, two-dome tank car, black; orange, blue, and white lettering, 1958.	23	65
6465	Lionel Lines, two-dome tank car, 1958-59.		
	(A) Black, white lettering.	5	15
	(B) Orange, black ends, black lettering.	5	15
(6465-60)	Gulf, two-dome tank car, gray, 1958.	10	20
6467	Bulkhead flatcar, red, black bulkheads, 1956.	20	50
6468-1	Baltimore & Ohio, auto boxcar, 1955.		
	(A) Tuscan, white lettering.	100	300
	(B) Blue, white lettering.	20	45

Gd   **Exc**

The 6519 Allis Chalmers flatcar with condensor load makes an interesting addition to any freight train.

		Gd	Exc
6468-25	New Haven, auto boxcar, orange, black doors, 1956-58.	10	25
	(A) Black "N" over white "H".	15	65
	(B) White "N" over black "H".	80	200
6469	Lionel Liquified Gases, bulkhead flatcar, red, black bulkheads, large white cylinder, 1963.	30	150
6470	Explosives car, red, white lettering, 1959-60.	10	30
6472	Refrigerator car, white, black lettering, 1950.	10	20
6473	Horse Transport car, yellow, red lettering, 1962-64.	10	20
6475	Heinz 57, vat car, tan car, brown roof, green vat labels, 1965- 66.	60	150
6475	Libby's Crushed Pineapple, vat car, light blue car, silver and white vat labels.	20	40
6475	Pickles, vat car, tan car, brown roof, yellow or light brown vats, 1960-62.	10	25
6476	Lehigh Valley, hopper, 1957-62.		
	(A) Red body.	5	9
	(B) Gray body.	5	9
	(C) Black body.	5	9
6476-85	Lehigh Valley, hopper, black.	5	9
6476-135	Lehigh Valley, hopper, yellow, black lettering, 1964-66, 1968.	5	14
6477	Bulkhead car with pipes, red, five pipes, 1957-58.	15	50
6480	Explosives car, red, white lettering.	10	30
6482	Refrigerator car, white, black lettering, 1957.	20	50
6500	Flatcar with Bonanza plane, black car, red and white plane, 1962-65.		
	(A) Plane has red top, white bottom, red wings.	325	575
	(B) Plane has white top, red bottom, white wings.	250	400
6501	Flatcar with jet boat, red, brown and white boat, 1963.	25	100
(6502-50)	Flatcar with bridge girder, blue or red, 1962.	15	45
(6502-75)	Flatcar with bridge girder, black, 1962.	20	60
6511	Flatcar with pipes, red or dark brown, 1953-56.	10	40
6512	Cherry Picker car, black, white lettering, 1962-63.	30	80
6517	Lionel Lines, bay window caboose, red, white lettering, 1955-59.	25	60
6517-75	Erie, bay window caboose, red, white lettering, 1966.	135	275
6517-1966	TCA, bay window caboose, 1966.	60	220

		Gd	Exc
6518	Transformer car, gray, black transformer, 1956-58.	25	90
6519	Allis Chalmers, flatcar with load, orange, gray condenser, 1958-61.	25	55
6520	Searchlight car, gray, 1949-51.		
	(A) Tan generator, gray light housing.	150	450
	(B) Green generator, black or gray light housing.	75	225
	(C) Maroon generator, gray light housing.	25	55
	(D) Orange generator, gray light housing.	25	55
6530	Fire fighting car, 1960-61.		
	(A) Red, white lettering.	25	60
	(B) Black, white lettering.	—	750
6536	M & St L, quad hopper, red, white lettering, 1955, 1963.	15	40
6544	Missile firing car, gray or brown frame, 1960-64.	25	60
6555	Sunoco, single-dome tank car, silver, 1949-50.	15	45
6556	MKT, cattle car, red, white lettering, 1958.	60	200
6557	Lionel, offset-cupola caboose, smoke, brown, 1958-59.	75	175
6560	Bucyrus Erie, crane, eight-wheel, 1955-58.		
	(A) Reddish-orange cab.	60	175
	(B) Black cab.	60	160
	(C) Gray cab.	40	80
	(D) Red cab.	20	50
	(E) Same as (D), but no lettering on frame.	35	110
6560-25	Bucyrus Erie, crane, eight-wheel, red cab, 1956.	40	105
6561	Reel car, gray or brown, 1953-56.	20	60
6562	NYC, gondola, 1956-58.		
	(A) Gray body.	7	25
	(B) Red body.	7	25
	(C) Black body.	7	25
6562-1	NYC, gondola	3	9
6572	Railway Express, refrigerator car, green, gold lettering, 1958- 59.	25	60
6630	IRBM rocket launcher, black, 1960-64.	20	75
6636	Alaska, quad hopper, black, orange-yellow lettering, 1959-60.	17	40
6640	USMC, rocket launcher, olive drab, 1960.	75	225
6646	Lionel Lines, stock car, orange, black lettering, 1957.	10	30
6650	IRBM rocket launcher, red, blue superstructure, 1959-63.	20	45
6650-80	Missile, 1960.	1	4
6651	USMC, cannon car, olive drab, 1960-61.	40	100
6656	Lionel Lines, stock car, yellow, black lettering, 1949-55.		
	(A) With brown "ARMOUR" decal.	35	85
	(B) Without decal.	5	15
6657	Rio Grande, offset-cupola caboose, 1957-58.	50	125
6660	Flatcar with crane, dark red, black crane, 1958.	20	65
6670	Flatcar with boom, red, yellow boom, 1959-60.	20	50

	Gd	Exc

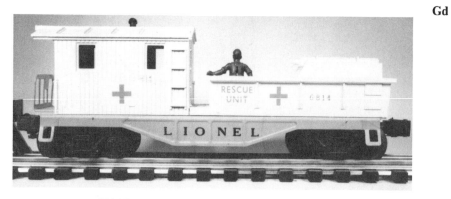

6814 Rescue Unit caboose —ready for action!

		Gd	Exc
6672	Santa Fe, refrigerator car, white, brown roof, 1954-56.		
	(A) Black lettering.	20	50
	(B) Blue lettering.	20	50
	(C) Black lettering, three lines of small data at right.	60	250
6736	Detroit & Mackinac, quad hopper, 1960-62.	17	35
6800	Flatcar with airplane, red; black and yellow Bonanza plane, 1957-60.		
	(A) Plane with black top, yellow bottom.	75	150
	(B) Plane with yellow top, black bottom.	75	150
6801	Flatcar with boat, red car, 1957-60.		
	(A) Boat with blue hull.	30	50
	(B) Boat with brownish-yellow hull.	30	50
	(C) Boat with white hull.	30	50
6802	Flatcar with bridge, red, black bridges, 1958-59.	10	25
6803	Flatcar with gray tank and truck, 1958-59.	50	120
6804	Flatcar with gray USMC trucks, red, 1958-59.	50	120
6805	Atomic Disposal, flatcar, red, gray containers, 1958-59.	35	100
6806	Flatcar with gray USMC trucks, red, 1958-59.	25	85
6807	Lionel flatcar with boat, red, gray amphibious DKW, 1958-59.	35	75
6808	Flatcar with gray USMC trucks, red, 1958-59.	60	125
6809	Flatcar with gray USMC trucks, red, 1958-59.	60	125
6812	Track maintenance car, red, superstructure with two blue men, 1959. Must be completely intact (with no repairs) to obtain Exc prices.		
	(A) Dark yellow-gold superstructure.	15	100
	(B) Black base and gray top.	10	85
	(C) Gray base, black top.	10	85
	(D) Cream base and top.	40	150
	(E) Light yellow base and top.	25	100
6814-1	Lionel, work caboose, white, "RESCUE UNIT", two stretchers, oxygen unit, figure, 1959-61.	30	125
6816	Flatcar with bulldozer, 1959-60.		
	(A) Red car.	75	275
	(B) Black car.	200	600

		Gd	Exc
6816-100	Allis Chalmers, tractor, 1956-60.	25	75
6817	Flatcar with scraper, 1959-60.		
	(A) Red car.	20	80
	(B) Black car.	200	600
6817-100	Allis Chalmers, scraper, 1959-60.	25	75
6818	Transformer car, red, white lettering, black transformer, 1958.	10	40
6819	Flatcar with helicopter, red, 1959-60.	15	40
6820	Flatcar with helicopter, 1960-61.		
	(A) Light blue flatcar.	60	225
	(B) Darker blue flatcar.	40	150
6821	Flatcar with crates, red, 1959-60.	10	20
6822	Searchlight car, red, blue man, 1961-69.		
	(A) Black lighting unit base, gray searchlight housing.	20	50
	(B) Gray lighting unit base, black searchlight housing.	20	50
6823	Flatcar with IRBM missiles, red, two red and white missiles with blue tips, 1959-60.	20	65
6824	USMC, work caboose, olive drab, "RESCUE UNIT", two stretchers, oxygen unit, figure, 1960.	50	160
6825	Flatcar with bridge, red, black or gray trestle bridge, 1959-60.	15	45
6826	Flatcar with trees, red, scrawny trees, 1959-60. Must have original trees for price in excellent condition.	30	110
6827-100	Harnischfeger shovel, yellow and black, 1960.	5	9
6827	Flatcar with steam shovel, black car, crane with yellow cab, 1960-63.	40	90
6828-100	Harnischfeger crane, yellow and black, 1960.	15	45
6828	Flatcar with crane, black car, crane with yellow cab, 1960-63, 1968.	40	90
6830	Flatcar with submarine, blue, gray "U.S. NAVY" submarine, 1960-61.	40	90
6844	Flatcar with missiles, 1959-60.		
	(A) Black flatcar, gray missile superstructure.	15	60
	(B) Red flatcar, light gray missile superstructure.	—	800
63132	(See 3464)		
64173	(See 6427 Lionel)		
65400	(See 2454 or 6454)		
81000	(See 6417 PRR)		
96743	(See 6454)		
159000	(See 3464)		
477618	(See 2457 or 2472)		
536417	(See 6417 PRR)		
546446	(See 6446-1 or 6446-25)		
576427	(See 6427-500)		
641751	(See 6417-50)		
576419	(See 6419-57)		
336155	(See 3361-55)		
576419	(See 6419-57)		

		Gd	Exc
A	Transformer, 90 watts, 1947-48.	8	10
ECU-1	Electronic control unit, 1946.	10	40
KW	Transformer, 190 watts.	75	95
LW	Transformer, 125 watts, 1955-56.	30	40
Q	Transformer, 75 watts, 1946.	8	12
R	Transformer, 110 watts, 1946-47.	15	20
RW	Transformer, 110 watts, 1948-54.	30	40
SP	Smoke pellets, bottle, 1948-69.	—	10
SW	Transformer, 130 watts, 1961-66.	40	50
TW	Transformer, 175 watts, 1953-60.	40	50
V	Transformer, 150 watts, 1946-47.	40	50
VW	Transformer, 150 watts, 1948-49.	80	100
Z	Transformer, 250 watts, 1945-47.	60	75
ZW	Transformer, 250 watts, 1948-49.	125	185
ZW	Transformer, 275 watts, 1950-60.	125	185
No Number	Caboose, offset-cupola, olive drab.	1	2
No Number	Caboose. (See 6057)		
No Number	Caboose, red, offset-cupola. (See 6167-50)		
No Number	Caboose, yellow, offset-cupola. (See 6167-50)		
No Number	Caboose, work, yellow. (See 6120)		
No Number	Flatcar. (See 1877)		
No Number	Flatcar, olive drab. (See 6401-50)		
No Number	Gondola, blue.	1	2
No Number	Gondola, green.	1	2
No Number	Hopper, gray. (See 6076)		
No Number	Hopper, yellow. (See 6176)		
No Number	Rolling stock. (See 1877, 3309, 3349)		
No Number	Turbo missile car. (See 3309)		
No Number	Turbo missile car. (See 3349)		

Track & Such Not Listed

011-11	Fiber pins (O), 1946-50.	.03	.05
011-11	Insulating pins (O), 1940-60.	.03	.05
011-43	Insulating pins dozen (O), 1961.	.40	1
020	90° crossover (O), 1945-61.	1.50	4
020X	45° crossover (O), 1946-59.	1.50	4
022-500	Adapter set (O), 1957-61.	1	2
025	Bumper (O), 1946-47.	3	8
026	Bumper, 1948-50.	3	8
31	Curved track (Super O), 1957-66.	.30	.60
32	Straight track (Super O), 1957.	.35	.75

		Gd	Exc
33	Half curved track (Super O), 1957-66.	.25	.85
34	Half straight track (Super O), 1957-66.	.25	.75
40	Hookup wire, 1950-51, 1953-63.	1	3
40-25	Conductor wire, 1956-59.	1	4
40-50	Cable reel, 1960-61.	1	3
41	Contactor.	.40	.80
48	Insulated straight track (Super O), 1957-66.	.75	1.50
61	Ground lockon (Super O), 1957-60.	.25	.50
62	Power lockon (Super O), 1957-66.	.25	.50
88	Controller, 1946-60.	.50	1
90	Controller.	.25	.75
91	Circuit breaker, 1957-60.	1	3
92	Circuit breaker controller, 1959-66, 1968-69.	.50	1
145C	Contactor, 1950-60.	.50	1.50
147	Whistle controller, 1961-66.	.50	1
153C	Contactor.	.50	2
390C	Switch, d.p.d.t., 1960-64.	.50	2
1013	Curved track (O27), 1945-69.	.10	.20
1013-17	Steel pins (O27), 1946-60.	—	.05
1013-42	Steel pins (O27), 1961-68.	—	.60
1018-1/2	Straight track (O27), 1955-59.	.10	.30
1018	Straight track (O27), 1945-69	.10	.30
6149	Remote-control uncoupling track (O27), 1964-69.	.25	1
CTC	Lockon (O and O27), 1947-69.	.20	.75
LTC	Lockon (O and O27), 1950-69.	3	5
OC	Curved track (O), 1945-61.	.15	.40
OCS	Curved insulated track (O), 1946-50.	1	2
OC1/2	Half section curved track (O), 1945-66.	.20	.40
OS	Straight track (O), 1945-61.	.20	.40
OSS	Straight insulated track, 1946-50.	1	2
OTC	Lockon track (O and O27).	1	3
RCS	Remote-control track (O), 1945-48.	1	3
TOC	Curved track (O), 1962-66, 1968-69.	.15	.40
TOC1/2	Half section straight track (O), 1962-66.	.20	.40
TOC51	Steel pins /dozen (O), 1962-69.	.20	.50
TOS	Straight track (O), 1962-69.	.20	.40
UCS	Remote-control track (O), 1945-69.	3	8
UTC	Lockon (O, O27, Standard), 1945.	.25	.75

Highlights of Lionel Modern Era History

From 1970 to 1985 Fundimensions, a subsidiary of General Mills, manufactured and marketed Lionel trains under an exclusive license from The Lionel Corporation. When General Mills divested itself of its toy divisions in 1985, Lionel (trains) became a subsidiary of Kenner-Parker, Inc. Within a short time the license was sold again, this time to real estate developer Richard Kughn. Kughn incorporated his train business as Lionel Trains, Inc. and developed an entrepreneurial style of management not entirely unlike Joshua Lionel Cowen's.

When Fundimensions took over production of Lionel trains in 1970, its managers realized that a whole new generation awaited the production and rediscovery of these trains. To appeal to these hobbyists, the trains would have to be colorful and fun, and they would have to reflect the contemporary diesel locomotives on American railroads. The new management succeeded in reviving children's interest in Lionel trains.

For many years, however, collectors had been an important and perhaps unrecognized part of Lionel's market. Many men (remember Lionel's original marketing bias) who had theoretically outgrown trains continued to collect and/or operate them with great pleasure. In 1973 Fundimensions enjoyed its first major success in the collector market when it offered a special edition locomotive in honor of General Motors' fiftieth anniversary making locomotives for the real railroads. From that point on, Lionel has addressed both markets: the newcomers (adults and children alike) seeking the traditional pleasure of toy trains, and collectors.

Business proved so good that Fundimensions expanded the line beyond the original Lionel tooling it had received. In 1974 a new General Electric U36B diesel locomotive was introduced in both a Bicentennial scheme and also painted for the Chessie System. A few years later the company made a special edition of this locomotive featuring Mickey Mouse to complement its train of Disney-inspired cars. Today the Disney items are very desirable, with both Disney and Lionel collectors seeking them. Fundimensions also resurrected models of the famous GG-1 and F-3 locomotives; in some cases, the Fundimensions versions are more desirable than the original postwar Lionel models!

With the collector market providing something of a safety net, Fundimensions also found plenty of reasons to reintroduce a number of steam locomotives. Although some certainly landed in the hands of enthusiastic youngsters, a great many more quenched the nostalgic yearnings of adult fans. In 1985 the company revived one of the great favorites of all the Lionel steamers — the twenty-wheel Pennsylvania 6-8-6 steam turbine.

Under Kenner-Parker management in 1985-1986, the company made a trial effort at direct-mail marketing of its special trains for collectors. This arrangement, unfortunately, took many collectors by surprise and naturally upset dealers who felt that they were being circumvented by the company.

In April 1987 real estate developer Richard Kughn purchased the Lionel license from Kenner-Parker. A long-time train collector and enthusiast, Kughn guides the business with a entrepreneurial slant. The company quickly released an all-new model of a Rock Island "Northern" (4-8-4) style steam locomotive that greatly impressed collectors.

In 1988 sales of Lionel trains, under Kughn's management, reached an all-time high. The company has gained respect from collectors, who have been impressed by the many new creations: new locomotives and cars, colorful new schemes on older items, and RailScope — a

Exc   LN

video camera mounted within a locomotive to provide a view-from-the-cab for the operator. In 1989-1990 Lionel created a clever new electronic device to accurately reproduce railroad sounds; the device has been incorporated in several locomotives and cars.

Presently, Lionel trains are enjoyed by a very wide audience. On the one hand, all Lionel collectors have a common bond, yet there exist strong factions. Some favor prewar, some postwar, some modern era; others collect a sampling from all groups. Some individuals espouse Joshua Lionel Cowen's notion that the trains should be operated with enthusiasm and enjoyed to the fullest extent. Others feel that Lionel trains should be kept in their original boxes or in glass display cabinets and touched only with white gloves.

Whatever your interest in Lionel trains, or however you enjoy them, it remains clear that Lionel trains are "Not just a toy — a tradition."

Lionel Modern Era (1970-Present)

		Exc	LN
1-700E	New York Central, scale Hudson steam locomotive, black, 1990.	—	1395
3	(See 8104 Union Pacific or 8701 W & A RR)		
4	(See 18008 Disney locomotive)		
0104	Wheat Thins, reefer, yellow and white, black lettering, 1984.		NRS
0124	Oreo, reefer, white and gray, black doors, 1984.		NRS
303	Stauffer Chemical, tank, gray and black, orange logo, 1985.	50	75
350E	Hiawatha, locomotive (See O Gauge Classics)		
484	(See 8587)		
491	Norfolk & Western, diner (See 7203)		
0511	TCA club, St. Louis baggage car, dark green, black roof, 1981.	—	75
0512	NYC, Toy Fair reefer, 1981.	90	125
550C	Curved track, 1970.	.75	1.25
550S	Straight track, 1970.	.75	1.25
577-582	Norfolk & Western (See 9562-9567)		
634	Santa Fe, NW-2 switcher, 1970.	55	100
659	Chicago & Alton (See 8101)		
665E	Johnny Cash Blue Train, steam.		NRS
700E	(See 5390 steam locomotive)		
779	(See 8215)		
0780	Lionel RR Club, boxcar, white and red, red and black lettering, 1982.	75	100
0781	Lionel RR Club, flatcar with two vans, black car, silver vans, 1983.	75	100
0782	Lionel Railroader Club, tank car, maroon, white lettering, 1985.	75	100
783	New York Central (See 8406)		
0784	Lionel Railroader Club, hopper, white, black cover and lettering, 1984.	60	80
784	(See 8608)		
785	(See 18002)		
882-884	(See O Gauge Classics)		
1018-1979	TCA Ceremony, boxcar, tan and yellow; multicolor lettering.	80	95

		Exc	LN

1975 TCA Bicentennial passenger car for the Train Collectors Association.

		Exc	LN
1100	Happy Huff 'n Puff, 1975.	30	40
1200	Gravel Gus, 1975.	35	55
1203	Boston & Maine, NW-2 switcher, body only, blue, white lettering, 1972.	—	80
1278	PHD LOTS club, boxcar, 1989.	—	100
1300	Gravel Gus Junior, 1975.		NRS
1359	Train display case, set 1355, 1983.	—	40
1400	Happy Huff 'n Puff Junior, 1975.	40	65
1776	B & A, GP-9 powered (with caboose), red, white, and blue, 1976.	120	160
1776	Norfolk & Western, N5C caboose, red and white, gold lettering, 1976.	30	45
1776	Norfolk & Western, GP-9 powered; red, white, and blue, 1976.	100	125
1776	Seaboard/Bicentennial, U36B powered; red, white, and blue, 1976.	100	140
1970	(See 8615)		
1973	TCA Convention, auto carrier, black, gold logo, 1973.	45	55
1973	TCA Bicentennial, passenger car; red, white, and blue, 1973.	40	60
1974	TCA Bicentennial, passenger car; red, white, and blue, 1974.	40	60
1975	TCA Bicentennial, passenger car; red, white, and blue, 1975.	40	60
1976	Seaboard, U36B diesel; red, white, and blue, 1976.	—	150
1980	The Rock, GP-20, LCCA, 1980 (See 8068)		
1983	Nabisco Brands, NW-2 switcher, blue and white, 1983.	—	200
1984	Ritz, boxcar, red and yellow, 1984.		NRS
1987	Mopar steam 4-4-2.	—	50
1987	Mopar Express, gondola, 1987.	—	50
1987	Mopar, boxcar.	—	50
1987	Mopar, flatcar with vans, tuscan, white lettering, 1987.	—	100
1987	Mopar, caboose.	—	50
1900	(See 18502 diesel)		
1990	(See 19708 caboose)		
2110	Graduated trestle, 1971-83, 1985-88.	10	12
2111	Elevated trestle, 1971-83, 1985-88.	10	12
2113	Tunnel portals (2), 1984-87.	8	12
2115	Dwarf signal, 1985-87.	11	13
2117	Block target signal, 1984-88.	17	21

		Exc	LN
2122	Extension bridge, 1977-83, 1986-87.	30	45
2125	Whistling freight station, 1971.	40	60
2126	Whistling freight shed, 1976-83, 1985-87.	30	35
2127	Diesel horn shed, 1976-83, 1985-87.	30	35
2128	Automatic switchman, 1983, 1985-86.	25	30
2129	Illuminated freight station, 1983, 1985-86.	20	30
2133	Illuminated freight station, 1972-83.	20	25
2140	Automatic banjo signal, 1970-84.	15	20
2145	Automatic gateman, 1970-84.	30	40
2146	Crossing gate, 1970-71.	15	20
2151	Automatic semaphore, 1978-84.	20	25
2152	Crossing gate, 1977-83.	20	25
2154	Highway flasher, 1970-83, 1985-87.	15	20
2156	Station platform, 1970-71.	35	60
2162	Gate and signal, 1970-83, 1985-87.	35	40
2163	Block target signal, 1970-78.	20	25
2170	Street lamps (3), 1970-83, 1985-87.	20	25
2171	Goose neck lamps (2), 1980-84.	20	25
2175	Sandy Andy kit, 1976-79.	20	40
2180	Road sign set, 1977-83, 1985-88.	2	3
2181	Telephone poles, 1977-81, 1983, 1985-88.	2	4
2195	Floodlight tower, 1970-72.	40	50
2199	Microwave tower, 1972-75.	30	50
2214	Girder bridge, 1970-83, 1985-87.	5	8
2256	Station platform, 1973-81.	6	10
2256	Station platform TCA, 1975.	20	30
2260	Bumpers (3), 1970-73.	25	40
2260	Bumpers (3), 1986.	—	3
2280	Bumpers (3), 1973-80, 1983	3	5
2281	Black bumpers (3), 1983.	15	18
2282	Bumpers (pair), 1983.	20	25
2283	Die-cast bumpers, red (pair), 1984-88.	10	12
2290	Lighted bumpers (pair), 1974-83, 1985-86.	6	8
2292	Station platform, 1985-87.	4	6
2300	Operating oil drum loader, 1985-87.	90	110
2301	Operating sawmill, 1981-1985.	65	90
2302	Union Pacific, gantry crane kit, 1981-82.	15	25
2303	Santa Fe, gantry crane kit, 1981-82.	20	40
2305	Operating oil derrick, 1981-86.	100	150
2306	Operating icing station and car, 1982-83.	145	200
2307	Billboard light, 1982-83, 1985-86.	15	20
2308	Animated newsstand, 1982-83.	90	120

		Exc	LN
2309	Mechanical gate, 1982-83, 1985-88.	2	4
2310	Gate and signal, 1973-75.	3	5
2311	Mechanical semaphore, 1982-84, 1986-88.	2	4
2312	Mechanical semaphore, 1973-75.	5	6
2313	Floodlight tower, 1975-84, 1986.	20	25
2314	Searchlight tower, 1975-85.	20	30
2315	Operating coaling station, 1984-86.	95	135
2316	Operating Norfolk & Western, gantry crane, 1984.	90	120
2317	Operating drawbridge, 1975-81.	95	125
2318	Operating control tower, 1984-86.	55	65
2319	Watchtower, illuminated, 1975-80.	20	30
2320	Flagpole kit, 1983-88.	8	10
2321	Operating sawmill, 1986-87.	85	125
2323	Operating freight station, 1985-87.	50	65
2324	Operating switch tower, 1985-87.	55	65
2383	Illuminated bumpers, die-cast, 1987.	—	12
2390	Lionel mirror, 1982.	50	65
2494	Rotary beacon, 1972-74.	40	50
2671	Cleveland TCA, 1975.	75	125
2709	Rico station kit, 1981-88.	15	25
2710	Billboards (5), 1970-83.	5	6
2714	Tunnel, 1975-77.	5	7
2716	Short extension bridge, 1988.	10	15
2717	Short extension bridge, 1977-87.	3	5
2718	Barrel platform kit, 1977-83, 1985.	2	7
2719	Signal tower kit, 1977-83, 1986-87.	2	7
2719	Watchman's shanty kit, 1985-87.	2	7
2720	Lumber shed kit, 1977-83, 1986-87.	2	7
2721	Operating log mill, 1979.		NRS
2722	Barrel loader, 1979.	3	5
2723	Barrel loader, 1984.	3	5
2783	Manual freight station kit, 1981-83.	7	10
2784	Freight platform kit, 1981-83, 1985-88.	6	9
2785	Engine house kit, 1974-77.	30	40
2786	Freight platform kit, 1974-77.	4	7
2787	Freight station kit, 1974-77.	7	10
2788	Coaling station kit, 1975-77.	40	60
2789	Water tower kit, 1975-80, 1985.	7	12
2790	Building kit assortment, 1983.		NRS
2791	Cross country set, 1970-71.	10	25
2792	Layout starter pack, 1980-83.	10	25
2792	Whistle stop set, 1970-71.	15	25

		Exc	LN
2793	Alamo junction set, 1970-71.	—	25
2796	Grain elevator kit, 1977.	50	75
2797	Rico station kit, 1976.	30	45
2900	Lockon, 1970-87.	1	1.25
2901	Track clips (12), 1970-87.	2	5
2905	Lockon and wire, 1972-87.	.85	1.50
2909	Smoke fluid, 1977-87.	1.50	3
2927	Maintenance kit, 1977-87.	3	5
2951	Track book, 1976-80, 1983, 1985-86.	.75	2
2952	Track accessories manual, 1985.	.75	1
2953	Track and accessories manual, 1977-83, 1985-86.	1.25	2
2960	Lionel 75th Anniversary book, 1976.	10	15
2980	Magnetic conversion coupler, 1979.	1	2
2985	The Lionel Train Book, 1986.	—	7
3080	Train display layout.	175	250
3100	Great Northern, 4-8-4 steam, dark green/silver, smoke deflectors, 1981.	495	575
3764	Kahn's refrigerator, LOTS club car, tan sides, red or brown roof, 1981.	25	50
4044	Transformer 45-W, 1970-71.	3	5
4045	Safety transformer, 1970-71.	3	5
4050	Safety transformer, 1972-79.	3	5
4060	Power Master, transformer, 1980-83, 1985-88.	12	30
4065	Commando set, DC transformer, 1986.	15	25
4065	DC hobby transformer, 1981-83.	3	4
4090	Power Master, transformer, 1978-81, 1983.	40	55
4125	Transformer 25-W, 1972.	3	4
4150	Trainmaster transformer, 1976-78.	6	12
4250	Trainmaster transformer.	6	12
4449	(See 8307)		
4651	Trainmaster transformer, 1978-79.	2	3
4690	Transformer, Type MW, solid-state, 1987-88.	—	90
4501	(See 8309)		
4851	Transformer, 1987-88.	3	4
4870	DC hobby transformer and throttle controller, 1977-78.	3	4
5001	Curved track (O27), 1985.		NA
5012	Curved track (O27), 1980-88.	2.20	3.50
5013	Curved track (O27).	.50	.55
5014	Half-curved (O27), 1980-88.	.50	.75
5016	Three-foot straight track (O27), 1987.	—	2.25
5017	Straight track (O27), 1980-88.	—	3.50
5018	Straight track (O27).	.50	.75
5019	Half-straight track (O27), 1986-88.	.50	.75
5020	90° crossover (O27), 1970-88.	3.50	4.75

		Exc	LN
5021	Manual left switch (O27), 1986-88.	8	13
5022	Manual right switch (O27), 1986-88.	8	13
5023	45° crossover (O27), 1970-88.	4	6.50
5024	Straight track.	—	2.25
5025	Manumatic uncoupler, 1971.	1	2
5027	Manual switches, pair (O27).	15	25
5030	Track expander set, 1972.	—	25
5030	Layout set, 1978-80, 1983, 1985.	17	25
5033	Curved track (O27), 1986-88.	.30	.75
5038	Straight track (O27), 1986-88.	.30	.75
5042	Steel pins (eight/pack) (O27), 1986-88.	.40	.75
5044	Curved track ballast (O42), 1987-88.	—	2.25
5045	Wide radius track ballast (O27), 1987-88.	—	2.25
5046	Curved track ballast (O27), 1987-88.	—	2.25
5047	Straight track ballast (O27), 1987-88.	—	2.25
5049	Curved track (O42).	—	1.10
5090	Manual switches (three pair), 1983, 1985.	60	80
5100	(See 18001)		
5113	Wide radius curved track (O27), 1986-87.	1.10	1.50
5121	Left remote-control switch (O27), 1986-88.	15	20
5122	Right remote-control switch (O27), 1986-88.	15	20
5125	Remote-control switches, pair (O27), 1986.	25	40
5132	Remote-control right switch (O27), 1986-88.	30	40
5133	Remote-control left switch (O), 1986-88.	30	40
5149	Remote-control uncoupling track (O), 1986-88.	3	7
5165	O72 wide radius remote switches, 1987-88.	—	50
5166	O72 wide radius remote switches, 1987-88.	—	50
5167	Remote switch (O42), right.	—	25
5168	Remote switch (O42), left.	—	25
5193	Remote-control switches (3 pair) (O27), 1983.	90	110
5380	(See 1-700E)		
5484	TCA steam 4-6-4, dark green, white lettering, 1985.	500	575
5500	Straight track (O), 1983-88.	.75	1.25
5501	Curved track (O), 1983-88.	.75	1.25
5502	Remote-control track, 10", 1971.	5	8
5504	Half-curved (O), 1983, 1985-88.	—	1.05
5505	Half-straight (O), 1983, 1985-88.	—	1.05
5510	Curved track (O).	.75	1.25
5520	90° crossover (O), 1971.	5	7
5522	Three-foot straight track, 1987.	—	3.75
5523	Straight track, 40-inch.	—	5
5530	Remote uncoupling section (O), 1986-88.	11	13

		Exc	LN
5540	90° crossover (O), 1981-88.	7	8
5545	45° crossover (O), 1982-88.	—	13
5572	Wide radius curved track (O72), 1986-88.	1.25	2
5600	Curved track, 1973.	—	1.75
5601	Card of four curved track, 1973.	—	7
5602	Card of four roadbed ballast, curved track, 1973-74.	4	7
5605	Straight track, 1973.	1	2
5606	Card of four straight track, 1973.	4	8
5607	Card of four roadbed ballast, straight track, 1973.	4	8
5620	Left manual switch, 1973-74.	—	25
5700	Oppenheimer, woodside reefer, blue-green "weathered" paint, 1981.	25	45
5701	Dairymen's League, reefer, white "weathered" paint, 1981.	20	25
5702	National Dairy Despatch, reefer, red and silver "weathered" paint, 1981.	20	25
5703	North American Despatch, reefer, yellow and brown, 1981.	20	25
5704	Budweiser, woodside reefer, dark green "weathered" paint, 1981.	45	55
5705	Ball Glass Jars, woodside reefer, yellow "weathered" paint, 1981.	25	30
5706	Lindsay Bros., woodside reefer, tuscan "weathered" paint, 1981.	30	35
5707	American Refrigerator, reefer, yellow "weathered" paint, 1981.	20	25
5708	Armour, woodside reefer, yellow, tuscan roof and ends, 1982- 83.	17	20
5709	REA, woodside reefer, medium green, 1982-83.	30	45
5710	Canadian Pacific, woodside reefer, tuscan, white lettering, 1982-83.	17	20
5711	Commercial Express, woodside reefer, two-tone brown, 1982-83.	17	20
5712	Lionel, woodside reefer, bright orange, blue roof and ends, 1982.	200	275
5713	Cotton Belt, woodside reefer, yellow, brown roof and ends, 1983.	15	20
5714	Michigan Central, reefer, white, brown roof and ends, 1983.	15	20
5715	Santa Fe, reefer, orange, tuscan roof and ends, 1983.	25	30
5716	Vermont Central, reefer, silver-gray, black roof and ends, 1983.	15	20
5717	AT & SF, bunk car, gray, 1984	40	55
5718	(See 9849)		
5719	Canadian National, reefer, gray, red lettering, 1984.	15	20
5720	Great Northern, reefer, dark green, gold lettering, 1985.	85	125
5721	SOO Line, woodside reefer, orange, brown roof and ends, 1985.	15	20
5722	Nickel Plate, woodside reefer, yellow, brown roof and ends, 1985.	15	20
5724	Pennsylvania, bunk car, light yellow, black lettering, 1985.	20	25
5726	Southern, bunk car, dark green, white lettering, 1985.	30	40
5727	US Marines, bunk car, olive and yellow-gray camouflage, 1985.	15	20
5728	Canadian Pacific, bunk car, maroon, white lettering, 1986.	15	20
5730	Strasburg RR, reefer, tuscan, yellow lettering, 1985-86.	15	20
5731	Louisville & Nashville, woodside reefer, tuscan, white lettering, 1985-86.	12	15
5732	Central of New Jersey, reefer, tuscan, white lettering, 1985-86.	20	30
5733	Lionel Lines, bunk car, orange and blue, blue and black lettering, 1986.	40	50
5734-85	TCA, club REA reefer, dark green body, black roof and ends, 1985.	100	150

Exc   LN

6207 Southern gondola.

		Exc	LN
5735	New York Central, bunk car, gray, black lettering, 1985-86.	35	45
5739	B & O, tool car, gray, black lettering, 1986.	40	50
5745	AT & SF, bunk car, red and silver, yellow lettering, 1986.	40	50
5760	AT & SF, tool car, red and silver, yellow lettering, 1986.	40	50
5823	45° O Gauge crossover.	4	6
5900	AC/DC converter, 1979-81, 1983.	4	6
5745	AT & SF, bunk car, 1986.	40	50
5760	AT & SF, tool car, 1986.	40	50
6014-900	Frisco, boxcar, white, black lettering, 1975.	50	75
6076	Lehigh Valley, short hopper, black, white lettering, 1970.		NRS
6100	Ontario Northland, quad hopper, blue sides, yellow lettering, 1981-82.	40	50
6101	Burlington Northern, quad hopper, green, white lettering, 1981, 1983.	15	25
6102	Great Northern, quad hopper (FARR #3), tuscan, white lettering, 1981.	35	50
6103	Canadian National, quad hopper, gray, maroon cover, 1981.	25	35
6104	Southern, quad with coal (FARR #4), green, gold lettering, 1984-85.	75	85
6105	Reading, operating short hopper, tuscan, white lettering, 1982.	55	65
6106	Norfolk & Western, quad hopper, gray, black cover and lettering, 1982.	35	45
6107	Shell, quad hopper, yellow, black and red lettering, 1982.	15	20
6109	Chesapeake & Ohio, operating short hopper, black, white lettering, 1983.	25	40
6110	MoPac, quad hopper, black, white lettering, 1983.	15	25
6111	Louisville & Nashville, quad hopper, gray, red lettering, 1983.	15	25
6112	Commonwealth Edison, hopper, tuscan, black and white lettering, 1983.	80	120
6113	Illinois Central, short hopper, black, white lettering, 1985.	10	15
6114	C & NW, quad hopper, dark green, yellow lettering, 1983.	105	125
6115	Southern, quad with coal, gray, red lettering, 1983.	10	20
6116	SOO Line, ore car, tuscan, white lettering, 1985.	40	50
6117	Erie, operating short hopper, black, white lettering, 1985.	25	35
6118	Erie-Lackawanna, quad hopper, gray, black lettering, 1985.	45	50
6122	Penn Central, ore car, black, white lettering, 1985.	40	50
6123	Pennsylvania, quad hopper (FARR #5), gray, black lettering, 1985.	45	55
6124	D & H, quad hopper, red, yellow lettering, 1984.	15	25

		Exc	LN
6126	Canadian National, ore car, tuscan, white lettering, 1986.	25	30
6127	Northern Pacific, ore car, black, white lettering, 1986.	30	35
6131	Illinois Terminal, quad hopper, yellow, red lettering, 1985- 86.	17	25
6134	Burlington Northern, ACF short hopper, green, white lettering, 1986.	125	200
6135	C & NW, ACF hopper, gray, black and yellow lettering, 1986.	125	200
6137	Nickel Plate Road, hopper, gray, black lettering, 1986.	10	15
6138	B & O, quad hopper, gray, black lettering, 1986.	20	30
6150	Norfolk & Western, short hopper, black, 1970.	125	150
6150	Santa Fe, hopper, blue, yellow lettering, 1985-86.	10	15
6177	Reading, short hopper, tuscan, yellow lettering, 1986.	20	25
6200	FEC, gondola, orange, yellow lettering, 1981.	15	30
6201	Union Pacific, gondola, yellow, cop and hobo figures, 1982-83.	25	35
6202	Western Maryland, gondola with coal, black, white lettering, 1982.	35	45
6205	Canadian Pacific, gondola, tuscan, white lettering, 1983.	25	30
6206	C & I M, gondola, red, white lettering, 1985.	10	15
6207	Southern, gondola, (O27), black; two red canisters, 1984.	6	8
6208	B & O "Chessie," gondola, blue, two gray canisters, 1983-84.	25	30
6209	New York Central, gondola w/coal (Std. O), black, white lettering, 1985.	50	75
6210	Erie-Lackawanna, gondola, black, two gray atomic containers, 1985.	20	30
6211	Chesapeake & Ohio, gondola (O27), black, two yellow canisters, 1984.	—	10
6214	Lionel Lines, gondola, orange and blue, 1985.	25	40
6230	Erie, reefer (Std. O), orange, silver roof, black ends, 1986.	125	150
6231	Railgon, gondola (Std. O), black and yellow, 1986.	140	200
6232	Illinois Central, boxcar (Std. O), 1986	125	150
6233	CP, flatcar with stakes (Std. O), black, white lettering, 1986.	100	140
6234	Burlington Northern, boxcar (Std. O), green, white lettering, 1985.	30	50
6235	Burlington Northern, boxcar (Std. O), green, white lettering, 1985.	30	50
6236	Burlington Northern, boxcar (Std. O), green, white lettering, 1985.	30	50
6237	Burlington Northern, boxcar (Std. O), green, white lettering, 1985.	30	50
6238	Burlington Northern, boxcar (Std. O), green, white lettering, 1985.	30	50
6239	Burlington Northern, boxcar (Std. O), green, white lettering, 1986.	50	75
6251	New York Central, operating dump car, black, white lettering, 1985-86.	15	20
6254	Nickel Plate Road, gondola, black, two silver canisters, 1986.	10	12
6258	AT & SF, gondola, dark blue, two silver canisters, 1985-86.	—	6
X6260	New York Central, gondola, gray, two black canisters, 1985.	15	18
6272	AT & SF, long gondola, gray, two black canisters, 1985.	20	25
6300	Corn Products, three-dome tank car, dark yellow, black lettering, 1981.	20	35
6301	Gulf, single-dome tank car, white, orange logo, 1981-82.	30	35
6302	Quaker State, three-dome tank car, dark green, white lettering, 1981-82.	30	40
6304	Great Northern, single-dome tank car (FARR #3), dark green, 1981.	45	65
6305	British Columbia, single-dome tank car, light green, white lettering, 1981.	65	85
6306	Southern, single-dome tank car, silver, black lettering, 1984-85.	60	75

Exc   LN

The 6405 Amtrak passenger coach was produced in 1976-1977.

		Exc	LN
6307	Pennsylvania, single-dome tank car, maroon, white lettering, 1985.	60	75
6308	Alaska, single-dome short tank car, blue, yellow lettering, 1982.	25	35
6310	Shell, two-dome tank car (O27), yellow, red lettering, 1983.	15	20
6312	Chesapeake & Ohio, tank car (O27), blue, yellow lettering, 1984.	25	30
6313	Lionel Lines, single-dome tank car, orange, blue ends, 1985.	40	65
6314	B & O, three-dome tank car, dark blue, yellow lettering, 1986.	40	65
6315	TCA, 18th Convention, tank, orange, black dome and lettering, 1972.	75	95
6317	Gulf, two-dome tank car (O27), white, orange lettering, 1984.	15	20
6323	Virginia Chemicals, single-dome tank, LCCA, black, 1985.	40	75
6326	N & B, bay window caboose.	—	30
6357	Frisco, single-dome tank car, black, white lettering, 1983.	65	85
6358	Phillips Petroleum, single-dome tank car, silver, 1984.	35	45
6401	Virginian, bay window caboose, blue and yellow, 1981.	35	40
6403	Amtrak, Vista Dome, aluminum, red and blue stripes, 1976-77.	45	65
6404	Amtrak, Pullman, aluminum, red and blue stripes, 1976-77.	45	65
6405	Amtrak, Pullman, aluminum, red and blue stripes, 1976-77.	45	65
6406	Amtrak, observation, aluminum, red and blue stripes, 1976- 77.	45	65
6410	Amtrak, Pullman, aluminum, red and blue stripes, 1977-78.	30	50
6411	Amtrak, Pullman, aluminum, red and blue stripes, 1977-78.	30	50
6412	Amtrak, Vista Dome, aluminum, red and blue stripes, 1977-78.	30	50
6420	Reading, maintenance caboose, dark yellow cab, green base, 1981-82.	15	20
6421	Cowen, bay window caboose, gold and tuscan, 1982.	35	40
6422	Duluth Missabe, bay window caboose, tuscan, yellow stripes, 1981-82.	20	25
6425	Erie-Lackawanna, bay window caboose, gray, maroon band, 1984.	35	40
6426	Reading, maintenance caboose, green cab, yellow base, 1982- 83.	10	12
6427	Burlington Northern, maintenance. caboose, green and black, 1983.	10	15
6428	C & NW, maintenance caboose, yellow cab, green base, 1985.	12	15
6430	Santa Fe, caboose, red and gold, 1983.	6	8
6431	Southern, bay window caboose (FARR #4), dark red, 1983-84.	35	45
6432	Union Pacific, caboose, silver and black, multicolor lettering, 1981.	10	12
6433	CP bay window caboose, gray and maroon, maroon lettering, 1981-82.	40	60
6434	SS RR, 1983.	6	8
(6435)	Commando Set, security caboose, unlettered, olive drab, 1983.	—	20

		Exc	LN
6438	Great Northern, b/w caboose (FARR #3), orange and green, 1981.	35	50
6439	Reading, caboose, green and yellow, yellow lettering, 1985- 86.	20	30
6441	Alaska, bay window caboose, blue, yellow lettering, 1982-83.	25	30
6446-25	Norfolk & Western, quad hopper, blue, 1970.	150	175
6446-50	Minneapolis & St. Louis boxcar, 1970.	—	500
6449	Wendy's, N5C caboose, red and yellow, multicolor lettering, 1981-82.	40	50
6464-500	Timken, boxcar, black lettering, 1970.		
	(A) Yellow.	—	250
	(B) Orange.	100	150
6464-1970	TCA, special boxcar, yellow, red door, white lettering, 1970.	125	160
6464-1971	TCA, special boxcar, white, orange-yellow doors, Disney logo, 1971.	200	250
6481	Rio Grande, caboose, 1983.	6	8
6482	Nibco Express, caboose, red, silver and black lettering, 1982.	—	80
6483	LCCA, caboose, red, white lettering, 1982.	—	50
6485	Chessie, caboose, yellow, blue lettering, 1984-85.	—	10
6486	Southern, caboose, green and white, 1985.	8	12
6491	Erie-Lackawanna, transfer caboose, dark red, black base, 1985-86.	—	12
6493	L & C, bay window caboose, blue, gray roof, white lettering, 1986-87.	20	25
6494	AT & SF, four-wheel. bobber caboose, blue, silver frame, 1986.	8	10
6496	AT & SF, work caboose, red cab, black base, 1986.	—	30
6504	LASER, flatcar with helicopter, black, 1981-82.	12	30
6505	LASER, flatcar with satellite tracking housing, black, 1981- 82.	12	30
6506	LASER, security car, 1981-82	15	30
6507	LASER, flat with missile, black, 1981-82.	12	30
6508	Canadian Pacific, crane, twelve-wheel, gray and maroon, 1981.	45	70
6509	Lionel 16-whl. flatcar with girders, gray, maroon girders, 1981.	60	85
6510	Union Pacific, crane, yellow, silver, and gray, 1982.	50	75
6515	Union Pacific, flatcar, yellow, blue lettering, 1986.	—	10
6521	New York Central, flatcar with stakes (Std. O), tuscan, white lett., 1985.	55	70
6522	C & NW, searchlight car, black and gray, white lettering, 1984- 85.	20	25
6524	Erie-Lackawanna crane, 12-wheel, yellow and maroon, 1985.	45	70
6526	US Marines, searchlight car, camouflage colors, 1985.	15	20
6529	New York Central, searchlight car, black and gray, 1985-86.	20	25
6531	Express Mail, flatcar with vans, blue car, blue and orange vans, 1985-86.	25	35
6560	Bucyrus Erie, crane , eight-whl., dk. blue and red, 1971; must have box.	125	200
(6561)	Flatcar with cruise missile, unlettered, olive drab, 1983-84.	—	25
(6562)	Flatcar with barrels, unlettered, olive drab, 1983-84.	—	25
(6564)	Flatcar with two USMC tanks, unlettered, olive drab, 1983- 84.	—	25
6567	Illinois Central Gulf, crane, LCCA, gray and orange, 1986.	60	75
6573	Redwood Valley Express, flatcar with log bin, 1984-85.	—	15
6574	Redwood Valley Express, short crane, tuscan, yellow, and gray, 1984.	—	15
6575	Redwood Valley Express, flatcar with crates, 1984-85.	—	15

		Exc	LN

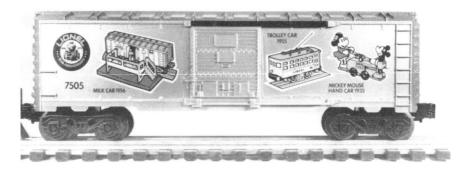

The 7505 boxcar is part of a series made to commemorate Lionel's 75th anniversary.

		Exc	LN
6576	AT & SF, short crane, dark blue and gray, 1985-86.	—	12
6579	New York Central, crane, black, black, white lettering, 1985-86.	50	70
6582	TTOS, flatcar, brown, yellow lettering, 1986.		NRS
6585	Pennsylvania, flatcar with fences, black, yellow fences, 1986.	—	10
6587	W&A, flatcar, tuscan, yellow lettering, 1986.	20	30
6593	AT & SF, crane, black and red, 1986.	—	50
6700	Union Pacific/Southern Pacific, reefer, orange, 1982-83 (part of 2306).	50	65
6900	Norfolk & Western, wide-vision caboose, 1982	100	145
6901	Ontario Northland, wide-vision caboose, yellow and blue, 1982.	50	75
6903	Santa Fe, wide-vision caboose, blue and yellow, 1983.	110	140
6904	Union Pacific, wide-vision caboose, yellow, silver roof, 1983.	100	150
6905	Nickel Plate, wide-vision caboose, dark red, black roof, 1984.	75	100
6906	Erie-Lackawanna, wide-vision caboose, gray and maroon, 1985.	100	120
6907	New York Central, woodside caboose, tuscan and black, 1986.	150	200
6908	Pennsylvania, N5C caboose, maroon and black, yellow cupola, 1985.	65	95
6910	New York Central, wide-vision caboose, red and gray, 1985.	100	135
6912	Redwood Valley, express caboose, tuscan, yellow lettering, 1983-84.	—	20
6913	Burlington Northern, caboose; green, yellow, and gray, 1986.	85	115
6916	New York Central, work caboose, gray cab, black base, 1985-86.	12	15
6917	J C, wide-vision caboose, dark green, cream lettering, 1986.	60	75
6918	B & O, caboose, blue, yellow lettering, 1986.	—	15
6919	Nickel Plate, caboose, red, white lettering, 1986.	—	10
6920	B & A, woodside caboose, tuscan, black and white lettering, 1986.	100	200
6921	Pennsylvania, caboose, red, white lettering, 1986.	—	10
6926	TCA, wide-vision caboose, white, blue roof, red heart, 1986.	50	75
7100	Huff 'n Puff Booklet, 1975	—	.25
7200	Quicksilver, coach, blue and silver, 1982-83.	20	40
7201	Quicksilver, coach, blue and silver, 1982-83.	20	40
7202	Quicksilver, observation, blue and silver, 1982-83.	20	40
7203	Norfolk & Western, "491" diner, maroon, black roof, 1984.	400	550
7204	Southern Pacific Daylight, diner; red, orange, black, and white, 1984.	500	600

		Exc	LN
7205	TCA Denver, combine, dark green, gold lettering, 1982.	—	75
7206	TCA Louisville, Pullman, dark green, gold lettering, 1983.	—	75
7207	New York Central, diner, gray and black, white lettering, 1984.	175	300
7208	Pennsylvania, diner, aluminum, maroon stripes, 1984.	125	225
7210	Union Pacific, diner, yellow and gray, red lettering, 1985.	125	225
7211	Southern Pacific, Vista Dome; red, orange, black, and white, 1984.	300	400
7212	TCA Convention Pitts. pass. car, dark green, gold lettering, 1984.	—	75
7215	B & O, old time coach, blue and gray, white lettering, 1983.	30	50
7216	B & O, old time coach, blue and gray, white lettering, 1983.	30	50
7217	B & O, old time baggage, blue and gray, white lettering, 1983.	30	50
7220	Illinois Central, baggage car, brown, orange and gold striping, 1986.	75	100
7221	Illinois Central, combine, brown, orange and gold striping, 1986.	75	100
7222	Illinois Central, coach, brown, orange and gold striping, 1986.	75	120
7223	Illinois Central, coach, brown, orange and gold striping, 1986.	75	120
7224	Illinois Central, diner, brown, orange and gold striping, 1986.	75	120
7225	Illinois Central, twelve-wheel observation, brown, matches above, 1986.	75	120
7227	Wabash, twelve-wheel diner, dark blue, gold lettering, 1986-87.	75	100
7228	Wabash, twelve-wheel baggage car, dark blue, gold lettering, 1986-87.	75	100
7229	Wabash, twelve-wheel combine, dark blue, gold lettering, 1986-87.	75	100
7230	Wabash, twelve-wheel coach, dark blue, gold lettering, 1986-87.	75	100
7231	Wabash, twelve-wheel coach, dark blue, gold lettering, 1986-87.	75	100
7232	Wabash, twelve-wheel observation, dark blue, gold lettering, 1986-87.	75	100
7241	W & A, coach, yellow, tuscan roof, 1986.	30	50
7242	W & A, baggage car, yellow, tuscan roof, 1986.	30	50
7301	Norfolk & Western, stock car, brown, white lettering, 1982.	40	50
7302	Texas & Pacific, stock car (O27), brown, white lettering, 1983-84.	—	10
7303	Erie-Lackawanna, stock car, blue, white lettering, 1985.	45	50
7304	Southern, "9459" stock car, dark green and tuscan, 1983.	60	75
7309	Southern, short stock car, tuscan, white lettering, 1985-86.	10	15
7312	W & A, stock car, tuscan, yellow lettering, 1986.	20	25
7401	Chessie, stock car (O27), red, white lettering, 1984.	8	10
7403	LNAC, boxcar, LCCA, dark blue-gray, 1984.	30	55
7404	Jersey Central, boxcar, dark green, cream lettering, 1986.	40	50
7500	Lionel 75th Anniv., U36B powered; red, silver, and black, 1975.	80	100
7501	Lionel 75th Anniv., boxcar, blue and silver, "Cowen", 1975.	15	20
7502	Lionel 75th Anniv., reefer, yellow and blue, Lionel innovations, 1975.	15	20
7503	Lionel 75th Anniv., reefer, orange and brown, famous engines, 1975.	15	20
7504	Lionel 75th Anniv., quad hopper, blue, red cover, 1975.	20	25
7505	Lionel 75th Anniv., boxcar, silver and red, shows accessories, 1975.	15	20
7506	Lionel 75th Anniv., boxcar, green and gold, shows catalogues, 1975.	15	20
7507	Lionel 75th Anniv., reefer, blue and white, famous logos, 1975.	15	20
7508	Lionel 75th Anniv., caboose, N5C, 1975.	20	30

	Exc	**LN**

The 7701 Camel boxcar features multicolor graphics.

		Exc	LN
7509	Kentucky Fried Chicken, reefer, brownish-red, white lettering, 1981-82.	15	20
7510	Red Lobster, reefer, white, black roof and ends, 1981-82.	20	30
7511	Pizza Hut, reefer, white, red roof and ends, 1981-82.	20	25
7512	Arthur Treacher's, reefer, yellow, green roof and ends, 1982.	25	30
7513	Bonanza, reefer, white, red roof and ends, 1982.	25	30
7514	Taco Bell, reefer, white, brown roof and ends, 1982.	25	30
7515	Denver Mint, car, light gold, silver bullion, 1982.	85	95
7517	Philadelphia Mint, car, bronze, silver bullion, 1982.	45	55
7518	Carson City Mint, car, black, silver bullion, 1983.	35	50
7519	Toy Fair, reefer, white; red roof, ends, and doors, 1982.	150	175
7520	Nibco, boxcar, green and white, multicolor lettering, 1982.	—	545
7521	Toy Fair, reefer, white sides, blue roof and ends, red doors, 1983.	150	175
7522	New Orleans Mint, car, dark blue, silver bullion, 1985.	40	50
7523	Toy Fair, refrigerator, white and red body, blue doors, 1984.	150	175
7524	Toy Fair, reefer, light brown sides, brown roof and ends, 1985.	175	200
7525	Toy Fair, boxcar, white, blue roof, ends, and doors, 1986.	150	175
7530	Dahlonega Mint, car, orange, silver bullion, 1986.	65	75
7600	Frisco N5C "Spirit", caboose; red, white, and blue, 1975-76.	—	50
7601	Delaware, boxcar, light yellow, blue roof, 1975-76.	15	20
7602	Pennsylvania, boxcar, light blue, orange roof, 1975-76.	30	35
7603	New Jersey, boxcar, light green, gold roof, 1975-76.	30	35
7604	Georgia, boxcar, light blue, red roof, 1975-76.	30	35
7605	Connecticut, boxcar, pale blue, dark blue roof, 1975-76.	30	35
7606	Frisco, N5C caboose, 1974.	45	55
7606	Massachusetts, boxcar, light yellow, white roof, 1975-76.	30	35
7607	Maryland, boxcar, light yellow, black roof, 1975-76.	30	35
7608	South Carolina, boxcar, mustard yellow, brown roof, 1975-76.	35	45
7609	New Hampshire, boxcar, dark yellow, green roof, 1975-76.	35	45
7610	Virginia, boxcar, orange, dark blue roof, 1976.	200	250
7611	New York, boxcar, light yellow, dark blue roof, 1976.	60	75
7612	North Carolina, boxcar, mustard yellow, black roof, 1976.	30	50

		Exc	LN
7613	Rhode Island, boxcar, green, gold roof, 1976.	50	65
7700	Uncle Sam, boxcar, white, red roof, 1976.	60	70
7701	Camel, boxcar, yellow; multicolor lettering, 1976-77.	15	20
7702	Prince Albert, boxcar, red and yellow, multicolor lettering, 1976-77.	15	20
7703	Beechnut, boxcar, red, white and blue, 1976-77.	15	20
7704	Welcome Toy Fair, boxcar, white sides, red roof and ends, 1976-77.	125	200
7705	Toy Fair, boxcar, white sides, red roof and ends, 1976 (Canadian).	250	350
7706	Sir Walter Raleigh, boxcar, orange, blue roof, 1977-78.	15	20
7707	White Owl, boxcar, white, brown roof, gold door, 1977-78.	15	20
7708	Winston, boxcar, red, gold roof and door, multicolor lett., 1977-78.	15	20
7709	Salem, boxcar, green and gold, 1978.	15	20
7710	Mail Pouch, boxcar, white and red, tuscan doors, 1978.	25	30
7711	El Producto, boxcar, white and red, yellow doors, 1978.	25	30
7712	AT & SF, FARR #1 boxcar, yellow and silver, black lettering, 1979.	35	45
7714	Northern Pacific, boxcar, 1980.	12	15
7784	TCA Museum, 1984	30	35
7800	Pepsi, boxcar; red, white, and blue, 1977.	25	45
7801	A & W, boxcar; yellow, orange, and brown, 1977.	15	30
7802	Canada Dry, boxcar, green and gold, white and gold lettering, 1977.	20	30
7803	Trains' n Truckin', boxcar, white and gold, green and gold lett., 1978.	20	35
7806	Season's Greetings, boxcar, silver, green door, 1976.	125	150
7807	Toy Fair, boxcar, green sides, gold roof, ends, and doors, 1977.	150	200
7808	NP, stock car, brown, silver roof, black door, 1977.	50	65
7809	Vernors, boxcar, dark green and yellow, dark green lettering, 1978.	15	20
7810	Orange Crush, boxcar, orange and light green, 1978.	15	20
7811	Dr. Pepper, boxcar, orange and maroon, white lettering, 1978.	15	20
7812	TCA Houston, stock car, brown, yellow plaque, 1977.	25	30
7813	Season's Greetings, boxcar, white and gold, red doors, 1977.	150	175
7814	Season's Greetings, boxcar, white and blue, red and blue lett., 1978.	125	175
7815	Toy Fair, boxcar, silver sides, red roof and ends, white doors, 1978.	125	175
7816	Toy Fair, boxcar, white, gold roof, ends, and doors, 1979.	125	175
7817	Toy Fair, boxcar, white sides, red roof and ends, 1980.	125	175
7900	Outlaw car, orange, outlaw and sheriff figures, 1982-83.	11	14
7901	Cop & Hobo car, red, two figures, 1982-83.	30	35
7902	AT & SF, boxcar (O27), red, white lettering, 1982-83.	6	8
7903	Rock, boxcar (O27), blue, white lettering, 1983.	6	8
7904	San Diego Zoo car (O27), red, yellow giraffe, 1983.	55	65
7908	Tappan, boxcar (O), red, white lettering, 1982.	50	70
7909	Louisville & Nashville boxcar (O27), blue, yellow lettering, 1983.	10	15
7910	Chessie, boxcar (O27), dark blue, yellow lettering, 1984.	10	15
7912	Geoffrey car, white, giraffe figure, 1982-83.	100	125
7913	Turtleback Zoo giraffe car, green, with giraffe, 1986.	35	40

	Exc	**LN**

The 8142 Chesapeake & Ohio steam locomotive has a "4-4-2" wheel arrangement, which indicates that there are four small leading wheels, four driving wheels, and two trailing wheels. The wheels on the tender are not included in the count.

		Exc	LN
7914	Geoffrey car with giraffe, operating, 1985.	100	135
7920	Sears Centennial, boxcar, white, green and blue lettering, 1985-86.	50	60
7925	Erie-Lackawanna, boxcar, light gray, maroon lettering, 1986.	8	12
7926	Nickel Plate Road, boxcar, yellow, black lettering, 1986.	8	11
7930	True Test.	—	60
7931	Town House TV & Appliances, boxcar, gray, black lettering, 1986.	—	50
7932	Kay Bee Toys, boxcar, white, 1986.	—	50
7979	True Value, boxcar, 1986.	—	50
8001	Nickel Plate, steam, 2-6-4, DC motor, 1980.	50	60
8002	Union Pacific, steam, 2-8-4, two-tone gray, black and yellow trim, 1980.	450	575
8003	Chessie System, steam, 2-8-4, dark gray, yellow and orange trim, 1980.	500	600
8004	RI & P, steam, 4-4-0, chrome boiler, brown cab and tender, 1980, 1982.	150	170
8004	(See 18004)		
8005	AT & SF, steam, 4-4-0, red and maroon, gold trim, 1980, 1982.	30	40
8006	ACL, steam, 4-6-4 (J.C. Penney's Special), gray and black, 1980.	650	850
8007	New York N H & H, steam, 2-6-4, gold stripe, 1980.	40	50
8008	Chessie, steam, 4-4-2, blue, yellow and orange trim, 1980.	50	75
8010	AT & SF, NW-2 switcher, blue, yellow lettering, 1970.	40	75
8020	Santa Fe, Alco A unit, red and silver, 1970-76.		
	(A) Powered unit.	75	100
	(B) Dummy unit.	50	70
8021	Santa Fe, Alco B, silver and red, 1971-76.	60	75
8022	Santa Fe, Alco A powered, blue, yellow striping and lettering, 1971.	75	125
8023	Canadian National, Alco A, green, yellow striping and lettering, 1970.	60	75
8025	Canadian National, Alco AA, black, orange nose, white striping, 1971.	150	225
8030	Illinois Central, GP-9 powered, orange and white, 1970-71.	85	125
8031	Canadian National, GP-7 powered, black, orange nose, 1970-71.	70	125
8040	Nickel Plate, steam, 2-4-2, black, white lettering, 1970.	20	30
8040	Canadian National steam, 2-4-2, black, white lettering, 1971.	50	100
8041	New York Central, steam, 2-4-2, gray, white lettering, 1970.	30	50
8042	Grand Trunk, steam, 2-4-2, black, white lettering, 1970.	30	40
8043	Nickel Plate, steam, 2-4-2, black, white lettering, 1970.	50	75
8050	D & H, U36C powered, gray and blue, yellow lettering, 1980.	125	175

		Exc	LN
8051	D & H, U36C dummy, matches 8050, 1980.	100	125
8054/8055	C & S Burlington F-3 AA, silver, black and red markings, 1980.	350	450
8056	C & NW, Trainmaster, yellow and green, 1980-81.	300	395
8057	Burlington, NW-2 powered switcher, red and gray, 1980.	75	150
8059	Pennsylvania, F-3 B dummy, green, gold stripes, 1980.	300	450
8060	Pennsylvania, F-3 B dummy, tuscan, gold stripes, 1980.	350	475
8061	WM/Chessie, U36C powered; yellow, orange, and blue, 1980.	145	175
8062	C & S Burlington, F-3 B dummy; silver, black, and red, 1980.	150	195
8063	Seaboard, SD-9 powered, dark green, yellow band, 1980.	125	175
8064	FEC, GP-9 powered, red and yellow, silver trucks, 1980.	125	150
8065	FEC, GP-9 dummy, red and yellow, silver trucks, 1980.	80	100
8066	TP & W, GP-20 powered, orange and white, white lettering, 1980.	100	125
8068	The Rock, GP-20 powered, LCCA special, blue, 1980.	125	150
8071	Virginian, SD-18 powered, blue and yellow, yellow lettering, 1980.	100	150
8072	Virginian, SD-18 dummy, blue and yellow, yellow lettering, 1980.	75	95
8100	Norfolk & Western, steam, 4-8-4, black/maroon, yellow trim, 1981.	1000	1400
8101	Chicago & Alton, steam, 4-6-4, maroon, gold striping, 1981.	500	600
8102	Union Pacific, steam, 4-4-2, dark gray, yellow trim, 1981-82.	60	75
8104	Union Pacific, steam, 4-4-0, chrome boiler, green and black trim, 1981.	300	395
8111	DT & I, NW-2 powered switcher, orange, black lettering, 1971- 74.	35	75
8140	Southern, steam, 2-4-0, 1971.	25	35
8141	Pennsylvania, steam, 2-4-2, 1971.	40	55
8142	Chesapeake & Ohio, steam, 4-4-2, black, white lettering, 1971.	55	65
8143	Milwaukee, steam, 4-4-2, black, orange stripe on tender, 1971.	30	40
8150	Pennsylvania, GG-1 powered, green, gold stripes, 1981.	450	650
8151	Burlington, SD-28 powered, red and gray, white lettering, 1981.	125	175
8152	Canadian Pacific, SD-24 powered, maroon and gray, yellow lett., 1981.	195	250
8153	Reading, NW-2 powered switcher, green and yellow, 1981.	100	125
8154	Alaska, NW-2 powered switcher, blue, yellow lettering, 1981- 82.	85	125
8155	Monon, U36B powered, dark blue and gold, white lettering, 1981-82.	75	100
8156	Monon, U36B dummy, matches 8155, 1981-82.	60	75
8157	Santa Fe, Trainmaster, blue and yellow, 1981.	400	495
8158	DM & IR, GP-35 powered, maroon, yellow band, white lett., 1981-82.	75	125
8159	DM & IR, GP-35 dummy, matches 8158, 1981-82.	60	75
8160	Burger King, GP-20 powered, yellow and red, 1981-82.	80	100
8161	LASER, gas turbine, bright chrome, blue lettering, 1981-82.	60	100
8162	Ontario Northland, SD-18 powered, blue and yellow, 1981.	150	175
8163	Ontario Northland, SD-18 dummy, blue and yellow, 1981.	100	150
8164	Pennsylvania, F-3 B unit, horn, green, 1981.	400	495
8182	Nibco, NW-2 powered switcher, white, blue-green lettering, 1982.	125	175
8190	Diesel horn kit, 1981.	—	40
8200	Kickapoo Dockside, steam, 0-4-0, black, gold lettering, 1972.	40	50

Exc　　LN

The 8363 Baltimore and Ohio F3 diesel is called an "A unit" because it has a cab for the crew. Matching "B units" without cabs were popular in the F3 design.

		Exc	LN
8203	Pennsylvania, steam, 2-4-2, black, red stripe, 1972.	30	40
8204	Chesapeake & Ohio, steam, 4-4-2, black, 1972.	60	70
8206	New York Central, steam, 4-6-4, black, 1972-74.	225	275
8206	(See also 18206 Santa Fe diesel)		
8209	Pioneer Dockside, steam, black, 0-4-0, 1972-76. Add $5-10 to price if four-wheel tender is present.	40	50
8210	Cowen, steam, 4-6-4, burgundy and gold, 1982.	450	550
8212	Black Cave, steam, 0-4-0, black; glow-in-the-dark decals, 1982.	30	50
8213	Rio Grande, steam, 2-4-2, 1982-83.	60	70
8214	Pennsylvania, steam, 2-4-2, 1982-83.	60	75
8215	Nickel Plate, steam, 2-8-4, black, white stripe, 1982.	600	650
8250	Santa Fe, GP-9 powered, black and yellow, 1972-75, 1982.	50	100
8251/8250	Horn/whistle controller, 1972-74	2	3
8252	D & H, Alco A unit powered, dark blue and silver, 1972.	100	125
8253	D & H, Alco B unit dummy, dark blue and silver, 1972.	50	75
8254	Illinois Central, GP-9 dummy, orange and white, black lett., 1972.	60	75
8255	Santa Fe, GP-9 dummy, black and yellow, yellow lettering, 1972.	60	75
8258	Canadian National, GP-7 dummy, black and orange, white lett., 1972.	60	75
8260-8262	Southern Pacific, F-3 AA, "Daylight" scheme; sold as set,1982.	675	795
8261	Southern Pacific, F-3 B unit dummy, "Daylight" scheme, 1982.	700	1000
8263	Santa Fe, GP-7 powered, blue and yellow, 1982.	75	100
8264	Canadian Pacific, snowplow, gray and maroon, yellow lett., 1982.	100	135
8265	Santa Fe, SD-40 powered, blue and yellow, 1982.	275	425
8266	Norfolk & Western, SD-24 powered w/horn, maroon, yellow trim, 1982.	150	200
8268	Texas & Pacific, Alco A unit powered, dark blue, silver stripe, 1982-83.	50	85
8269	Texas & Pacific, Alco A unit dummy, dark blue, silver stripe, 1982-83.	30	50
8272	Pennsylvania, EP-5, tuscan, gold ends and striping, 1982.	275	350
8300	Santa Fe, steam, 2-4-0, black, 1976.	20	25
8302	Southern, steam, 2-4-0, green, 1973-76.	25	30
8303	Jersey Central, steam, 2-4-2, two-tone blue, 1973-74.	40	50
8304	Baltimore & Ohio, steam, black, white lettering, 4-4-2, 1975.	90	125
8304	Chesapeake & Ohio, steam, 4-4-2, black, gold lettering, 1974-77.	90	125

		Exc	LN
8304	Pennsylvania, steam, 4-4-2, black, gold lettering, 1974.	90	125
8304	Rock Island, steam, 4-4-2, black, white lettering, 1973-74.	100	150
8305	Milwaukee Road, steam, 4-4-2, black, red and gold stripes, 1973.	90	125
8306	Pennsylvania, steam, 4-4-2, black, 1974.	30	40
8307	Southern Pacific, steam, 4-8-4 GS-4 "4449"; black/white/orange, 1983.	1800	2200
8308	Jersey Central, steam, 2-4-2, black, gold lettering, 1973-74.	40	50
8309	Jersey Central, steam, 2-4-2, 1974.	40	50
8309	Southern, steam, 2-8-2 (FARR #4), "4501", green, gold lettering, 1984.	525	600
8310	AT & SF, steam, 2-4-0, black, gold lettering, 1974-75.	30	40
8310	Jersey Central, steam, 2-4-0, black, gold lettering.	30	60
8310	Jersey Central, steam, 0-4-0, black, 1974-75.	30	60
8310	Nickel Plate, steam, 2-4-0, black, gold lettering, 1974-75.	30	60
8311	Southern, steam, 0-4-0, black, 1973.	30	40
8313	Santa Fe, steam, 0-4-0, black, gold trim, 1983.	15	20
8314	Southern, steam, 2-4-0, dark green, white lettering, 1983.	20	25
8315	B & O, steam, 4-4-0, blue, white lettering, 1983.	85	120
8350	US Steel, gas turbine, maroon, silver lettering, 1974-75.	20	30
8351	Santa Fe, Alco A powered, blue and silver, 1973-74.	50	70
8352	Santa Fe, GP-20 powered, blue and yellow, yellow lettering, 1973-75.	80	125
8353	Grand Trunk, GP-7 powered, blue and orange, white lettering, 1974-75.	80	125
8354	Erie, NW-2 powered switcher, black, gold lettering, 1973-75.	125	175
8355	Santa Fe, GP-20 dummy with horn, blue and yellow, 1973-75.	60	80
8356	Grand Trunk, GP-7 dummy, blue and orange, white lettering, 1974-75.	30	40
8357	Pennsylvania, GP-9 powered, dark green, gold lettering, 1973-75.	125	150
8358	Pennsylvania, GP-9 dummy, dark green, gold lettering, 1973-75.	35	50
8359	Chessie, GP-7 powered, gold, blue lettering, 1973.	100	150
8360	Long Island, GP-20 powered, charcoal-gray, silver lettering, 1973-74.	90	125
8361	WP, Alco A powered, silver and orange, 1973-74.	100	125
8362	WP, Alco B dummy, silver and orange, 1973-74.	50	75
8363	B & O, F-3 A; blue, white, and gray; yellow lettering, 1973- 75.	250	285
8364	B & O, F-3 A dummy, matches 8363, 1973-75.	120	200
8365 / 8366	CP, F-3 AA set, brown and gray, yellow lettering, 1973.	650	950
8367	Long Island, GP-20 dummy with horn, charcoal gray, silver lett., 1973.	75	100
8368	Alaska RR, motorized unit, yellow and blue, blue lettering, 1983.	100	140
8369	Erie-Lackawanna, GP-20 powered, gray and tuscan, 1983.	100	125
8370/8371/8372	New York Central, F-3 ABA, two-tone gray, 1983.	500	700
8374	Burlington Northern, NW-2 switcher, green and black, white lett., 1983.	75	145
8375	C & NW, GP-7 powered, green and yellow, red and white herald, 1983.	100	125
8376	Union Pacific, SD-40, Magnetraction, yellow and gray, red stripe, 1983.	450	550
8377	US, switcher with decal sheet, olive drab, 1983.	60	100
8378	Wabash, FM Trainmaster, blue, gray and white striping, 1983.	1100	1500
8379	Pennsylvania, motorized fire fighter, tuscan, gold lettering, 1985.	140	175
8380	Lionel Lines, SD-28 powered, blue and orange, blue lettering, 1983.	150	250

		Exc	**LN**

The 8460 MKT diesel is called an NW-2 switcher; it is bright red.

No.	Description	Exc	LN
8402	Reading, steam, 4-4-2, black, silver lettering, 1984.	60	75
8403	Chessie, steam, 4-4-2, blue, yellow lettering, 1974-75.	60	75
8404	Pennsylvania, 6-8-6, steam, green, gray trim, white lettering, 1984-85.	500	575
8406	New York Central, semi-scale Hudson, 4-6-4, black, 1985.	950	1200
8410	Redwood, steam, 4-4-0, tuscan and yellow, gold trim, 1984- 85.	40	60
8452	Erie, Alco A powered, green, yellow lettering, 1974.	75	100
8453	Erie, Alco B dummy, green, yellow lettering, 1974.	50	75
8454	Rio Grande, GP-7 powered, black, orange lettering, 1974-75.	100	125
8455	Rio Grande, GP-7 dummy, black, orange lettering, 1974-75.	50	80
8456	Norfolk Southern, GP-7, gray; red and white logo, 1974.	60	75
8458	Erie-Lackawanna, SD-40, twin motors, gray and maroon, 1985.	375	450
8459	Rio Grande, rotary snowplow, black and yellow, yellow lettering, 1984.	100	135
8460	MKT, NW-2 powered switcher, red, white lettering, 1973-75.	50	75
8463	Chessie, GP-20 powered, blue and yellow, 1974.	125	150
8464 / 8465	Rio Grande, F-3 AA set, yellow, silver roof, black lettering, 1974.	225	350
8466	Amtrak, F-3 A powered, silver and black, red and blue logo, 1974-75.	275	350
8467	Amtrak, F-3 A dummy, matches 8467, 1974-75.	125	200
8468	B & O, F-3 B dummy, blue, yellow lettering, 1974.	150	175
8469	CP, F-3 B dummy, brown and gray, 1974.	175	225
8470	Chessie, U36B powered; blue, orange, and yellow, 1974.	100	150
8471	Pennsylvania, NW-2 powered switcher, dk. green, yellow lett., 1973-74.	200	295
8473	Coca-Cola, NW-2 powered switcher, red, white lettering, 1975.	100	125
8474	Rio Grande, F-3 dummy, yellow and green, silver roof, 1975.	125	150
8475	Amtrak, F-3 B dummy, silver, black roof, red and blue logo, 1975.	125	175
8477	New York Central, GP-9 powered, black, gray stripe, white lett., 1985.	300	395
8480/8481/8482	Union Pacific, F-3 ABA units, yellow, red, and gray, 1985.	400	550
8485	US Marines, NW-2 switcher, olive drab and black camouflage, 1984.	75	100
8500	Pennsylvania, steam, 2-4-2, black, gold lettering, 1976.	20	35
8502	Santa Fe, steam, 2-4-0, black, gold lettering, 1975.	20	25
8503	(See 18503 diesel switcher)		
8506	Pennsylvania, steam, 0-4-0, black, gold lettering, 1975-77.	100	150

		Exc	LN
8507	AT & SF, steam, 2-4-0, black, gold lettering, 1975.	25	30
8510	Pennsylvania, steam, 0-4-0, 1975.	20	30
8512	Santa Fe, steam, 0-4-0, blue, yellow lettering, 1985-86.	25	35
8516	New York Central, steam, 0-4-0, black, white lettering, 1985-86.	125	150
8550	Jersey Central, GP-9 powered, red and white, white lettering, 1975.	125	150
8551	Pennsylvania, EP-5 powered, tuscan, gold stripes, 1975.	200	275
8552/8553/8554	Southern Pacific, Alco ABA, two-tone orange, 1975-76.	250	350
8555/8557	Milwaukee Rd., F-3 AA set, gray and orange, yellow lett., 1975.	300	450
8556	Chessie, NW-2 powered switcher, yellow and blue, 1975-76.	225	300
8558	Milwaukee Road, EP-5, powered; maroon, orange, and black, 1976.	175	200
8560	Chessie, U36B dummy, orange and yellow, 1975.	75	100
8561	Jersey Central, GP-9 dummy, red and white, 1975-76.	80	100
8562	MoPac, GP-20 powered, blue, white lettering, 1975-76.	105	125
8563	Rock Island, Alco A powered, red, white lettering, 1975.	75	100
8564	Union Pacific, U36B powered, gray and yellow, 1975.	150	200
8565	MoPac, GP-20 dummy, blue, white lettering, 1975-76.	80	100
8566	Southern, F-3 A powered, green, gray stripes, 1975-77.	275	400
8567	Southern, F-3 A dummy, green, gray stripes, 1975-77.	125	200
8568	Preamble Express, F-3 A powered; red, white, and blue, 1975.	100	125
8569	SOO, NW-2 powered switcher, red, white lettering, 1975-77.	75	100
8570	Liberty Special, Alco A powered; red, white, and blue, 1975.	75	100
8571	Frisco, U36B powered, red and white, 1975-76.	75	100
8572	Frisco, U36B dummy, red and white, 1975-76.	60	75
8573	Union Pacific, U36B dummy, gray and yellow, 1975.	200	275
8575	Milwaukee Road, F-3 B dummy, gray and orange, yellow lett., 1975.	100	175
8576	Penn Central, GP-7 powered, black, white lettering, 1975-76.	125	150
8578	New York Central, ballast tamper powered, yellow, 1985, 1987.	100	125
8580/8581	Illinois Central, F-3 AA, brown; orange and yellow striping, 1985-87.	400	475
8582	Illinois Central, F-3 B with horn, brown/orange/yellow, 1985, 1987.	150	200
8585	Burlington Northern, SD-40 twin motors, horn, green and black, 1985.	350	450
8587	Wabash, GP-9 (J. C. Penney Spec.), blue and gray, white lett., 1985.	300	395
8600	New York Central, steam, 4-6-4, black, white lettering, 1976.	250	300
8601	Rock Island, steam, 0-4-0, black, white lettering, 1976-77.	20	25
8602	Pennsylvania, (See 18602)		
8602	Rio Grande, steam, 2-4-0, black, white lettering, 1976-78.	25	30
8603	Chesapeake & Ohio, steam, 4-6-4, black, white lettering, 1976-77.	225	300
8604	Jersey Central, steam, 2-4-2, black, gold lettering, 1976.	40	45
8606	Boston & Albany, 773 Hudson, black, white trim, 1986.	1500	2150
8609	(See 18609 steam)		
8610	Wabash, 4-6-2 steam, dark blue, silver smokebox, white lettering, 1986-87. (Listed as 18610 in 1990.)	500	650
8612	(See 18612)		
8615	Berkshire, 2-8-4 steam (J. C. Penney Special), black, 1986.	950	1350

Exc   **LN**

Many children enjoyed the 8502 ATSF steam locomotive offered in 1975.

		Exc	LN
8616	AT & SF, steam, 4-4-2, black, white lettering, 1986.	65	75
8617	Nickel Plate, steam, 4-4-2, black, yellow stripe and lettering, 1986.	65	75
8625	Pennsylvania, steam, 2-4-0, black, white lettering, 1986.	25	35
8630	W & A, steam 4-4-0, General, black and red, 1986.	—	135
8635	AT & SF, steam, 0-4-0, black, white lettering, 1986.	120	145
8650	Burlington Northern, U36B powered, black and green, 1976-77.	125	150
8651	Burlington Northern, U36B dummy, black and green, 1976-77.	90	100
8652	Santa Fe, F-3 A powered, red and silver, 1976-77.	300	400
8653	Santa Fe, F-3 A dummy, red and silver, 1976-77.	225	300
8654	Boston & Maine, GP-9 powered; blue, white, and black, 1976.	115	150
8655	Boston & Maine, GP-9 dummy; blue, white, and black, 1976.	80	100
8656/8657/8658	Canadian National, Alco ABA (3) units; orange/black/white, 1976.	300	400
8656	Canadian National, Alco A unit powered; orange, black and white, 1976.	150	200
8657	Canadian National, Alco B dummy unit; orange, black, and white, 1976.	75	100
8658	Canadian National, Alco A dummy unit; orange, black, and white, 1976.	75	100
8659	Virginian, rectifier, blue, yellow stripe, 1976-77.	125	175
8660	CP Rail, NW-2 switcher, red, white lettering, 1976-77.	100	125
8661	Southern, F-3 B dummy, green and gray.	125	200
8662	B & O, GP-7, blue, yellow stripe and lettering, 1986.	100	125
8664	Amtrak, Alco A powered; silver, black, and red, 1976-77.	100	150
8666	Northern Pacific, GP-9 powered, black and gold, red stripe, 1976.	125	150
8667	Amtrak, Alco B dummy, silver and black, 1976-77.	100	150
8668	NP, GP-9 dummy, black and gold, red stripe, 1976.	100	125
8669	Illinois Central, U36B powered, white and orange, black lett., 1976.	125	150
8670	Chessie, gas turbine, yellow, blue trim, 1976.	20	35
8679	Northern Pacific, GP-20, black and gold, red stripe, 1986.	100	125
8687	Jersey Central, FM diesel, olive green, cream striping and lett., 1986.	360	525
8690	Lionel Lines, trolley car, orange, blue roof, 1986.	100	125
8700	Rock Island (See 18700)		
8701	W & ARR General, black and red, yellow lettering, 1978.	150	200
8702	Crescent Limited, steam, 4-6-4, 1977.	375	475
8702	V & T (See 18702)		

		Exc	LN
8703	Wabash steam, 2-4-2, black, white lettering, 1977.	—	25
8750	The Rock, GP-7 powered, blue and white, 1977.	100	125
8751	The Rock, GP-7 dummy, blue and white, 1977.	50	75
8753	Pennsylvania, GG-1, tuscan, gold stripes, 1977.	500	600
8754	New Haven, rectifier; orange, black, and white, 1977-78.	175	250
8755	Santa Fe, U36B powered, blue and yellow, 1977-78.	150	175
8756	Santa Fe, U36B dummy, blue and yellow, 1977-78.	90	100
8757	Conrail, GP-9 powered, blue, white lettering, 1977-78.	100	150
8758	Southern, GP-7 dummy, green and white, 1978.	80	100
8759	Erie-Lackawanna, GP-9 powered; gray, tuscan, and yellow, 1977- 79.	120	150
8760	Erie-Lackawanna, GP-9 dummy; gray, tuscan, and yellow, 1977- 79.	100	125
8761	Grand Trunk Western, NW-2 switcher; blue/white/orange, 1977- 78.	125	250
8762	Great Northern, EP-5, dark green and orange, 1977-78.	175	225
8763	Norfolk & Western, GP-9 powered, black, white lettering, 1977-78.	100	125
8764	B & O, Budd RDC powered, silver, blue lettering, 1977.	125	175
8765	B & O, Budd RDC dummy, silver, blue lettering, 1977.	100	125
8766	B & O, Budd RDC powered; with 8767, 8768, 1977.	300	450
8767	B & O, RDC dummy, 1977 (See 8766).		
8768	B & O, RDC dummy, 1977 (See 8766).		
8769	Republic Steel, gas turbine, blue, yellow lettering, 1977.	20	40
8770	EMD, NW-2 powered switcher, blue and white, 1977.	50	95
8771	Great Northern, U36B powered; black, white, and blue, 1977.	100	120
8772	GM & O, GP-20 powered, red and white, 1977.	100	120
8773	Mickey Mouse, U36B pow., orange and white, Disney characters, 1977-78.	300	500
8774	Southern, GP-7 powered, green and white, gold stripes, 1977-78.	150	200
8775	Lehigh Valley, GP-9 powered, red, yellow lettering, 1977-78.	150	200
8776	C & NW, GP-20 powered, yellow and green, 1977-78.	75	225
8777	Santa Fe, F-3 B unit dummy, red and silver, 1977-78.	175	250
8778	Lehigh Valley, GP-9 dummy, red, yellow lettering, 1977-78.	100	125
8779	C & NW, GP-20 dummy, yellow and green, 1977-78.	125	150
8800	Lionel Lines, steam, 4-4-2, black, 1978, 1981.	100	125
8800	Lehigh Valley, GP-9 (See 18800).		
8801	Blue Comet steam, 4-6-4, two-tone blue, gold trim, 1979-80.	400	500
8801	Santa Fe, U36B (See 18801).		
8802	Southern, GP-9 (See 18802).		
8803	Santa Fe, steam, 0-4-0, black, silver boiler front, 1979.	10	20
8806-8808	(See 18806-18808 locomotives)		
8850	Penn Central, GG-1, black, white lettering, 1979.	450	525
8851/8852	New Haven, F-3, AA, pair; white, orange, and black, 1978- 79.	275	375
8854	CP Rail, GP-9 powered, red, white, and black, 1978-79.	85	125
8855	Milwaukee Road, SD-18 powered, orange and black, 1978.	115	150
8857	Northern Pacific, U36B powered; black, orange, and yellow, 1978-80.	100	125

Exc   LN

9018 DT & I open-top hopper car.

		Exc	LN
8858	NP, U36B dummy, black, orange band, yellow end, 1978-80.	55	85
8859	Conrail, rectifier, blue, white lettering, 1978-80, 1982.	150	195
8860	Rock, NW-2 powered switcher, blue, black and white lett., 1978-79.	100	125
8861	Santa Fe, Alco A powered, red and silver, 1978-79.	75	100
8862	Santa Fe, Alco A dummy, red and silver, 1978-79.	40	50
8864	New Haven, F-3 B dummy; white, orange, and black, 1978.	125	150
8866	M & StL, GP-9 powered, red and white, blue cab roof, 1978.	100	125
8867	M & StL, GP-9 dummy, red and white, blue cab roof, 1978.	75	100
8868	Amtrak, Budd RDC powered, silver, blue lettering, 1978, 1980.	150	200
8869	Amtrak, Budd RDC dummy, silver, blue lettering, 1978, 1980.	70	100
8870	Amtrak, Budd RDC dummy, silver, blue lettering, 1978, 1980.	70	100
8871	Amtrak, Budd RDC dummy, silver, blue lettering, 1978, 1980.	70	100
8872	Santa Fe, SD-18 powered, yellow and blue, 1978-79.	100	150
8873	Santa Fe, SD-18 dummy, yellow and blue, 1978-79.	75	100
8900	AT & SF, steam, 4-6-4, black, silver front, tuscan cab roof, 1979.	350	425
8902	ACL, steam, 2-4-0, black, 1979-82.	15	20
8903	Rio Grande, steam, 2-4-2, black, white lettering, 1979.	20	25
8904	Wabash, steam, 2-4-2, black, white lettering, 1979, 1981.	35	40
8905	Unlettered steam, 0-4-0, 1979.	10	20
8950	Virginian, Trainmaster, cream and red, 1978.	350	495
8951	Southern Pacific, Trainmaster; black, red, orange, and white, 1979.	500	695
8952/8953	Pennsylvania, F-3, AA, green, gold stripes, 1979.	450	650
8955	Southern, U36B powered, green and white, gold striping, 1979.	125	175
8956	Southern, U36B dummy, green and white, gold striping, 1979.	70	100
8957	Burlington Northern, GP-20 powered, black and green, white lett., 1979.	150	200
8958	Burlington Northern, GP-20 dummy, black and green, white lett., 1979.	100	125
8960	Southern Pacific, U36C, pair, red and yellow, white lettering, 1979.	80	100
8961	Southern Pacific, U36C dummy, red and yellow, white lettering, 1979.	60	75
8962	Reading, U36B, green and yellow, 1979.	150	200
8970/8971	Pennsylvania F-3, AA, pair, tuscan, gold stripes, 1979- 80.	400	500
8977	(See 18000)		

		Exc	LN
9001	Conrail, boxcar, blue, white lettering, 1986.	12	15
9010	Great Northern, hopper, blue, white lettering, 1971.	6	8
9011	Great Northern, hopper, white lettering, 1971, 1979.		
	(A) Medium blue.	3	6
	(B) Deep royal blue.	—	120
9012	TA & G, short hopper, white lettering, 1971-72, 1979.		
	(A) Medium or navy blue.	8	15
	(B) Bright royal blue.	—	50
9013	Canadian National, hopper, red, 1972-74, 1979.	4	6
9014	Trailer Train flatcar (O27), yellow, black lettering, 1978.	4	6
9015	Reading, short hopper, brown, yellow lettering, 1973-74, 1979.	20	25
9016	Chessie, short hopper, yellow, blue lettering, 1975-79.		
	(A) Regular production.	4	6
	(B) "LCCA 1979-80" overstamp.	—	25
9017	CP, short hopper, tuscan, gold lettering, 1971.	6	8
9017	Wabash, gondola (O27), red, three canisters, 1978, 1980-81.	6	8
9018	DT & I, short hopper, yellow, black lettering, 1978, 1981.	5	8
(9019)	Unlettered flatcar (O27), 1978.	1	2
9020	Union Pacific, flatcar (O27), yellow, blue or black lettering, 1970-77.	2	4
9021	Santa Fe, work caboose, black frame, yellow lettering, 1970-74.		
	(A) Red caboose	3	7
	(B) Orange caboose	12	20
9022	AT & SF, bulkhead flatcar, red or black, yellow lettering, 1971, 1977.	3	8
9023	MKT bulkhead flatcar, black, white lettering, 1974, 1978.	10	20
9024	Chesapeake & Ohio, flatcar, (O27), yellow; blue lettering, 1974.	3	4
9025	DT & I, short hopper, yellow or orange, black lettering, 1978.	—	5
9025	DT & I, work caboose, red cab, black frame, 1971-74.	8	10
9025	DT & I, flatcar, 1978.		NRS
9026	Republic Steel, flatcar, blue, white lettering, 1975-77, 1980.	3	4
9027	SOO, work caboose, red cab, black frame, white lettering, 1975.	8	10
9028	B & O, short hopper, 1978.		NRS
9030	Kickapoo, black base, 1972, 1979.		
	(A) Green bin.	2	5
	(B) Red bin.	1	3
	(C) Yellow bin.	2	4
9031	Nickel Plate, gondola, brown, white lettering, 1974, 1979, 1983.	5	7
9032	Southern Pacific, gondola (O27), red, white lettering, 1975, 1978.	3	4
9033	Penn Central, gondola, green, white lettering, 1977, 1979, 1981-82.	3	4
9034	Lionel Leisure, short hopper (O27), white, multicolor lettering, 1977.	35	50
9035	Conrail, boxcar (O27), blue, white lettering, 1978-82.	10	15
9036	Mobilgas, single-dome tank, white, red lettering, convention overstamp, 1978-80.	10	15
9037	Conrail, boxcar (O27), brown or blue; white lettering, 1978- 81.	10	15

Exc LN

"Chessie" is one of the most popular and widely-recognized heralds in contemporary railroading — even in miniature! Here is the 9038 B&O/Chessie coal hopper.

		Exc	LN
9038	Chessie, short hopper, blue, yellow lettering, 1975-79.	8	10
9039	Cheerios, boxcar (O27), yellow, black lettering, 1971-72.	6	8
9039	Mobilgas, single-dome tank, white, red lettering, 1978, 1980.	10	15
9040	Wheaties, boxcar (O27), orange, white and blue lettering, 1970.	7	10
9041	Hershey's, boxcar (O27), brown, white lettering, 1971.	12	20
9042	Autolite, boxcar (O27), white, black and orange lettering, 1972.	8	12
9043	Erie-Lackawanna, boxcar (O27), gray, maroon lettering, 1973- 74.	8	10
9044	D & RGW, boxcar (O27), orange, black lettering, 1975, 1979.	6	8
9045	Toys 'R Us, boxcar (O27), white, orange lettering.	40	50
9046	True Value, boxcar (O27), white, red and black lettering, 1976.	40	50
9047	Toys 'R Us, boxcar (O27), white, orange lettering.	35	50
9048	Toys 'R Us, boxcar (O27), white, orange lettering.	35	50
(9049)	Toys 'R Us, boxcar, white, orange and black lettering, "GEOFFREY POWER", 1979.	35	50
9050	Sunoco, single-dome short tank, yellow, 1970-71.		
	(A) Blue lettering.	15	25
	(B) Green lettering.	—	40
9051	Firestone, single-dome tank, white, blue lettering, 1974-75.	15	25
9052	Toys 'R Us, short boxcar, white, orange and black lettering, 1977.	30	40
9053	True Value, short boxcar, green, multicolor lettering, 1978.	35	50
9054	JC Penney, short boxcar, orange, black lettering.	35	50
9055	Republic Steel, gondola (O27), yellow, three silver canisters, 1977-81.	10	12
9057	CP Rail, caboose, yellow and black, black lettering, 1978-79.	9	11
9058	Lionel Lines, caboose, orange, black lettering, 1978-79.	6	8
9060	Nickel Plate, caboose, brown, white lettering, 1970-71.	6	8
9061	AT & SF, caboose, red, yellow lettering, 1970-71, 1978.	6	8
9062	Penn Central, caboose, green, white lettering, 1970-71.	5	9
9063	Grand Trunk Western, caboose, white lettering, 1970.		
	(A) Orange body.	8	15
	(B) Maroon body.	15	25
9064	Chesapeake & Ohio, caboose, yellow, red stripe, blue lettering, 1971.	7	10
9065	Canadian National, caboose, maroon, white lettering, 1971-72.	20	25

		Exc	LN
9066	Southern, caboose, red, white lettering.	8	10
9067	Kickapoo Valley, bobber caboose; red, yellow, or green; 1972.	7	10
9068	Reading, bobber caboose, green, yellow lettering, 1973-75.	6	8
9069	Jersey Central, caboose, brown, white lettering, 1973-74.	6	8
9070	Rock Island, caboose, gray, black and gray lettering, 1973- 74.	10	15
9071	AT & SF, bobber caboose, red, white lettering, 1974-75.	8	10
9073	Coca-Cola, caboose, red, white lettering, 1973.	10	20
9075	Rock Island, caboose, red, white lettering, 1973-74.	10	15
9076	We the People, caboose; red, white, and blue, 1975.	20	40
9077	Rio Grande, caboose, orange, black lettering, 1977-79, 1981.	6	8
9078	Rock Island, bobber caboose, red, white lettering, 1977-79.	6	8
9079	Grand Trunk Western, short hopper, blue, white lettering, 1977.	9	12
9080	Wabash, caboose, red, black roof, white lettering, 1977.	10	11
9085	AT & SF, work caboose, 1980-81.	5	6
9090	Mini-Max, four-wheel car, blue and white, 1971.	30	40
9100-9106	(See 19100-19106)		
9106	Easy Cheese, vat car, dark blue, white lettering, 1984-85.		NRS
9106	Miller Beer, vat car, dark blue, white lettering, 1984.	20	30
9107	Dr. Pepper, vat carrier, 1986-87	20	30
9110	B & O, quad hopper, black, 1971.		
	(A) Gray lettering.	—	50
	(B) White lettering.	25	40
9111	Norfolk & Western, quad hopper, brown, white lettering, 1972.	15	20
9112	D & RGW, quad hopper, orange, black lettering, 1972-73.	15	20
9113	Norfolk & Western, quad hopper, gray, black lettering, 1973.	25	40
9114	Morton Salt, quad hopper, navy blue, yellow cover, 1975-76.	15	25
9115	Planter's, quad hopper, dark blue, yellow cover and lettering, 1974-76.	15	25
9116	Domino Sugar, quad hopper, gray, blue cover and lettering, 1974-76.	15	25
9117	Alaska, quad hopper, black, yellow cover, 1974-76.	15	25
9118	LCCA Corning, quad hopper, white and green, 1974.	100	125
9119	Detroit & Mackinac, quad hopper, red, white lettering, 1975.		
	(A) Regular production.	35	45
	(B) "SEASON'S GREETINGS" overstamp for TCA.	—	45
9120	Northern Pacific, flatcar with vans, green car, white vans, 1970-71.	30	50
9121	L & N, brown flatcar w/yellow dozer or scraper, 1974, 1976, 1978-79.	30	45
9122	NP, flatcar with vans, 1972-75.		
	(A) Tuscan car, gray vans.	30	35
	(B) Green body, white vans.	40	50
9123	Chesapeake & Ohio, auto carrier, 1974.		
	(A) Three-tier black body, yellow lettering.	10	25
	(B) Three-tier blue body, yellow lettering.	5	15
9124	P & LE, flatcar with logs, green, 1973.	8	15

		Exc	LN

9153 Standard Oil Company tank car.

		Exc	LN
9125	Norfolk & Western, auto carrier, white lettering, 1974.		
	(A) Blue body.	15	30
	(B) Black body.	20	40
9126	C & O, auto carrier, yellow, blue lettering, 1973-74.	10	15
9128	Heinz, vat car, gray and red, yellow vats, 1974-76.	15	25
9129	Norfolk & Western, auto carrier, brown, white lettering, 1975.	30	55
9130	B & O, quad hopper, blue, white lettering, 1970-71.	15	25
9131	Rio Grande, gondola, orange, black lettering, 1974.	4	8
9132	Libby's, vat car, green and gray, yellow vats, 1975-77.	10	20
9133	Burlington Northern, flatcar with vans, green, white lettering, 1976, 1980.	10	25
9134	Virginian, quad hopper, silver, blue cover and lettering, 1976-77.	25	30
9135	Norfolk & Western, quad hopper, blue, 1971.		
	(A) Royal blue or light blue body.	8	12
	(B) Purple body.	15	30
9136	Republic Steel, gondola, blue, white lettering, 1976-79.	6	8
9138	Sunoco, three-dome tank, black, white lettering, 1978.	25	40
9139	Penn Central, auto carrier, green, white lettering, 1977.	20	30
9140	Burlington, gondola, green, white lettering, 1970-71, 1980-81.	5	10
9141	Burlington Northern, gondola, green, white lettering, 1970-71, 1980-81.	3	4
9142	Republic Steel gondola, green, white lettering, 1971.		
	(A) Regular production.	3	4
	(B) "1977-78 MEET SPECIAL" overstamp.	—	25
9143	Canadian National, gondola, maroon, white lettering, 1973.	20	25
9144	Rio Grande, gondola, black, yellow lettering, 1974.	4	5
9145	Illinois Central Gulf, auto carrier, orange, black lettering, 1977.	20	35
9146	Mogen David, vat car, silver and blue, tan vats, 1977-79.	15	25
9147	Texaco, single-dome tank, chrome and black, red and black lett., 1977.	20	40
9148	Dupont, three-dome tank, cream-yellow and green, red logo, 1977-79, 81.	25	35
9149	CP Rail, flatcar with vans, red car, silver vans.	40	45
9150	Gulf, single-dome tank car, white; black and orange lettering, 1970-71.	30	35

		Exc	LN
9151	Shell, single-dome tank car, yellow, red lettering, 1972.	30	35
9152	Shell, single-dome tank car, yellow, black ends, red lettering, 1973-74.	25	30
9153	Chevron, single-dome tank car, silver and blue, blue lettering, 1974-76.	25	35
9154	Borden, single-dome tank car, chrome and black, black lettering, 1975-76.	30	40
9155	LCCA, Monsanto single-dome tank car, white, red logo, 1977.	60	75
9156	Mobilgas, single-dome tank car, chrome, red and blue lettering, 1976-77.	15	30
9157	Chesapeake & Ohio, blue flatcar w/ yellow P&H crane, 1976-78, 1981.	30	50
9158	Penn Central, green flatcar w/ yellow steam shovel, 1976-77, 1980.	30	50
9159	Sunoco, single-dome tank car, chrome and blue, blue lettering, 1975.	45	60
9160	Illinois Central, N5C caboose, orange, black and white lett., 1970-72.		
	(A) Regular production.	20	35
	(B) With large "ITT" sticker.		NRS
9161	Canadian National, caboose, orange and black, white lettering, 1971-72.	20	35
9162	Pennsylvania, N5C caboose, tuscan, white lettering, 1972-76.	40	55
9163	AT & SF, N5C caboose, red, white lettering, blue herald, 1973-76.	15	25
9165	Canadian Pacific, N5C caboose, red, white lettering, 1973.	25	40
9166	Rio Grande, caboose, yellow and silver, black lettering, 1974.	12	20
9167	Chessie, N5C caboose, yellow and silver, orange and blue trim, 1974-76.	40	55
9168	Union Pacific, N5C caboose, yellow, red lettering, 1975-76.	15	30
9169	Milwaukee Road, caboose, brown and black, red lettering, 1975.	15	25
9170	Norfolk & Western (See 1776, 1976)		
9171	MoPac, caboose, red, white lettering, 1975-77.	15	20
9172	Penn Central, caboose, black, white lettering, 1975-77.	40	55
9173	Jersey Central, caboose, red, white lettering, 1975-77.	15	20
9174	P & LE, bay window caboose, green and black, white lettering, 1976.	75	90
9175	Virginian, N5C caboose, blue and yellow, yellow lettering, 1975-77.	20	30
9176	BAR, N5C caboose; red, white, and blue, 1976.	20	35
9177	NP, bay window caboose, green and yellow, silver roof, black lett., 1976.	20	30
9178	Illinois Central, caboose, orange, silver roof, black lettering.	15	25
9179	Chessie, bobber caboose, yellow, blue lettering, 1979.	6	10
9180	The Rock, N5C caboose; blue, black, and white, 1977, 1978.	15	25
9181	B & M, N5C caboose; blue, black, and white, 1977.	15	25
9182	Norfolk & Western, N5C caboose, black, white lettering, 1977-80.	15	30
9183	Mickey Mouse, N5C caboose, white, red-orange roof, 1977-78.	40	60
9184	Erie, bay window caboose, red, white lettering, 1977-78.	20	30
9185	Grand Trunk Western, N5C caboose, blue, orange ends, white lett., 1977.	15	30
9186	Conrail, N5C caboose, blue, black roof, white lettering, 1977-78.	25	45
9187	G M & O, caboose, red, black roof, white lettering, 1977-78.	15	30
9188	Great Northern, bay window caboose, blue and white, black roof, 1977.	30	45
9189	Gulf, single-dome tank car, chrome and black, blue lettering, 1977.	35	50
9189	Norfolk Southern, NC5 caboose, red, black and white logo, 1974.	12	15
9193	Budweiser, vat car, red, silver roof, red and white vats, 1983.	25	40

Exc   LN

Although cabooses are no longer used extensively on America's railroads, they are likely to remain popular with model railroaders for many years to come. This is the 9167 C & O/Chessie system caboose produced from 1974-1976.

		Exc	LN
9195	Rolling stock asstortment (O27), 1988.		NA
9200	Illinois Central, boxcar, orange; black and white lettering, 1970-72.	25	35
9201	Penn Central, boxcar, green, white lettering, 1970.	25	35
9202	Santa Fe, boxcar, red, white lettering, 1970.		
	(A) Silver door.	30	50
	(B) Gray door.	32	60
9203	Union Pacific, boxcar, yellow, blue lettering.	35	50
9204	Northern Pacific, boxcar, green; black and white lettering.	30	45
9205	Norfolk & Western, boxcar, blue, white lettering.	20	25
9206	Great Northern, boxcar, blue, white lettering.	20	25
9207	SOO, boxcar, red, white lettering.	20	25
9208	CP Rail, boxcar, yellow, black lettering.	20	32
9209	Burlington Northern, boxcar, green, white lettering.	20	25
9210	B & O, automobile boxcar, black body and doors, white lettering.	20	30
9211	Penn Central, boxcar, jade, silver-painted doors, white lettering.	30	35
9212	LCCA, flatcar with vans, Atlanta, 1976.	35	40
9213	M & St L, quad hopper, red, white lettering, 1978.	25	35
9214	Northern Pacific, boxcar, maroon, black and white lettering.	25	35
9215	Norfolk & Western, boxcar, blue, gray doors, white lettering.	30	35
9216	Great Northern, auto carrier, blue, white lettering, 1978.	25	40
9217	SOO Lines, operating boxcar, brownish-maroon, white lettering, 1982-83.	—	20
9218	Monon, operating boxcar, tuscan, script lettering at top, 1981-82.	15	25
9219	MP, operating boxcar, blue and gray, 1983.	25	35
9220	Borden, operating milk car set, white, brown roof and ends, 1985-86.	80	100
9221	Poultry Dispatch, brown, gray doors, white lettering, 1985-86.	30	35
9222	Louisville & Nashville, flatcar with vans, tuscan car, gray vans, 1983.	15	20
9223	Reading, operating boxcar, tuscan, white lettering, 1985.	25	30
9224	Louisville, operating horse car set, yellow, tuscan roof, 1985.	75	90
9225	Conrail, operating barrel car, tuscan, white lettering, 1984-85.	35	50
9226	D & H, flatcar with vans, blue, yellow lettering, 1985.	—	20
9227	Canadian Pacific, boxcar, 1986.	20	25

		Exc	LN
9228	Canadian Pacific, boxcar, 1986.	20	30
9229	Express Mail, operating boxcar, dark blue and orange, 1985- 86.	25	35
9230	Monon, boxcar, brown, white lettering, 1972.	15	25
9231	Reading, bay window caboose, green and yellow, 1979.	30	40
9232	Allis Chalmers, flatcar with load, orange base, gray reactor, 1980.	25	60
9233	Die-cast transformer flatcar, tuscan, red transformer, 1980.	35	60
9234	Radioactive Waste car, red, containers with flashing lights, 1980.	30	50
9235	Union Pacific, flatcar with derrick, yellow and black, 1983.	10	15
9236	C & NW, derrick car, black and yellow, 1985.	15	20
9238	NP, operating log dump, dark green, white lettering, 1985.	15	20
9239	Lionel Lines, N5C caboose, orange, blue roof, 1985.	75	95
9240	New York Central, hopper car, tuscan, white lettering, 1986.	30	40
9241	Pennsylvania, operating log dump car, tuscan, gold lettering, 1985-86.	15	20
9250	Waterpoxy, three-dome tank car, white; blue and green lettering, 1971.	30	35
X9259	Southern, bay window caboose, red, white or gold lettering, 1977.	35	50
9260	Reynolds, quad hopper, blue, silver cover and lettering, 1975-78.	15	20
9261	Sun-Maid Raisins, quad hopper, red, yellow cover, 1975-76.	15	20
9262	Ralston-Purina, quad hopper, white; red and black cover, 1975-76.	65	90
9263	Pennsylvania, quad hopper, tuscan, black cover, white lett., 1975-77.	40	50
9264	Illinois Central quad hopper, orange, black lettering, 1975-77.		
	(A) Regular production.	25	30
	(B) Overstamped "TCA MUSEUM EXPRESS".	—	100
9265	W M /Chessie, quad hopper, yellow, blue cover and lettering, 1975-77.	25	30
9266	Southern, "Big John" quad hopper, silver, red cover, 1976.	60	75
9267	Alcoa, quad hopper, silver, blue lettering, 1975.	30	40
9268	NP, bay window caboose, black and gold; yellow and red trim, 1977-78.	30	40
9269	Milwaukee Road, caboose, orange and black, red logo, 1978.	35	60
9270	NP, N5C caboose, orange, white lettering, 1978, 1980.	15	25
9271	M & StL, bay window caboose, red, blue roof, white lettering, 1978-79.	20	30
9272	New Haven, bay window caboose, dark red, 1978-80.	15	25
9273	Southern, bay window caboose, green and white, gold stripes, 1978.	40	55
9274	Santa Fe, bay window, red, black roof, white lettering, 1978.	50	65
9275	Santa Fe, bay window, red, 1978		NRS
9276	Peabody open quad hopper, yellow, green lettering, 1978.	25	35
9277	Cities Service three-dome tank car, green, 1977.	40	50
9278	Lifesavers single-dome tank car, multicolor five-flavors label, 1978-79.	75	110
9279	Magnolia three-dome tank car, white and black, 1978-79.	15	20
9280	AT & SF, horse transport, red, white lettering, 1978-80.	10	20
9281	AT & SF, two-level auto carrier, red, white lettering, 1978- 79.	20	30
9282	Great Northern, flatcar with vans, orange, green vans, 1978, 1981-82.	35	50
9283	Union Pacific, gondola, yellow, red lettering, 1977.	8	10
9284	AT & SF, gondola, red and yellow, two canisters, 1977-78.	20	25

| | Exc | LN |

The 9250 Waterpoxy tank car (1971) comes from the "early days" of Modern Era production.

		Exc	LN
9285	Illinois Central Gulf, black flatcar with silver vans, 1977.	35	60
9286	B & LE, quad hopper, orange, black lettering, 1977.	15	25
9287	Southern, N5C caboose, red, white lettering, 1978.	15	25
9288	Lehigh Valley, N5C caboose, red, yellow roof and lettering, 1978, 1980.	20	30
9289	C & NW, N5C caboose, yellow and green, black lettering, 1978, 1980.		
	(A) Regular production.	20	30
	(B) Overstamped "TCA MUSEUM EXPRESS".	—	85
9290	Union Pacific, operating barrel car, black, yellow lettering, 1983.	55	85
9300	Penn Central, dump car, green, 1970-73	15	20
9301	Operating U. S. Mail car, red, white, and blue, 1975-83.	15	30
9302	Louisville & Nashville, searchlight car, brown and gray, 1973- 74.	12	15
9303	Union Pacific, operating log dump, yellow, red lettering, 1974, 1979.	10	15
9304	Chesapeake & Ohio, oper. coal dump, blue, yellow lettering, 1973-76.	15	20
9305	Santa Fe, animated stock, 1980, 1982	15	20
9306	AT & SF, animated stock car, 1980.	15	20
9307	Erie, animated gondola, red, cop and hobo figures, 1979-83, 1985.	35	55
9308	Aquarium car, green, gold lettering, 1981-83, 1985.	70	85
9309	TP & W, bay window caboose, orange, silver roof, black lett., 1980-81.	20	35
9310	AT & SF, log dump, red, yellow lettering, 1978-79, 1981-82.	10	15
9311	Union Pacific, operating coal dump, yellow, 1978-82.	10	15
9312	Conrail, searchlight car, blue, white lettering, 1978-83.		
	(A) Gray superstructure.	—	15
	(B) Orange superstructure.	—	20
9313	Gulf, three-dome tank car, black, orange and black logo, 1979.	45	60
9315	Southern Pacific, gondola, brown, white lettering, 1979.	20	30
9316	Southern Pacific, bay window caboose, silver, black roof, 1979.	60	85
9317	AT & SF, bay window caboose, blue and yellow, yellow lettering, 1979.	25	35
9319	TCA Silver Jubilee, silver, coin slot on top, 1979.	250	325
9320	Fort Knox Gold Bullion car, silver, coin slot on top, 1979.	250	300
9321	AT & SF, tank car (FARR #1), silver; black and white logo, 1979.	30	45

		Exc	LN
9322	AT & SF, quad hopper (FARR #1), red, white lettering, 1979.	70	80
9323	AT & SF, bay window caboose, tuscan, black roof, white lettering, 1979.	30	45
9324	Tootsie Roll, single-dome tank, brown and white, 1979, 1981- 82.	40	55
9325	Norfolk & Western, flatcar with fence, black, 1980-81.	5	10
9325	Norfolk & Western, flatcar with cab, red, 1978-79.	5	10
9325	Norfolk & Western, log dump (See 9363)		
9325	USMC Security, caboose, black, white lettering, 1983.	5	10
9326	Burlington Northern, caboose, green, black roof, white lettering, 1979-80.	20	25
9327	Bakelite, single-dome tank car, red and white, red lettering, 1980.	10	20
9328	Western Maryland Chessie, bay window caboose, yellow/silver, 1980.	30	50
9329	Western Maryland Chessie, crane, blue; yellow and silver cab, 1980.	40	70
(9330)	Kickapoo Valley, dump car, unlettered, various colors, 1972.	3	5
9331	Union 76, single-dome tank car, dark blue, orange lettering, 1979.	40	60
9332	Reading, bay window caboose, 1979.	50	75
9332	Reading, crane, green and yellow, silver roof, 1979.	35	55
9333	Southern Pacific, flatcar with vans, tuscan car, white vans, 1980.	40	50
9334	Humble, single-dome tank car, silver, red and blue lettering, 1979.	20	30
9335	B & O, operating log dump, 1986.	—	20
9336	CP Rail, gondola, red, white lettering, 1979.	20	25
9338	Penn. Power & Light, quad hopper, brown, yellow lettering, 1979.	50	75
9339	Great Northern, boxcar (O27), 1979-81, 1983.	5	10
9340	Illinois Central, gondola (O27), 1979-81.		
	(A) Orange, black lettering, yellow canisters.	5	10
	(B) Red, white lettering, no canisters.	—	20
9341	Atlantic Coast Line, SP caboose, red, white lettering, 1979- 82.	6	10
9344	Citgo, three-dome tank, white, red and blue lettering, 1980.	35	55
9345	Reading, searchlight car, dark green, cream superstructure, 1985.	20	25
9346	NYNH & H, caboose, red, black roof, white lettering, 1980-81.	6	8
9346	Wabash, caboose, red, black roof, white lettering, 1979.	6	10
9347	Niagara Falls TTOS single-dome tank, blue, black lettering, 1979.	40	50
9348	Santa Fe, crane, blue, yellow lettering, 1979.	55	70
9349	San Francisco Mint, dark maroon, gold lettering, gold bullion, 1980.	110	150
9351	Pennsylvania, auto carrier, tuscan, gold lettering, 1980.	20	40
9352	C & NW, flatcar with vans, green car, yellow vans, 1980.	60	95
9353	Crystal, three-dome tank car, red, white lettering, 1980.	15	25
9354	Pennzoil, single-dome tank car, chrome; yellow and black logo, 1981.	20	35
9355	D & H, bay window caboose, blue and gray, yellow stripe, 1980.	20	25
9356	Life Savers Stik-O-Pep, tank car, 1980.	Not Manufactured	
9357	Smokey Mountain, bobber caboose, black frame, 1979.		
	(A) Red or green body.	5	10
	(B) Yellow body.	7	15
9358	LCCA Sands of Iowa, quad hopper, blue and black, 1980.	25	40

Exc   LN

The 9341 caboose features the attractive herald of the Atlantic Coast Line, which is now part of the CSX Transportation system.

		Exc	LN
9359	National Basketball, boxcar, white and red, 1980.	20	30
9360	National Hockey League, boxcar, white and orange, 1980.	20	30
9361	C & NW, bay window caboose, yellow, green roof, 1980.	45	60
9362	Major League Baseball, boxcar, white and blue, 1980.	20	30
9363	Norfolk & Western, op. dump car, lettered "9325", black and blue, 1979.	25	30
9364	Norfolk & Western, crane car, black, yellow cab, 1978.	8	10
9365	Toys 'R Us, boxcar (O27), white, orange logo, 1979.	40	50
9366	Union Pacific, hopper (FARR #2), silver/black, multicolor lett., 1980.	25	35
9367	Union Pacific, single-dome tank car (FARR #2), silver, black lett., 1980.	35	45
9368	Union Pacific, bay window caboose (FARR #2), yellow and red, 1980.	35	45
9369	Sinclair, single-dome tank car, green tank, white lettering, 1980.	60	75
9370	Seaboard, gondola, tuscan, three silver canisters, 1980.	20	25
9371	Lantic Sugar, quad hopper, yellow, multicolor lettering, 1980.	25	35
9372	Seaboard, bay window caboose, red, black roof, white lettering, 1980.	30	40
9373	Getty, single-dome tank, white, red dome, red and orange logo, 1980-81.	40	50
9374	Reading, quad hopper, black; red and white lettering, 1980- 81.	60	75
9376	T & P, caboose, 1981.	20	25
9378	Lionel, flatcar with yellow derrick, red, 1981.	15	20
9379	AT & SF, gondola, black and yellow, two gray canisters, 1980.	30	35
9380	NYNH & H (New Haven), caboose, silver, black roof and lettering, 1980.	10	12
9381	Chessie, caboose, yellow; silver roof, blue lettering, 1980.	8	10
9382	Florida East Coast, caboose, red and yellow, silver stripe, 1980.	25	35
9383	Union Pacific, flatcar with vans (FARR #2), gray car, yellow vans, 1980.	30	40
9384	Great Northern, operating hopper, green, multicolor lettering, 1981.	55	75
9385	Alaska, gondola, yellow, four white canisters, 1981.	30	40
9386	Pure Oil, single-dome tank car, cream, dark blue lettering, 1981.	30	50
9387	Burlington, bay window caboose, red, white lettering, 1981.	35	45
9388	Toys 'R Us, boxcar (O27), white, orange logo, 1981.	40	50
9389	Radioactive Waste car, maroon car, tan containers, 1981.	35	50
9398	Pennsylvania, operating coal dump, tuscan, gold lettering, 1983.	20	25
9399	C & NW, coal dump, black, gray bin, 1983-84.	15	20

		Exc	LN
9400	Conrail, boxcar, brown, white lettering, 1978.	15	20
9401	Great Northern, boxcar, green; black and white lettering, 1979.	15	20
9402	Susquehanna, boxcar, green, gold lettering, 1978.	30	35
9403	SCL, boxcar, black, yellow lettering, 1978.	15	20
9404	Nickel Plate, boxcar, maroon and silver, 1978-79.	30	40
9405	Chattahoochie, boxcar, silver; orange and black lettering, 1978-79.	15	20
9406	D & RGW, boxcar, white and brown; black and red lettering, 1978-79.	15	20
9407	Union Pacific, cattle car, gray and yellow, black doors, 1978.	25	35
9408	Lionel Lines Circus car, white and red, 1978.	30	40
9411	Lackawanna "Phoebe Snow", boxcar, tuscan, white lettering, 1978.	60	75
9412	RF & P, boxcar, blue, silver doors, white lettering, 1979.	12	18
9413	Napierville Jct., boxcar, yellow and red, black lettering, 1979-80.	12	15
9414	Cotton Belt, boxcar, tuscan, white lettering, 1980.	15	20
9415	P & W, boxcar, red; white and black lettering, 1979.		
	(A) Regular production.	10	15
	(B) NETCA overprint.	—	20
9416	MD & W, boxcar, white and green, 1979, 1981.	10	15
9417	CP Rail, boxcar, black; red and white logo, 1980.	35	45
9418	FARR, boxcar, gold and red, multiple logos, 1979.	75	100
9419	Union Pacific, boxcar (FARR #2), tuscan and black, 1980.	25	35
9420	B & O "Sentinel", boxcar, blue and silver, 1980.		
	(A) Regular production.	25	35
	(B) "WORLD'S LONGEST... TRAIN" overprint.	—	75
9421	Maine Central, boxcar, green and yellow, 1980.	12	20
9422	EJ & E, boxcar, green and orange, 1980.	15	25
9423	NYNH & H (New Haven), boxcar, tuscan, black roof, white lettering, 1980.		
	(A) Regular production.	20	35
	(B) NETCA overprint.	—	20
9424	TP & W, boxcar, orange and silver, white lettering, 1980.	15	20
9425	British Columbia, auto boxcar, green, white lettering, 1980.	20	25
9426	Chesapeake & Ohio, boxcar, blue and yellow, silver roof and ends, 1980.	20	35
9427	Bay Line, boxcar, green; yellow stripe and lettering, 1980-81.	10	20
9428	TP & W, boxcar, green and cream, 1980.	35	50
9429	The Early Years, boxcar, light yellow, red roof and ends, 1980.	25	30
9430	Standard Gauge Years, boxcar, silver sides, maroon roof and ends, 1980.	25	30
9431	The Prewar Years, boxcar, gray sides, black roof and ends, 1980.	25	30
9432	The Postwar Years, boxcar, tan sides, green roof and ends, 1980.	85	125
9433	The Golden Years, boxcar, gold sides, blue roof and ends, 1980.	85	125
9434	Joshua Lionel Cowen, boxcar, yellow sides, brown roof and ends, 1980.	70	100
9435	LCCA, Central of Georgia, black, silver doors, 1981.	40	50
9436	Burlington, boxcar, red, white lettering, 1981.	40	55
9437	Northern Pacific, cattle car, dark green, black doors, 1981.	30	50

		Exc	LN
9438	Ontario Northland, boxcar, blue, yellow ends and lettering, 1981.	20	25
9439	Ashley Drew & Northern, boxcar, green, white doors and lettering, 1981.	10	20
9440	Reading, boxcar, yellow and green, green lettering, 1981.	40	70
9441	Pennsylvania, boxcar, tuscan, white and red lettering, 1981.	40	70
9442	Canadian Pacific, boxcar, silver and black, red lettering, 1981.	15	20
9443	FEC, boxcar, tuscan, silver roof and ends, white lettering, 1981.	15	20
9444	Louisiana Midland, boxcar, white and blue, red and blue lettering, 1981.	15	20
9445	Vermont Northern, boxcar, yellow and silver, black lettering, 1981.	15	20
9446	Sabine River, boxcar, red and silver, white lettering, 1981.	15	20
9447	Pullman Standard, boxcar, silver, black lettering, 1981.	15	20
9448	AT & SF, cattle car, brown, white lettering, 1981.	40	55
9449	Great Northern, boxcar, (FARR #3), green; green and orange, 1981.	35	50
9450	Great Northern, cattle, (FARR #3), red; red and black, 1981.	75	100
9451	Southern, boxcar (FARR #4), tuscan, white lettering, 1984.	40	55
9452	Western Pacific, boxcar, tuscan, white lettering, 1982-83.	15	20
9453	MPA, boxcar, blue, yellow lettering, 1982-83.	10	15
9454	New Hope & Ivyland, boxcar, green, white lettering, 1982-83.	10	15
9455	Milwaukee Road, boxcar, yellow, black lettering, 1982-83.	15	20
9456	PRR, auto boxcar (FARR #5), tuscan, white lettering, 1985.	35	50
9460	DT & SL, auto boxcar, LCCA, blue, white lettering, 1982.	30	60
9461	Norfolk & Southern, boxcar, tuscan, yellow doors, 1983.	35	60
9462	Southern Pacific, boxcar, silver, black roof and ends, 1983-84.	20	25
9463	Texas & Pacific, boxcar, yellow and black, 1983-84.	12	15
9464	NC & StL, boxcar, red, white lettering, 1983-84.	12	15
9465	AT & SF, boxcar, green, yellow lettering, 1983.	12	25
9466	Wanamaker, boxcar, maroon, gold door and lettering, 1982.	115	150
9467	Tennessee World's Fair, boxcar, white, tuscan roof and ends, 1982.	35	45
9468	Union Pacific, auto boxcar, tuscan, yellow lettering, 1983.	40	50
9469	New York Central Pacemaker, boxcar (Std. O), red and gray, 1985.	110	125
9470	Chicago Beltline, boxcar, green, yellow lettering, 1984.	15	20
9471	Atlantic Coast Line, boxcar, tuscan, white lettering, 1984.	15	20
9472	Detroit & Mackinac, boxcar, white and red, 1985.	20	25
9473	Lehigh Valley, boxcar, green and silver, 1984.	15	20
9474	Erie-Lackawanna, boxcar, tuscan, white lettering, 1985.	45	55
9475	D & H "I Love N.Y.", boxcar, blue and white, red heart, 1984-85.	25	40
9476	Pennsylvania, boxcar, tuscan, white lettering, 1985.	40	50
9480	MN & S, boxcar, blue, white lettering, red logo, 1985-86.	15	20
9481	Seaboard System, boxcar, tuscan, white lettering, 1985-86.	15	20
9482	Norfolk Southern, boxcar, gray, black lettering, 1985-86.	15	20
9483	Manufacturers Railway, boxcar, white and black, 1985-86.	12	15
9484	Lionel 85th Anniv., boxcar, silver and black, multicolor trim, 1985.	20	30
9486	"I Love Michigan", boxcar, white and purple, multicolor trim, 1986.	15	20

		Exc	LN
9491	Christmas car, silver and red, multicolor trim, 1986.	**35**	**40**
9492	Lionel Lines, boxcar, orange and blue, multicolor trim, 1986.	**30**	**50**
9500	Milwaukee Road, Pullman, orange and maroon, 1973.	**40**	**60**
9501	Milwaukee Road, Pullman, orange and maroon, 1973.	**25**	**40**
9502	Milwaukee Road, observation, orange and maroon, 1973.	**40**	**60**
9503	Milwaukee Road, Pullman orange and maroon, 1974.	**40**	**60**
9504	Milwaukee Road, Pullman, orange and maroon, 1974.	**25**	**40**
9505	Milwaukee Road, Pullman, orange and maroon, 1974.	**25**	**40**
9506	Milwaukee Road, combine, orange and maroon, 1975.	**25**	**40**
9507	Pennsylvania, Pullman, tuscan, black roof, gold lettering, 1974.	**40**	**60**
9508	Pennsylvania, Pullman, tuscan, black roof, gold lettering, 1974.	**40**	**60**
9509	Pennsylvania, observation, tuscan, black roof, gold lettering, 1974.	**50**	**75**
9510	Pennsylvania, combine, tuscan, black roof, gold lettering, 1975.	**30**	**50**
9511	Milwaukee Road, Pullman, orange and maroon, 1974.	**30**	**50**
9512	Summerdale Junction TTOS, passenger car, 1974.	**40**	**50**
9513	Pennsylvania, Pullman, tuscan, black roof, gold lettering, 1975.	**30**	**50**
9514	Pennsylvania, Pullman, tuscan, black roof, gold lettering, 1975.	**30**	**50**
9515	Pennsylvania, Pullman, tuscan, black roof, gold lettering, 1975.	**30**	**50**
9516	Baltimore & Ohio, Pullman, blue and gray, yellow lettering, 1975.	**25**	**40**
9517	Baltimore & Ohio, coach, blue and gray, yellow lettering, 1975.	**40**	**60**
9518	Baltimore & Ohio, observation, blue and gray, yellow lettering, 1975.	**50**	**75**
9519	Baltimore & Ohio, combine, blue and gray, yellow lettering, 1975.	**75**	**100**
9520	TTOS, combine car, 1975.	**30**	**50**
9521	Pennsylvania, baggage, tuscan and black, 1975.	**100**	**125**
9522	Milwaukee Road, baggage, orange and maroon, 1975.	**100**	**125**
9523	Baltimore & Ohio, baggage, blue and gray, yellow lettering, 1975.	**60**	**85**
9524	Baltimore & Ohio, Pullman, blue and gray, yellow lettering, 1976.	**30**	**50**
9525	Baltimore & Ohio, Pullman, blue and gray, yellow lettering, 1976.	**30**	**50**
9526	TTOS, observation car, 1976.	**30**	**50**
9527	Milwaukee Road, campaign observation, red/white/blue bunting, 1976.	**50**	**65**
9528	Pennsylvania, campaign observation, red/white/blue bunting, 1976.	**60**	**75**
9529	Baltimore & Ohio, campaign observation, red/white/blue, 1976.	**55**	**60**
9530	Southern, baggage, two-tone green, gold lettering, 1978.	**30**	**50**
9531	Southern, combine, two-tone green, gold lettering, 1978.	**30**	**50**
9532	Southern, Pullman, two-tone green, gold lettering, 1978.	**30**	**50**
9533	Southern, Pullman, two-tone green, gold lettering, 1978.	**30**	**50**
9534	Southern, observation, two-tone green, gold lettering, 1978.	**30**	**50**
9535	TTOS, observation, 1977.	**30**	**50**
9536	Blue Comet, baggage, two-tone blue, cream band, gold lettering, 1978.	**30**	**50**
9537	Blue Comet, combine, two-tone blue, cream band, gold lettering, 1978.	**30**	**50**
9538	Blue Comet, Pullman, two-tone blue, cream band, gold lettering, 1978.	**30**	**60**
9539	Blue Comet, Pullman, two-tone blue, cream band, gold lettering, 1978.	**30**	**60**

Exc   **LN**

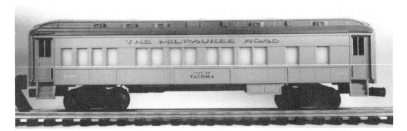

Like many passenger cars, the 9504 Milwaukee Road Pullman features a name (City of Tacoma) as well as a number.

9540	Blue Comet, observation, two-tone blue, cream band, 1978.	30	50
9541	Santa Fe, baggage, tan and red, black lettering, 1980, 1982.	20	30
9542	Baltimore & Ohio, Pullman, 1976	30	50
9544	TCA Chicago, Pullman, dark green, black roof, gold lettering, 1980.	—	75
9545	Union Pacific, baggage, yellow, gray roof, red lettering, 1985.	70	100
9546	Union Pacific, combine, yellow, gray roof, red lettering, 1985.	70	100
9547	Union Pacific, observation, yellow, gray roof, red lettering, 1985.	75	100
9548	Union Pacific, "Placid Bay" yellow, gray roof, red lettering, coach, 1985.	75	100
9549	Union Pacific, "Ocean Sunset" coach, yellow and gray, 1985.	75	100
9551	W & A, baggage, yellow, tuscan roof, 1977-79.	30	50
9552	W & A, coach, yellow, tuscan roof.	30	50
9553	W & A, flatcar with fences, brown, gold lettering, six horses, 1978-79.	45	60
9554	Alton Limited, baggage, maroon, red, and silver, gold lettering, 1981.	40	60
9555	Alton Limited, combine, maroon, red, and silver, gold lettering, 1981.	40	60
9556	Alton Limited, coach, maroon, red, and silver, gold lettering, 1981.	50	80
9557	Alton Limited, coach, maroon, red, and silver, gold lettering, 1981.	50	80
9558	Alton Limited, observation, maroon, red, and silver, gold lettering, 1981.	50	80
9559	Rock Island, combine, gold, tuscan roof, 1981.	35	50
9560	Rock Island, coach, gold, tuscan roof, 1981.	35	50
9561	Rock Island, coach, gold, tuscan roof, 1981.	35	50
(9562)	Norfolk & Western, "577" baggage, maroon and black, gold trim, 1981.	90	125
(9563)	Norfolk & Western, "578" combine, maroon and black, gold trim, 1981.	90	125
(9564)	Norfolk & Western, "579" coach, maroon and black, gold trim, 1981.	110	150
(9565)	Norfolk & Western, "580" coach, maroon and black, gold trim, 1981.	110	150
(9566)	Norfolk & Western, "581" observation, maroon and black, 1981.	90	125
(9567)	Norfolk & Western, "582" Vista Dome, maroon and black, 1981.	425	575
9569	Pennsylvania, combine, aluminum, maroon stripes, 1981.	125	150
9570	Pennsylvania, baggage, aluminum, maroon stripes, 1979.	125	150
9571	Pennsylvania, Pullman, aluminum, maroon stripes, 1979.	140	175
9572	Pennsylvania, Pullman, aluminum, maroon stripes, 1979.	140	175
9573	Pennsylvania, Vista Dome, aluminum, maroon stripes, 1979.	140	175
9574	Pennsylvania, observation, aluminum, maroon stripes, 1979.	140	175

		Exc	LN
9575	Pennsylvania, "Edison", aluminum, maroon stripes, 1979.	135	175
9576	Burlington, baggage, aluminum, 1980.	70	100
9577	Burlington, coach, aluminum, 1980.	80	110
9578	Burlington, coach, aluminum, 1980.	80	110
9579	Burlington, Vista Dome, aluminum, 1980.	80	110
9580	Burlington, observation, aluminum, 1980.	80	110
9581	Chessie, baggage; yellow, gray, blue, and vermilion, 1980.	60	80
9582	Chessie, combine; yellow, gray, blue, and vermilion, 1980.	60	80
9583	Chessie, coach; yellow, gray, blue, and vermilion, 1980.	60	80
9584	Chessie, coach; yellow, gray, blue, and vermilion, 1980.	60	80
9585	Chessie, observation; yellow, gray, blue, and vermilion, 1980.	60	80
9586	Chessie, diner; yellow, gray, blue, and vermilion, 1986.	110	125
9588	Burlington, Vista Dome, aluminum, 1980.	110	150
9589	Southern Pacific, baggage; red, orange, black, and white, 1982.	100	125
9590	Southern Pacific, combine; red, orange, black, and white, 1982.	100	125
9591	Southern Pacific, Pullman; red, orange, black, and white, 1982-83.	100	125
9592	Southern Pacific, Pullman; red, orange, black, and white, 1982-83.	100	125
9593	Southern Pacific, observation; red, orange, black, and white, 1982-83.	100	125
9594	New York Central, baggage, gray, black roof, white lettering, 1983.	100	125
9595	New York Central, combine, gray, black roof, white lettering, 1983.	115	150
9596	New York Central, Pullman, gray, black roof, white lettering, 1983.	115	150
9597	New York Central, Pullman, gray, black roof, white lettering, 1983.	115	150
9598	New York Central, observation, gray, black roof, white lettering, 1983.	100	125
9599	Alton Limited, diner; maroon, red, and silver; gold lettering, 1986.	120	135
9600	Chessie, hi-cube, blue, yellow door and lettering, 1976.	15	25
9601	Illinois Central, hi-cube, orange, black door and lettering, 1976-77.	20	25
9602	AT & SF, hi-cube, red, white lettering, 1977.	20	25
9603	Penn Central, hi-cube, green, silver door, white lettering, 1976-77.	25	30
9604	Norfolk & Western, hi-cube, black, silver door, white lettering, 1976-77.	20	25
9605	New Haven, hi-cube, orange, black door, white lettering, 1976-77.	30	35
9606	Union Pacific, High-cube, yellow, blue lettering, 1976-77.	20	25
9607	Southern Pacific, hi-cube, red and gray, white lettering, 1976-77.	20	25
9608	Burlington Northern, hi-cube, green, white lettering, 1977.	20	25
9610	Frisco, hi-cube, yellow, black lettering, 1977.	30	50
9611	TCA, hi-cube, light blue, black roof and ends, 1978.	35	50
9620	NHL Wales, boxcar, white and black, 1980.	15	30
9621	NHL Campbell, boxcar, white and orange, 1980.	15	30
9622	NBA Western, white and silver, 1980.	15	30
9623	NBA Eastern, white and blue, 1980.	15	30
9624	National League, white and red, 1980.	15	30
9625	American League, white and gold, 1980.	15	30
9626	AT & SF, hi-cube, red, white door and lettering, 1982-83.	10	15

	Exc	**LN**

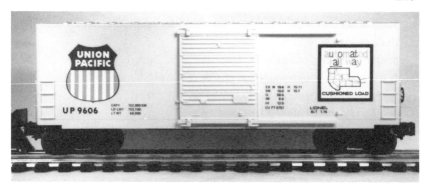

The 9606 Union Pacific boxcar is typical of contemporary "hi-cubes."

		Exc	LN
9627	Union Pacific, hi-cube, yellow, white door, red lettering, 1982-83.	10	15
9628	Burlington Northern, hi-cube, green, white door and lettering, 1982-83.	10	15
9629	Chessie, System, hi-cube, blue, yellow lettering, 1983.	15	20
9660	Mickey Mouse, hi-cube, white and yellow, 1977-78.	40	50
9661	Goofy, hi-cube, white and red, 1977-78.	40	45
9662	Donald Duck, hi-cube, white and green, 1977-78.	40	50
9663	Dumbo, hi-cube, white and red, 1978.	40	70
9664	Cinderella, hi-cube, white and lavender, 1978.	55	75
9665	Peter Pan, hi-cube, white and orange, 1978.	40	60
9666	Pinocchio, hi-cube, white and blue, 1978.	125	200
9667	Snow White, hi-cube, white and green, 1978.	350	500
9668	Pluto, hi-cube, white and brown, 1978.	150	200
9669	Bambi, hi-cube, white and green, 1978.	60	100
9670	Alice in Wonderland, hi-cube, white and green, 1978.	50	75
9671	Fantasia, hi-cube, white and blue, 1978.	30	40
9672	Mickey Mouse "50th", hi-cube, white and gold, 1978.	395	500
9678	TTOS, hi-cube, white, red roof and ends, 1978.	40	50
9700	Southern, boxcar, red, white lettering, 1972-73.	20	30
9701	B & O, automobile boxcar, various door colors, 1971-73.		
	(A) Regular production, silver.	30	40
	(B) Black.	85	125
	(C) LCCA overprint.	—	125
9702	SOO boxcar, white, black roof, red door, 1972-73.	25	35
9703	CP Rail, boxcar, red, black lettering, 1970-71.	55	65
9704	Norfolk & Western, boxcar, brown, white lettering, 1972.	15	25
9705	D & RGW, boxcar, orange, silver doors, black lettering, 1972-73.	15	25
9706	Chesapeake & Ohio, boxcar, blue, yellow door and lettering, 1972-74.	20	30
9707	MKT, cattle car, red, yellow doors, white lettering, 1972-74.	20	30
9708	US Mail, boxcar, red; white and black lettering, 1972-74.		
	(A) Regular production.	15	25
	(B) "Toy Fair '73" overprint.	—	150

		Exc	LN
9709	State of Maine, boxcar, blue and red, 1973-74.	40	50
9710	Rutland, boxcar, yellow and green, 1973-74.	30	40
9711	Southern, boxcar, brown, white lettering, 1974.	20	25
9712	B & O, automobile boxcar, blue, yellow door and lettering, 1973-74.	30	40
9713	CP Rail, boxcar, green, black lettering, 1973-74.		
	(A) Regular production.	20	35
	(B) Overprinted "SEASON'S GREETINGS '74".	—	125
9714	D & RGW, boxcar, silver, red doors and lettering, 1973-74.	20	25
9715	Chesapeake & Ohio, boxcar, black, yellow door, 1973-74.	20	25
9716	Penn Central, boxcar, green, white lettering, 1973-74.	30	35
9717	Union Pacific, boxcar, yellow and black, black lettering, 1973-74.	20	30
9718	Canadian National, boxcar, tuscan, yellow door, 1973-74.	30	40
9719	New Haven, automobile boxcar, orange, black door.		
	(A) Black and white lettering.	30	40
	(B) Black overprinted on white lettering.	—	75
	(C) White overprinted on black lettering.	—	75
9723	Western Pacific, boxcar, orange, black lettering, 1974.		
	(A) Regular edition.	30	50
	(B) Gold overstamping "SEASON'S GREETINGS 1974".	—	125
9724	Missouri Pacific, boxcar, blue, yellow and silver doors, 1974.	35	50
9725	MKT, cattle car, yellow, black door, 1974-75.	15	20
9726	Erie-Lackawanna, boxcar, blue, white lettering, 1978.	25	35
9727	TAG, LCCA, boxcar, maroon, white lettering, 1973.	200	260
9728	Union Pacific, cattle car, LCCA, yellow, silver roof and ends, 1978.	35	45
9729	CP Rail, boxcar, black, red and white logo, 1979.	40	60
9730	CP Rail, boxcar, silver, 1974-75.		
	(A) White lettering.	10	25
	(B) Black lettering.	10	30
9731	Milwaukee Road, boxcar, red, white lettering, 1974-75.	20	25
9732	Southern Pacific, boxcar, silver and black, 1979.	40	50
9733	Airco, LCCA, boxcar with tank, orange and white, 1979.	40	55
9734	Bangor & Aroostock, boxcar, red, white lettering, 1979.	35	45
9735	Grand Trunk Western, boxcar, blue, white lettering, 1974-75.	15	20
9737	Central of Vermont, boxcar, tuscan, white lettering, 1974- 75.	20	25
9738	Illinois Terminal, boxcar, yellow and green, 1982.	55	70
9739	D & RGW, boxcar, yellow and silver, 1975.		
	(A) With black stripe.	20	25
	(B) Without black stripe.	90	125
9740	Chessie, boxcar, yellow, blue lettering, 1974-75.	15	20
9742	M & St L, boxcar, green, gold lettering, 1975.	30	40
9743	Sprite, boxcar, green, dark green lettering, 1974.	25	45
9744	Tab, boxcar, magenta, white lettering, 1974.	25	40

Exc   LN

This two-tone 9739 Rio Grande boxcar is the scarcer version with the black stripe.

		Exc	LN
9745	Fanta, boxcar, orange, black lettering, 1974.	25	40
9747	Chessie System, boxcar, blue, yellow lettering, 1975-76.	20	30
9748	CP Rail, boxcar, blue, white lettering, 1975-76.	20	30
9749	Penn Central, boxcar, green, white and red lettering, 1975.	20	30
9750	DT & I, boxcar, green, yellow lettering, 1975-76.	20	30
9751	Frisco, boxcar, red, white lettering, 1975-76.	15	25
9752	Louisville & Nashville, boxcar, blue, yellow lettering, 1975-76.	15	25
9753	Maine Central, boxcar, yellow, green lettering, 1975-76.		
	(A) Regular production.	25	35
	(B) NETCA overprint.	—	35
9754	New York Central Pacemaker, boxcar, red, white lettering, 1976-77.		
	(A) Regular production.	35	50
	(B) METCA overprint.	—	25
9755	Union Pacific, boxcar, tuscan, white lettering, 1975-76.	20	30
9757	Central of Georgia, boxcar, tuscan, silver doors, red lettering, 1974.	30	40
9758	Alaska, boxcar, blue, yellow lettering, 1976-77.	35	45
9759	Paul Revere, boxcar, white and red, blue door and lettering, 1975-76.	40	55
9760	Liberty Bell, boxcar, red, white, and blue, 1975-76.	40	55
9761	George Washington, boxcar; red, white, and blue, 1975-76.	40	55
(9762)	Welcome Toy Fair, boxcar, 1975	150	200
9763	Rio Grande, cattle car, orange, black door and lettering, 1976.	25	35
9764	Grand Trunk Western, auto boxcar, blue, white lettering, 1976-77.	20	25
9767	Railbox, boxcar, yellow, black door and lettering, 1976-77.	20	25
9768	Boston & Maine, boxcar, blue, black and white lettering, 1976-77.	20	30
9769	B & LE, boxcar, orange, black and white lettering, 1976-77.	15	20
9770	Northern Pacific, boxcar, orange, black and white lettering, 1976-77.	15	22
9771	Norfolk & Western, boxcar, blue, white lettering, 1976-77.		
	(A) Regular production.	30	40
	(B) TCA museum dedication overprint.	—	50
9772	Great Northern, boxcar, green and orange, 1975.	65	90
9773	New York Central, cattle car, yellow, black door and lettering, 1976.	25	35

		Exc	LN
9774	Southern Belle TCA, boxcar, orange, silver, and green, 1975.	35	50
9775	M & St L, boxcar, red, white lettering, 1975.	30	45
9776	Southern Pacific, "Overnight" boxcar, black, 1975.	60	75
9777	Virginian, boxcar, blue, yellow lettering, 1976-77.	15	20
9778	Season's Greetings, boxcar, blue, silver doors and lettering, 1975.	225	300
9779	TCA Philadelphia, boxcar, white, red roof and ends, blue doors, 1976.	35	50
9780	Johnny Cash, boxcar, silver and black, black lettering, 1976.	35	45
9781	Delaware & Hudson, boxcar, yellow, blue lettering, 1977-78.	20	25
9782	The Rock, boxcar, blue, white lettering, 1977-78.	20	25
9783	B & O "Time Saver", boxcar, blue and silver, 1977- 78.	30	40
9784	AT & SF, boxcar, red and black, white lettering, 1977-78.	25	35
9785	Conrail, boxcar, blue, white lettering, 1977-79.	20	25
9786	C & NW, boxcar, brown, white lettering, 1977-79.	30	40
9787	Central of NJ, boxcar, green, gold lettering, 1977-79.	15	35
9788	Lehigh Valley, boxcar, cream color, black lettering, 1977- 79.	15	20
9789	Pickens, boxcar, blue, white lettering, 1977.	25	40
9801	B & O Sentinel, boxcar (Std. O), silver and blue, 1975.	30	50
9802	Miller High Life, reefer (Std. O), white, red lettering, 1975.	20	30
9803	Johnson's Wax, boxcar (Std. O); red, white, and blue, 1975.	25	40
9805	Grand Trunk, reefer (Std. O), silver, black lettering, 1975.	25	40
9806	Rock Island, boxcar (Std. O), tuscan, white lettering, 1975- 76.	75	110
9807	Stroh's Beer, reefer (Std. O), red, gold and white lettering, 1975-76.	80	150
9808	Union Pacific, boxcar (Std. O), yellow, 1975-76.	100	150
9809	Clark, reefer (Std. O), red, blue lettering, 1975-76.	40	50
9811	Pacific Fruit Express, reefer, yellow, tuscan roof, 1980.	25	35
9812	Arm & Hammer, reefer, yellow, red roof and ends, 1980.	15	20
9813	Ruffles, reefer, light blue, blue roof and ends, 1980.	15	20
9814	Perrier, reefer, dark green, yellow roof and ends, 1980.	20	25
9815	New York Central, reefer (Std. O), orange, tuscan roof, 1985.	70	90
9816	Brachs, reefer, white, tuscan roof and ends, magenta doors, 1980.	15	20
9817	Bazooka Gum, reefer, white, orange roof and ends, 1980.	15	20
9818	Western Maryland, reefer, orange, black roof and edns, 1980.	25	35
9819	Western Fruit Express, reefer, yellow, 1981.	25	35
9820	Wabash, gondola, black (Std. O), black, white lettering, 1973-74.	40	50
9821	Southern Pacific, gondola, (Std. O), white lettering, 1973-74.		
	(A) Brown body.	40	50
	(B) Black body.	—	275
9822	Grand Trunk Western, gondola, (Std. O), blue, coal load, 1974.	40	50
9823	AT & SF, flatcar with crates (Std. O), tuscan, tan crates, 1976.	80	125
9824	New York Central, gondola, (Std. O), black, coal load, 1975.	60	85
9825	Schaefer, reefer (Std. O), white, red roof, 1976-77.	60	80
9826	P & LE, boxcar (Std. O), green, white lettering, 1976-77.	90	125

Exc   LN

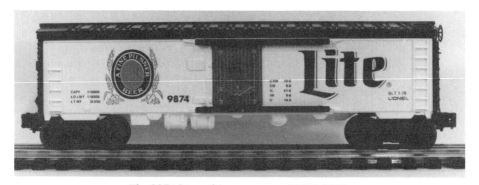

The 9874 Lite refrigerator car of 1978-1979.

		Exc	LN
9827	Cutty Sark, reefer, yellow, black roof and ends, 1984.	15	20
9828	J & B, reefer, yellow-green, white roof and ends, 1984.	15	20
9829	Dewars, reefer, white, red roof and ends, 1984.	15	20
9830	Johnny Walker Red Label, reefer, yellow, maroon roof and ends, 1984.	15	20
9831	Pepsi Cola, reefer, white, light blue roof and ends, 1982.	30	40
9832	Cheerios, reefer, yellow, black lettering, 1982.	15	25
9833	Vlasic Pickles, reefer, white, yellow roof and ends, 1982.	15	20
9834	Southern Comfort, reefer, white, gold roof and ends, 1983.	20	30
9835	Jim Beam, reefer, white, red roof and ends, 1983.	20	30
9836	Old Grand-Dad, reefer, orange, gold roof and ends, 1983.	20	30
9837	Wild Turkey, reefer, yellow, brown roof and ends, 1983.	20	30
9840	Fleischmann's Gin, reefer, yellow, maroon roof and ends, 1985.	15	20
9841	Calvert Gin, reefer, dark blue, silver roof and ends, 1985.	15	20
9842	Seagram's Gin, reefer, cream, dark blue roof and ends, 1985.	15	20
9843	Tanqueray Gin, reefer, white, dark green roof and ends, 1985.	15	20
9844	Sambuca, reefer, dark blue, silver roof and ends, 1986.	15	20
9845	Baileys Irish Cream, reefer, dark green, tuscan roof and ends, 1986.	20	25
9846	Seagrams Vodka, reefer, dark gray, black roof and ends, 1986.	15	20
9847	Wolfschmidt Vodka, reefer, dark green, gold roof and ends, 1986.	15	20
9849	Lionel, reefer, orange, blue roof, 1984.	50	70
9850	Budweiser, reefer, white, red roof, 1973-76.	15	30
9851	Schlitz, reefer, white, brown roof, 1973-76.	15	30
9852	Miller, reefer, white, brown roof, 1973-76.	15	30
9853	Cracker Jack, reefer, brown roof, 1973.		
	(A) Caramel color body.	25	50
	(B) White body, black border around "Cracker Jack".	15	20
9854	Baby Ruth, reefer, white, red roof, 1973-76.	15	20
9855	Swift, reefer, silver, black roof, 1974-76.	20	30
9856	Old Milwaukee, reefer, red, gold roof, 1974-76.	15	30
9858	Butterfinger, reefer, orange, blue roof, 1973-76.	15	25
9859	Pabst, reefer, white, blue roof, 1974-75.	15	30

		Exc	LN
9860	Gold Medal, reefer, white, orange roof and ends, 1973-76.	15	20
9861	Tropicana, reefer, white, green or white, 1976-77.	25	30
9862	Hamm's, reefer, blue, white roof, red and white lettering, 1975-76.	15	30
9863	REA, reefer, green, gold lettering, 1975-76.	30	40
9864	TCA Seattle, reefer, white, blue roof, ends, and door, 1974.	60	75
9866	Coors, reefer, white, brown roof, black and yellow lettering, 1977.	20	40
9867	Hershey's, reefer, maroon, silver roof and ends, silver door, 1976-77.	20	40
9868	TTOS, reefer, yellow, blue roof and ends, 1980.	60	75
9869	Santa Fe, reefer, white, brown roof and door, black lettering, 1975.	35	50
9870	Old Dutch Cleanser, reefer, yellow and red, multicolor, 1977-78.	15	20
9871	Carling's, reefer, dark red, black roof, 1977-78, 1980.	20	25
9872	Pacific Fruit Express, reefer, orange, silver roof, 1977-78.	25	35
9873	Ralston Purina, reefer, white sides, blue ends and roof, 1978.	20	30
9874	Miller Lite Beer, reefer, white sides, blue roof and ends, 1978-79.	35	45
9875	A & P, reefer, mustard-yellow, brown roof, 1979.	20	25
9876	Central Vermont, reefer, silver, black roof, green lettering, 1978.	30	40
9877	Gerber's, reefer, two-tone blue; black and white print, 1979-80.	30	45
9878	Good and Plenty, reefer, white, magenta roof, candy box, 1979.	15	20
9879	Hills Bros., reefer, red sides, yellow roof and ends, 1979- 80.	15	20
9880	Santa Fe, reefer, orange, tuscan roof and ends, gold diamond, 1979.	35	50
9881	Rath Packing, reefer, yellow sides, tuscan roof and ends, 1979.	30	40
9882	NYRB "Early Bird", reefer, orange sides, tuscan roof and ends, 1979.	30	40
9883	Nabisco, reefer, gray sides, blue roof, Oreo package, 1979.	45	60
9884	Fritos, reefer, yellow-orange sides, red roof and ends, 1981-82.	20	25
9885	Lipton Tea, reefer, red and yellow sides, brown roof and ends, 1981-82.	20	25
9886	Mounds, reefer, white sides, red roof and ends, 1981-82.	15	20
9887	Fruit Growers Express, reefer, yellow, green roof and ends, 1984.	35	45
9888	Green Bay & Western, reefer, gray sides, red roof and ends, 1983.	50	70
12700	Erie, magnetic crane, 1987.	175	225
12701	Operating fuel station, 1987-88.	75	90
12702	Operating control tower, 1987.	50	75
12703	Icing station, 1988.	—	65
12704	Dwarf signal, 1988.	—	18
12705	Lumber shed, 1988.	—	6
12706	Barrel loader building, 1987-88.	—	7
12707	Billboard set, 1987-88.	5	6
12708	Street lamps, 1988.	—	8
12709	Banjo signal, 1987-88.	—	25
12710	Engine house, 1987-89.	—	23
12711	Water tower, 1987.	—	12
12712	Automatic ore loader, 1987.	—	22
12713	Automatic gateman, 1987-88.	—	36

		Exc	LN
12714	Automatic crossing gate, 1987-88.	—	23
12715	Illuminated bumpers, 1987-88.	—	6
12716	Searchlight tower, 1987.	—	26
12717	Non-illuminated bumpers, 1987.	—	3
12718	Barrel shed, 1987-88.	—	6
12719	Refreshment stand, 1988.	—	65
12720	Rotary beacon (metal), 1988.	—	36
12721	Illuminated extension bridge, 1989.	—	30
12722	Roadside diner with smoke, 1988.	—	40
12723	Microwave tower, 1988.	—	20
12724	Signal bridge, 1988.	—	40
12725	Lionel truck and trailer, 1988-89.	—	10
12726	Grain elevator kit, 1988.	—	22
12727	Automatic operating semaphore, 1989.	—	25
12728	Illuminated freight station, 1989.	—	30
12729	Mail pickup set, 1988.	—	19
12730	Plate girder bridge, 1988.	—	7
12731	Station platform, 1988.	—	7
12732	Coal bag, 1988.	—	2.50
12733	Watchman's shanty, 1988.	—	6
12734	Passenger/freight station, 1989.	—	15
12735	Diesel horn shed, 1988.	—	30
12736	Coaling station, 1988.	—	22
12737	Whistling freight shed, 1988.	—	30
12739	Tractor and tanker, 1989.	—	15
12740	Log package (3 logs), 1988.	—	2.50
12741	Intermodal crane, 1989.	—	220
12742	Gooseneck street lamps, 1989.	—	12
12743	O track clips, 1989.	—	4
12744	Rock piers, 1989.	—	7
12745	Barrel pack (6), 1989.	—	3
12746	O27 operating/uncoupling track, 1989.	—	13
12748	Illuminated station platform, 1989.	—	17
12749	Rotary radar antenna, 1989.	—	30
12750	Crane kit, 1989.	—	7
12751	Shovel kit, 1989.	—	6
12752	Historical VHS tape, 1989.	—	18
12753	Ore load to fit ore car, 1989.	—	3
12754	Graduated trestle set (22), 1989.	—	13
12755	Elevated trestle set (10), 1989.	—	11
12759	Floodlight tower, 12" tall, 1990.	—	27
12760	Automatic highway flasher, 8-7/8" tall, 1990.	—	35

		Exc	LN
12761	Animated billboard, messages alternate, 1990.	—	29
12763	Single signal bridge, two lights, 1990.	—	33
12765	Die-cast automobile assortment, 1990.	—	10
12768	Burning switch tower, smoke generator, 1990.	—	83
12770	Arch under bridge, 1990.	—	14
12771	Roadside diner, operating smokestack, 1990.	—	42
12772	Illuminated extension bridge, rock piers, 1990.	—	28
12773	Freight platform, deep red and gray, 1990.	—	10
12774	Lumber loader kit, 1990.	—	6
12777	Chevron tractor and tanker, die-cast vehicle, 1990.	—	10
12778	Conrail trackor and trailer, die-cast vehicle, 1990.	—	10
12779	Lionelville tractor and grain rig, die-cast vehicle, 1990.	—	10
12780	RS-1 transformer, solid-state, 1990.	—	118
12781	Intermodal crane, unloads trailers from flatcars, 1990.	—	230
16000	Pennsylvania, Vista Dome, tuscan, black roof, 1987-88.	—	25
16001	Pennsylvania, coach, tuscan, black roof, gold lettering, 1987-88.	—	25
16002	Pennsylvania, coach, tuscan, black roof, gold lettering, 1987-88.	—	25
16003	Pennsylvania observation, tuscan, black roof, gold lettering, 1987-88.	—	25
16009	Pennsylvania, combine, tuscan, black roof, gold lettering, 1988.	—	25
16010	Dry Gulch, passenger, 1988.	—	35
16011	Dry Gulch, passenger, 1988.	—	35
16012	Dry Gulch, passenger, 1988.	—	35
16013	Amtrak, lighted combine, silver; red, white, and blue trim, 1988.	—	25
16014	Amtrak, lighted Vista Dome, silver; red, white, and blue trim, 1988.	—	25
16015	Amtrak, lighted observation, silver; red, white, and blue trim, 1988.	—	25
16016	New York Central, baggage, 1989.	—	25
16017	New York Central, combine, 1989.	—	25
16018	New York Central, coach, 1989.	—	25
16019	New York Central, Vista Dome, 1989.	—	25
16020	New York Central, coach, 1989.	—	25
16021	New York Central, observation, 1989.	—	25
16022	Pennsylvania, baggage, 1989.	—	22
16023	Amtrak, coach, 1989.	—	23
16023	Amtrak, lighted coach, 1988.	—	25
16031	Pennsylvania, dining car, brown, 1990.	—	24
16033	Amtrak, baggage car, silver; red, white, and blue trim, 1990.	—	24
16034	Northern Pacific, baggage car, two-tone green, 1990.	—	24
16035	Northern Pacific, combine, two-tone green, 1990.	—	24
16036	Northern Pacific, passenger car, two-tone green, 1990.	—	24
16037	Northern Pacific, Vista Dome, two-tone green, 1990.	—	24
16038	Northern Pacific, passenger car, two-tone green, 1990.	—	24
16039	Northern Pacific, observation car, two-tone green, 1990.	—	24

		Exc	LN
16102	Southern, three-dome tank, dark green, gold lettering, 1987.	—	45
16103	Lehigh Valley, two-dome tank, gray, black lettering, 1988.	—	25
16104	Santa Fe, two-dome tank car, 1989.	—	18
16107	Sunoco, two-dome tank car, black, multicolor lettering, 1990.	—	19
16124	Rio Grande, two-tier auto carrier, orange and yellow, 1990.	—	30
16125	Conrail, two-tier auto carrier, brown and yellow, 1990.	—	30
16200	Rock Island, boxcar, red, white lettering, 1987.	—	10
16201	Wabash, boxcar, blue, white lettering, 1988.	—	10
16204	Hawthorne, boxcar (appliance store).	—	75
16208	Pennsylvania, auto rack with cars, 1989.	—	40
16209	Disney Magic '88 Sears set, 1988.	—	75i
16211	Hawthorne, boxcar, 1988.	—	70
16213	Shop Rite, boxcar, 1988.	—	75
16300	Rock Island, flatcar with fences, red, white lettering, 1987.	6	8
16301	Lionel, barrel ramp car, blue and white, yellow lettering, 1987.	—	15
16302	Lehigh Valley, flatcar with yellow derrick, green, 1987.	—	15
16303	PRR, flatcar with trailers, tuscan, gold lettering, 1987.	—	45
16304	Rail Blazer, gondola, red, two black cable reels, 1987.	5	7
16305	Lehigh Valley, ore car, gray, black lettering, 1987.	—	95
16306	Santa Fe, barrel ramp, red, white lettering, 1988.	—	15
16307	Nickel Plate, flatcar with vans, blue car, silver vans, 1988.	—	15
16308	Burlington Northern, flatcar with one trailer, 1989.	—	40
16309	Wabash, gondola, 1988.	5	7
16313	PRR, gondola with cable reels, 1989.	5	7
16314	Wabash, flatcar with trailers (2), 1989.	—	25
16315	Pennsylvania, flatcar with fences, 1989.	—	20
16317	Pennsylvania, barrel ramp car, 1989.	—	16
16318	Lionel Lines, depressed flatcar with wire reels, 1989.	—	20
16320	Great Northern, barrel ramp car, orange and black, 1990.	—	17
16322	Sealand, articulated flatcar with two trailers, 1990.	—	55
16323	Lionel Lines, gray flatcar with two blue trailers, 1990.	—	21
16324	Pennsylvania, depressed flatcar with cable reels, 1990.	—	20
16400	Pennsylvania, two-bay hopper, 1989.	—	25
16402	Southern, hopper, 1987.	—	35
16500	Rock Island, bobber caboose, 1987.	—	25
16501	Lehigh Valley, caboose, 1987.	—	15
16503	New York Central, transfer caboose, gray cab, black base, 1987.	—	12
16504	Southern, caboose, red and yellow, black roof, 1987.	—	35
16505	Wabash, caboose, red, white lettering, 1988.	8	10
16506	Santa Fe, bay window caboose, blue and yellow, yellow lettering, 1988.	25	30
16510	New Haven, bay window caboose, 1989.	—	30
16511	Penn, bobber caboose, 1989.	5	7

		Exc	LN
16513	Union Pacific, SP type caboose, 1989.	—	22
16516	Lehigh Valley, caboose, red, black and white lettering, 1990.	—	22
16519	Rock Island, transfer caboose, blue and black, 1990.	—	21
16600	Illinois Central, coal dump, tuscan, orange bin, 1988.	—	19
16601	Canadian National, searchlight car, maroon, gray superstructure, 1988.	—	22
16602	Erie, coal dump, gray, maroon lettering, 1987.	—	25
16603	Detroit Zoo, giraffe car, tuscan, white lettering, 1987.	—	35
16603	Lehigh Valley, searchlight car, black, gray superstructure, 1987.	—	15
16604	New York Central, log dump, black, white lettering, 1987.	—	25
16605	Bronx Zoo, operating giraffe car, blue, yellow giraffe, 1988.	—	35
16606	Southern, searchlight car, green, gray superstructure, 1987-88.	—	25
16607	Southern, coal dump, black, dark green bin, 1987.	—	35
16609	Lehigh Valley, derrick, 1987.	20	25
16610	Lionel track maintenance car, gray, blue superstructure, 1987-88.	—	20
16611	San Francisco, log dump, black, yellow log cradle, 1988.	—	19
16612	SOO Line, log dump car, 1989.	—	20
16613	Katy, coal dump car, 1989.	—	20
16614	Reading, cop and hobo car, 1989.	—	30
16615	Lionel Lines, extension searchlight car, 1989.	—	25
16617	C & NW, boxcar with end of train device, 1989.	—	25
16618	Santa Fe, track maintenance car, 1989.	—	20
16619	Wabash, coal dump car, brown and black, 1990.	—	20
16620	Chesapeake & Ohio, track maintenance car, yellow and black, 1990.	—	19
16621	Alaska, railroad, log dump car with logs, yellow, 1990.	—	20
16622	CSX, boxcar with blinking end-of-train-device, 1990.	—	25
16624	New Haven, cop and hobo operating boxcar, 1990.	—	32
16625	New York Central, searchlight car with extension cord, 1990.	—	27
16631	Rock Island, boxcar with sound unit, green, 1990.	—	139
16632	Burlington Northern, boxcar with sound unit, yellow, 1990.	—	139
16701	Southern, tool car, green and black, gold lettering, 1987.	—	75
16707	Southern, coal dump, 1987.	—	25
16800	Lionel Railroader Club, ore car, yellow, black lettering, 1986.	—	100
16801	Lionel Railroader Club, bunk car, blue, yellow lettering, 1988.	—	45
16802	Lionel Railroader Club, tool car, 1989.	—	45
17002	Conrail, ACF hopper, gray, black lettering, 1987.	90	110
17003	DuPont, ACF hopper, red, multicolor lettering, 1990.	—	25
17100	Chessie, hopper, yellow, blue lettering, 1988.	—	55
17101	Chessie, hopper, yellow, blue lettering, 1988.	—	55
17102	Chessie, hopper, yellow, blue lettering, 1988.	—	55
17103	Chessie, hopper, yellow, blue lettering, 1988.	—	55
17104	Chessie, hopper, yellow, blue lettering, 1988.	—	55
17107	Sclair, covered hopper, 1989.	—	100

		Exc	LN
17108	Santa Fe, centerflow hopper, brown, white lettering, 1990.	—	90
17200	CP Rail, boxcar, 1989.	—	60
17201	Conrail, boxcar (O), tuscan, white lettering, 1987.	—	70
17202	Santa Fe, boxcar with railsounds, 1990.	—	90
17300	CP Rail, reefer (O), 1989.	—	75
17301	Conrail, reefer (O), blue, white lettering, black roofwalk, 1987.	—	50
17302	Santa Fe, reefer, yellow and black w/ blinking end-of-train device, 1990.	—	50
17400	CP Rail, gondola with coal load, 1989.	—	40
17401	Conrail, gondola (O), brown, white lettering, coal load, 1987.	—	40
17402	Santa Fe, gondola, brown, white lettering, coal load, 1990.	—	30
17500	CP Rail, flatcar with logs, 1989.	—	55
17501	Conrail, flatcar (O), brown, white lettering, 1987.	—	40
17502	Santa Fe, black flatcar with silver trailer, 1990.	—	60
17600	New York Central, caboose, brown, white lettering, 1987.	—	95
17601	Southern, woodside caboose, red, black roof, yellow lettering, 1988.	—	75
17602	Conrail, caboose, blue, black roof, white lettering, 1987.	—	75
17603	Rock Island, caboose, maroon, white lettering, 1988.	—	60
17604	Lackawanna, caboose, brown, white lettering, 1988.	—	60
17605	Reading, low-cupola woodside caboose, 1989	—	60
17606	New York Central, caboose with smoke, 1990.	—	71
17607	Reading, caboose with smoke, brown, 1990.	—	71
17870	LCCA club, boxcar, orange, cream stripe, black lettering, 1987.	—	100
17871	TTOS club, flatcar with Kodak and Xerox trailers, 1985.	—	300
17872	TTOS club, Anaconda ore, 1988.	—	90
17873	LCCA club, Ashland Oil tank car, black, white lettering, 1988.	—	70
17874	LOTS club Milwaukee Road flatcar, 1988.	—	125
17875	LOTS club, 1989 car.	—	100
17876	LCCA club, CN & L boxcar, 1989.	—	50
17877	TTOS club, tank car, 1989.	—	100
17878	TTOS club, Magma ore, 1989.	—	100
17900	Santa Fe, tank car, black, white lettering, 1990.	—	49
17901	Chevron, tank car, white, multicolor lettering, 1990.	—	49
18000	Pennsylvania, B6 0-6-0 switcher, 1989.	—	650
18001	Rock Island, 4-8-4 steam, dark gray, white lettering, 1987.	500	650
18002	New York Central, 4-6-4 steam, "785" on cab, gun-metal gray, 1987.	950	1100
18003	Lackawanna, 4-8-4, "1501" on cab, black and gray, white lett., 1988.	—	650
18004	Reading Pacific, 4-6-2 steam locomotive, 1989.	—	350
18008	Disneyland RR, 35th anniv., 4-4-0 locomotive w/display case, 1990.	—	350
18090	D & RG, LCCA club, steam, 2-6-4, 1989.	—	450
18200	Conrail, SD-40, blue, white lettering, 1987.	—	325
18201	Chessie, SD-40, yellow, vermilion, and dark blue, 1988.	—	300
18203	CP Rail, SD-40, 1989.	—	295

		Exc	LN
18205	Union Pacific, GE-8 40C, 1989.	—	375
18206	Santa Fe, Dash-8 40B diesel, blue and yellow, 1990.	—	325
18300	Pennsylvania, GG-1 electric, bronze, black striping, red keystone, 1987.	—	500
18301	Southern, FM Trainmaster w/caboose, green and white, 1988.	—	395
18302	Great Northern, engine, electric, 1988.	—	250
18303	Amtrak, GG-1, 1989.	—	395
18400	Santa Fe, 2-4-2 snowplow, 1987.	—	145
18401	Lionel, hand car, 1987-88.	—	50
18402	Burro crane, 1988.	—	120
18403	Santa Claus, hand car, 1988.	—	50
18404	San Francisco, trolley, 1988.	—	150
18405	Santa Fe, operating Burro crane, 1989.	—	100
18406	Lionel, operating track maintenance car, 1989.	—	90
18407	Snoopy and Woodstock, handcar, cartoon characters, 1990.	—	48
18408	Santa, hand car, 1989.	—	50
18410	Pennsylvania, burro crane, powered, 1990.	—	110
18411	Canadian Pacific, fire fighter car, powered, 1990.	—	92
18500	Milwaukee Road, GP-9, 1987.	—	225
18501	Western Maryland, NW-2 switcher, 1989.	—	295
18502	Lionel 90th Anniversary, GP-9 diesel; red, white and blue, 1990.	—	300
18503	Southern Pacific, diesel switcher, gray, 1990.	—	300
18600	Atlantic Coast Line, steam, 4-4-2, 1987.	—	95
18601	Great Northern, 4-4-2, "8601" on cab, dark green and silver, 1988.	—	95
18602	PRR, steam, 4-4-2, black, white lettering, 1987.	—	90
18604	Wabash, 2-4-2, "8604" on cab, white stripe, 1988.	—	80
18606	New York Central, 2-6-4, 1989.	—	165
18607	Union Pacific, 2-6-4, 1989.	—	150
18609	Northern Pacific, 2-6-4 steam, black, 1990.	—	170
18610	Rock Island, 0-4-0 steam, black, 1990.	—	180
18612	Chicago & North Western, 2-6-4, 1989.	—	100
18615	Grand Trunk Western, 4-4-2, steam, black, 1990.	—	105
18700	Rock Island, steam, 0-4-0, bright red, white lettering, 1987.	—	25
18702	V & TRR, steam, 4-4-0, "8702" on cab, dark maroon, gold trim, 1988.	—	100
18800	Lehigh Valley, GP-9, 1987.	—	110
18801	Santa Fe, U36-B, 1987.	—	85
18802	Southern, GP-9 diesel, 1987.	—	100
18803	Santa Fe, RS-3 diesel, 1988-89.	—	100
18804	SOO Line, RS-3 diesel, 1988-89.	—	100
18805	Union Pacific, RS-3, 1989.	—	105
18806	New Haven, SD-18 diesel, 1989.	—	105
18807	Lehigh Valley, RS-3 diesel, red, multicolor trim, 1990.	—	110
18808	Atlantic Coast Line, SD-18 diesel, black and yellow, 1990.	—	105

		Exc	LN
18901	Pennsylvania, Alco A powered (price with 18902), 1988.	—	125
18902	Pennsylvania, Alco A dummy, sold with 18901.		
18903	Amtrak, Alco A powered (price with 18904), 1988.	—	125
18904	Amtrak, Alco A dummy, sold with 18903.		
19000	Blue Comet, diner, two-tone blue, cream stripe, gold lettering, 1987.	—	85
19001	Southern Crescent, diner, two-tone green, gold striping, 1987.	—	85
19002	Pennsylvania, diner, tuscan, black roof, gold lettering, 1988.	—	50
19003	Milwaukee Road, diner, orange and maroon, 1988.	—	50
19100	Amtrak, baggage car, 1989.	—	150
19101	Amtrak, combine, 1989.	—	150
19102	Amtrak, coach, 1989.	—	150
19103	Amtrak, Vista Dome, 1989.	—	150
19104	Amtrak, dining car, 1989.	—	150
19106	Amtrak, observation car, 1989.	—	150
19200	Tidewater Southern, boxcar, tuscan, yellow lettering, 1987.	—	15
19201	Lancaster & Chester, boxcar, blue, gray, and white, 1987.	—	65
19202	Pennsylvania, boxcar, green, red and white trim, 1987.	—	50
19203	Detroit & Toledo Shoreline, boxcar, yellow, red lettering, 1987.	—	15
19204	Milwaukee Road, boxcar, brown, yellow stripe, 1987.	—	40
19205	Great Northern, boxcar, green and orange, red and white logo, 1988.	—	40
19206	Seaboard, boxcar, black, gold lettering, 1988.	—	20
19207	CP Rail, boxcar, burnt orange, black lettering, 1988.	—	20
19208	Southern, boxcar, tuscan, white lettering, 1988.	—	20
19209	Florida East Coast, boxcar, dark blue, yellow lettering, 1988.	—	20
19210	SOO Line, boxcar, 1989.	—	20
19211	Vermont Railway, boxcar, 1989.	—	20
19212	Pennsylvania, boxcar, 1989.	—	25
19213	SP & S, boxcar, 1989.	—	20
19214	Western Maryland, boxcar, 1989.	—	30
19215	Union Pacific, boxcar, yellow, multicolor lettering, 1990.	—	18
19216	Santa Fe, boxcar, brown, white and yellow lettering, 1990.	—	18
19217	Burlington, boxcar, red, black and white lettering, 1990.	—	18
19218	New Haven, boxcar, black, orange door, 1990.	—	18
19219	Lionel comm., boxcar, orange and white, blue door, railsounds, 1990.	—	90
19220	Lionel commemorative, boxcar, orange and white, blue door, 1990.	—	30
19221	Lionel commemorative, boxcar, orange and white, blue door, 1990.	—	30
19222	Lionel commemorative, boxcar, orange and white, blue door, 1990.	—	30
19223	Lionel commemorative, boxcar, orange and white, blue door, 1990.	—	30
19300	Pennsylvania, ore car, tuscan, white lettering, 1987.	—	20
19301	Milwaukee Road, ore car, oxide red, white lettering, 1987.	—	20
19302	Milwaukee Road, hopper, yellow, black lettering, coal load, 1987.	—	30
19303	Lionel Lines, hopper, orange and blue, multicolor lettering, 1987.	35	50

		Exc	LN
19304	Great Northern, covered hopper, light gray, black lettering, 1988.	—	40
19305	Chessie, ore car, dark blue, yellow lettering, 1988.	—	18
19307	B & LE, ore car, 1989.	—	17
19308	Great Northern, ore car, 1989.	—	17
19309	Seaboard, covered hopper, 1989.	—	20
19310	Lancaster & Chester, covered hopper, 1989.	—	20
19311	Southern Pacific, covered hopper, gray, red lettering, 1990.	—	20
19312	Reading, hopper with coal load, black, 1990.	—	20
19313	B & O, ore car with load, black, white lettering, 1990.	—	18
19400	Milwaukee Road, gondola, brown, two black cable reels, 1987.	—	30
19401	Great Northern, gondola, black, white lettering, coal load, 1988.	—	40
19402	Great Northern, crane car, black, orange cab, 1988.	—	50
19403	Western Maryland, gondola with coal load, 1989.	—	25
19404	Western Maryland, flatcar with trailers, 1989.	—	30
19500	Milwaukee Road, reefer, yellow sides, brown roof and ends, 1987.	—	35
19502	C & NW, refrigerator, green and yellow, 1987.	—	40
19503	B & A, refrigerator, blue and white sides, red roof, ends, and door, 1987.	—	35
19504	Northern Pacific, refrigerator, yellow sides, red roof and ends, 1987.	—	30
19505	Great Northern, refrigerator, green and orange, 1988.	—	45
19506	Thomas Newcomen, reefer, white, bright red roof and ends, 1988.	—	25
19507	Thomas Edison, reefer, light tan sides, brown roof and ends, 1988.	—	25
19508	Leonardo Da Vinci, woodside reefer, 1989.	—	20
19509	Alexander Graham Bell, woodside reefer, 1989.	—	20
19511	Western Maryland, reefer, 1989.	—	30
19512	Wright Brothers, reefer, green and white, 1990.	—	20
19513	Ben Franklin, reefer, red and white, 1990.	—	20
19600	Milwaukee Road, single-dome tank, orange and black, logo, 1987.	—	55
19601	Western Maryland, single-dome tank, 1989.	—	55
19602	Erie, coal dump, 1987.	—	25
19651	AT & SF, tool car, gray, black lettering, 1987.	—	25
19652	Jersey Central, bunk car, brown, white lettering, 1988.	—	25
19653	Jersey Central, tool car, brown, white lettering, 1988.	—	25
19654	Amtrak, bunk car, 1989.	—	30
19655	Amtrak, tool car, orange and gray, black lettering, 1990.	—	27
19656	Milwaukee Road, bunk car with smoke, brown and yellow, 1990.	—	50
19700	C & O, caboose, yellow, blue roof, blue lettering, 1988.	—	50
19701	Milwaukee Road, N5C caboose, orange, black roof, 1987.	—	50
19702	Pennsylvania, N5C caboose, bronze, black lettering, 1987.	—	75
19703	Great Northern, caboose, dark red, black roof, white lettering, 1988.	—	50
19704	Western Maryland, wide-vision caboose, 1989.	—	65
19705	CP Rail, wide-vision caboose, 1989.	—	45
19706	Union Pacific, wide-vision caboose, 1989.	—	65

		Exc	LN
19707	Southern Pacific, searchlight caboose with smoke, 1990.	—	89
19708	Lionel commemorative, b/w caboose, white, orange, and blue, 1990.	—	50
19709	Pennsylvania, work caboose, 1989.	—	80
19800	Lionelville, cattle car set, tan and gray, with corral and cattle, 1988.	—	100
19801	Poultry Dispatch, boxcar, red, black lettering, 1987.	—	35
19802	Carnation, operating milk car, yellow and brown, 1987.	—	100
19803'	Reading, ice car, white sides, black roof and ends, 1987.	—	50
19804	Wabash, hopper, black, white lettering, 1987.	—	35
19805	Santa Fe, boxcar, red, white lettering, 1987.	—	40
19806	Pennsylvania, operating hopper, red-brown, white lettering, 1988.	—	32
19807	Pennsylvania, smoking caboose, tuscan, gold lettering, 1988.	—	65
19808	New York Central, ice car, orange sides, maroon roof and ends, 1988.	—	45
19809	Erie-Lackawanna, operating boxcar, 1988.	—	35
19810	Bosco, milk car, yellow sides, silver roof, ends, and doors, 1988.	—	90
19811	Monon, operating brakeman car with telltale, 1990.	—	59
19900	Toy Fair, boxcar, red, silver roof and ends, 1987.	—	150
19901	I Love Virginia, boxcar, yellow and blue, pink and blue lettering, 1987.	—	25
19902	Toy Fair, boxcar, 1988.	—	125
19903	Christmas car, white and green, red doors, multicolor printing, 1987.	—	30
19904	Christmas car, white and red, 1988.	—	35
19905	I Love California, blue and gold, yellow lettering, 1988.	—	20
19906	I Love Pennsylvania, boxcar, 1989.	—	20
19909	I Love New Jersey, boxcar, green and gold, 1990.	—	20
33000	Lionel Lines, RailScope diesel, 1988.	—	250
33001	HO RailScope diesel, 1988.	—	200
33002	RailScope diesel with black and white television, 1988.	—	375
33003	HO RailScope with black and white television, 1988.	—	375
59629	LOTS club, Milwaukee Road, log carrier, 1988.	—	100
81487	(See 19417)		
97330	(See 9733)		
3739469	MKT single-dome tank, TTOS, 1989.	—	50

O Gauge Classics

350E/350WX/883-884	(See 51000 set)		
892-895	(See 51202-51)		
893	(See 51203-51205)		
8814-8820	(See 51400, 51500, 51700, 51800)		
13001	Freight Express train, includes 1318E locomotive, 5130, 5140, 5150, and 5160, 1990.	—	900
51000	Milwaukee Road, Hiawatha set (350E locomotive, 350WX coach, 83 Center coach, 884 coach), 1988.	—	1000

		Exc	LN
51001	Lionel "#44 Freight Special", set w/51100, 51500, 51800, 51400, 51700.	—	750
51100	Lionel electric engine, originally a No. 4 (sold with 51001).		
51202	Lionel Lines, Rail Chief combo car, numbered "892", 1990.	—	185
51203	Lionel Lines, Rail Chief coach, numbered "893", 1990.	—	185
51204	Lionel Lines, Rail Chief coach, numbered "894", 1990.	—	185
51205	Lionel Lines, Rail Chief observation, numbered "896", 1990.	—	185
51400	Lionel Lines, boxcar, numbered "8814" (sold with 51001).		
51500	Lionel Lines, hopper, numbered "8816" (sold with 51001).		
51700	Lionel Lines, caboose, numbered "8817" (sold with 51001).		
51800	Lionel Lines, searchlight car, "8820" (sold with 51001).		

Standard Gauge Classics

7E	(See 13104)		
183-185	(See 13413-3415)		
323-325	(See 13400-3402)		
390E	(See 13100)		
1115	(See 13800)		
11990	LCCA D & RG, steamer, 1990.	—	NRS
13100	"390E" 2-4-2 locomotive, 1988.	—	550
13103	Blue Comet, 1400E locomotive, 1990.	—	1000
13104	"No. 7E" 4-4-0 locomotive, brass and nickel plated, 1990.	—	N/A
13400	"323" baggage car, 1988.	—	200
13401	"324" Pullman, 1988.	—	200
13402	"325" observation, 1988.	—	200
13408	Blue Comet, set of three cars: 1420, 1421, 1422; 1990.	—	1500
13413	"183" parlor/baggage car, cream and orange, 1990.	—	250
13414	"184" parlor car, cream and orange, 1990.	—	250
13415	"185" observation car, cream and orange, 1990.	—	150
13800	"1115" passenger station, 1988.	—	300
13802	Lionel Runabout, windup speedboat, 1990.	—	450
51900	"440N" signal bridge/control panel, 1989.	—	300

Highlights of American Flyer Prewar History

In many ways, American Flyer and Lionel began business in very opposite ways. Lionel began its train production as an outgrowth of Joshua Lionel Cowen's interest in electrical models (remember, electricity was a very new concept in the early 20th century), while American Flyer introduced its trains as clockwork (windup) toys. Additionally, Lionel began with large-size trains (first 2-7/8" Gauge, then Standard Gauge) and later introduced its O Gauge line. American Flyer began with O Gauge and later added its premium Wide Gauge line to compete with Lionel's Standard Gauge.

It is generally believed that the Edmonds-Metzel Manufacturing Company began producing and selling American Flyer trains in 1927. The company was founded by William O. Coleman in partnership with John Hafner. In the 1910 catalogue, the company identified itself as the American Flyer Manufacturing Company. The company's first locomotives were O Gauge models powered by clockwork motors. It was not until 1918 or 1919 that the company built electrically-powered trains. The majority of the clockwork locomotives had cast-iron boilers, although some were made with stamped-steel bodies.

The company clearly favored passenger cars in its early days — O Gauge freight cars were not shown in the catalogue until 1910. Even then, freight sets were outnumbered by passenger sets twelve to one. Nevertheless, the company went on to produce a wide selection of freight and passenger cars. Today, the more common freight and passenger cars carry almost equal values.

American Flyer introduced electrically-powered O Gauge steam locomotives in 1918-1919 and electric-outline locomotives in 1920. The first of the new steam locomotives had cast-iron boilers with little semblance of scale, but by the late 1930s they had undergone a transition first through a phase of nicely-proportioned stamped-steel models and then into very fine die-cast models. The electric-outline locomotives produced from 1920 through 1934 resembled the most modern locomotives operating in the New England Corridor on the New York Central and New Haven railroads. These models were produced in various configurations with a variety of construction techniques: lithographed steel, enameled steel, cast-iron, and die-cast metal.

In 1925 American Flyer introduced a premium line of larger trains called Wide Gauge. Although Lionel had introduced this size (using its trademarked Standard Gauge name) in 1906, Wide Gauge did not come into its own until the early 1920s, when Lionel, Ives, American Flyer, Boucher, and Dorfan actively competed for the upper end of the market — the 1920s was a great boom time preceding the Great Depression.

American Flyer's Wide Gauge trains were widely advertised, and they were indeed very elegant. Steam locomotives were offered with cast-iron or steel bodies; electric locomotives with lithographed or enameled steel bodies. Once again showing its preference for passenger cars, Flyer introduced those in 1925 and freight cars a year later. The first year's freight cars were Lionel bodies mounted on American Flyer trucks. In 1927 Flyer introduced its own series of freight cars to complement its selection of passenger cars.

In 1929 and 1930 several Ives items crept into the product line, as American Flyer and Lionel jointly purchased the troubled firm. The result, in a simplified view, was an intermin-

Gd   Exc

gling of parts from three different product lines offered under three different trade names. However, in 1930 Lionel bought out American Flyer's part-ownership in Ives.

The Great Depression took its toll on American Flyer's sales, notably the premium Wide Gauge line. Reportedly, W. O. Coleman axed the Wide Gauge line in 1932, with remaining stock being sold until 1936. As the Wide Gauge line disappeared and the "Classic Period" of Wide/Standard Gauge ended, American Flyer focused its attention on O Gauge streamliners and the "NEW" Hudson.

In 1938 A. C. Gilbert of New Haven purchased the American Flyer line and moved it to Gilbert's Connecticut factory. In addition to the actual product line, Gilbert brought senior staff from Chicago to help with the line, which soon matured to included nicely- detailed 3/16" scale trains. Gilbert's momentum, however, was interrupted by the onset of World War II and the collateral shift of American factories from private production to war-time production.

Please note: Trains lettered "Overland Flyer" are Hafner products (see short essay near end of book), not American Flyer.

The complexity of equipment and the frequent changes to equipment as recorded [in the Greenberg Guides] are the fascinating consequence of Mr. Coleman's continual changes to his line so that a store buyer could have a train at whatever price he wanted to pay. The trains were just as confusing to our production and cost accounting departments as they are to collectors today. Si V. Chaplin, Engineer, Chicago Flyer, 1929-1938.

O Gauge Clockwork-powered Steam Locomotives

All of the clockwork locomotives have four driving wheels unless noted. Specific identification of the earliest models requires careful comparison of many criteria, which may be found in *Greenberg's Guide to American Flyer Prewar O Gauge*. It should be noted that several unmarked Hafner locomotives look similar to some of the American Flyer engines. The clockwork mechanism is different between the two manufacturers.

		Gd	Exc
c. 1907-1914	Cast-iron body, 0-4-0, with or without drive rods. The very earliest models bring higher prices, but identification is complex; wheels are lead.	250	750
c. 1916	Cast-iron body, 0-4-0, no ventilation hatch on cab roof, several sizes.	100	200
c. 1917-1921	Cast-iron body, 0-4-0, open hatch on cab roof, several sizes.	70	150
c. 1921	Cast-iron body, 0-4-0, "A.F." on cab side, open ventilation hatch on cab roof, several sizes.	70	150
c. 1921-1922	Cast-iron body, 0-4-0, open ventilation hatch on cab roof.		
	(A) No markings on cab side.	65	125
	(B) "A.F. 10" on cab side.	65	125
	(C) "A.F. 11" on cab side.	65	125
	(D) "A.F. 12" on cab side.	65	125
c. 1923-1924	Cast-iron body, 0-4-0, no ventilation hatch on roof.		
	(A) No markings on cab side.	65	125
	(B) "A.F. 13" on cab side.	65	150

	Gd	**Exc**

Here is an example of American Flyer's quaint windup locomotives of the early 20th century.

		Gd	Exc
	(C) "A.F. 16" on cab side.	100	225
c. 1925-1933	Cast-iron body, 0-4-0, no ventilation hatch on cab roof.		
	(A) No markings on cab side.	50	100
	(B) "A.F." on cab side.	50	100
	(C) "A.F. 10" on cab side.	50	100
	(D) "A.F. 14" on cab side.	75	175
c. 1933-1935	Stamped-steel body, 0-4-0, red, battery-operated headlight.	50	100
Tenders	A variety of four-wheel stamped-steel tenders were made to accompany iron and steel locomotives. Value each:	25	60

O Gauge Electrically-Powered Steam Locomotives

American Flyer produced electrically-powered steam locomotives from 1918 through 1924 and from 1929 to 1939. These locomotives were made in a variety of subtly different designs and with a chaotic numbering system. The following descriptions will help provide a basic identification of your pieces. Value of tender is included with each locomotive.

		Gd	Exc
c. 1918-1924	7-1/2" long cast-iron body, 0-4-0, open ventilation hatch on cab roof, with or without operating headlight.	100	225
c. 1930-1931	7-5/8" long cast-iron body, 0-4-0, no ventilation hatch on cab roof, body cast in two halves riveted together.	60	150
1931	Cast-iron body, 2-4-0, no ventilation hatch on cab roof, body cast in two halves riveted together.	50	125
1931-1936	Cast-iron body, 2-4-2, closed ventilation hatch on roof, one-piece body casting, eight-wheel Vanderbilt tender.		
	(A) 1931 version, visor on headlight, thin driver rims.	110	250
	(B) 1932-1936 versions, no visor on headlight, thick driver rims.	90	200
1932-1938	Cast-iron body, 2-4-2, no ventilation hatch on roof, body cast in two halves riveted together.	60	125
1932-1939	Stamped-steel body, several variations of body shape, produced in 0-4-0, 2-4-0, and 2-4-4 wheel arrangements.	25	5035

		Gd	Exc
1935	"Aeolus", streamlined locomotive-tender combination, 0-4-0 with four-wheel truck under rear, one-piece aluminum casting, 13-1/4" long.	700	1200
1936-1939	Torpedo-style streamlined locomotive, stamped-steel body with rounded contours, gray.		
	(A) 0-4-2 wheel arrangement.	50	100
	(B) 2-4-4 wheel arrangement.	60	130
1936-1938	Hudson style locomotive, die-cast body, scale-like appearance, 2-6-2 (rear truck designed to look like four-wheel model).	125	275
1936-1937	"Hiawatha", stamped-steel body, streamlined appearance, orange and beige, 4-4-2 (made to look like 4-4-4).	400	1000
1938-1939	Die-cast locomotive, scale-like appearance.		
	(A) 2-4-2 wheel arrangement.	90	175
	(B) 2-6-4 wheel arrangement.	90	175
1938-1940	Switcher, body die-cast in two halves, scale-like appearance, 0-6-0, tender has tendency to warp.	250	450
1938-1940	Atlantic, die-cast body, scale-like appearance, 4-4- 2.	350	1000
1938-1940	Pacific, die-cast body, scale-like appearance, 4-6- 2.	300	850

O Gauge Electrically-powered Electric-outline Locomotives

American Flyer produced electric-outline locomotives from 1920 through 1934. These models reproduced the real electrically-powered trains found on the railroads in the northeast corridor.

Trains in this section are arranged according to catalogue number, as many of them have brass plates, rubber-stamped numerals, or other identifying marks that correspond to these numbers.

		Gd	Exc
1090	Box cab locomotive, 0-4-0, dark orange, 6-1/2" long, 1928-29.	50	100
1093	Box cab locomotive, 0-4-0, green or red, 6-1/2" long, 1930.	50	100
1094	Box cab locomotive, 0-4-0, lithographed, red, 6-1/2" long, 1928.	50	100
1095	Box cab locomotive, 0-4-0, brown or green, 6-1/2" long, 1922-24.	50	100
1096	Box cab locomotive, 0-4-0, 1925-27.		
	(A) Green or black enamel finish, 1925.	50	100
	(B) Red or maroon lithographed body, 1926-27.	65	125
1097	Box cab locomotive, 0-4-0, lithographed, red or dark orange sides, green roof, 1929.	75	125
1101	Box cab locomotive, 0-4-0, black, c. 1924.	60	125
1196	Box cab locomotive, 0-4-0, "EMPIRE EXPRESS", lithographed, red.	70	150
1201	Steeple cab locomotive, 0-4-0, 1921-24.		
	(A) Black body.	50	100
	(B) Dark green.	65	125
1211	Steeple cab locomotive, 0-4-0, dark green.	65	125

Gd **Exc**

1201 steeple cab locomotive lettered for "AMER. FLYER LINES". Models of real electrically-powered locomotives were more popular before World War II than they are today.

1217	Steeple cab locomotive, 0-4-0, various colors: black, brown, dark green, 1920-21.	65	125
1218	Steeple cab locomotive, 0-4-0.		
	(A) Dark yellow or orange body, rubber-stamped "MOTOR 1218".	100	200
	(B) Other colors: red, green, maroon, or black.	75	150
1270	Steeple cab locomotive, black, 0-4-0.	60	125
3011	Box cab locomotive, 0-4-0, painted or lithographed finish, 1926-27.	60	125
3012	Box cab locomotive, 0-4-0, painted or lithographed finish, various colors, 1925-27.	60	140
3013	Box cab locomotive, 0-4-0, lithographed, blue, 1927.	90	200
3014	Box cab locomotive, 0-4-0, black or green, 1925-27.	90	125
3015	Box cab locomotive, 0-4-0, medium green, 1927.	70	150
3019	Box cab locomotive, 0-4-0, 1923-24.		
	(A) Black body, maroon window frames.	75	150
	(B) Dark green body, dark red window frames.	95	200
3020	Box cab locomotive, 4-4-4 or 0-4-0, 1922-25.		
	(A) Black body and window frames, 4-4-4.	175	300
	(B) Black body, 4-4-4, dark red window frames.	150	300
	(C) Green body, 4-4-4, various color window frames.	150	300
	(D) Brown/maroon body, 4-4-4, orange window trim.	160	400
	(E) Green, 0-4-0, cast-iron frame.	150	300
3100	Box cab locomotive, 0-4-0, red, 1930-33.	50	90
3103	Steeple cab locomotive, 0-4-0, red, 1930.	75	150
3105	Box cab locomotive, 0-4-0, blue, 1930-31.	75	150
3107	Box cab locomotive, 0-4-0, 1930-32.		
	(A) Medium green body.	80	140
	(B) Medium blue body.	90	175
3109	Center cab locomotive, 0-4-0, medium green body, beige frame, 1930-31.	125	375
3110	Steeple cab locomotive, 0-4-0, green, black, or red, 1928- 29.	60	125
3112	Box cab locomotive, 0-4-0, lithographed, orange, 1928-29.	60	125
3113	Box cab locomotive, 0-4-0, 1928-29.		

		Gd	Exc
	(A) Blue lithographed body.	80	175
	(B) Dark blue-painted body.	150	300
3115	Box cab locomotive, 0-4-0, two-tone blue, 1928-30, 1932-34.	90	200
3116	Center cab locomotive, 0-4-0, green and tan, 1928-29, 1931.	175	250
3117	Center cab locomotive, 0-4-0, red, 1928-29.	250	400
3185	Box cab locomotive, 0-4-0, two-tone blue, 1928-30.	175	250
3186	Center cab locomotive, 0-4-0, green and tan, 1928-29.	175	250
3187	Center cab locomotive, 0-4-0, red, 1928-32.	250	500
7010	Steeple cab locomotive, 0-4-0, medium green, 1929.	125	200
7011	Steeple cab locomotive, 0-4-0, green, 1929.	125	250

O Gauge Early Chicago and 102 O Gauge Passenger Cars

Pullman/Chicago   Three-window, four-wheel lithographed car, "PULLMAN" above windows, "CHICAGO" below windows; the three large windows are not punched out on this version.

(A) Red, white details.	200	450
(B) Blue, white details.	200	450

American Flyer/Chicago   Three-window, four-wheel lithographed car, "AMERICAN FLYER", "CHICAGO" below windows; the three large windows are punched out on this version; various colors.   **200   450**

American Flyer/Chicago   Four-window, four-wheel lithographed car, "AMERICAN FLYER" above windows, "CHICAGO" below windows; the four large windows are punched out; various multicolor schemes.   **200   450**

American Flyer/Chicago   Five-window, eight-wheel lithographed car, "AMERICAN FLYER" above windows, "CHICAGO" below windows; the five large windows are punched out; light blue.   **NRS**

American Flyer/102   Four-window, four-wheel lithographed car, "AMERICAN FLYER" above windows, "102" below windows at each end; four large windows punched out; red or dark green.   **125   250**

O Gauge 1107/1108/1120 Passenger Cars

Note: All cars are four-wheel lithographed cars. In this area there are many subtle variations far too complex to describe in this abbreviated format. Some of these subtle differences affect prices, while others merely add interest for dedicated collectors.

1107	No name, number at either end, winged-engine herald, various colors, c. 1930.	20	50
1107	American Flyer, lettered with name above windows and number at each end below windows, c. 1914-34. See also "Jefferson" cars.		
	(A) Coach, wood-grain lithography, "AMERICAN FLYER LINE" above windows, various colors.	60	150

Gd   **Exc**

One of the numerous variations of 1108 baggage car, this example is lettered for the "AMERICAN FLYER LINE". This one is ornamented with two of the "winged locomotive" heralds that American Flyer collectors recognize immediately.

		Gd	Exc
(B)	Coach, plain lithography, "AMERICAN FLYER LINE" above windows, various colors, no winged-engine herald.	20	50
(C)	Coach, plain lithography, "AMERICAN FLYER" above windows, various colors, winged-engine herald.	20	50
(D)	Coach, very plain, no lettering across top.	20	50
(E)	Observation car (with end platform), "AMERICAN FLYER LINES" above windows, various colors.	20	50
1107	Baltimore & Ohio, coach, blue, c. 1917-27.	20	50
1107	Dominion Flyer, coach, maroon, 1925.		NRS
1107	Erie, coach, red, c. 1917-27.	20	50
1107	Jefferson, coach, orange, 1927-30.	20	40
1107	Nationwide Lines, coach, various colors, 1927-30.		NRS
1107	New York Central, coach, green, 1925-27.	30	75
1107	North-Western, coach, yellow, c. 1915-24.		
	(A) Wood-grain lithography.	50	100
	(B) Plain lithography.	40	100
1107	Pennsylvania, coach, brown, "PENNSYLVANIA R.R." above windows, c. 1915-26.		
	(A) Wood-grain lithography, blue or brown.	100	200
	(B) Plain lithography, brown.	35	70
1107	Santa Fe, coach, red, 1925-27.	40	80
1107	Union Pacific, coach, green, wood-sheath lithography, 1915.	100	250
1107	Yankee Flyer Lines, coach, lithographed, dark red, black roof.	150	400
1108	AF, baggage car, "AMERICAN FLYER LINE" above windows, various "EXPRESS BAGGAGE" insignias, various colors, c. 1914-34.		
	(A) Wood-grain lithography.	100	200
	(B) Plain lithography, no winged-engine herald.	20	40
	(C) Plain lithography, winged-engine herald.	20	50
	(D) Very plain, no lettering across top.	20	40
1108	Dominion Flyer, baggage car, maroon, 1925.		NRS
1108	Nationwide Lines, baggage car, various colors, 1927-30.		NRS
1108	New York Central, baggage car, green, 1925-26.	30	75

		Gd	Exc
1108	North-Western, baggage car, c. 1915-1924.		
	(A) Wood-grain lithography.	100	250
	(B) Plain lithography.	40	100
1108	Pennsylvania, baggage car, c. 1915-1926.		
	(A) Wood-grain lithography, "PENNSYLVANIA LINE" across top, blue.	100	200
	(B) Wood-grain lithography, "PENN. LINE" across top, brown.	100	200
	(C) Plain lithography, "PENNSYLVANIA R.R." across top, brown.	35	70
1108	Union Pacific, baggage car, green, wood-sheath lithography, 1915.	100	250
1120	American Flyer, coach or observation, various colors, c. 1926- 1930.	15	35

O Gauge 6-1/2" Passenger Cars

		Gd	Exc
1103	American Flyer, coach, lithographed, winged-engine herald on side, 1917.		
	(A) Four-wheel version, various colors.	35	75
	(B) Eight-wheel version, various colors.	35	75
1104	American Flyer, four-wheel baggage car, lithographed, winged- engine herald on side, yellow, 1917.		NRS
1105	American Flyer, baggage car, lithographed, 1914.		
	(A) Eight-wheel version, "AMERICAN FLYER LINE" above windows, dark green.	35	75
	(B) Four-wheel version, "AMERICAN FLYER" above windows, winged-engine herald, yellow.	35	75
1105	Dominion Flyer, baggage car, lithographed, 1914.		
	(A) Eight-wheel, no winged-engine herald, red.	100	200
	(B) Eight-wheel, winged-engine herald, green.	100	200
	(C) Four-wheel, winged-engine herald, red.	100	200
1106	American Flyer, eight-wheel coach, lithographed.		
	(A) "AMERICAN FLYER LINE" above windows, no winged-engine herald, dark green.	30	60
	(B) "AMERICAN FLYER" above windows, winged-engine herald, blue.	75	150
1106	Dominion Flyer, eight-wheel coach, lithographed, blue or red, 1914.	100	200
1106	Union Pacific, four- or eight-wheel coach, lithographed, green.	35	75
1200	American Flyer, four- or eight-wheel baggage car, lithographed, lightning bolt herald, red or brown.	35	75
1201	American Flyer, four- or eight-wheel coach, lithographed, lightning bolt herald, red or brown.	35	75
1202	American Flyer, four- or eight-wheel baggage car, lithographed, blue.	35	75
1203	American Flyer, four- or eight-wheel coach, lithographed, lightning bolt herald, blue.	35	75
1204	American Flyer, eight-wheel baggage car, lithographed, lightning bolt herald, brown.	40	80

		Gd	Exc
1205	American Flyer, four-wheel baggage car, lithographed, lightning bolt herald, green.	35	75
1205	American Flyer, four- or eight-wheel baggage car, lithographed, three faux windows.		
	(A) Dark blue.	35	75
	(B) Brown or red.	17	35
1205	Milwaukee, eight-wheel baggage car, lithographed, three faux windows, orange, red herald.	17	35
1206	American Flyer, eight-wheel coach, lithographed, red.	17	35
1206	Milwaukee, eight-wheel coach, lithographed, orange, red herald.	17	35
1207	American Flyer, eight-wheel observation, lithographed.	17	35
1306	American Flyer, four- or eight-wheel coach, litho., various colors.	17	35
Unnumbered Cars A variety of four-wheel and eight-wheel cars were made without numbers, average value:		17	35

O Gauge Wide/Low Profile Passenger Cars

		Gd	Exc
404	American Flyer, eight-wheel Pullman, blue or red, 8-1/4", 1939.	18	30
405	American Flyer, eight-wheel observation, blue or red, 8-1/4", 1939.	18	30
3140	American Flyer, four-wheel baggage car, red, 6-1/2", 1932- 33.	17	35
3141	American Flyer, four-wheel Pullman, red or green, 6-1/2", 1930-32.	17	35
3142	AF, four-wheel observation car, red or green, 6- 1/2", 1930-32.	17	35
3541	American Flyer, four-wheel Pullman, red, 6-1/2", 1933.	20	40
3542	American Flyer, four-wheel observation car, red, 6-1/2", 1933.	20	40
3150	American Flyer, eight-wheel baggage car, 6-1/2", 1930-33.		
	(A) Green.	30	60
	(B) Violet-blue.	45	100
	(C) Orange.	25	50
3151	American Flyer, eight-wheel Pullman, various colors, 6-1/2", 1930-33.	25	50
3152	AF, eight-wheel observation car, various colors, 6-1/2", 1930-33.	30	60
3161	American Flyer, eight-wheel Pullman, green or blue, 6-1/2", 1930-33.	30	60
3162	American Flyer, eight-wheel observation car, green or blue, 6-1/2", 1930-33.	30	60
3171	American Flyer, eight-wheel Pullman, 8-1/4", 1930-38.		
	(A) Tan, green, or blue.	30	50
	(B) Red.	20	35
3172	American Flyer, eight-wheel observation car, various colors, 8-1/4", 1930-38.	30	50
3176	American Flyer, eight-wheel Pullman, tan, 8-1/4", 1931, 1937.	30	50
3177	American Flyer, eight-wheel observation car, tan, 8-1/4", 1931, 1937.	30	50
3178	American Flyer, eight-wheel Pullman, cadmium plated, 8-1/4", 1935.	300	600
3179	American Flyer, eight-wheel observation car, cadmium plated, 8-1/4", 1935.	300	600

		Gd	Exc

The 3380 "AMBASSADOR" club car.

		Gd	Exc
3180	"THE POTOMAC", eight-wheel club car, rookie tan, 8- 1/4", 1928-30.	60	100
3181	"THE POTOMAC", eight-wheel Pullman, rookie tan, 8-1/4", 1928-30.	60	100
3182	"THE POTOMAC" eight-wheel observation, rookie tan, 8-1/4", 1928-30.	60	100
3280	AF, eight-wheel club car, blue or blue-green, 9-1/4", 1928- 31.	60	125
3281	AF, eight-wheel Pullman, blue or blue-green, 9-1/4", 1928- 31.	60	125
3282	American Flyer, eight-wheel obs., blue or blue-green, 9-1/4", 1928-31.	60	125
3380	American Flyer, eight-wheel club car, red, 11", 1928-35.	75	150
3381	American Flyer, eight-wheel Pullman, red, 11", 1928-35.	75	150
3382	American Flyer, eight-wheel observation, red, 11", 1928- 35.	75	150

O Gauge "Hummer" Locomotives and Cars

		Gd	Exc
Locomotive	Four-wheel, stamped-steel model, clockwork mechanism, came with tender marked "No. 50" or "No. 513" or unmarked, 1916-25.	55	100
Pass. Cars	Stamped-steel, simple lithography.		
	(A) Marked "THE HUMMER", with or without car number.	30	45
	(B) Marked "EMPIRE EXPRESS", with or without car number.	30	60
	(C) Marked "PENNSYLVANIA LINES/500".	15	30
	(D) Marked "NEW YORK EXPRESS".	50	100
	(E) Marked "CONTINENTAL LTD.", also Canadian Nat'l herald.	45	75
American Flyer Lines	Cattle car, green, stamped-steel.	10	20
American Flyer Lines	Caboose, red, stamped-steel.	10	20
Flyer Lines	Sand car, yellow, stamped-steel.	10	20
Flyer Lines	Boxcar, yellow, stamped-steel.	10	20
513	American Flyer Line, coach, yellow or orange, stamped-steel.	10	20
515	American Flyer Line, observation car, yellow or orange, stamped-steel.	10	20

		Gd	**Exc**

O Gauge 5", 5-1/2", 6", and 6-1/2" Freight Cars

Note: The 241-series cars are unmarked and thus difficult to properly identify without experience or comparison to catalogue illustrations.

No number	Sand car, four-wheel car, brown, 5-1/2".	60	100
241	Log car, four-wheel car, no markings, black, 5-1/2".	200	250
242	Coal car, no details available, 5", 1910.		NRS
243	Boxcar, four-wheel car, lithographed, "8965/LOADED FOR AMERICAN FLYER R.R.", red or yellow, 5", 1910.	200	300
244	Oil tank car, four-wheel car, wooden tank and dome, various colors, 5", 1910.	200	300
1106	Log car, four-wheel car with load, black, 6-1/2", 1928-32.	10	25
1109	American Flyer, four-wheel sand car, 5-1/2", 1915-17.		
	(A) Red.	35	75
	(B) Light brown.	30	60
1109	E J & E, four-wheel sand car, gray, 5-1/2", 1925-32.	35	75
1109	Illinois Central, four-wheel sand car, dark green, 5-1/2", 1925-32.	35	75
1109	Lehigh Valley, four-wheel sand car, red, 5-1/2", 1925-35.	35	75
1109	Milwaukee, four-wheel sand car, orange, 5-1/2", 1925-32.	35	75
1110	Baltimore & Ohio, four-wheel boxcar, lithographed, "B. & O. 170090" on side, red, with or without doors, 5-1/2", 1916, 1918-19.	50	100
1110	Illinois Central, four-wheel boxcar, lithographed, red, with or without doors, 5-1/2", 1914-15.	50	110
1110	Morris & Company, four-wheel boxcar, lithographed, yellow, various dairy products, with or without doors, 5-1/2", 1919-35.	60	150
1111	ICRR, four-wheel caboose, lithographed, brown, 5-1/2", 1915-29.	25	50
1112	American Flyer, four-wheel boxcar, red, 6-1/2".	12	25
1112	Canadian Pacific, four-wheel boxcar, yellow, 6-1/2".	75	200
1112	NYC & HR, four-wheel boxcar, white, 6-1/2".	75	200
1112	Southern, four-wheel boxcar, dark green, 6-1/2".	75	150
1114	American Flyer, four-wheel caboose, red, 6-1/2", 1919-33.	9	25
1115	American Flyer, eight-wheel boxcar, red or orange, 6-1/2".	18	40
1115	SP, eight-wheel boxcar, dark green, 6-1/2".	75	150
1116	American Flyer, eight-wheel sand car, dark green, 6-1/2".	45	100
1116	CB & Q, four- or eight-wheel sand car, red, 6-1/2".	10	25
1116	NYC, four- or eight-wheel sand car, dark green, 6-1/2".	10	25
1116	PRR, four- or eight-wheel sand car, dark green, 6-1/2".	10	25
1117	American Flyer, four- or eight-wheel caboose, red, 6-1/2", 1919-33.	9	25
1118	American Flyer, eight-wheel tank car, gray tank, 6-1/2", 1921-29.	25	50
1119	American Flyer, four-wheel stock car, various colors, 5-1/2", 1921-24.	25	50
1127	Caboose, four-wheel caboose, red, 1935.	10	20
1128	Texaco, four-wheel tank car, red, 1935.	10	20

Gd   Exc

A boxcar full of breakfast for the "Champions" — American Flyer's Wheaties boxcar.

		Gd	Exc
1141	Log car, four-wheel car with lumber, black, 5-1/2", 1925.	25	50
1146	Log car, eight-wheel car with lumber, black, 6-1/2", 1928- 29.	9	25
1228	Sinclair, eight-wheel tank car, green and red, 1935.	10	20
3004	Caboose, four-wheel, red, 6-1/2", 1930-35.	9	25
3006	Log car, four-wheel car with lumber, black, 6-1/2", 1933-35.	9	25
3008	Tank car, four-wheel, yellow, 6-1/2", 1933-34.	9	25
3009	Dump car, four-wheel, peacock blue, 6-1/2", 1934-35.	25	40
3012	AFL, four-wheel boxcar, orange, 6-1/2", 1930-35.	9	25
3013	AFL, four-wheel sand car, green, 6-1/2", 1930-35.	9	25
3014	Caboose, four-wheel, red, 6-1/2", 1930-35.	9	25
3015	AF, eight-wheel boxcar, orange and green, 6- 1/2", 1930-38.	9	25
3016	AFL, eight-wheel sand car, green or orange, 6-1/2", 1930-38.	8	20
3017	American Flyer, eight-wheel caboose, red, 6-1/2", 1930-35.	8	20
3018	Tank car, eight-wheel, 6-1/2", 1930-38.		
	(A) Gray tank.	9	25
	(B) Yellow tank.	20	50
3019	American Flyer, eight-wheel dump car, blue-green, 6-1/2", 1934-38.	20	50
3045	American Flyer, eight-wheel crane, red, 6-1/2", 1930-31.	80	200
3046	Log car, eight-wheel car w/ lumber, black or orange, 6-1/2", 1930-35.	9	25
10001	Container car, four-wheel car with simulated container load, containers marked "10001/10002/10003/10004/10005", green and red, 1935.	10	20
311122	American Flyer, four-wheel boxcar, yellow, 1935.	10	20
311131	American Flyer, four-wheel sand car, yellow, 1935.	10	20
311267	Pennsylvania, eight-wheel hopper car, red, 1935.	10	20
Wheaties	Four-wheel boxcar, yellow, orange and blue Wheaties boxes, 1935.	50	100

O Gauge 9-1/2" Freight Cars

		Gd	Exc
406	American Flyer, log car w/ lumber, light green or orange, 9- 1/2", 1939.	6	18
407	American Flyer, sand car, light green, 9-1/2", 1939.	7	20
408	American Flyer, boxcar, light orange, peacock roof, 9-1/2", 1939.	10	30

		Gd	Exc

3208 American Flyer Lines boxcar with sliding door.

		Gd	Exc
409	Dump car, light green 9-1/2", 1939.	8	25
410	American Flyer, tank car, silver or green tank, 9-1/2", 1939- 40.	18	45
411	American Flyer, caboose, red, 9-1/2", 1939-40.	7	20
412	Milk car, white tank, 9-1/2", 1939-40.	18	40
415	American Flyer, floodlight car, silver, red, and gray, 9- 1/2".	22	50
416	Wrecker crane, yellow, red, and green, 9-1/2", 1939.	22	50
3006	American Flyer, log car, black, 9-1/2", 1924-27.	90	150
3007	Illinois Central, sand car, red-orange, 9-1/2", 1927.	75	150
3007	New York Central, sand car, dark green, 9-1/2", 1925-27.	75	150
3007	Pennsylvania, sand car, dark red, 9-1/2", 1925-27.	75	150
3007	Union Pacific, sand car, yellow, 9-1/2", 1925-26.	75	150
3008	American Refrigerator Transit, refrigerator car, yellow, 9- 1/2", 1927.	170	350
3008	Baltimore & Ohio, boxcar, brown, 9-1/2", 1925-27.	170	350
3008	Great Northern, boxcar, dark green, 9-1/2", 1925-26.	170	350
3008	Nickel Plate, boxcar, dark green, 9-1/2", 1925-27.	170	350
3010	American Flyer, tank car, gray, 9-1/2", 1925-27.	95	200
3025	American Flyer, Crane, green and red, 9-1/2", 1936-38.	17	50
3206	American Flyer, flatcar, orange, no load, 9-1/2", 1928-35.	6	15
3207	American Flyer, sand car, medium green, 9-1/2", 1928-38.	4	12
3208	American Flyer, boxcar, light orange or dark cream, peacock roof, 9-1/2", 1928-38.	5	15
3210	American Flyer, tank car, 9-1/2", 1928-38.		
	(A) Green tank.	7	20
	(B) Dark blue tank.	18	45
	(C) Yellow tank.	20	50
3212	Borden's, milk car, white tank, 9-1/2", 1936-38.	7	25
3213	Searchlight, silver, red, and gray, 9-1/2", 1938.	18	50
3216	American Flyer, log car with lumber, orange, 9-1/2", 1930- 38.	7	20
3219	American Flyer, dump car, blue body, 9-1/2", 1938.	8	25

Gd   Exc

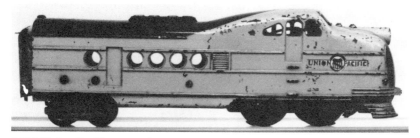

1684 Union Pacific streamline power car. The wheels on these units are often decayed.

O Gauge Streamline Trains

Burlington Zephyr equipment:

			Gd	Exc
Burlington Zephyr		Four-unit streamline train, shorter engine, 1935.	200	350
Burlington Zephyr		Five-unit streamline train, longer engine, 1935.	300	450
9910		Power car, aluminum, black lettering, 11-3/4".	75	150
9911		Baggage-Combination car, aluminum, black lettering, 9-1/2".	25	50
9912		Observation car, aluminum, black lettering, 10-1/2" long.	25	50
9913		Coach, aluminum, black lettering, 9-1/2" long.	25	50
9914		Power car, aluminum, black lettering, 13" long.	125	250

Union Pacific equipment:

			Gd	Exc
Union Pacific		Four-unit streamline train, die-cast, yellow and brown, 1936-37.	150	400
Union Pacific		Five-unit streamline train, die-cast, yellow and brown, 1938-39.	175	450
1621Y		Coach, die-cast, yellow and brown, no whistle, 12" long.	20	50
1632Y		Observation car, die-cast, yellow and brown, 14" long.	20	50
1636Y		Coach, die-cast, yellow and brown, whistle, 12" long.	30	75
1684		Power car, die-cast, yellow and brown, 13" long, excellent price requires unbroken, unwarped wheels.	60	150

Illinois Central equipment:

			Gd	Exc
9954		Coach, sheet metal, green and tan, 1935.	40	100
9955		Observation car, sheet-metal, green and tan, 1935.	40	100
9962		Power car, sheet-metal, die-cast nose, spoked driving wheels, 1935.	100	250

	Gd	Exc

Milwaukee Road Hiawatha equipment:

		Gd	Exc
Loco. w/ tender	Deluxe, die-cast, orange/maroon/gray, whistle in tender, 1936-37.	400	1000
1641	Coach, Stamped-steel, orange, maroon, and gray, 12" long, 1936-37.	50	150
1642	Observation car, Stamped-steel, orange, maroon, and gray, 12" long, 1936-37.	50	150

Streamline cars:

		Gd	Exc
1621B	Coach, blue, 12" long, 1936-37.	60	150
1621C	Coach, chrome-plated, 12" long, 1938.	60	150
1621G	Coach, green, 12" long, 1936-37.	60	150
1621R	Coach, red, 12" long, 1936-37.	55	110
1622B	Observation, blue, 13-1/2" long, 1936-37.	60	150
1622C	Observation, chrome-plated, 13-1/2" long, 1938.	60	150
1622G	Observation, green, 13-1/2" long, 1936-37.	60	150
1622R	Observation, red, 13-1/2" long, 1936-37.	55	110

Lithographed Burlington Zephyr sets:

		Gd	Exc
Three-unit Set	Power car with electric motor, coach, observation, lithographed sheet metal, 1935.	55	125
Three-unit Set	Power car with clockwork motor, coach, observation, lithographed sheet metal, 1935.	65	150
Four-unit Set	Power car with clockwork motor, two coaches, observation, lithographed sheet metal, 1935.	80	175
Five-unit Set	Power car with reversible electric motor, three coaches, observation, lithographed sheet metal, 1935.	80	175
562	Power car, lithographed, silver, black details, electric or clockwork motor.		
	(A) 10-1/2" long.	35	75
	(B) 9" long.	10	25
564	Observation car, lithographed, silver, black details, 10" long.	10	25
Comet Streamlined Train	Lithographed, blue, silver, gray, and black, includes power car, coach, trailing car, c. 1935.	150	400

Sheet Metal Hiawatha equipment:

		Gd	Exc
Passenger Set	Lithographed, sheet metal, orange, locomotive, tender, three cars.	80	175
Freight Set	Lithographed, sheet metal, orange, locomotive, tender, and cars.	80	175

		Gd	Exc

Minne-Ha-Ha sets:

816	Steam streamline set, burnt orange and silver, clockwork locomotive, two coaches, observation.	80	175
960-T	New York Central set, locomotive with built-in tender, coach, observation, 1935.	80	175
964-T	Minne-Ha-Ha set, locomotive with built-in tender, two coaches, observation, 1935.	80	175

O Gauge 9-1/2" Passenger Cars

3000	United States Mail, baggage/post office car, 9-1/2".		
	(A) Brown body and roof.	55	100
	(B) Green body and roof.	20	50
3001	Columbia, produced in two different body styles.		
	(A) Pullman, brown, 9-1/2".	55	100
	(B) Observation, brown, 9-1/2".	55	100
3001	Illini, produced in two different body styles.		
	(A) Pullman, green, 9-1/2".	55	100
	(B) Observation, green, 9-1/2".	30	75
3181	Club car, Rookie tan, green roof, "POTOMAC" or "AMERICAN FLYER", 8-1/4", 1928-30.	40	85
3181	Pullman, Rookie tan, green roof, "POTOMAC", 8-1/4", 1928-30.	40	85
3182	Observation, Rookie tan, green roof, "POTOMAC" or "AMERICAN FLYER", 8-1/4", 1928-30.	40	85
3280	Club car, blue-green, various name plates, 9-1/2", 1928-31, 1934.	45	100
3281	Pullman, blue-green, various name plates, 9-1/2", 1928-34.	45	100
3282	Observation, blue-green, various name plates, 9-1/2", 1928- 34.	45	100
3390	Club car, red, various name plates, 11", 1928-35.	65	135
3381	Pullman, red, various name plates, 11".	75	150
3382	Observation, red, various name plates, 11".	65	135

3/16" Scale Locomotives

In February 1938 the American Flyer Manufacturing Company was acquired by the A. C. Gilbert Company of New Haven, Connecticut. Apparently, Gilbert had planned to enter the toy train field and chose to do so by acquiring another company. Under Gilbert's management, American Flyer introduced a series of O Gauge trains built to a scale of 3/16" to the foot. An identifying characteristic of these trains is the presence of large link couplers.

Collectors must be careful when acquiring 3/16" scale locomotives. Many of the cast-metal parts, such as locomotive boilers, frames, etc., are subject to serious "zinc rot" or decay.

Gd   **Exc**

496 Pullman passenger car. R. Bartelt photograph.

Many of these items were offered in both kit form and ready-to-run. The kit versions are similar to those listed, but they may have a "K" item number prefix on their boxes.

		Gd	Exc
531	New York Central, steam locomotive, 4-6-4, black, 18-1/2" with twelve-wheel tender, 1940-41.	60	150
533	Union Pacific, steam locomotive, 4-8-4, black, 1940-41.	125	275
534	Union Pacific, steam locomotive, 4-8-4, black, 21-1/2" with twelve-wheel tender, 1940.	120	350
553	AFL, streamlined locomotive, 4-4-2, gun-metal gray, 17" with tender, 1940.	35	95
556	Royal Blue, streamlined loco., 4-6-2, dark blue, 17" w/tender, 1940-41.	35	85
559	Pennsylvania, steam locomotive, 4-6-2, black, 17-3/4" w/tender, 1940-41.	45	100
561	Pennsylvania, steam locomotive, 4-6-2, black, 17-3/4" w/tender, 1940-41.	45	100
564	New York Central, steam locomotive, 4-6-4, black, 1939.	75	200
565	Reading, steam locomotive, 4-4-2, black, 1941-42.	30	50
568	Union Pacific, steam locomotive, 4-8-4, black, 21-1/2" w/tender, 1939.	150	400
570	New York Central, steam loco., 4-6-4, black, 19" w/tender, 1940-41.	70	150
571	Union Pacific, steam loco., 4-8-4, black, 21-1/2" w/tender, 1940-41.	250	500
572	Union Pacific, steam loco., 4-8-4, black, 21-1/2" w/tender, 1940-41.	250	500
574	Nickel Plate, steam locomotive, 0-8-0, 14-3/4" with tender; typically operates poorly, but collectible; 1941.	375	500

3/16" Scale Rolling Stock

		Gd	Exc
444	The Royal Blue, sheet-metal, baggage car, blue.	12	30
445	The Royal Blue, sheet-metal, coach, blue.	16	30
472	Flatcar with gray Tootsietoy armored car, sheet-metal, red and black flatcar with yellow ramp, 1940-41. Note: Must have Tootsietoy for these values.	60	125
474	AFL, sheet-metal, automatic coal dump car, red, 1941.	10	35
476	AFL, sheet-metal, gondola, green, 7-5/8", 1940-41.	5	10
478	AFL, sheet-metal, boxcar, white, red roof, 7-5/8", 1940-41, 1946.	5	10
480	Tank car, sheet-metal, various colors, Shell or American Flyer markings, 7-5/8", 1940.	5	13

		Gd	Exc
481	Crane, sheet-metal; green, red, and black; 7-5/8".	16	35
482	AFL, sheet-metal, log car, green or black, 7-5/8", 1940-41.	5	15
483	AFL, sheet-metal, flatcar, black with orange girder, 7-5/8", 1941.	7	20
484	AFL, sheet-metal, caboose, red, 6-1/2", 1940-46. Add $3-4 if lighted.	3	8
486	AFL, sheet-metal, hopper, yellow, 6-1/2", 1940-41.	7	20
488	AFL, sheet-metal, floodlight car, silver and red, 7-5/8", 1940-41.	9	20
490	AFL, sheet-metal, baggage car, gun-metal gray, 10-3/4", 1940.	30	75
490B	AFL, sheet-metal, baggage car, blue, 10-3/4".	30	75
492G	AFL, sheet-metal, baggage car, dark green, 10-3/4"; includes remote-control button and special track section.	15	50
492R	AFL, sheet-metal, baggage car, red, 10-3/4"; includes remote-control button and special track section.	15	50
492T	AFL, sheet-metal, baggage car, tuscan, 10-3/4"; includes remote-control button and special track section.	25	60
494B	AFL, sheet-metal, baggage car, blue, 10-3/4".	12	30
494G	AFL, sheet-metal, baggage car, green, 10-3/4".	12	30
494R	AFL, sheet-metal, baggage car, red, 10-3/4".	12	30
494T	AFL, sheet-metal, baggage car, tuscan, 10-3/4".	15	40
495B	AFL, sheet-metal, coach, blue. Add $2-5 if lighted.	12	30
495G	AFL, sheet-metal, coach, green. Add $2-5 if lighted.	12	30
495R	AFL, sheet-metal, coach, red. Add $2-5 if lighted.	12	30
495T	AFL, sheet-metal, coach, tuscan. Add $2-5 if lighted.	13	35
496GL	AFL, sheet-metal, coach, green, lighted, 10-3/4", c. 1946.	30	90
496RL	AFL, sheet-metal, coach, red, lighted, 10-3/4", c. 1946.	30	90
496T	AFL, sheet-metal, coach, tuscan, 10-3/4".	30	90
497GL	AFL, sheet-metal, coach, green, lighted, 10-3/4".	30	90
497R	AFL, sheet-metal, coach, red, with or without lights, 10-3/4".	30	90
497T	AFL, sheet-metal, coach, tuscan, with or without lights, 10-3/4".	30	90
504	Lehigh New England, gondola, die-cast, "LNE 15503", 7-1/2", 1939-41.		
	(A) Dark gray body.	20	85
	(B) Tuscan body.	25	100
506	Baltimore & Ohio, die-cast, boxcar, brown, 7-1/2", 1939-41.	20	85
508	Virginian, die-cast, hopper, gray, 6-1/2", 1939-41.	20	85
510	Missouri Pacific, stock car, die-cast, brown, 7-1/2", 1939-41.	20	88
512	Texaco, die-cast, tank car, silver or gray, "TCX 5802", 7-1/2", 1939-41.	20	85
514	Crane, sheet-metal cab; yellow/red/green, no lettering; 7-1/2", 1939-41.	50	150
516	NYC, die-cast, caboose, red, "N.Y.C. 5160", 6-1/2".	20	75
521	Pullman, die-cast, baggage-pass. car, green or tuscan, 12", c. 1939-41.	50	200
524	Pullman, die-cast, passenger car, green or tuscan, 12", 1939-41.	50	200
5160	NYC, see 516.		
5802	Texaco, see 512.		
15503	Lehigh New England (See 504).		

Wide Gauge Electric-outline Locomotives

The 4678 electric-outline locomotive has the NYC-style body.

		Gd	Exc
4000	NYC-style locomotive, 0-4-0, 14-1/2" long, 1925-27.		
	(A) Green cab, yellow or yellow-orange window frames.	125	250
	(B) Orange cab, blue window frames.	150	300
	(C) Red cab, blue window frames.	150	350
4019	NYC-style locomotive, 0-4-0, maroon cab, 14-1/2" long, 1925-27.		
	(A) Early version, yellow-orange windows on insert with black frame, 1925.	275	600
	(B) Later versions, individual yellow-orange windows.	125	250
4039	NYC-style locomotive, 0-4-0, buff cab, 15" long, 1926.	150	325
4633	St. Paul-style locomotive, 0-4-0, red, 13-1/4" long, 1930- 31.	150	300
4635	St. Paul-style locomotive, 0-4-0, red, 13-1/4" long, 1929- 30.	125	250
4637	St. Paul-style locomotive, 0-4-0, red, r/c reverse, 15" long, 1929-33.	225	500
4643	NH-style locomotive, 0-4-0, green cab, 12" long, 1927.	100	200
4644	NH-style locomotive, 0-4-0, 12" long, 1928-33.		
	(A) Green cab, black or gray frame.	75	175
	(B) Red cab, black or gray frame.	75	175
	(C) Red cab, black frame, "NATION / WIDE / LINES" plates in place of "AMERICAN FLYER".	200	400
4644R/C	NH-style locomotive, 0-4-0, red cab, r/c reverse, 12" long, 1931-33.	100	225
4653	NH-style locomotive, 0-4-0, orange cab, 12" long, 1927.	125	250
4654	NH-style locomotive, 0-4-0, orange cab, 12" long, 1928- 31.	100	200
4667	NYC-style locomotive, 0-4-0, red cab, 15" long, 1927.	150	300
4677	NYC-style locomotive, 0-4-0, buff cab, 15" long, 1927.	150	300
4678	NYC-style locomotive, 0-4-0, two-tone red cab, 15" long, 1928-29.	175	375
4683	St. Paul-style locomotive, 0-4-0, red cab, r/c reverse, 1930-31, 1933-34.	150	325
4684	NH-style locomotive, 0-4-0, r/c reverse, 12" long, 1928-31.		
	(A) Green cab, black or gray frame.	100	200

		Gd	Exc
	(B) Red cab, black or gray frame.	100	200
	(C) Orange cab, green and gray frame.	100	200
4685	St. Paul-style locomotive, 0-4-0, red cab, r/c reverse, 13-1/4" long, 1929-30.	125	275
4686	NYC-style locomotive, 4-4-4, blue cab, 18-1/2" long, 1928- 29.	450	1000

Note: *Original examples are difficult to distinguish from less-valuable reproductions of the 4686.*

4687	NYC-style locomotive, 4-4-4, blue cab, 18-1/2" long, 1927.	275	600
4689	NYC-style locomotive, 4-4-4, 18-1/2" long, 1928-34.		
	(A) Regular production, two-tone blue.	600	1500
	(B) Chrome-plated for "Mayflower" set.		NRS

Note: *Original examples of the chrome-plated locomotives and cars from the Mayflower set are very valuable. Unfortunately, they are virtually indistinguishable from the reproductions that have been made. Inexperienced dealers or collectors should exercise extreme caution when considering the purchase or sale of a Mayflower set.*

4743	NH-style locomotive, 0-4-0, red cab, uncatalogued.		NRS
4753	NH-style locomotive, 0-4-0, red cab, uncatalogued.		NRS

Wide Gauge Steam Locomotives

4664	Ives casting engine and tender, 4-4-2, 25" long w/ 4693 Vanderbilt tender, 1930.	450	900
4672	Cast-iron engine and tender, 23" long, 1931-32.		
	(A) 2-4-2 wheel arrangement, 4671 tender.	350	550
	(B) 4-4-2 wheel arrangement, 4671 tender.	350	550
	(C) 4-4-2 wheel arrangement, 4693 tender.	450	650
4675	Die-cast engine and tender, 4-4-2, single drive rod, 24-1/2" long, 1931-32.		
	(A) "AMERICAN FLYER" brass plate on cab.	350	550
	(B) "ANNAPOLIS" brass plate on cab.	350	575
4681	Brass piper locomotive and tender, 4-4-2, r/c reverse, ringing bell, 4671 tender, 24-1/2" long, 1933-35.	500	800
4682	Die-cast engine and tender, 4-4-2, triangular valve gear, 24-1/2" long, 1933.	375	600

This 4672 steam locomotive has a 2-4-2 wheel arrangement. The same design was also produced as a 4-4-2.

		Gd	Exc
4692	Ives casting engine and tender, 4-4-2, 26" long Ives "GOLDEN STATE" coal tender.	450	800
4693	Vanderbilt tender, sold with 4664 and 4694.		
4694(A)	Ives casting engine and tender, 4-4-2, 1929-30.	550	900
4694(B)	Die-cast engine and tender, 4-4-2 triangular valve gear, 27" long, 1931-34. Add $25 for ringing bell.	400	650
4696	Brass piper locomotive and tender, 4-4-2, r/c reverse and ringing bell, 4693 tender, 27" long, 1931-35.	600	900

Wide Gauge Passenger Cars

		Gd	Exc
4040	Mail and baggage, lithographed, 14" long, 1925-27.		
	(A) Maroon sides and doors.	40	100
	(B) Red sides and doors.	40	100
	(C) Dark or olive green sides and doors.	65	150
	(D) Medium green sides and doors.	40	100
4041	Pullman, "AMERICA", lithographed, 14" long, 1925-27.		
	(A) Maroon sides and doors.	40	100
	(B) Red sides and doors.	40	100
	(C) Dark or olive green sides and doors.	65	150
	(D) Medium green sides and doors.	40	100
4042	Observation, "PLEASANT VIEW", lithographed, 14" long, 1925-27.		
	(A) Maroon sides and doors.	40	100
	(B) Red sides and roof.	40	100
	(C) Red sides, maroon roof.	40	100
	(D) Medium green sides and roof.	40	100
	(E) Dark green sides and roof.	75	250
4080	Mail and baggage car, lithographed, buff, 19" long, 1926-27.	75	160
4081	Pullman, lithographed, buff, 19" long, 1926-27.	75	160
4082	Observation, lithographed, buff, 19" long, 1926-27.	65	160
4090	Mail and baggage car, lithographed, blue, 19" long, 1927.	125	275
4091	Pullman, lithographed, blue, 19" long, 1927.	125	275
4092	Observation, lithographed, blue, 19" long, 1927.	125	275
4141	Pullman, lithographed, 14" long, 1927.		
	(A) Green sides, "AMERICA".	35	80
	(B) Orange sides, "BUNKERHILL".	40	100
	(C) Red sides, "KNICKERBOCKER".	150	250
4142	Observation, lithographed, 14" long, 1927.		
	(A) Green sides, "AMERICA" or "PLEASANT VIEW".	40	100
	(B) Orange sides, "YORKTOWN".	40	100
	(C) Red sides, "HENRY HUDSON".	150	250
4151	Pullman, lithographed, 14" long, 1928-31.		

		Gd	**Exc**

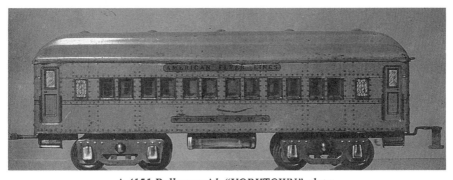

A 4151 Pullman with "YORKTOWN" plates.

		Gd	Exc
	(A) Green sides, "AMERICA".	35	80
	(B) Orange sides, various name plates.	40	100
	(C) Red sides, "EAGLE".	40	100
	(D) Green sides, "EAGLE".	40	100
4152	Observation, lithographed, 14" long, 1928-31.		
	(A) Green sides, "PLEASANT VIEW" or "EAGLE".	35	80
	(B) Orange sides, various name plates.	40	100
	(C) Red sides, "EAGLE".	40	100
4250	Club car, "LONE SCOUT", litho., bluish-green, 14" long, 1929-31.	60	130
4251	Pullman, "LONE SCOUT", litho., bluish-green, 14" long, 1929-31.	60	130
4252	Observation, "LONE SCOUT", litho., bluish-green, 14" long, 1929-31.	60	130
4331	Pullman, enameled, 14" long, 1931-36.		
	(A) Red body and roof.	40	100
	(B) Red body, dark red roof.	50	125
4332	Observation, enameled, 14" long, 1931-36.		
	(A) Red body and roof.	40	100
	(B) Red body, dark red roof.	50	125
4340	Club car, enameled, 14" long, 1928-32.		
	(A) Rookie tan, green roof.	75	175
	(B) Red body and roof.	70	150
	(C) Red body, darker red roof.	70	150
4341	Pullman, enameled, 14" long, 1928-32.		
	(A) Rookie tan, green roof.	75	175
	(B) Red body, dark red roof.	70	150
4342	Observation, enameled, 14" long, 1928-32.		
	(A) Rookie tan, green roof.	75	175
	(B) Red body, dark red roof.	70	150
4343	Dining car, enameled, Rookie tan, green roof, 14" long, 1928-32.	90	190
4350	Club car, enameled, bluish-green, 14" long, 1931.	50	120
4351	Pullman, enameled, bluish-green, 14" long, 1931.	50	120
4352	Observation, enameled, bluish-green, 14" long, 1931.	50	120

		Gd	Exc

All of the cars in the 4380/4390 series have been reproduced and are very difficult to tell from originals.

4380	Club car, enameled, 19" long, 1928-29, 1931-32.		
	(A) Dark blue sides.	200	450
	(B) Rookie tan sides.	200	450
4381	Pullman, enameled, 19" long, 1928-29, 1931-32.		
	(A) Dark blue sides.	200	450
	(B) Rookie tan sides.	200	450
4382	Observation, enameled, 19" long, 1928-29, 1931-32.		
	(A) Dark blue sides.	200	450
	(B) Rookie tan sides.	200	450
4390	Club car, enameled, 19" long, 1928-34.		
	(A) Two-tone blue.	300	600
	(B) Chrome-plated for Mayflower set.	500	1000
4391	Pullman, enameled, 19" long, 1928-34.		
	(A) Two-tone blue.	300	600
	(B) Chrome-plated for Mayflower set.	500	1000
4392	Observation, enameled, 19" long, 1928-34.		
	(A) Two-tone blue.	300	600
	(B) Chrome-plated for Mayflower set.	500	1000
4393	Diner, enameled, 19" long, 1928-34.		
	(A) Two-tone blue.	300	600
	(B) Chrome-plated for Mayflower set.	500	1000

Wide Gauge Freight Cars

4000	Flatcar, see 4012.		
4000	Caboose, see 4011.		
4005	Stock car, Lionel 13 body, green, 1926.	75	175
4006	Hopper, red, 14" long, 1931-36.	150	350
4007(A)	Rock Island, sand car, Lionel 12 body, gray, 1926.	75	175
4007(B)	American Flyer, sand car, maroon, 14" long, 1927.	75	175
4008(A)	CM & St P, boxcar, Lionel #14 body, orange, 1926.	75	175
4008(B)	American Flyer, boxcar, light orange, 14" long, 1927.	100	300
4010	Tank car, 14" long, 1928-36.		
	(A) Cream tank, blue frame.	100	225
	(B) Similar to (A), with "AIR SERVICE" decal.	225	450
	(C) Blue tank and frame.	225	450
4011(A)	NYC & HR, caboose, Lionel 17 body, red, black roof, 1926.	75	175
4011(B)	American Flyer, caboose, 14" long, 1927-32.		
	(A) Yellow sides, tan roof.	85	275
	(B) Red sides, dark red roof.	40	125
4012	Flatcar, blue, brass plates, 14" long, 1928-36.	125	250

Gd   **Exc**

4011(B) American Flyer caboose.

		Gd	Exc
4017	Sand car (gondola), 14" long, 1928-36.		
	(A) Green body, black frame.	30	60
	(B) Green body and frame.	30	60
	(C) Orange body and frame.	40	80
	(D) Maroon body, black frame.	85	250
4018	Automobile car, Rookie tan, 14" long, 1928-36.	90	200
4020	Stock car, Rolls Royce two-tone blue, 14" long, 1928-36.	90	200
4021	Caboose, red sides, dark red roof, 14" long, 1928-36.	75	150
4022	Machinery car, orange, five stakes per side, 14" long, 1928- 33.	30	70
4023	Log car, orange, rectangular wood load, 14" long, 1934-36.	45	90
4677	Sand car (see 4017).		
4677	Automobile car (see 4018).		
4677	Caboose (see 4021).		

Highlights of American Flyer Postwar History

While American Flyer's prewar history is that of a Chicago toy maker, the postwar history definitely belongs to A. C. Gilbert. Born in 1884 in Salem, Oregon, Gilbert was an energetic young man who excelled in athletics and in the performance of magic tricks. In fact, he helped fund his education in medicine at Yale University by performing magic demonstrations at parties.

In 1909 Gilbert set himself up in business in a rented shed near New Haven and began in earnest to manufacture and sell boxed magic tricks. From these humble beginnings the Mysto Manufacturing Company was born. Although Mysto did comparatively well selling the tricks, it was the introduction of Erector sets in 1912 (for the Christmas season) that launched the company. By 1915 the Erector and Mysto Magic lines had grossed three-quarters of a million dollars and had earned a net profit of $100,000. The following year the company was renamed the A. C. Gilbert Company.

In 1916 Gilbert co-founded the Toy Manufacturers Association with Harry Ives. At the time Gilbert's employees numbered approximately 1000, and he sought Congressional aid via an increased duty on foreign imports that would, in turn, spur further sales of American toy goods.

At the 1937 Toy Manufacturers Association meeting, A. C. Gilbert made arrangements with Chicago Flyer's W. O. Coleman, Jr. (son of the company's founder) that led to Gilbert's purchase of that company. In 1938 Gilbert moved Flyer production and at least a couple of key employees to the New Haven plant. The onset of World War II provided a somewhat convenient break. Gilbert had wanted to compete with Lionel by introducing a new gauge but feared repercussions from his existing customer base. The war provided a three-year hiatus in which American Flyer engineers could develop a distinctive new line for the train-hungry public.

With a staff of creative individuals and enthusiasts at work, the first postwar American Flyer trains rolled off the production line in 1946. Reasonably well scaled at 3/16" to the foot, the trains were heavily promoted and well received.

Gilbert's management excelled at getting publicity for its products. One large display layout was created exclusively for use on television shows. It featured two controls — a fake, handheld control for a show's host, and an active control used by an American Flyer employee carefully hidden from view! American Flyer trains appeared on the Dave Garroway Show (now The Today Show), The Price Is Right, Top Dollar, and American Bandstand with Dick Clark. Annual sales reached $17 million in the mid-1950s.

Numerous changes, both within the company and throughout the marketplace, began to undermine Gilbert's success in the late 1950s. Foremost was the advent of the chain discount store, such as Korvette's and Two-Guys from Harrison. These companies required low-cost merchandise that would be sold in a self-service environment without the benefit of knowledgeable salesmen or elaborate displays. Additionally, 1958 brought with it a severe recession and the end of retail price maintenance. Essentially, the traditional outlets for toy trains — privately-owned shops and toy departments in retail stores — were driven out of the toy train business.

Gd   Exc

Following the inevitable retirement of the company's founder, son A. C. Gilbert, Jr. was appointed president. But it was a case of too little too late. Although bright and articulate, A. C., Jr. lacked the drive and ambition his father had imparted on the company. In the face of a rapidly-changing marketplace, he simply could not turn the tides. Company sales skidded lower each year — all the way down to $10.7 million in 1962, with a loss of $5.7 million.

In 1962 Jack Wrather, president of a West Coast holding company that owned the Lassie and Lone Ranger television shows and a variety of other properties, purchased a 52 percent interest in Gilbert for $4 million and then replaced their senior staff with his own men. Under new management, the company made several attempts to recapture sales — including television promotions, new packaging, and gimmicky new products but ultimately failed. Finally, Gilbert went out of business in 1967.

Subsequent to Gilbert's failure, Lionel purchased the American Flyer trademark and tooling. Then, in 1969, Lionel itself ceased toy train production and licensed both the Lionel and American Flyer lines to Fundimensions, which a few years later sold off the license.

Today, a limited selection of new American Flyer trains is offered in each year's Lionel catalogue. American Flyer enthusiasts tend to be very dedicated — devoted to the underdog who never quite became the number one toy train producer. To some, the sale of American Flyer trains by Lionel is a great irony, perhaps even a bitter pill. To others, it is a welcome reflection of A. C. Gilbert's ingenuity.

S Gauge Trains

		Gd	Exc
Buffalo Hunt	Gondola, green, white lettering, 1963.	3	8
G. Fox & Co.	Boxcar, brown, white lettering, 1947.*		NRS
Freight Ahead	Caboose, red, white lettering.	2	5
20	(See 24720)		
30	(See 24730)		
40	(See 24740)		
50	(See 24750)		
55	(See (240)55)		
65	(See (245)65)		
88	(See (210)88)		
234	(See (21)234)		
282	CNW, steam, 4-6-2, black, white lettering, 1952-53.	15	45
283	CNW, steam, 4-6-2, black, white lettering, 1954-57.	15	45
285	CNW, steam, 4-6-2, black, white lettering, 1952.	25	90
287	CNW, steam, 4-6-2, black, white lettering, 1954.	15	45
289	CNW, steam, 4-6-2, black, white lettering, 1956.	60	160
290	American Flyer, steam, 4-6-2, black, white lettering, 1949- 51.	20	45
293	AF New Haven, steam, 4-6-2, black, white lettering, 1953-58.	20	60
295	American Flyer, steam, 4-6-2, black, white lettering, 1951.	30	85
296	American Flyer, steam, 4-6-2, black, white lettering, 1951.	50	190

		Gd	**Exc**

The 293 Pacific is lettered for both the "New Haven" (in fancy script) and for "AMERICAN FLYER LINES."

		Gd	Exc
299	AF Reading, steam, 4-4-2, black, white lettering, 1954.	45	100
300	AF Reading, steam, 4-4-2, black, white lettering, 1946-47, 1952.	10	30
300AC	AF Reading, steam, 4-4-2, black, white lettering, 1949-50.	15	30
301	AF Reading, steam, 4-4-2, black, white lettering, 1946-47, 1953.	10	30
302	AF Reading, steam, 4-4-2, black, white lettering, 1948, 1951- 53.	10	30
302AC	AF Reading, steam, 4-4-2, black, white lettering, 1948, 1951-52.	10	30
303	AF Reading, steam, 4-4-2, black, white lettering, 1954-56.	10	35
307	AF Reading, steam, 4-4-2, black, white lettering, 1954-57.	7	20
308	American Flyer, steam, 4-4-2, black, white lettering, 1956.	15	50
310	Steam, 4-6-2, black, silver lettering, "PENNSYLVANIA" or "AMERICAN FLYER LINES" on tender, 1946-47.	20	60
312	American Flyer / PRR, steam, 4-6-2, black, silver lettering, 1946, 1948, 1951-52.	30	85
312AC	American Flyer / PRR, steam, 4-6-2, black, white lettering, 1949-51.	30	85
313	American Flyer / PRR, steam, 4-6-2, black, white lettering, 1955-56.	40	120
314AW	American Flyer / PRR, steam, 4-6-2, black, white lettering, 1949-50.	70	185
315	American Flyer / PRR, steam, 4-6-2, black, white lettering, 1952.	40	135
316	American Flyer PRR, 4-6-2, black, white lettering, 1953-54.	40	130
320	New York Central, steam, 4-6-4, black, silver lettering, 1946-47.	40	100
321	New York Central, steam, 4-6-4, black, silver lettering, 1946-47.	75	150
322	New York Central, steam, 4-6-4, black, silver lettering, 1946-50.	40	95
322AC	New York Central, steam, 4-6-4, black, white lettering, 1949-50.	40	95
324AC	New York Central, steam, 4-6-4, black, white lettering, 1950.	45	110
325AC	New York Central, steam, 4-6-4, black, white lettering, 1951.	45	125
K325	New York Central, steam, 4-6-4, black, white lettering, 1952.	40	120
326	New York Central, steam, 4-6-4, black, white lettering, 1953-56.	40	125
332	Union Pacific, steam, 4-8-4, black; silver or white lettering, 1946-49.	75	240
332AC	Union Pacific, steam, 4-8-4, black, white lettering, 1950- 51.	80	250
332DC	Union Pacific, steam, 4-8-4, black, white lettering, 1950.	100	300
334DC	Union Pacific, steam, 4-8-4, black, white lettering, 1950.	100	350
K335	Union Pacific, steam, 4-8-4, black, white lettering, 1952.	100	250
336	Union Pacific, steam, 4-8-4, black, white lettering, 1953-56.	90	260

Gd   Exc

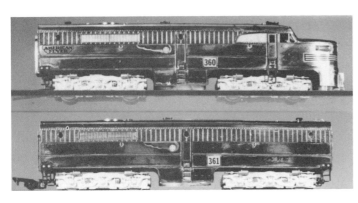

The 360 Santa Fe diesel is an Alco PA unit. The 361 is a dummy (nonpowered) PB unit with chrome finish.

		Gd	Exc
342	Nickel Plate Road, steam, 0-8-0, black, 1946-48, 1952.	80	225
342AC	Nickel Plate Road, steam, 0-8-0, black, white lettering, 1949-51.	65	85
342DC	Nickel Plate Road, steam, 0-8-0, black; silver or white lettering, 1948-50.	60	190
343	Nickel Plate Road, steam, 0-8-0, black, white lettering, 1953-58.	60	200
346	Nickel Plate Road, steam, 0-8-0, black, white lettering, 1955.	110	375
350	The Royal Blue, streamlined, 4-6-2, blue, white lettering, 1948-50.	35	85
353	American Flyer Circus, streamlined, 4-6-2, red, yellow lettering, 1950-51.	50	225
355	Chicago Northwestern, diesel switcher, green and yellow, 1956-57.	40	85
356	Silver Bullet, streamlined, 4-6-2, chrome, yellow and blue decals, 1953.	30	125
360	Santa Fe, Alco PA unit, 1950-52.		
	(A) With 361 dummy, chrome finish.	80	200
	(B) With 361 dummy, silver-painted finish.	70	150
	(C) With 364 dummy, silver-painted finish.	50	120
370	GM American Flyer, GP-7 diesel, silver; red, yellow, and blue lettering, 1950-53.	50	130
371	GM American Flyer, GP-7 diesel, dummy, silver, 1954.	60	130
372	Union Pacific, GP-7 diesel, yellow and gray, red trim, 1955-57.		
	(A) "BUILT BY GILBERT" on side.	75	165
	(B) "MADE BY AMERICAN FLYER" on side.	80	200
374/375	Texas & Pacific, GP-7 diesel and dummy, orange and black, 1955.	150	350
375	GM American Flyer, GP-7 diesel, silver; blue, yellow, and red lettering, beware of fakes, 1953.	300	1000
377/378	Texas & Pacific, GP-7 diesel and dummy, orange and black, 1956-57.	150	375
405	Silver Streak, Alco PA, chrome, red or yellow stripe, 1952.	60	150
466	Comet, Alco PA, 1953-55.		
	(A) Chrome-plated body.	50	175
	(B) Silver-painted body.	50	135
467	Comet, Alco PB, silver-painted body, beware of fakes, 1955.*		NRS
470/471/473	Santa Fe, Alco PA/PB/PA, 1953-57.		

		Gd	Exc
	(A) Chrome-finished shells.	120	350
	(B) Silver-painted shells, "CHIEF" nose decal.	100	275
	(C) Silver-painted, "SANTA FE" nose decal.	120	280
472	Santa Fe, Alco PA, silver, red, yellow, and black, 1956.	75	175
474/475	Rocket, Alco PA powered and dummy, green and yellow trim, 1953-55.		
	(A) Chrome-finished shells.	100	275
	(B) Silver-painted shells.	80	225
476	Rocket, Alco PB, forest green, yellow and silver, 1955.*		NRS
477/478	Silver Flash, Alco PA and PA, chocolate brown and orange trim, 1953-54.		
	(A) Chrome-finished shells.	120	400
	(B) Silver-painted shells.	120	350
479	Silver Flash, Alco PA diesel, silver, chocolate brown, and orange, 1955.	60	200
480	Silver Flash, Alco PB diesel, with diesel horn and roar, 1955.*		NRS
484/485/486	Santa Fe, Alco PA/PB/PA, blue, yellow, and black, 1956.	300	750
490/491/493	Northern Pacific, Alco PA/PB/PA, two-tone green, white trim, 1956.	300	750
494/495	New Haven, Alco PA powered and dummy, two-tone green, white trim, 1956.	150	450
497	New Haven, Alco PA diesel, black, orange and white trim, 1957.	80	225
499	New Haven, GE electric, black, orange and white trim, 1956- 57.	150	400
500	American Flyer, combine car, black lettering, 1952.		
	(A) Silver finish.	100	425
	(B) Chrome finish.	75	300
501	American Flyer, coach, silver finish, black lettering, 1952.	125	425
502	American Flyer, Vista Dome, black lettering, 1952.		
	(A) Silver finish.	100	425
	(B) Chrome finish.	75	300
503	American Flyer, observation, silver finish, black lettering, 1952.	100	425
605	American Flyer, flatcar with log load, gray, 1953.	5	20
606	American Flyer, crane, gray or blue base, yellow cab, 1953.	10	30
607	American Flyer, work caboose, gray base, brown cab, 1953.	5	20
613	Great Northern, boxcar, brown, white lettering, 1953.	7	20
620	Southern, black, white lettering, 1953.	6	20
622	GAEX, boxcar, green, yellow lettering, 1953.	7	20
623	Illinois Central, reefer, orange, dark green lettering, 1953.	6	12
625	Shell, tank car, 1946-51.		
	(A) Orange, "CAPACITY 8000" pounds (not "80000").*	300	500
	(B) Orange, "CAPACITY 80000".*	300	500
	(C) Black, silver lettering, "8000".	7	15
	(D) Silver, black lettering, "80000".	5	12

		Gd	Exc
	(E) Silver, black lettering, "100000".	5	10
625G	Gulf tank car, silver, orange logo, 1951-53.	5	13
627	American Flyer, gray flatcar w/ orange bridge girder, 1950.	5	15
627	C & NW, gray flatcar w/ orange bridge girder, 1946-50.	6	15
(628)	C & NW, flatcar w/ six logs, 1946-53.		
	(A) Gray pressed wood base (number does not appear on car).	5	35
	(B) Gray plastic or die-cast car.	5	15
	(C) White plastic frame.	5	20
629	Missouri Pacific, stock car, silver lettering, 1946-53.		
	(A) Red.	5	12
	(B) Maroon.	6	18
630	Reading, caboose, red, white or silver lettering.	3	8
630	American Flyer, caboose, red, white lettering.	4	6
631	Texas & Pacific, gondola, various colors, 1946-53.		
	(A) Dark green.	2	5
	(B) Dark gray.	30	75
	(C) Red.	25	50
(632)	Virginian, hopper, 1946.		
	(A) Gray or steel blue.	20	60
	(B) Cream.		NRS
632	Lehigh New England, hopper, white lettering, 1946-53.		
	(A) Gray, solid red dot in logo.	2	5
	(B) Gray, no red dot in logo.	25	85
	(C) Black, no red dot in logo.	25	85
633	Baltimore & Ohio, boxcar, 1946-53.		
	(A) White, brown roof and ends, black lettering.	7	15
	(B) Brown, white lettering.	6	12
	(C) Red, white lettering.	6	15
633	Baltimore & Ohio, reefer, 1952.		
	(A) Red, white lettering.	20	75
	(B) Brown, white lettering.	25	85
634	C & NW, floodlight car, 1946-49, 1953.		
	(A) Black lamp housing.	10	15
	(B) Silver lamp housing.	10	20
635	C & NW, crane, gray base, yellow cab, 1946-48.	9	25
(635)	C & NW, crane, gray base, yellow or red cab, 1948-49.		
	(A) Light yellow cab with chrome stack.	10	30
	(B) Red cab with chrome stack.	50	250
636	Erie, depressed-center reel car, gray, 1948-53.		
	(A) Die-cast metal frame.	6	20
	(B) Pressed-wood frame.	35	275
637	MKT, boxcar, yellow, black lettering, 1949-53.	6	20

		Gd	Exc

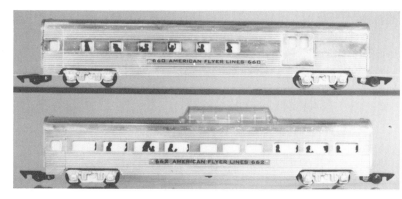

The 660 baggage car (top) and the 662 Vista Dome (bottom). The Vista Dome has a clear center section to provide panoramic views for miniature travelers.

No.	Description	Gd	Exc
638	American Flyer, caboose, red, white lettering.	2	4
639	American Flyer, boxcar, 1949-52.		
	(A) Yellow or mustard, black lettering.	4	8
	(B) Brown, white lettering.	15	45
639	American Flyer, reefer, black lettering, 1949-52.		
	(A) Yellow.	4	8
	(B) Cream (ivory) unpainted body.	30	125
640	American Flyer, hopper, 1949-53.		
	(A) Gray, white lettering.	2	5
	(B) Gray, black lettering.	3	6
	(C) White, black lettering.	15	50
640	Wabash, black, white lettering, 1953.	6	20
641	Frisco, brown, white lettering, 1953.	5	15
642	American Flyer, boxcar, 1951-52.		
	(A) Red, white lettering.	4	8
	(B) Brown, white lettering.	4	8
642	American Flyer, reefer, 1952.		
	(A) Red.	4	8
	(B) Brown.	5	10
642	Seaboard, boxcar, brown, white lettering, 1953.	6	11
(643)	American Flyer Circus, flatcar w/ two wagons and one trailer, 1950-53.		
	(A) Car with two wagons, one trailer, and wooden block loads. (Reproductions available)	45	150
	(B) Car only.	3	8
644	American Flyer, crane, gray base, red or black cab, 1950-53.	15	40
645	American Flyer, work caboose, gray base, red cab, brown or yellow stake sides.	7	20
645A	American Flyer, work caboose, gray base, red or brown cab, brown or yellow stake sides.	6	20
(646)	Erie, gray-painted base, 1950-53.		
	(A) Green die-cast generator, chrome or silver lamp housing.	25	150
	(B) Green or red plastic generator, chrome or silver lamp housing.	10	20

		Gd	Exc
647	Northern Pacific, reefer, orange sides, tuscan roof and ends, three-color logo, 1952-53.	10	30
648	American Flyer, track cleaning car, red or brownish-red, 1952- 54.	5	20
649	American Flyer Circus, coach, yellow, red lettering, 1950-52.	20	75
650	New Haven, Pullman, green or red, 1946-53.	10	35
651	New Haven, baggage, green or red, 1946-53.	10	35
652	Pullman, passenger car, 1949-53.		
	(A) Green, "PULLMAN".	20	85
	(B) Dark olive green, "PULLMAN".	20	150
	(C) Polished red, "PULLMAN".	20	85
	(D) Green, "PIKES PEAK".	20	95
	(E) Red, "PIKES PEAK".	25	95
653	Pullman, combine car, green or red, 1946-53.	20	85
654	Pullman, observation car, green or red, 1946-53.	20	85
655	Silver Bullet, coach, blue and gold decals, 1953.		
	(A) Chrome finish.	15	100
	(B) Satin aluminum finish.	15	75
655	American Flyer, green, red, or white, 1953.	20	45
660	American Flyer, baggage car, 1950-52.		
	(A) Extruded aluminum body.	20	40
	(B) Chrome-finished plastic body.	20	60
661	American Flyer, Pullman, 1950-52.		
	(A) Extruded aluminum body.	20	40
	(B) Chrome-finished plastic body.	20	60
662	American Flyer, Vista Dome, 1950-52.		
	(A) Extruded aluminum body.	20	40
	(B) Chrome-finished plastic body.	20	60
663	American Flyer, observation car, extruded aluminum, 1950-52.	20	40
0700	National Association S-Gaugers, boxcar, orange, white lettering, 1981.	—	40
714	Log unloading car, black, gray platform, 1951-54.	12	35
715	American Flyer, auto unloading car, black frame, red and yellow superstructure, 1946-54.		
	(A) With Tootsietoy armored car.	15	45
	(B) With Manoil coupe.	12	40
	(C) With Tootsietoy race No. 7.	12	40
716	American Flyer, red, black lettering, 1946-51.	8	20
717	American Flyer, log unloading car, black, yellow superstructure, three logs, 1946-52.	8	40
718	American Flyer, mail car, green or red, 1946-54.	20	45
719	CB & Q, coal dump car, black, base, 1950-54.		
	(A) Maroon body.	15	60
	(B) Red body.	10	75
732	American Flyer, operating baggage car, 1951-54.		

		Gd	Exc

The 936 Pennsylvania flatcar has a depressed center to provide clearance for the large load when the car passes through a tunnel or under a bridge.

		Gd	Exc
	(A) Green or red unpainted plastic.	20	50
	(B) Green-painted plastic.	20	75
734	American Flyer, operating boxcar, red or brown, white number, 1950-54.	10	35
735	Animated station coach, included with 776 animated station, red or maroon, 1952-54.		
736	Missouri Pacific, stock car, tuscan or red, white lettering, 1954.	7	25
(740)	Handcar, orange, two men with blue shirts, 1952-54.	10	50
741	Handcar and shed, includes 740 handcar and toolshed, must have original box, 1953.	30	125
(742)	Handcar, with reversing mechanism, orange, two men in blue shirts, 1955-56.	30	100
801	Baltimore & Ohio, hopper, black, white lettering, 1956-57.	8	15
802	Illinois Central, reefer, orange, dark green lettering, 1956- 57.	5	10
803	ATSF, boxcar, tuscan, white lettering, 1956-57.	10	20
804	N & W, gondola, black, white lettering, 1956-57.	5	10
805	Pennsylvania, gondola, tuscan, white lettering, 1956-57.		
	(A) Tuscan unpainted plastic.	3	8
	(B) Tuscan-painted plastic.	6	20
806	American Flyer, caboose, red, white lettering, 1956-57.	2	4
807	Rio Grande, boxcar, white, black lettering, red "Cookie Box", 1957.	7	20
812	(See (21)812)		
900	Northern Pacific, combine car, two-tone green, white trim, 1956-57.	100	275
901	Northern Pacific, coach, two-tone green, white trim, 1956-57.	100	275
902	Northern Pacific, Vista Dome, two-tone green, white trim, 1956-57.	100	275
904	American Flyer, caboose, red, white lettering, 1956.	3	7
905	American Flyer, flatcar with six logs, 1954.		
	(A) Gray base.	5	30
	(B) Blue base.	10	40
906	American Flyer, crane, yellow cab, 1954.		
	(A) Gray base.	10	30

		Gd	Exc
	(B) Blue base.	12	35
907	American Flyer, gray base, tuscan cab, 1954.	6	20
909	American Flyer, flatcar with orange bridge girder, 1954.		
	(A) Gray base.	5	30
	(B) Blue base.	10	40
910	Gilbert Chemical, green and yellow, dark green lettering, 1954.	45	150
911	Chesapeake & Ohio, black, white lettering, 1955-57.		
	(A) Six silver pipes.	5	25
	(B) Six brown pipes.	25	100
912	Koppers, black, orange or yellow lettering, 1955-56.	10	40
913	Great Northern, boxcar, tuscan, black and white lettering, 1953-58.	10	25
914	American Flyer, log unloading car, black with gray or silver bin, 1953-57.	10	45
915	American Flyer, auto unloading car, black or gray, Tootsietoy racer or Renwal gasoline truck, 1953-1956.	10	55
916	Delaware & Hudson, tuscan, white lettering, five canisters, 1955-56.	7	15
918	Mail car, 1953-58.		
	(A) Maroon or red, "AMERICAN FLYER".	25	60
	(B) Red, "NEW HAVEN".	25	70
919	CB & Q, coal dump car, black, white lettering, 1953-56.	15	50
920	Southern, black, white lettering, 1953-56.	5	20
921	CB & Q, coal dump car, black, white lettering, 1953-56.	5	20
922	GAEX, boxcar, green, yellow lettering, 1953-57.	10	30
923	Illinois Central, reefer, orange, dark green lettering, 1954- 55.	7	15
924	CRP, covered hopper, gray, black lettering, 1953-56.	6	15
925	Gulf, silver, orange logo, 1953-56.	3	12
926	Gulf, silver, orange logo, 1955-56.	10	30
928	New Haven, lumber car with four blocks of wood, black, 1956- 57.	5	15
929	Missouri Pacific, stock car, red or tuscan, white lettering, 1953-56.	6	20
930	American Flyer, caboose, red or brown, white lettering.	9	40
931	Texas & Pacific, green, white lettering, 1953-55.	3	7
933	Baltimore and Ohio, boxcar, white, brown roof and ends, black lettering, 1953-54.	10	35
934	American Flyer, caboose, red, white lettering.	10	35
934	C & NW, searchlight, gray base, black superstructure, silver lamp housing.	10	20
934	Southern Pacific, searchlight, brown base, black superstructure, silver lamp housing.	10	30
935	American Flyer, brown, white lettering, 1957.	10	55
936	Erie, depressed-center flatcar with cable reel, gray, 1953- 56.	6	25
936	Pennsylvania, depressed-center flatcar with cable reel, tuscan, 1953-57.	15	65
937	MKT, boxcar, yellow or yellow and brown, black lettering, 1953- 58.	8	30
938	American Flyer, caboose, red, white lettering.	2	4

	Gd	Exc

The 948 track cleaning car is a handy accessory on an S Gauge layout!

		Gd	Exc
940	Wabash, hopper, black, white lettering, 1953-56.	5	20
941	Frisco Lines, gondola, tuscan, white lettering, 1953-56.	4	10
942	Seaboard, boxcar, tuscan, white lettering, 1954.	7	20
944	American Flyer, crane, gray or green base, black cab, 1952-56.	15	40
945	American Flyer, work caboose, gray base, tuscan cab, red toolbox, 1953-57.	10	25
946	Erie, depressed-center floodlight car, gray base,1953-56.		
	(A) Red or green generator.	10	25
	(B) Yellow generator.	10	30
947	Northern Pacific, reefer, orange sides, brown roof and ends, three-color logo, 1953-58.	10	30
948	American Flyer, track cleaning car, tuscan, 1953-56.	7	20
951	American Flyer, baggage, green or red, 1953-57.	15	40
952	American Flyer, Pullman, green or red, 1953-58.	25	125
953	American Flyer, baggage and club car, green or red, 1953-58.	25	125
954	American Flyer, observation, green or red, 1953-56.	25	150
955	American Flyer, coach, 1954-55.		
	(A) Satin silver-finish.	25	65
	(B) Green or tuscan.	20	50
	(C) Red.	20	60
956	Monon, gray piggyback car, two red, white, and blue trailers, 1956.	15	55
957	Erie, operating boxcar, tuscan, black and white lettering, 1957.	20	95
958	Mobilgas, red, white lettering, 1957.	10	55
960	Columbus, combine car, 1953-56.		
	(A) Silver or chrome finish, with or without color band.	25	70
	(B) Satin silver finish with chestnut-color band.	35	110
961	Jefferson, Pullman, 1953-58.		
	(A) Silver or chrome finish, with or without color band.	25	70
	(B) Satin silver finish, chestnut-color band.	60	150
962	Hamilton, Vista Dome, 1953-60.		
	(A) Silver or chrome finish, with or without color band.	25	70
	(B) Satin silver finish, chestnut-color band.	35	110

		Gd	Exc
963	Washington, observation car, 1953-58.		
	(A) Silver or chrome finish, with or without color band.	25	70
	(B) Satin silver finish, chestnut-color band.	35	110
969	Rocket launcher, black car, red, white, and blue rocket, 1957.	10	45
970	Seaboard, operating boxcar, tuscan, red and white logo, 1956- 57.	15	50
971	Southern Pacific, lumber unloading car, tuscan, eight pieces of lumber, 1956.	25	100
973	Gilbert's Milk, operating boxcar, white, black lettering, 1956- 57.	30	45
974	American Flyer, operating boxcar, tuscan, white lettering, 1953-54.	20	65
974	Erie, operating boxcar, tuscan, white lettering, 1955.	30	100
975	Animated station coach, came with K766 animated station, dark red, 1955.	20	65
976	Missouri Pacific, operating stock car, tuscan, white lettering, 1953-62.	10	40
977	American Flyer, caboose, brown, white lettering, 1955-57.	8	30
978	Grand Canyon, action car, tuscan, 1956-58.	75	200
979	American Flyer, caboose, brown, yellow lettering, 1957.	10	75
980	Baltimore & Ohio, boxcar, blue, orange band, decal, 1956-57.	25	100
981	Central of Georgia, boxcar, black and silver, 1956.		
	(A) Shiny black paint.	30	85
	(B) Dull black paint.	35	125
982	State of Maine, boxcar, red, white, and blue, 1956-57.	20	70
983	MP Eagle, boxcar, blue, gray, and yellow, 1956-57.	20	100
984	New Haven, boxcar, red, black and white lettering, 1956-57.	20	65
985	BM, boxcar, blue, black door, black and white lettering, 1957.	20	75
988	American Refrigerator Transit, orange sides, silver roof and ends, 1956.	15	65
989	Northwestern, green and yellow, multicolor lettering/decals, 1956-58.	30	125
994	Union Pacific, stock car, yellow, silver roof, red lettering, 1957.	25	150
C1001	White's Discount Center, boxcar, yellow, red lettering, 1962.		NRS
C2001	Post, boxcar, white, orange logo, 1962.		
	(A) With "Hayjector" mechanism.	30	120
	(B) Without mechanism.	10	55
L2001	Casey Jones Game Train, steam, 4-4-0, black, white lettering, 1963.	5	15
L2002	Burlington Route, steam, 4-4-0, black, white lettering, 1963.	125	200
L2004	Rio Grande, F-9 diesel, red, white trim, 1962.	50	160
C2009	Texas & Pacific, green, white lettering, 1962-64.	4	8
2300	Oil drum loader, accessory, 1986-88.	—	85
2321	Operating saw mill, accessory, 1986-88.	—	89
5300T	Miners Work Train, handcar with three tipple cars, 1953-54.*	80	225
8007	(See 48007 diesel)		
8100/8101	(See 48100/8101)		

		Gd	Exc
8150/8152	Southern Pacific, twin Alco PA diesels, red, orange, and black, 1981.	—	250
8151	Southern Pacific, Alco PB unit with horn, 1981.	—	85
8153/8154/8155	Baltimore & Ohio, Alco PA/PB/PA diesels, blue and gray, yellow trim, 1981, 1983.	—	250
8251/8253	Erie, twin Alco PA diesels, two-tone green, yellow trim, 1982.	—	200
8252	Erie, Alco PB unit with horn, 1982.	—	85
8305	(See 48305 flatcar)		
8308	(See 48308 boxcar)		
8350	Boston and Maine, GP-7 diesel, blue, black, and white, 1983.	—	250
8458	Southern, GP-9 diesel, green and white, gold trim, 1985.	—	150
8459	B & O / Chessie, GP-20 diesel, yellow, orange, and blue, 1985.	—	225
8551	Santa Fe, GP-20 diesel, blue and yellow, yellow lettering, 1986.	—	225
8552	New York Central, GP-9 diesel, black, gray and white striping, 1986.	—	200
8706	(See 48706 caboose)		
8805	(See 48805 reefer)		
9000	B & O, gray flatcar with (2) blue and orange vans, 1981, 1983.	—	25
9001	(See 49001 searchlight)		
9002	Boston and Maine, yellow flatcar with six logs, 1983.	—	50
9004	Southern, dark green flatcar with (2) silver vans, 1985.	—	20
9005	New York Central / MDT, green flatcar with (2) silver vans, 1986.	—	27
9100	Gulf, tank car, white, orange lettering, 1979.	—	40
9101	Union 76, tank car, black, orange and white lettering, 1980.	—	20
9102	Baltimore & Ohio, tank car, yellow, black lettering, 1981, 1983.	—	20
9104	Boston and Maine, tank car, brown, white lettering, 1983.	—	50
9105	Southern, tank car, silver, black lettering, 1985.	—	20
9106	New York Central, tank car, black, white lettering, 1986.	—	25
9200	Baltimore & Ohio / Chessie, hopper, black, yellow lettering, 1979.	—	40
9201	Baltimore & Ohio, covered, hopper, blue and gray, yellow lettering, 1981, 1983.	—	20
9203	Boston and Maine, hopper, silver, black and white logo, 1983.	—	50
9204	Southern, hopper, gray, red lettering, 1985.	—	15
9205	Pennsylvania, covered, hopper, tuscan, white lettering, 1985.	—	15
9206	New York Central, covered hopper, gray, black lettering, 1985.	—	15
9207	Baltimore & Ohio, covered hopper, gray, white lettering, 1986.	—	25
9208	Santa Fe, covered hopper, tuscan; black and white logo, 1986.	—	21
9209	New York Central, hopper, brown, white lettering, 1986.	—	21
9300	Burlington, gondola, green, white lettering, 1980.	—	10
9301	Baltimore & Ohio, gondola, black, five gray containers, 1981, 1983.	—	20
9303	Southern, gondola, black, five red containers, 1985.	—	15
9304	New York Central, gondola, brown, five gray containers, 1986.	—	21
C-9400	Baltimore & Ohio / Chessie, caboose, yellow, silver roof, blue lettering, 1979.	—	20
C-9401	Baltimore & Ohio, caboose, red, black roof, white lettering, 1981, 1983.	—	25

		Gd	Exc
9402	B & M, caboose, blue, black roof, black and white lettering, 1983.	—	50
X9403	Southern, caboose, red, silver roof, white lettering, 1985.	—	20
9404	New York Central, caboose, dark red, black roof, white lettering, 1986.	—	31
9405	Santa Fe, caboose, red, black roof, yellow lettering, 1986.	—	31
9500	Southern Pacific, combine car, red and orange, white trim, 1981.	—	75
9501	Southern Pacific, coach, red and orange, white trim, 1981.	—	100
9502	Southern Pacific, Vista Dome, red and orange, white trim, 1981.	—	75
9503	Southern Pacific, observation, red and orange, white trim, 1981.	—	75
9504	Erie, combine car, two-tone green, yellow trim, 1982.	—	50
9505	Erie, Pullman, two-tone green, yellow trim, 1982.	—	75
9506	Erie, Vista Dome, two-tone green, yellow trim, 1982.	—	75
9507	Erie, observation car, two-tone green, yellow trim, 1982.	—	50
9700	AT & SF, boxcar, red, white lettering, 1979.	—	40
9701	The Rock, boxcar, blue; black and white lettering, 1980.	—	20
9702	Baltimore & Ohio, boxcar, blue and silver, multicolor logo, 1981.	—	25
9703	Boston and Maine, boxcar, blue, black door, black and white lettering, 1983.	—	50
9704	Southern, boxcar, brown, white lettering, 1985.	—	20
9705	Pennsylvania, boxcar, brown, white lettering, 1985.	—	25
9706	New York Central, boxcar, red and gray, white lettering, 1985.	—	20
9707	Rail Box, boxcar, yellow, red and blue logo, 1985.	—	25
9708	Conrail, boxcar, blue, white lettering, 1985.	—	20
9709	Baltimore and Ohio, boxcar, silver, black lettering, 1986.	—	25
9710	ATSF, boxcar, brown; black and white lettering, 1986.	—	25
9711	Southern Pacific, boxcar, silver; orange and black lettering, 1986.	—	25
9712	Illinois Central, boxcar, orange; black and white lettering, 1986.	—	25
9713	New York Central, green, black ends, multicolor lettering, 1986.	—	25
21004	American Flyer / PRR, steam, 0-6-0, black, white lettering, 1957.	100	225
21005	American Flyer / PRR, steam, 0-6-0, black, white lettering, 1957-58.	100	275
21084	Chicago Northwestern, steam, 4-6-2, black, white lettering, 1957.	35	95
(210)88	Franklin, steam, 4-4-0, green, black, red, and yellow, 1959.	40	75
(21089)	Washington, steam, 4-4-0, blue and gold, red trim, 1960- 61.	60	175
21095	New Haven, steam, 4-6-2, black, white lettering, 1957.		NRS
21099	New Haven, steam, 4-6-2, black, white lettering, 1958.	75	225
21100	Reading, steam, 4-4-2, black, white lettering, 1957.	7	20
21105	Reading, steam, 4-4-2, black, white lettering, 1957-58.	7	20
21106	Reading, steam, 4-4-2, "MADE FOR SEARS" on tender, black; white lettering, 1964.	40	100
21107	Steam, 4-4-2, black, white lettering, various names on tenders, 1964.	10	30
21115	American Flyer / PRR, steam, 4-6-2, black, white lettering, 1958.	100	450
21129	New York Central, steam, 4-6-4, black, white lettering, 1958.	100	700

Gd   **Exc**

One of the most beautiful paint schemes in railroading —real or model —is the two-tone green scheme once used by the Northern Pacific, which advertised itself as the "Main Street of the Northwest."

		Gd	Exc
21130	New York Central, steam, 4-6-4, black, white lettering, 1959- 60, 1962-63.	70	225
21139	Union Pacific, steam, 4-8-4, black, white lettering, 1958- 59.	150	450
21140	Union Pacific, steam, 4-8-4, black, white lettering, 1960.	180	1000
21145	Nickel Plate Road, steam, 0-8-0, black, white lettering, 1958.	150	400
21155	Dockside switcher, steam, black, white lettering, no tender, 1958.	75	200
21156	Dockside switcher, steam, black, white lettering, no tender, 1959.	60	165
21158	Dockside switcher, steam, blue, white lettering, 1959.	30	85
21160	Reading, steam, 4-4-2, black, white lettering, 1958-60.	10	20
21161	Reading, steam, 4-4-2, black, white lettering, 1960.		
	(A) Only "AMERICAN FLYER LINES" on tender.	7	20
	(B) "PRESTONE CAR CARE EXPRESS" also on tender.	40	120
21165	American Flyer, steam, 4-4-0, black, white lettering, various names on tender, 1961-62.	7	15
21166	Burlington Route, steam, 4-4-0, black, white lettering, 1963- 64.		
	(A) "Burlington Route" in white on tender.	5	15
	(B) "Burlington Route" in black letters on white field.	80	175
21168	Southern, steam, 4-4-0, black, white lettering, 1961-63.	15	30
21205/21205-1	Boston and Maine, F-9 powered and dummy, blue, white trim, 1961.	70	170
21206/21206-1	Santa Fe, F-9 powered and dummy, red, white trim, 1962.	80	180
21207/21207-1	Great Northern, F-9 powered and dummy, orange, green trim, 1963-64.	90	170
21210	Burlington, F-9 diesel, red, white trim, 1961.	40	150
21215/21215-1	Union Pacific, F-9 powered and dummy, yellow, gray and red trim, 1961-62.	70	180
(21)234	Chesapeake & Ohio, GP-7 diesel, blue, yellow trim, 1961- 62.	125	350
(21514)	(See 470)		
21551	Northern Pacific, two-tone green, white trim, 1958.	125	350
(21552/21556)	Northern Pacific, Alco PA powered and dummy, two-tone green, white trim, 1957.	150	375
(21560)	(See 497)		

		Gd	Exc
21561	New Haven, Alco PA, black, orange and white trim, 1957-58.	80	225
(21570)	(See 499)		
(21571)	(See 499)		
21573	New Haven, GE electric, black, orange and white trim, 1958- 59.	150	400
21720	Santa Fe, Alco PB, blue, yellow, and black, 1958.	250	900
21801	Chicago Northwestern, "355" on side. (See 355)		
21801	Chicago Northwestern, diesel switcher, green and yellow, "21801" on side, 1957-58.	50	120
21801-1	Chicago Northwestern, dummy switcher, green and yellow, 1958.	60	150
21808	Chicago Northwestern, diesel switcher, green and yellow, 1958.	40	90
(21)812	Texas & Pacific, diesel switcher, black and orange, 1959- 60.	70	150
21813	M St. L, diesel switcher, red, white trim, 1958.	150	450
(21821)	See 372)		
21831	Texas & Pacific, GP-7 diesel, black and orange, 1958.	150	200
(21908)	(See 377 and 378)		
21910/21910-1/21910-2	Santa Fe, Alco PA/PB/PA; blue, yellow, and black, 1957-58.	250	550
21918/21918-1	Seaboard, diesel switcher, black; red and yellow trim, 1958.	150	350
21920/21920-1	Missouri Pacific, Alco PA powered and dummy, silver and blue, yellow trim, 1958.	250	700
21920	Missouri Pacific, Alco PA diesel, silver and blue, yellow trim, 1963-64.	150	450
21922/21922-1	Missouri Pacific, Alco PA powered and dummy, silver and blue, yellow trim, 1959.	200	600
21925/21925-1	Union Pacific, Alco PA powered and dummy, yellow and gray, red trim, 1959-60.	200	600
21927	Santa Fe, Alco PA, silver and red, yellow and black trim, 1960-62.	150	250
23743	Track maintenance car, yellow, black trim, man with turquoise shirt.	50	110
24003	ATSF, boxcar, tuscan, white lettering, 1958.	15	45
24016	MKT, boxcar, yellow sides, brown roof, 1958.	150	600
24019	Seaboard, boxcar, tuscan, white lettering, 1958.	15	35
24023	Baltimore & Ohio, boxcar, dark blue, orange band, decal, 1958-59.	30	150
24026	Central of Georgia, boxcar, black and silver, 1958.	30	125
24029	State of Maine, boxcar; red, white, and blue, 1957-60.	35	125
24030	MKT, boxcar, yellow, black lettering, 1958.	10	20
24033	MP Eagle, boxcar, blue, gray, and yellow, 1958.	40	110
24036	New Haven, boxcar, orange; black and white lettering, 1958.	20	75
24039	Rio Grande, boxcar, white; black and red lettering, 1959.	10	30
24043	BM, boxcar, blue and black, black and white lettering, 1958- 60.	25	80
24045	Maine Central, boxcar, dark green, yellow lettering.		NRS
24047	Great Northern, boxcar, red, white lettering, 1959.	50	200
24048	M St L, boxcar, red, white lettering, 1959-62.	40	100
24052	United Fruit Growers, boxcar, various colors, 1961.	5	10

Gd **Exc**

The utilitarian 24203 B & O coal hopper.

		Gd	Exc
24054	Santa Fe, red, white lettering, 1962-64.	10	40
(240)55	The Gold Belt Line, boxcar, yellow and red.	12	45
24056	BM, boxcar, blue and black, black and white lettering, 1961.	25	110
24057	Mounds, boxcar, red lettering, 1962.		
	(A) White.	5	10
	(B) Ivory.	7	20
24058	Post, boxcar, white or ivory, red lettering, 1963-64.	5	10
24059	BM, boxcar, blue, black and white lettering, 1963.	40	160
24060	M St L, boxcar, red, white lettering, 1963-64.	30	110
24065	New York Central, boxcar, green, white lettering, 1960-64.	30	60
24066	Louisville & Nashville, boxcar, blue, yellow lettering, 1960.	50	150
(24067)	Keystone, boxcar, orange, black lettering, 1960.*		NRS
24068	Planters Peanut, boxcar, white, red and blue lettering, 1961.*		NRS
24069	Olney Bologna, refrigerator, white, green and black lettering, 1961.	4	8
24076	Union Pacific, stock car, yellow, silver roof and ends, red lettering, 1957-60.	12	40
24077	Northern Pacific, stock car, red, silver roof and ends, multicolor logo, 1959-62.	60	160
24103	Norfolk & Western, gondola, black, white lettering, 1958, 1963-64.	4	10
24106	Pennsylvania, gondola, tuscan, white lettering, 1960.	4	8
24109	Chesapeake & Ohio, gondola, black, white lettering, six pipes, 1957-60.		
	(A) Silver plastic pipes.	6	25
	(B) Silver cardboard pipes.	6	35
	(C) Brown plastic pipes (reproductions available).	20	100
	(D) Orange cardboard pipes.	20	50
24110	Pennsylvania, gondola, tuscan, white lettering, 1959.	4	8
24113	Delaware & Hudson, gondola, brown, white lettering, silver and gray containers, 1957-59.	7	30
24116	Southern, gondola, black, white lettering, 1957-60.	10	30
24120	Texas & Pacific, gondola, dark green, white lettering, 1960.	10	25
24124	Boston and Maine, gondola, blue, white lettering, 1963-64.		
	(A) Aqua blue.	3	5

		Gd	Exc
	(B) Dark blue.	9	18
24125	Bethlehem Steel, gondola, gray, 1960-64.		
	(A) Light gray unpainted plastic, no load, red or orange lettering.	4	8
	(B) Medium or light gray-painted, two small rail holders and four T-rails in car, red lettering.	20	85
24126	Frisco, gondola, tuscan, white lettering, 1961.	20	100
24127	Monon, gondola, light gray, dark red lettering, 1961-65.	5	10
(24130)	Pennsylvania, gondola, brown, white lettering, 1960.	4	8
24203	Baltimore & Ohio, hopper, black, white lettering, 1958, 1963-64.	5	20
24206	CB & Q, hopper, brown, white lettering, 1958.	15	50
24209	CRP, covered hopper, gray, black lettering, 1957-60.	15	50
24213	Wabash, hopper, black, white lettering, 1958-60.	10	25
24216	Union Pacific, hopper, tuscan, yellow lettering, 1958-60.	12	40
24219	Western Maryland, hopper, tuscan, white lettering, 1958-59.	15	50
24221	Chicago & Eastern Illinois, hopper, gray, red lettering, 1959-60.	25	75
24222	Domino Sugars, covered hopper, yellow, black lettering, 1963-64.*	50	150
24225	Santa Fe, hopper, red, white lettering, 1960-65.	6	25
24230	Peabody, hopper, cream, green lettering, 1961-64.	12	30
24309	Gulf, tank car, silver, orange logo, 1957-58.	6	20
24310	Gulf, tank car, silver, orange logo, 1958-60.	8	20
24313	Gulf, tank car, silver, orange logo,		
24316	Mobilgas, tank car, red, white lettering, 1956-61, 1965-66.	5	20
24319	Pennsylvania Salt, tank car, blue, red and yellow lettering, 1958.*	125	350
24320	Deep Rock, tank car, black, yellow lettering, 1960.	100	260
24321	Deep Rock, tank car, black, yellow lettering, 1959.	10	40
24322	Gulf, tank car, silver, black lettering 1959.	10	40
24323	Baker's Chocolate, tank car, white, Baker's lady in brown and white dress, 1959-60.		
	(A) White ends, "SINCE 1780" in red-printed band.		NRS
	(B) Gray ends, "SINCE 1780" on red sticker.	50	160
24324	Hooker, tank car, orange and black, 1959-60.	18	55
24325	Gulf, tank car, silver, orange logo, 1960.	5	15
24328	Shell, tank car, yellow, red lettering, 1962-66.	5	10
24329	Hooker, tank car, orange, white lettering, 1964-65.	10	25
(24329)	Hooker, tank car, orange, with or without black band, 1961- 65.	10	20
24330	Baker's Chocolate, tank car, white, black and brown lettering, 1961-62.	15	45
24403	Illinois Central, orange, dark green lettering.	7	15
24409	Northern Pacific, orange, brown roof and ends.	200	1000
24413	American Refrigerator Transit, orange, silver roof, 1957- 60.	25	70
24416	Northwestern, green and yellow, multicolor lettering/decal, 1958.	350	1200
24419	Canadian National, gray, dark red lettering, green leaf, 1958- 59.	50	200
(24420)	Simmons Carload Bargains Sale, orange, black lettering, 1958.*		NRS

Gd   **Exc**

The unusual 24619 American Flyer Lines caboose has both a cupola and a bay window.

		Gd	Exc
24422	Great Northern, boxcar, light green, white lettering, 1963- 65.	35	120
24422	Great Northern, reefer, green, white lettering, 1963-66.		
	(A) Plug door.	4	9
	(B) Opening door.	20	85
	(C) Plug door, two-tone green.	40	175
24425	BAR, reefer, orange; red, white, and blue trim, 1960.	75	350
24426	Rath Packing, reefer, orange, multicolor logo, 1960-61.	75	350
24516	New Haven, lumber car, black, four-piece load, 1957-59.	7	20
24519	Pennsylvania, depressed flatcar with cable reel, tuscan, 1958.		NRS
24529	Erie, searchlight, gray base, yellow generator, 1957-58.	10	30
24533	American Flyer, track cleaning car, brown, 1958-66.	6	15
24536	Monon, gray piggyback car; two red, white, and blue trailers, 1958.		NRS
24537	New Haven, flatcar with three pipes, black, 1958.	15	45
24539	New Haven, flatcar with three pipes, black, 1958-59, 1963- 64.	10	30
24540	New Haven, flatcar with three pipes, black, 1960.		NRS
24543	American Flyer, crane, gray base, black cab, 1958.	10	30
24546	American Flyer, work caboose, gray base, tuscan shed, yellow and brown stake sides, 1958-64.		
	(A) "AMERICAN FLYER" only.	6	25
	(B) "AMERICAN FLYER LINES".	10	30
24547	Erie, floodlight car, brown base, yellow generator, 1958.		NRS
24549	Erie, floodlight car, brown base, 1958-66.		
	(A) Yellow generator, die-cast lamp brackets, silver light.	10	20
	(B) Red generator, silver light.	20	50
	(C) Yellow generator, steel lamp brackets, various housing colors.	5	10
24550	Monon, gray piggyback car, two red, white, and blue trailers, 1959-64.	12	55
24553	Rocket Transport, olive drab car with two red, white, and blue rockets, 1958-60.	15	75
24556	Rock Island, black car, four axles as a load, 1959.	13	45
24557	US Navy, flatcar, gray with black superstructure, two olive drab Tootsietoy jeeps, 1959-61.	25	85

		Gd	Exc
24558	Canadian Pacific, black flatcar with four Christmas trees, 1959-60.		
	(A) Trees: fiber material on metal wire.	30	175
	(B) Trees: rubber.	30	175
	(C) Car only, no trees.	5	25
24559	New Haven, flatcar without load, black, 1959.		NRS
24561	American Flyer, crane, gray base, black cab.	10	25
24562	New York Central, flatcar without load, black, 1960.	12	35
(24564)	New Haven, flatcar with three pipes, black, 1960.	10	35
(245)65	FY & PRR, cannon car, yellow, spoked-wheel cannon (reproductions available), 1960-61.	50	125
24566	New Haven, auto transport car, black; blue or red tractor, silver trailer with five autos, 1961-64.	15	40
24566	National Car Co., auto transport car, black, white truck with five autos, 1961-65.	15	45
24569	American Flyer, crane, gray base, black cab.	7	15
24572	US Navy, gray flatcar with two red or olive drab jeeps, 1961.	40	125
24574	US Air Force, rocket fuel transport, blue and red, silver tanks, 1960-61.	20	70
24575	National Car Co., milk container car, black, white tanks, 1960-66.	7	30
(24575)	Unlettered black milk car, two white Borden's tanks, 1966.	4	30
24577	Illinois Central, jet engine transport, black, silver containers, 1960-61, 1963-64.	10	65
24578	New Haven, Corvette transport car, black frame, unassembled Corvette kit, 1962-63.	50	250
24579	Illinois Central, tuscan and red, silver tanks, 1960-61.	20	75
24603	American Flyer, caboose, red, white lettering.	1	3
24610	American Flyer, caboose, red, white lettering.	1	3
24619	American Flyer, caboose, brown, yellow lettering, 1958.	10	65
24626	American Flyer, caboose, yellow, silver roof and ends, red stripe, black lettering.	3	7
24627	American Flyer, caboose, red, white lettering.	2	4
24630	American Flyer, caboose, red, white lettering.	1	3
24631	American Flyer, caboose, yellow, silver roof and ends, red stripes, black lettering.	3	15
24632	American Flyer, caboose, yellow, silver roof and ends, red stripes, black lettering.	15	50
24633	American Flyer, silver, red lettering, 1959-62.	10	55
24634	American Flyer, caboose, red, 1963-66.	8	40
24636	American Flyer, caboose.		
	(A) Red, white lettering.	1	3
	(B) Yellow, silver roof and ends, red stripe, black lettering.	200	300
24638	American Flyer, caboose, silver.	8	55
(247)20	FY & PRR, frontier-type coach, yellow, 1959-61.	15	45
(247)30	FY & PRR, frontier-type baggage car, yellow, 1959-60.	15	45

	Gd	Exc

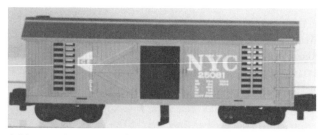

Add some fun to your layout with the 25081 NYC operating boxcar. Notice the activating mechanism visible at bottom.

		Gd	Exc
(247)40	FY & PRR, frontier-type combine car, yellow, 1960.	15	45
(247)50	FY & PRR, frontier-type combine car, red, 1960-61.	30	85
24773	Columbus, combine car, aluminum finish, 1957-58, 1960-62.	30	125
24776	Columbus, combine car, orange stripe, 1959.	40	110
24793	Jefferson, Pullman, aluminum finish, 1957-58, 1960-62.	30	125
24794	American Flyer, Pullman, aluminum finish, 1959.		
	(A) "JEFFERSON", red stripe.		NRS
	(B) "WASHINGTON", orange stripe.	40	110
24796	Jefferson, Pullman, aluminum finish, orange stripe, 1959.	40	110
24813	Hamilton, Vista Dome, aluminum finish, red stripe, 1957-58, 1960-62.	40	125
24816	Hamilton, Vista Dome, aluminum finish, orange stripe, 1959.	40	110
24833	Washington, observation car, aluminum, red stripe, 1957-58, 1960-62.	20	125
24836	Washington, observation car, aluminum, orange stripe, 1959.	40	125
24837	Union Pacific, combine, yellow and gray, red trim, 1959-60.	100	275
24838	Union Pacific, Pullman, yellow and gray, red trim, 1959-60.	100	275
24839	Union Pacific, Vista Dome, yellow and gray, red trim, 1959- 60.	100	275
24840	Union Pacific, observation car, yellow and gray, red trim, 1959-60.	100	275
24843	Northern Pacific, combine, two-tone green, white trim, 1958.	80	175
24846	Northern Pacific, Pullman, two-tone green, white trim, 1958.	80	175
24849	Northern Pacific, Vista Dome, two-tone green, white trim, 1958.	80	175
24853	Northern Pacific, observation car, two-tone green, white trim, 1958.	80	175
24856	Eagle Hill (Missouri Pacific), combine, silver, blue, and yellow, 1958, 1963-64.*		
	(A) Blue stripe extends through narrow passenger door.	125	300
	(B) Blue stripe ends at edge of passenger door.	100	275
24859	Eagle Lake (Missouri Pacific), coach, silver, blue, and yellow, 1958, 1963-64.*		
24863	Eagle Creek (Missouri Pacific), coach, silver, blue, and yellow, 1958, 1963-64.*		
	(A) Blue stripe extends through passenger doors.	125	300

		Gd	Exc
	(B) Blue stripe ends at edge of passenger doors.	100	275
24866	Eagle Valley (Missouri Pacific), observation car, silver, blue, and yellow, 1958, 1963-64.		
	(A) Blue stripe extends through passenger doors.	125	300
	(B) Blue stripe ends at edge of passenger doors.	100	275
24867	American Flyer, combine, silver finish, red stripe, 1958, 1960.	50	150
24868	American Flyer, observation car, silver finish, red stripe, 1958, 1960.	50	150
24869	American Flyer, coach, silver finish, red stripe, 1958, 1960.	50	150
25003	American Flyer, log unloading car, black base, aluminum bin, four logs, 1957-60.	20	75
25016	Southern Pacific, lumber unloading car, tuscan, black superstructure, 1957-60.	20	85
25019	Gilbert's Milk, operating boxcar, white, black lettering, 1957-60.	40	125
25025	CB & Q, dump car, black, white lettering, 1958-60.	35	130
25042	Erie, operating boxcar, brown; black and white logo, 1958.	40	150
25045	Rocket launcher, black, tuscan toolbox; red, white, and blue rocket, 1957-60.	12	55
25046	Rocket launcher, black car; red, white, and blue rocket, 1960.	15	60
25049	Rio Grande, operating boxcar, white; black and red lettering, 1958-60.	40	225
25052	American Flyer, caboose, silver, 1958.	15	75
(25056)	USM, two-car operating boxcar and rocket launcher set, both yellow, 1959.	70	350
25057	TNT, exploding boxcar, black, silver roof, yellow and red lettering, 1960.	30	200
25058	Southern Pacific, lumber loading car, tuscan, black superstructure, 1961-64.	20	85
25059	Rocket Launcher, black car; red, white, and blue, 1960-62.	10	50
25060	CB & Q, dump car, black, white lettering, 1961-64.	45	150
25061	TNT, exploding boxcar, black; yellow and red lettering, 1961.	35	250
25062	Mine Carrier, exploding boxcar, yellow sides, brown or silver roof, red and black lettering, 1962-64.	40	300
25071	American Flyer, tie car, brown bin sides, 1961-64.	7	20
25081	New York Central, operating boxcar, light green, white lettering, 1961-64.	10	35
25082	New Haven, operating boxcar, black and white lettering, 1961- 64.	10	35
25301	American Flyer, caboose, brown, white lettering.		NRS
25515	USAF, rocket transport, black car, yellow, red, and blue rocket, 1960-64.	35	125
42597	(See 634)		
48000	Southern Pacific, GP-20 diesel, gray, orange, and white, 1987.	—	180
48001	Illinois Central, GP-20 diesel, white and orange, brown lettering, 1987.	—	180
48002	Southern Pacific, GP-9 dummy, gray, orange, and white, 1988.	—	140
48003	Santa Fe, GP-9 dummy, blue and yellow, 1988.	—	140

		Gd	Exc
48004	Chessie, GP-9 dummy, yellow, orange, and blue, 1988.	—	140
48007	Burlington Northern, GP-20 diesel, green and black, 1990.		NA
48100/8101	Wabash, twin Alco PA diesels, light gray, blue, and white, 1988.	—	225
48300	Southern Pacific, boxcar, black, multicolor lettering, 1987.	—	23
48301	Denver & Rio Grande, boxcar, yellow and silver, black lettering, 1987.	—	23
48302	Canadian Pacific, boxcar, silver, red lettering, 1987.	—	23
48303	Chessie, boxcar, yellow, blue lettering, 1987.	—	23
48304	Burlington Northern, boxcar, green, white lettering, 1987.	—	23
48305	Wabash, boxcar, brown, red and white logo, 1988.	—	23
48305	Illinoic Central Gulf, flatcar with bulkheads, 1990.		NA
48306	Seaboard Coast Line, boxcar, light yellow, red door, 1988.	—	23
48307	Western Pacific, boxcar, brown, yellow lettering, red feather, 1988.	—	23
48308	Maine Central, boxcar, dark green, yellow lettering, 1990.		NA
48400	Southern Pacific, tank car, black, white lettering, 1987.	—	25
48500	Southern Pacific, gondola, brown, five gray containers, 1987.	—	20
48501	Southern Pacific, brown flatcar with (2) white trailers, 1987.	—	26
48502	Wabash, dark blue flatcar with two dark blue trailers, 1988.	—	26
48503	Wabash, gondola, black, five white canisters, 1988.	—	20
48600	Southern Pacific, hopper, brown, white lettering, 1987.	—	20
48601	Union Pacific, covered hopper, gray, red lettering, 1987.	—	20
48602	Erie, covered hopper, black, yellow and white logo, 1987.	—	20
48603	Wabash, hopper, gray, black lettering, 1988.	—	20
48604	Milwaukee Road, covered hopper, white, black lettering, 1988.	—	20
48605	Burlington Northern, light gray, black lettering, 1988.	—	20
48700	Southern Pacific, caboose, brown, silver roof, yellow lettering, 1987.	—	30
48701	Illinois Central, caboose, orange, brown lettering, 1987.	—	30
48702	Wabash, caboose, red, white lettering, 1988.	—	30
48703	Union Pacific, caboose, white, black roof, red lettering, 1988.	—	30
48706	Burlington Northern, caboose; green, yellow and silver, 1990.		NA
48800	Wabash, reefer, red, white lettering, 1988.	—	23
48801	Union Pacific, reefer, yellow, red lettering, 1988.	—	23
48802	Pennsylvania, reefer, brown, yellow lettering, 1988.	—	23
48805	National Dairy, reefer, red and silver, 1990.		NA
49001	NYC, operating serachlight car, 1990.		NA
49600	Union Pacific set, twin Alcos and five cars, 1990.		NA

Note: Prices on new 1990 items not available at press time. Consult your hobby shop for current prices.

Highlights of Marx History

When a collector refers to "Marx," he or she may be referring to the toys, the trains, the company, or the man behind the company, for they are all closely related. Louis Marx, a self-made millionaire and son of German immigrants, stands out as one of the figureheads in American toy history.

Born August 14, 1896 in Brooklyn, New York, Marx graduated from high school at age fifteen. Aspiring to earn a considerable salary, Marx began his career in 1912 as an office boy for toy-maker Ferdinand Strauss. Within four years, he became manager of Strauss' East Rutherford, New Jersey plant.

In 1917 Marx joined the Army as a private. Before returning to civilian life in 1918, he attained the rank of sergeant. Of the many military toys Marx eventually produced most represented Army prototypes. Marx became a salesman for a Vermont wood products company, where he caused an astronomical boost in sales, before forming his own corporation, Louis Marx & Company, Inc., with his brother David in 1919. The two became middlemen offering to secure production of a company's current toy at a lower cost.

Marx's corporate success quickly accelerated after the purchase of dies for two successful toys, the Alabama Minstrel Dancer and Zippo the Climbing Monkey, from the now-distressed Strauss. Marx availed himself of every opportunity to expand both his production — including a number of corporate acquisitions — and his distribution — with long-lasting relationships with such retail giants as Sears-Roebuck, Montgomery Ward, JC Penney, and others.

By the mid-1930s Marx toys dominated most dime store toy counters, large chains, and mail order firms. It was during these years that Marx hit his stride as a train manufacturer. Volume was up, production costs down. His goal was to produce an inexpensive electric train set that "every kid could own."

Marx trains provide an interesting challenge to the collector and hobbyist. Marx concerned himself with producing each item at the lowest possible cost and made changes as needed. It is up to the collectors and historians to determine the outcome of Marx's efforts. This study produces many heated debates as to whether a certain item is a "legitimate" variation of Marx production, or whether it has been modified by a collector seeking notoriety or peculiarity in his collection.

The trains were produced in many, many varieties as needed to meet the cost criteria of various customers. Four-wheel cars were offered in the lowest-priced sets, eight-wheel cars in moderate- priced sets, and deluxe eight-wheel cars (with additional details, better proportions, etc.) in the higher-priced sets. Locomotives were similarly varied. Clockwork and battery-powered engines were the cheapest. Electric engines were more, with some having extra features as a premium.

Marx collectors fall into several categories. Some prefer the brightly-colored and often quaint tinplate trains, while others enjoy the plastic models in their various forms.

The era of Louis Marx & Company came to an end on March 10, 1972, when an agreement was reached with the Quaker Oats Company of Stamford, Connecticut for the sale of the domestic toy plants. However, Quaker Oats discontinued production of Marx toys in September 1975. Louis Marx passed away on February 5, 1982 at the age of 85.

Because Marx trains varied so often and so widely, those who have an interest in developing a large collection or those wishing to sell a large collection should consult *Greenberg's Guide to Marx Trains*, Volumes I and II. These books provide an excellent visual guide along with detailed text.

Identification

Once you have identified a train as a Marx product, you may still face something of a challenge. More often than not, the number (if any) on a Marx train differs from the catalogue number. Because of the challenge this presents, we have divided the Marx listings into categories that should make the process somewhat easier. So, begin by scanning the headings. Is your item a locomotive or a freight car? What length is it? How many wheels does it have? Use these features to help you locate your trains in the listings. If you still have difficulty, consult the collector guides described above and use the extensive photographs as a reference.

"Joy Line" Electric Steam Locomotives

These are electrically-operated models of real steam locomotives; 0-4-0 wheel arrangement.

(101)	Locomotive, cast-iron, black, 1930-31.	**50**	**80**
(106)	Locomotive, steel, black, red frame, 1932-35.	**30**	**50**

"Joy Line" Windup Steam Locomotives

These are windup models of real steam locomotives; 0-4-0 wheel arrangement.

(102)	Locomotive, cast-iron, black, 1930-31.	**30**	**50**
(103)	Locomotive, steel, red, 1933-35.	**25**	**40**
(104)	Locomotive, steel, black, 1933-35.	**25**	**40**
(105)	Locomotive, steel, red, black frame, 1932-35.	**25**	**45**
(105)	Locomotive, non-powered, coupler on pilot for doubleheading.		**NRS**
(107)	Bunny locomotive, pink steel body shaped like a rabbit, moving rear feet, 1935-36.	**450**	**600**
350	"The Joy Line", red and blue, 1927-30.	**175**	**275**

"Joy Line" Tenders

These tenders (coal cars) may be used with steam locomotives from either group; all cars have four wheels.

(351)	Tender, steel, 1927-35.		
	(A) "KOAL KAR" and "351" on side, yellow.	**50**	**75**
	(B) Short black body, embossed coal load.	**15**	**22**

		Gd	Exc
(C) Short red body, embossed coal load.		35	50
(D) Long black body, two-level top deck.		25	40

"Joy Line" Rolling Stock

			Gd	Exc
352	"VENICE GONDOLA", light blue, 1927-34.		25	65
(352)	Gondola, orange body, black or blue frame, 1934.		50	75
(352)	Gondola, red body, blue frame, 1934.		40	60
(352)	"BUNNY EXPRESS", chicks and ducklings shown, multi-color, 1935-36.		60	85
353	"EVERFUL TANK CAR", gold, 1927-34.		20	35
354	"CONTRACTOR DUMP CAR", yellow, 1927-34.		25	35
355	"HOBO REST", boxcar, red, 1927-34.		25	35
356	"EAGLE EYE CABOOSE", red, 1926-34.		20	35
357	"THE JOY LINE COACH", green, 1931-34.			
	(A) Yellow roof.		30	75
	(B) Red or orange roof.		15	20
458	"OBSERVATION", green; red or orange roof, 1931-34.			
	(A) Plain deck railing without drumhead sign.		20	30
	(B) Illuminated "JOY LINE" drumhead at rear.		35	50

Early Six-Inch Cars

All cars have four wheels unless noted.

			Gd	Exc
201	"OBSERVATION", cherry red, cut-out windows, open platform, 1934-36.		15	30
245	"BOGOTA", cherry red, 1934-36.		15	20
246	"MONTCLAIR", cherry red, 1934-36.		15	20
547	"EXPRESS BAGGAGE", cherry red, 1934-36.		30	45
(550)	"WRECKER" crane, New York Central, orange cab, 1934-36.		20	35
(551)	New York Central tender, black, 1934-36.		5	10
552	Rock Island, gondola, cherry red, 1934-36.		10	20
553	Middle State Oil, tank car, yellow, 1934-36.		10	20
(559)	Floodlight car, red and black base, two tinplate floodlights.		35	50
694	New York Central, caboose, cherry red, 1934-36.		10	20
1678	General Coal Co., hopper, olive bronze and red, 1934-36.		15	25
1935	"U.S. MAIL CAR", dark green, 1934-36.		35	50
91453	Colorado & Southern, refrigerator, yellow, 1934-36.		15	20

Gd   **Exc**

The 246 Montclair Pullman is characteristic of the quaint lithographed cars made by Marx.

Six-Inch Four-Wheel Cars

Eight-wheel cars with the same car numbers are listed in the next section. Values for flatcars include loads, subtract 25% for missing loads. All cars have black frames unless noted.

		Gd	Exc
Rail Car	Two coupled flatcars with 12 rails, U-shaped stakes, no lettering.	75	100
Wheel Car	Black car with six pairs of wheels as load, no lettering.	25	35
59	Union Pacific, stock car, brown.		
	(A) Lithographed sides.	8	12
	(B) Slotted sides.	15	20
201	Observation, cherry red.	15	30
245	"BOGOTA", Pullman, cherry red.	10	20
246	"MONTCLAIR", Pullman, cherry red.	10	20
246	Canadian Pacific "MONTREAL", wine-maroon, gold lettering.	60	100
247	Canadian Pacific "TORONTO", wine-maroon, gold lettering.	60	100
248	Canadian Pacific "QUEBEC", wine-maroon, gold lettering.	60	100
249	Canadian Pacific "OTTAWA", wine-maroon, gold lettering.	60	100
250	Canadian Pacific "WINNIPEG", wine-maroon, gold lettering.	60	100
251	Canadian Pacific "VANCOUVER", wine-maroon, gold lettering.	60	100
252	Canadian Pacific "CALGARY", wine-maroon, gold lettering.	60	100
253	Canadian Pacific "HAMILTON", wine-maroon, gold lettering.	60	100
(298/6)	(See 552M)		
547	N.Y.C. Lines, baggage car, red, 1936-37.	20	45
(548)	"GUERNSEY MILK", gondola, blue, cream interior, load of four milk cans, 1939-40.	30	50
(550)	New York Central, crane, red or orange cab.	7	13
(552)	"Rock Island", gondola, red interior, 1937.		
	(A) Red exterior.	5	8
	(B) Green exterior with black trim, red and white frame.	15	22
	(C) Green exterior with red trim, black frame.	2	4
	(D) Blue exterior.	2	4
	(E) Same as (C), but red and white or silver frame.	10	15

	Gd	Exc

Simple but fun, the 552 Rock Island gondola has plenty of room for your favorite cargo. R. Bartelt photograph.

		Gd	Exc
552C	(See 91257 or 241708)		
552G	"GROCERIES and SUNDRIES", gondola, yellow and brown, cardboard box load.	25	40
552M	"ORDNANCE DEPT", military gondola, olive drab, wooden bombshells.	75	100
553	Santa Fe, tank car, 1937.		
	(A) Yellow tank, black frame.	6	10
	(B) Silver tank, black frame.	2	5
	(C) Silver tank, silver or red/white frame.	6	10
(553A)	(See 19847)		
553C	Union Tank Car Co., silver, black frame.		
	(A) Tin dome and tank ends.	3	5
	(B) Black dome and tank ends.	8	15
554	Northern Pacific, high-side gondola, red, yellow interior, 1938-40, 1946, 1950.		
	(A) Black frame.	3	5
	(B) Silver or red/white frame.	7	12
554	Northern Pacific, hopper, 1937-38.		
	(A) Blue, red interior, black frame.	3	5
	(B) Blue, red interior, red and white frame.	6	9
	(C) Blue, red interior, silver frame.	10	15
	(D) Red, yellow interior, black frame.	3	5
	(E) Red, yellow interior, silver frame.	7	10
555	"COLORADO & SOUTHERN", refrigerator, 1937-42, 1953-54.		
	(A) Red roof, sliding doors.	10	20
	(B) Red roof, non-operating doors, black or silver frame.	100	150
	(C) Blue roof, sliding doors.	3	6
	(D) Blue roof, non-opening doors, black or silver frame.	60	80
	(E) Same as (C), but silver or red/white frame.	10	20
556	New York Central, caboose, red, with or without Marx logo.		
	(A) No lights.	2	5
	(B) Illuminated.	20	30

Gd   **Exc**

The 1935 NYC Lines US Mail Car is ready for service on your tinplate layout. R. Bartelt photograph.

		Gd	Exc
	(C) Same as (A), but silver or red/white frame.	6	12
(557M)	"RADIO CAR", military coach, olive drab.	15	25
(558A)	Passenger car, scarlet red, several lettering patterns.		
	(A) "OBSERVATION", non-illuminated, black frame.	5	10
	(B) "OBSERVATION", illuminated, silver or red and white frame.	15	25
	(C) "BOGOTA", non-illuminated, black frame.	5	10
	(D) "BOGOTA", illuminated, silver or red and white frame.	15	25
	(E) "MONTCLAIR", non-illuminated, black frame.	5	10
	(F) "MONTCLAIR", illuminated, silver or red and white frame.	15	25
558	Pullman.		
	(A) Red, white lettering.	5	10
	(B) Green, yellow lettering.	15	20
	(C) Blue, white lettering.	35	50
(558M)	"OFFICIAL CAR", military observation car, olive drab.	12	22
(559)	Floodlight, no lettering, two silver or black lights.		
	(A) Red deck, black frame.	9	12
	(B) Copper deck.	16	20
	(C) Black deck, red and white frame.	25	30
	(D) Red deck, red and white frame.	35	40
(561)	Searchlight, no lettering, large single light.		
	(A) Copper metal light, copper deck.	25	30
	(B) Metal light, red deck.	12	15
	(C) Metal light, black deck, red and white frame.	15	25
	(D) Plastic light, red deck.	12	15
(561M)	"SEARCHLIGHT", military car, olive drab.		
	(A) Operating light.	12	25
	(B) Non-operating mirrored light.	25	35
(562)	Flatcar, no lettering, single dump truck or stake body in various colors as load.	25	35
(563)	Lumber car, black car with four-piece load, U-shaped stakes.	9	15
(566)	Cable car, black car and reel with white cord.	15	25

Gd   Exc

20102 NYC caboose. Although no longer required on most US railroads, cabooses remain extremely popular with toy and model train enthusiasts. R. Bartelt photograph.

		Gd	Exc
567	New York Central, dump car, yellow, brown or tank interior.		
	(A) Black frame.	6	10
	(B) Red and white frame.	18	25
(572)	Field gun, military flatcar with crank-operated gun, olive drab, 1940.	35	45
(572A)	Black flatcar with airplane, various color airplanes.		
	(A) Red airplane.	60	80
	(B) Blue or yellow airplane.	75	100
(572A)	Olive drab flatcar with airplane, military version, red or olive drab airplane, 1940.	50	75
(572AA)	Anti-aircraft gun, military flatcar with 5/16"-bore gun, olive drab, 1940.	35	60
(572D)	Military flatcar with dump truck or canopy truck, olive drab car and load.	40	80
(572G)	Siege gun, military flatcar with 5/8"-bore gun, olive drab, 1940.	45	60
(572M)	Olive drab military flatcar with various truck loads, 1957.	30	55
(572MG)	Machine gun, military flatcar, 1940.	40	60
(572ST)	Military flatcar with detachable tank, olive drab, 1940.	45	75
(574)	Barrel car, black, seven wooden barrels, wire railings.	15	25
(663)	Pole car, black, fifteen wooden poles.	9	15
694	New York Central, caboose, red.	4	8
956	Seaboard Air Lines, caboose, green and yellow.	20	35
1678	Northern Pacific, hopper, olive bronze, red interior, 1936.	5	10
1935	New York Central, postal car, 1936.		
	(A) Green.	25	40
	(B) Red.	20	35
2071	New York Central, coach, silver, blue lettering.	20	30
2072	New York Central, observation, silver, blue lettering.	20	30
3824	Union Pacific, caboose, yellow and brown.		
	(A) Black frame.	3	5
	(B) Brown frame.	10	15
4485-4500	"BANGOR AND AROOSTOOK", boxcar, red, white, and blue, various numbers in series, 1960, 1962.	5	10
5011-5026	New York Central, postal car, blue and gray, various numbers in series, 1957.	20	35

		Gd	Exc
5563	Kansas City Southern, caboose, red, yellow, and black.	35	50
10961-10976	Fruit Growers Express, refrigerator, yellow, gray roof, various numbers in series, 1940-49, 1954- 56.	25	50
19847	Sinclair, tank car.		
	(A) Black tank and ends.	6	10
	(B) Green tank and ends.	25	30
20102	NYC, caboose, red and gray.		
	(A) No lights.	1	3
	(B) Illuminated.	15	25
28500	Lehigh Valley, high-side gondola, green, silver interior, 1953, 1960.	4	7
31055	Monon, caboose, red and gray.	20	30
37960-37975	Pennsylvania, boxcar, red and gray, various numbers in series, 1954.	4	8
46010	Cotton Belt, boxcar, various colors, 1940.	20	30
51998	Chicago and North Western, boxcar, various colors, 1939-40, 1955.	17	25
86000	Lackawanna, high-side gondola, blue, red interior, 1956.	15	25
86000	Lackawanna, hopper, blue, red interior, 1953.	3	5
90170	B & LE, boxcar, various colors, 1940, 1948, 1953, 1955.		
	(A) Sliding door.	15	20
	(B) Solid door.	10	15
91257	Seaboard, gondola, black interior, 1957.		
	(A) Chestnut brown exterior.	5	10
	(B) Red exterior.	3	6
	(C) Dark blue exterior.	15	25
91453	Colorado & Southern, refrigerator, yellow, 1936-38.	8	12
174580-174595	New York Central, boxcar, red and gray, various numbers in series.	15	25
241708	Baltimore & Ohio, gondola, yellow exterior, 1953.	2	4
384299	B & O, boxcar, various colors, 1940, 1954-55, 1957.	15	20
738701	Pennsylvania, gondola, red, silver lettering, 1940, 1952, 1954.	3	5
738701	Pennsylvania, hopper, brown, brown or black interior, 1940.	3	5

Six-Inch, Eight-Wheel Cars

Note: For military cars see 2552, 2561, and 2572 series. All cars have black frames unless noted; equipped with automatic one-way or hook couplers.

59	Union Pacific, stock car, brown.		
	(A) Lithographed sides.	5	10
	(B) Slotted sides.	15	20
246	Canadian Pacific, "MONTREAL" coach, maroon, gold lettering.	60	100
247	Canadian Pacific, "TORONTO" coach, maroon, gold lettering.	60	100
248	Canadian Pacific, "QUEBEC" coach, maroon, gold lettering.	60	100

		Gd	Exc
249	Canadian Pacific, "OTTAWA" coach, maroon, gold lettering.	60	100
250	Canadian Pacific, "WINNIPEG" coach, maroon, gold lettering.	60	100
251	Canadian Pacific, "VANCOUVER" coach, maroon, gold lettering.	60	100
252	Canadian Pacific, "CALGARY" coach, maroon, gold lettering.	60	100
253	Canadian Pacific, "HAMILTON" coach, maroon, gold lettering.	60	100
547	NYC Lines, baggage car, red, yellow lettering.	25	40
548	Guernsey Milk, gondola, blue, cream interior, four silver milk cans.	35	60
552	Rock Island, gondola, green, red interior.		
	(A) Black frame.	6	10
	(B) Red frame.	12	20
552G	Groceries and Sundries, gondola, yellow and brown, white interior, loaded with cardboard cartons.	35	50
553	Santa Fe, tank car, silver; red and black lettering.	8	15
554	Northern Pacific, high-side gondola, red, yellow or white lettering.	10	15
554	Northern Pacific, hopper, red, yellow or white lettering.	10	15
555	Colorado and Southern, refrigerator, cream, red or blue roof.	10	15
556	New York Central, caboose, red.		
	(A) Black frame.	8	12
	(B) Red frame.	12	20
567	New York Central, side dumping car, yellow, brown interior.	20	30
1935	NYC Lines, Post Office car, red, yellow lettering.	25	40
2548	(See 548)		
(2550)	New York Central, wrecker crane, orange cab, red boom, no number on car.	10	20
(2552M)	Ordnance Dept., gondola, olive drab, black and white lettering, silver and gold wooden bullets.	75	100
2555B	(See 46010, 51998, 90171)		
2556-2556B	(See 556)		
(2557)	Bogota, Pullman car, red, white lettering, 1938.	10	15
(2557)	Montclair, Pullman car, red, white lettering, 1938.	10	15
(2558)	Observation, Pullman car, red, white lettering, 1938- 41.	12	20
(2561)	Searchlight, red deck and light housing, black frame, no number on car.	40	75
(2561MC)	Field gun, olive drab, clicking gun.	35	50
(2561MD)	Searchlight, olive drab, dummy searchlight.	25	40
(2562)	Flatcar, stake or dump truck load in various colors.		
	(A) Black flatcar.	30	40
	(B) Red flatcar.	50	75
(2563)	Lumber car, four pieces of wooden lumber, U-shaped stakes.		
	(A) Black car.	8	15
	(B) Red car.	35	50
(2566)	Cable car, black, reel with cable.	20	35
2567	(See 567)		

		Gd	Exc
(2572)	Deluxe Delivery, end-loading car with two four-wheel stake body trailers and stake truck.	50	70
(2572AA)	Anti-aircraft gun, olive drab; yellow, black, and red detail on gun (5/8" bore).	40	60
(2572G)	Siege gun, olive drab, cannon-like gun (5/8" bore).		NRS
(2572H)	Ramp car, end-loading flatcar with tank, olive drab.		NRS
(2572I)	Ramp car, end-loading flatcar with dark red tank, olive drab.	50	70
(2572MG)	Machine gun, olive drab flat, yellow and black detail on gun.	45	65
(2572ST)	Flatcar with tank, olive drab.	50	70
(2574)	Barrel car, black, seven dark brown wood barrels.	20	35
(2663)	Pole car, flatcar with fifteen wooden poles.		
	(A) Black flatcar.	8	15
	(B) Red flatcar.	35	50
46010	Cotton Belt, boxcar, various colors.	25	35
51998	Chicago and North Western, boxcar, various colors.	25	35
90171	Bessemer, boxcar, various colors.	20	25
384299	Baltimore & Ohio, boxcar, various colors.	20	30
738701	Pennsylvania, high-side gondola, brown, white lettering.		NRS
738701	Pennsylvania, hopper, brown, white lettering.	10	20

Articulated Streamliners, 1934-1954

M10000 Power Cars

		Gd	Exc
M10000	UP, diesel, many variations, mechanical or electric, 1934- 37.		
	(A) Brown top, yellow sides.	22	30
	(B) Green top, cream sides.	15	25
	(C) Maroon top, silver sides.	15	25
	(D) Olive top, yellow sides.	25	40
	(E) Tan top, light tan sides.	20	30
	(F) Tan top, yellow sides.	25	40

Passenger Cars for M10000 Sets

		Gd	Exc
657	UP, "Coach", four-wheel unless noted otherwise, 1934- 37.		
	(A) Brown top, yellow sides.	15	25
	(B) Green top, cream sides.	10	15
	(C) Maroon top, silver sides, two- or four-wheel.	10	15
	(D) Olive top, yellow sides.	20	30
	(E) Tan top, light tan sides.	12	20
	(F) Tan top, yellow sides.	20	30

		Gd	Exc
658	UP, "Coach-Buffet", observation car, illuminated or non-illum. jewels, 1934-37.		
	(A) Brown top, yellow sides.	15	25
	(B) Green top, cream sides.	10	15
	(C) Maroon top, silver sides, two- or four-wheel.	10	15
	(D) Olive top, yellow sides.	20	30
	(E) Tan top, light tan sides.	12	20
	(F) Tan top, yellow sides.	20	30

M10005 Power Cars and Dummies

		Gd	Exc
732	Mechical or electric, cream with green and orange trim, 1936- 40.	12	20
732GM	Mechanical, cream with green and orange trim, 1937-40, 1948.	12	20
732GMD	UP, electric, white with green and orange trim.	12	20
735	Mechanical, yellow and brown, red or orange trim, 1948- 50.	15	25
735D	Mech. with dummy, yellow with brown and orange trim, 1951. Pair:	35	50
791	Mechanical or electric, silver, red and blue trim, 1940, 1948- 52.	10	20

Passenger Cars for M10005 Sets

		Gd	Exc
(657G)	Cream, green roof, orange trim, 1936-40.	5	10
(658G)	UP, "Squaw Bonnet", observation.	6	12
(757)	Yellow, brown roof, orange trim, 1937-40.		
	(A) Various city names.	6	12
	(B) "Diner".	75	100
(757A)	White, green roof, orange trim, 1948-50.	5	10
(757A)	Silver, red roof, blue trim.	4	7
(758)	UP, "Squaw Bonnet", observation.	8	15
(758A)	UP, observation, various colors, 1948-50.	6	12

Passenger Cars for Mercury Sets

		Gd	Exc
(657)	Gray body and roof, white trim, various names, 1938- 40.	10	15
(657CQ)	Copper body and roof, black trim, illum. or non-illum., various names, 1939-41.	12	18
(657RA)	NYC, "Coach", red, white trim, various names, 1937- 40.	10	15
(658)	NYC, "Detroit", observation, gray.	10	15
(658CQ)	NYC, "Detroit", observation, copper.	12	18
(658RA)	NYC, "Detroit", observation, red.	10	15

Gd   **Exc**

The No. 1 Wm. Crooks steam locomotive captures the "old-fashioned" look that many people associate with toy trains.

Steam Locomotives

		Gd	Exc
1	Wm. Crooks, old-fashioned locomotive, plastic, electric motor, black, 1959-60, 1973.	30	50
1	Wm. Crooks, old-fashioned locomotive, plastic, windup motor, black, 1962.	35	60
(198)	Marlines, plastic, electric motor, red or black.	15	25
(198)	Marlines, plastic, windup motor, 1962.		
	(A) Black.	10	25
	(B) Red.	20	40
(232)	Commodore Vanderbilt, streamlined, sheet metal, windup motor, 1938-48.		
	(A) Silver.	75	100
	(B) Green.	50	100
	(C) Red.	20	30
	(D) Black.	20	25
(233)	(See 635)		
(235)	Canadian Pacific, streamlined, sheet metal, windup motor, various colors, 1936, 1939.	150	200
333	Locomotive, die-cast, electric motor, black, 1949-58.	25	40
391	Canadian Pacific, streamlined, sheet metal, electric motor, black cab, 1938-42.	12	18
396	Canadian Pacific, streamlined, sheet metal, electric motor, black cab, 1941-42.		
	(A) Copper boiler, 2-4-2 or 0-4-0.	25	35
	(B) Black boiler, 2-4-2.	12	18
397	Canadian Pacific, streamlined, sheet metal, electric motor, black cab, 1941.		
	(A) Black boiler, silver sideboards.	20	35
	(B) Copper boiler, blue and yellow sideboards.	35	50
	(C) All black engine.	20	25
	(D) Copper boiler and sideboards.	20	25

		Gd	Exc
400	Locomotive, plastic, electric motor, 1953-54.		
	(A) Black.	5	10
	(B) Olive drab.	20	35
400	Locomotive, plastic, windup motor, black, 1952-56, 1958, 1965-76.	10	15
(401)	Marlines, plastic, windup motor, black, 1962.	10	15
(490)	Locomotive, plastic, black, 1962-75.	10	15
(494)	Canadian Pacific, various boiler and cab colors.	20	30
(495)	Marlines, streamlined, sheet metal, electric motor, black cab and boiler; silver, red, and black sideboards, 1939, 1946-52.	20	30
500	Army Supply Train, streamlined, sheet metal, electric motor, olive drab, 1938-42.	35	50
(591)	Locomotive, stamped steel, electric motor, black, 1953-60.	6	12
(591)	Locomotive, stamped steel, windup motor, black, 1950-58.	6	12
(593)	Locomotive, stamped steel, electric motor, black, 1953-60.	6	12
(595)	Locomotive, stamped steel, electric motor, 1959-60.	6	12
(597)	Commodore Vanderbilt, streamlined, sheet metal, electric motor, 1934-52.		
	(A) Black boiler, cab, and boiler front.	20	30
	(B) Gray boiler, cab, and boiler front.	40	65
	(C) Red boiler, cab, and boiler front.	20	35
	(D) Black boiler and cab, black or chrome boiler front.	10	20
	(E) Olive drab boiler, cab, and boiler front.	75	100
(635)	Mercury, streamlined, sheet metal, electric motor.		
	(A) Black boiler and cab, copper boiler front.	25	45
	(B) Gray boiler, cab, and boiler front.	25	45
	(C) Red boiler, cab, and boiler front.	25	45
	(D) Red boiler and cab, chrome boiler front.	25	45
(635)	Mercury, streamlined, sheet metal, windup motor, 1938-52.		
	(A) Gray.	25	40
	(B) Black.	15	25
	(C) Blue.	50	75
	(D) Red.	20	35
666	Locomotive, die-cast, electric motor, 1955.		
	(A) Black.	10	15
	(B) Olive drab.	20	35
666	Locomotive, die-cast, windup motor.		NRS
734	Mickey Mouse, sheet metal, multicolor lithograph with Disney characters, windup motor, 1950-52.	75	100
735	Locomotive, stamped steel, windup motor, black, 1950-52.	10	15
(833)	Locomotive, stamped steel, electric motor, black, 1947-52.	8	15
(833)	Locomotive, stamped steel, windup motor, black.	8	15
897	Locomotive, stamped steel, electric motor, 1939.		
	(A) Olive drab, black and white lithography.	75	100

		Gd	Exc

The streamlined 3000 Canadian Pacific steam locomotive with 2-4-2 wheel arrangement and eight-wheel tender. R. Bartelt photograph.

		Gd	Exc
	(B) Black, gray and white lithography.	8	12
897	Locomotive, stamped steel, windup motor, 1940.		
	(A) Olive drab, lithographed.	100	125
	(B) Black and white lithography.	35	50
898	Locomotive, stamped steel, electric motor, black, 1946-52.	8	12
898	Locomotive, stamped steel, windup motor, black, 1940.	25	35
994	Locomotive, stamped steel, electric motor, black.	10	15
994	Locomotive, stamped steel, windup motor.		
	(A) Black.	10	15
	(B) Red.		NRS
995	Locomotive, stamped steel, electric motor.		
	(A) Black.	10	15
	(B) Red.		NRS
999	Locomotive, die-cast, electric motor, black.		
	(A) Open-spoked cowcatcher.	30	50
	(B) Solid cowcatcher.	15	25
999	Locomotive, die-cast, windup motor, black, 1949.		NRS
1666	Locomotive, plastic, electric motor, gray or black.	15	25
1829	Locomotive, plastic, electric motor, black.	20	35
3000	Canadian Pacific, streamlined, sheet metal, electric motor, black cab, 1939-41, 1946-52.		
	(A) Red boiler, 0-4-0.	20	40
	(B) Gray boiler, 2-4-2.	22	30
	(C) Gray boiler, blue and yellow sideboards, 0-4-0.	50	75
3000	Canadian Pacific, streamlined 0-4-0, sheet metal, windup motor, black cab, gray boiler, various trim colors.	75	100

Tenders for Steam Locomotives

198A	Marlines, plastic, square-type four-wheel.		
	(A) Blue.	25	30

		Gd	Exc
	(B) Black.	10	15
	(C) Black, made in Hong Kong, plastic couplers.	1	2
(451)	Canadian Pacific, stamped steel, black body, 1937-39.		
	(A) Gold lettering on maroon background.	10	15
	(B) Yellow lettering on maroon background.	10	15
	(C) Yellow lettering on light blue background.	25	35
	(D) Red lettering on silver background.	10	15
(451)	Pennsylvania, stamped steel, black body, white lettering, 1940-41.	10	15
(461)	Canadian Pacific, stamped steel, black body, 1938-39.		
	(A) Yellow lettering on light blue background.	25	35
	(B) Yellow lettering on maroon background.	6	12
	(C) Red lettering on silver background.	6	20
500	Army Supply Train, stamped steel, four-wheel, olive drab, 1938-40.	20	35
551	New York Central, four-wheel, 1934-41, 1950-55.		
	(A) Black, detail and road names vary.	2	4
	(B) NYC, red, black or orange/white detail.	10	20
	(C) NYC, blue.	20	30
	(D) NYC, gray.		NRS
551	New York Central, eight-wheel, black, 1939-40.	5	10
851M	(See 500)		
(941)	Nickel Plate Road, seven-inch, four-wheel, black.	5	10
(941)	Mickey Mouse Meteor, seven-inch, four-wheel, blue, multicolor lithograph, 1950-52.	50	75
(951)	Four-wheel, stamped steel, black.		
	(A) NYC, without searchlight.	5	10
	(B) NYC, with searchlight.	25	35
	(C) Nickel Plate Road.		NRS
(951)	New York Central, eight-wheel, stamped steel, black.	10	20
(952)	Army Supply Train, stamped steel, olive drab, 1940.	50	70
(961)	Slope-back tender, plastic, eight-wheel, black unless noted.		
	(A) New York Central.	3	6
	(B) Union Pacific.	3	6
	(C) Allstate.	5	10
	(D) Southern Pacific.	5	10
	(E) Penn Central.	3	6
	(F) Santa Fe, gray.	3	6
	(G) Santa Fe, gray, with sound mechanism.	12	20
(971)	New York Central, articulated, stamped steel, lithographed stripes, 1938-40.		
	(A) Gray or red, white lettering.	10	20
	(B) Copper, black lettering.	15	25
(1951)	Four-wheel, plastic, black unless noted.		
	(A) No road name.	1	3
	(B) Southern Pacific Lines.	2	4

	Gd	Exc

Commonly called a "coal car" by non-railroaders, the 2731 Santa Fe is an example of what railroaders call a '"tender." R. Bartelt photograph.

		Gd	Exc
	(C) Marlines.	5	10
	(D) New York Central.	1	2
	(E) Santa Fe, gray or black.	2	4
	(F) Penn Central.	2	4
	(G) Union Pacific.	2	4
	(H) Bessemer and Lake Erie.	10	20
	(I) Cape Canaveral Express.	30	50
(1951)	Eight-wheel, plastic, black unless noted.		
	(A) Southern Pacific.	3	6
	(B) Santa Fe.	3	6
	(C) New York Central.	3	6
	(D) US Army.	15	25
	(E) Canadian Pacific.	30	40
	(F) Allstate.	3	6
	(G) Rio Grande.	30	40
(2451)	Canadian Pacific, stamped steel, black, 1937-38.		
	(A) Gold lettering on maroon background.	6	12
	(B) Yellow lettering on red background.	25	35
(2451)	Pennsylvania, stamped steel, black, white lettering, 1941.	15	30
2461SB	(See 461)		
2731	Santa Fe, eight-wheel, plastic, 1953, 1955, 1959-60.	8	12
(3551)	"1st Div. St.P. & P.R.R.", four-wheel, embossed coal pile, black, various years from 1956 to 1967.	15	25
(3651)	William Crooks, old-time, plastic, simulated wood pile, 1959-62, 1973.		
	(A) Tales of Wells Fargo.	10	15
	(B) 1st Div. St.P. & P.R.R.	10	15
(3991)	New York Central, die-cast, black, 1949-54.	25	35
04551	(See 2731)		

	Gd	Ex

Diesel Locomotives

The alphabetical cross-reference provided at the beginning of this section will help you locate items that do not have numbers on them.

		Gd	Ex
Allstate	See (51) or (1998)		
Illinois Central Gulf	See (801)		
Kansas City Southern	See (55)		
Marxtronic	Diesel switcher, plastic, battery- powered, black, 1959.	50	75
Missouri Pacific	See (800)		
New Haven	See (2003)		
Rock Island	See (99X)		
Santa Fe	See (1096)		
Seaboard	See (4001)		
Union Pacific	See (52)		
Western Pacific	See (902)		
21	Santa Fe, FT diesel, lithographed, silver with red war bonnet, 1950-54.		
	(A) Powered locomotive.	15	30
	(B) Dummy locomotive.	12	25
(51)	Allstate, E-7 diesel, plastic, orange and black, 1957-59.		
	(A) A unit, powered or dummy.	65	85
	(B) B unit, dummy.	75	95
(52)	Union Pacific, E-7 diesel, plastic, orange and black, 1960.		
	(A) A unit, powered or dummy.	50	75
	(B) B unit, dummy.	60	80
54	Kansas City Southern, FM diesel, lithographed, red, black, and yellow, 1956-60.		
	(A) Powered locomotive.	20	35
	(B) Dummy locomotive.	20	40
(55)	Kansas City Southern, FM B unit diesel, lithographed; red, black and yellow; dummy, 1957-60.	20	35
62	Baltimore & Ohio, F-3 diesel, lithographed, blue and silver, 1953-54, 1958, 1967.		
	(A) Powered locomotive.	15	20
	(B) Dummy locomotive.	10	15
81	Monon, FM diesel, lithographed, red and gray, 1955-56, 1958- 59.	15	20
(81)	Monon, FM B unit, lithographed, red and gray, 1958- 59.	18	25
99	Rock Island, E-7 diesel, powered or dummy, plastic, black and red, 1958-74.	15	30
(99X)	Rock Island, E-7 B unit, dummy, plastic, black and red, 1958-68.	18	35
112	Lehigh Valley, diesel switcher, plastic, red, 1974-76.	15	20
588	New York Central, diesel switcher, 1958-62.		
	(A) Black body.	10	15
	(B) Maroon body.	25	35
	(C) Gray body.	35	45

		Gd	Exc

1998 Northern Pacific S-3 diesel.

		Gd	Exc
702	Western Pacific, diesel switcher, plastic, green, 1972- 74.	**15**	**25**
799	Western Pacific, diesel switcher, green.	**35**	**50**
(800)	Missouri Pacific, diesel switcher, blue, 1975- 76.	**25**	**45**
(801)	Illinois Central Gulf, diesel switcher; white, orange, and black, 1974-75.	**15**	**20**
901	Western Pacific, E-7 diesel, plastic, 1956-60.		
	(A) Green body, powered or dummy.	**20**	**35**
	(B) Gray body, powered or dummy.	**50**	**75**
(902)	Western Pacific, E-7 B unit, dummy, plastic, 1957-58.		
	(A) Green body.	**20**	**30**
	(B) Gray body.	**75**	**90**
1095	Santa Fe, E-7 diesel, powered or dummy, plastic, gray and red, 1952.	**10**	**25**
(1096)	"Santa Fe", E-7 B unit, plastic, gray and red, 1955-71.	**12**	**30**
1798	Cape Canaveral Express, diesel switcher, plastic; red, white, and blue, 1959-64.	**50**	**75**
1998	Allstate, S-3 diesel, blue, white lettering, 1959.	**100**	**125**
1998	AT & SF, S-3 diesel, 1955-62.		
	(A) Maroon body.	**30**	**50**
	(B) Black body.	**35**	**60**
1998	Rock Island, S-3 diesel, powered or dummy, red and gray, 1962.	**40**	**70**
1998	Northern Pacific, S-3, two-tone scheme, gold stripes.	**15**	**30**
1998	Union Pacific, S-3 diesel, yellow, 1955-62.		
	(A) Powered locomotive.	**15**	**30**
	(B) Dummy locomotive.	**25**	**45**
2002	New Haven, E-7 diesel, powered or dummy, plastic; red, white, and black, 1960-74.	**25**	**40**
(2003)	New Haven, E-7 B unit, dummy; red, white, and black, 1960-74.	**20**	**45**
2124	Boston & Maine, RDC, plastic, powered, gray, 1956- 59.	**150**	**175**
4000	New York Central, E-7 diesel, plastic, powered or dummy, black and white, 1953-55, 1959-69, 1971-74.	**35**	**55**

		Gd	Ex
4000	Penn Central, E-7 diesel, powered or dummy, plastic, turquoise, 1971-73.	125	150
4000	Seaboard, FM diesel, lithographed, green and yellow, 1955- 62.	20	30
(4001)	Seaboard, FM B unit, lithographed, green and yellow, 1962.	125	150
6000	Southern Pacific, F-3 diesel, lithographed, orange, 1950-54.		
	(A) Powered locomotive, silver band.	18	25
	(B) Dummy locomotive, silver band.	10	15
	(C) Powered locomotive, white band.	25	35
	(D) Dummy locomotive, white band.	25	35

3/16" Scale Metal Passenger Cars

New York Central   See (236)

234	New York Central, two-tone gray.		
	(A) Coach.	25	40
	(B) Vista Dome.	25	40
(236)	New York Central, observation car, two-tone gray.	25	40
1007	Western Pacific, observation car, silver.	25	40
1217	Western Pacific, silver.		
	(A) Coach.	40	75
	(B) Vista Dome.	25	50
3152	Santa Fe, silver.		
	(A) Coach.	12	20
	(B) Vista Dome; dome covers only part of roof.	12	20
	(C) Vista Dome; full-length dome.	15	30
3197	Santa Fe, observation car, silver.	12	20
3557	New York Central, silver.		
	(A) Coach.	40	60
	(B) Vista Dome.	40	60
3558	New York Central, observation car, silver.	40	70

3/16" Scale Metal Freight Cars

New York Central   See (3550)
Searchlight   See (3591A)

256	Niacet Chemical Corp., tank car, silver.	5	10
652	Shell, tank car, orange, red lettering.	6	12
1950	GAEX, boxcar, green, yellow lettering.	5	10
2532	Cities Service, tank car, green.	5	10
2700	NYC & St. L, flatcar, black.	15	20
3200	New York, New Haven & Hartford, boxcar, brown, black ends.	6	12

		Gd	Exc
(3550)	New York Central, plastic cab and body, "MARX" embossed on boom.		
	(A) Red body.	25	35
	(B) Gray body.	5	10
(3591A)	Searchlight, red body, black base, Marx logo on plastic housing.	20	30
9100	Union Pacific, red sides, black roof and ends.	6	12
13079	LNE, hopper, black.	15	20
13549	AT & SF, stock car, orange sides, brown roof, black ends.	10	15
17899	T & P, gondola, light blue-gray.	5	10
20102	New York Central, caboose, red and gray sides, black roof.	5	10
33773	Boston & Maine, flatcar, black.	15	20
35461	Pacific Fruit Express, refrigerator car, yellow sides, brown roof, black ends.	10	30
44572	Chesapeake & Ohio, gondola, black.	6	10
53941	Pennsylvania, stock car, brown, black ends.	150	175
70311	Pennsylvania, boxcar, brown, black ends.	6	12
71499	Nickel Plate Road, gondola, black.	6	12
80410	Chesapeake & Ohio, flatcar, black.	20	30
92812	Reading, caboose, red.	6	10
174580	New York Central, boxcar, red and gray sides, black roof and ends.	6	10
254000	Baltimore & Ohio, gondola, gray.	5	10

Seven-Inch Cars, 1950-1962

These cars measure 7-1/4" long over the base. Most cars are four-wheel, some are found in either four- or eight-wheel variations.

		Gd	Exc
1	St. Paul & Pacific, four- or eight-wheel baggage car, yellow, black roof, 1959-62.	15	30
3	St. Paul & Pacific, four- or eight-wheel coach, yellow, black roof, 1959-62.	15	30
C504-C518	Baltimore and Ohio, caboose, four- or eight-wheel, sky blue and black, various numbers in series.	10	15
956	Nickel Plate Road, caboose, red and gray, 1950-58.	6	12
969-980	Kansas City Southern, caboose; yellow, red, and black, 1956-57.	15	35
1235	Southern Pacific, caboose, red and silver, 1952-55.	5	10
1476	Disney characters, boxcar, yellow; decorated with Dumbo, Jiminy Cricket, etc.	75	125
1951	AT & SF, eight-wheel caboose, red and silver, 1952-55.	5	10
3855	Monon, caboose; red, gray, and white, 1956-57.	10	30
4484	State of Maine, boxcar; red, white, and blue, 1956-57.	6	15
20110-20124	NYC Pacemaker, four- or eight-wheel boxcar, red and gray body, black roof, various numbers in series, 1954-58.	5	10
36000	Chesapeake & Ohio, gondola, brown, 1956-57.	5	10

		Gd	Ex
37950-37959	Pennsylvania, boxcar, red and gray, various numbers in series, 1950-58.	5	10
80982	Wabash, gondola, yellow, 1950-58.	5	8
691521	Mickey Mouse Meteor, caboose, orange, red roof, characters include Pluto, Pinocchio, etc., 1950-51.	50	80

Plastic Freight Cars

These cars were made in three major versions. Four-wheel and eight-wheel cars are plastic with little or no extra detail. "Deluxe" eight-wheel cars measure about 8-1/2" long. They have sliding doors, metal railings and ladders, and separate cast parts. These cars were sold in Marx's best sets by Sears, Wards, and others.

		Gd	Ex
Allstate	See (2225), (4588), (5543), (5553), or (9553)		
AT & SF	See (4587), (4590) or (05571)		
Cities Service	See (5543)		
Crane	Eight-wheel, no lettering, silver-gray body.	5	10
Erie	Flatcar, four-wheel.		
	(A) Maroon body, two red farm tractors, 1960.	15	25
	(B) Maroon body, Sears trailer.	30	40
	(C) Maroon body, Walgreen trailer.	25	35
	(D) Maroon body, NYC trailer.	20	40
	(E) Maroon body, Burlington trailer.	20	30
	(F) Maroon body, lumber load, 1973.	8	12
	(G) Blue, green, or maroon body, two automobiles, 1974.	10	15
Erie	See (586), (05544), or (05594); also see following listings.		
Erie	Eight-wheel flatcar with load, maroon, 1974.		
	(A) Two red, gray, or yellow farm tractors.	12	25
	(B) Sears, Allstate, Western Auto, or Walgreen tractor- trailer.	30	40
Erie	Deluxe eight-wheel flatcar, maroon, stake sides, 1973.	10	15
Erie	Searchlight car, maroon body, black or gray searchlight, 1962.	20	30
Exxon	See (5553)		
Gulf Oil	See (5543) or (9553)		
Marlines	Gondola, yellow body, 1952.	10	15
Milk	See (5553)		
Missile Launcher	Deluxe eight-wheel flatcar, blue; gray racks, vertical launcher.	50	100
NYC	See (4589) or the following listing.		
NYC	Four- or eight-wheel crane, black or silver-gray body and boom.	5	10
Santa Fe	See (1972)		
Searchlight	See (05571)		
Southern Pacific	See (4556)		

Gd   **Exc**

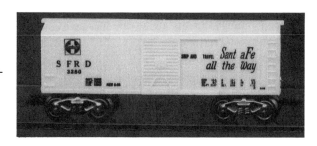

3280 Santa Fe eight-wheel boxcar.

		Gd	Exc
USAF	Eight-wheel flatcar, "MISSILE LAUNCHER", white body, blue star, 1959.	50	100
24	No name, deluxe eight-wheel searchlight, black, gray serachlight, 1974.	20	30
45	William Crooks, deluxe eight-wheel caboose, brown, 1973.	25	35
56	William Crooks, eight-wheel flatcar maroon, yellow stake sides, six-piece lumber load, 1973.	20	30
234	US Army, eight-wheel caboose, olive drab, 1957.	15	25
X-246	Chemical Rocket Fuel, four- or eight-wheel tank car, white or off-white.	5	10
284	UTLX, deluxe eight-wheel tank car, gray, 1954, 1964.	5	10
C-350	Monon, four- or eight-wheel caboose, tuscan or red body.	10	15
X-467	Rocket Computing Center, four- or eight-wheel caboose, red body.	30	40
504	Baltimore & Ohio, four-wheel caboose, blue.	35	40
564	Allstate, eight-wheel caboose, tuscan, 1959.	5	10
(586)	Erie, flatcar, maroon body, stake sides.	2	4
586	Rock Island, deluxe eight-wheel work caboose, tuscan.	7	12
586	USA, deluxe eight-wheel flatcar, olive drab, 1957.	25	35
C-635	New Haven, eight-wheel caboose, brown body.	3	6
C-678	New Haven, eight-wheel caboose, brown.	3	6
643	Western Pacific, caboose, green body, 1973.		
	(A) Yellow lettering, four-wheel.	10	20
	(B) Gold lettering, four-wheel.	5	10
	(C) Green, bay window, eight-wheel deluxe.	35	50
(929)	Erie, eight-wheel automobile carrier, blue.	10	15
967	NYC, four-wheel side dump car, 1957-58.		
	(A) Black body.	35	60
	(B) Blue body.	35	60
969	Kansas City Southern, four- or eight-wheel caboose, red body, 1958.	20	40
1015	ICG, deluxe eight-wheel work caboose, orange cab, 1974.	15	20
1020	IC, eight-wheel crane, orange cab.	15	20
1024	IC, eight-wheel deluxe flatcar, black, yellow stakes, lumber load, 1974.	10	15

		Gd	Ex
1231	Missouri Pacific, four-wheel caboose, blue or white body.	10	15
01500	Rio Grande, eight-wheel caboose, orange, 1974.	25	35
1796	Rocket Launcher, four- or eight-wheel flatcar, white, blue star, three missiles, 1959-60.	30	40
1796	Missile Launcher Danger, deluxe eight-wheel flatcar, blue, white star, 1959-60.	30	40
1799	USAX, four- or eight-wheel gondola, "DANGER HIGH EXPLOSIVES", blue or black body, 1959.	35	45
1963	USAX, deluxe eight-wheel work caboose, red and blue, 1963.	12	15
(1972)	Santa Fe, eight-wheel caboose, tuscan or red, 1974.	3	6
1977	AT & SF, four- or eight-wheel caboose, tuscan or gray/red/yellow, 1973-75.	2	4
1988	B & LE, four-wheel caboose, orange body, 1974.	10	15
2130	USA, deluxe eight-wheel work caboose, olive drab, tank.	75	100
(2225)	Allstate, deluxe eight-wheel caboose, bay window, orange or blue, 1958-59.	18	25
2225	Santa Fe, deluxe eight-wheel caboose, bay window, red or tuscan, 1958-59.	18	25
2236	USA, eight-wheel gondola, olive drab, 1957.	30	40
2246	USA, deluxe eight-wheel flatcar, olive drab, jeep or army truck, 1957.	40	50
2366	Canadian Pacific, eight-wheel deluxe caboose, bay window, tuscan, 1956.	25	35
2532	Cities Service, four- or eight-wheel tank car, green body, 1966-70.	3	5
2824	USA or USAF, deluxe eight-wheel gondola, yellow or olive drab, 1961-62.	25	35
2858	USA Ordnance, boxcar, olive drab.	100	150
3280	SFRD/Santa Fe, four- or eight-wheel boxcar; orange, white, or yellow body.	2	5
3824	Union Pacific, eight-wheel deluxe caboose, bay window or work caboose, tuscan, 1956.	25	35
3900	Union Pacific, four- or eight-wheel caboose.		
	(A) Yellow body, four- or eight-wheel.	15	20
	(B) Orange or brown body.	2	5
4427	Santa Fe, deluxe eight-wheel caboose, red, 1952-59.	10	15
4528	Erie, eight-wheel deluxe flatcar, maroon or orange, with tractors or stake sides, 1956.	15	30
4546	NYC, deluxe eight-wheel caboose, tuscan.	20	30
(4556)	Southern Pacific, four- or eight-wheel caboose; brown, dark red, or green body, 1952-75.	2	3
4566	CWEX, deluxe eight-wheel flatcar, blue, two cable reels, 1955.		
	(A) Gray cable reels.	25	30
	(B) Yellow cable reels.	75	100
4571	WECX, deluxe eight-wheel searchlight, red, 1955-65.	15	20
4581	BKX, deluxe eight-wheel searchlight, red.	15	20

Gd   **Exc**

34178 Great Northern eight-wheel boxcar.

		Gd	Exc
4583	GEX, deluxe eight-wheel searchlight, black, 1955.	18	25
4586	UP, deluxe eight-wheel work caboose, tuscan, 1957-58.	18	25
(4587)	AT & SF, deluxe eight-wheel work caboose, tuscan, 1962.	15	20
(4588)	Allstate, deluxe eight-wheel work caboose, tuscan, 1955.	25	35
(4589)	NYC, deluxe eight-wheel work caboose, tuscan, gray tank, 1957.	35	50
(4590)	AT & SF, deluxe eight-wheel work caboose, tuscan and red, 1955-62.	10	15
5532	Allstate, four- or eight-wheel tank car, blue or turquoise body, 1959, 1962.	5	10
(5543)	Allstate, deluxe eight-wheel tank car, white tanks, maroon base.	35	50
(5543)	Cities Service, deluxe eight-wheel tank car, green tanks, maroon base.	18	25
(5543)	Gulf, deluxe eight-wheel tank car, orange tanks, blue base.	75	100
(05544)	Erie, deluxe eight-wheel flatcar, maroon.		
	(A) Sears or Allstate tractor trailer.	30	40
	(B) Burlington tractor trailer.	15	20
5545	CB & Q, deluxe eight-wheel flatcar, maroon, 1957-60.		
	(A) Two Allstate or Walgreen trailers.	50	75
	(B) Two Burlington trailers.	18	25
	(C) Erie bridge girder.	12	18
	(D) Two Western Auto trailers.	45	65
(5553)	Allstate, deluxe eight-wheel tank car, blue.	10	15
(5553)	Exxon, deluxe eight-wheel tank car, white, 1974.	65	90
(5553)	Milk, deluxe eight-wheel tank car, cream, 1960.	150	200
5561	WECX, deluxe eight-wheel searchlight, red.	10	20
(05571)	Atomic Light Generator, eight-wheel searchlight car, red body, white star herald, 1959.	20	30
(05571)	AT & SF, eight-wheel searchlight car, maroon, 1965.	20	30
(05571)	USAF, eight-wheel searchlight car, red body, white star herald, 1959.	25	35
5586	WP, deluxe eight-wheel work caboose, tuscan, 1957.	12	18
5590	NYC, deluxe eight-wheel crane, die-cast base, black.	20	30
(05594)	Erie, eight-wheel log car, maroon, five logs.	10	15
5595	Farm Master Brand, deluxe eight-wheel refrigerator, white or cream, 1959.	7	15

		Gd	Ex
(9553)	Gulf Oil Corp, four-wheel tank car, orange body, 1974.	25	35
(9553)	Allstate Motor Oil, four-wheel tank car, light or dark blue.	5	12
(9553)	Allstate Rocket Fuel, eight-wheel tank car, white, 1959- 74.	5	12
13975	AT & SF, four- or eight-wheel stock car, various colors.	2	8
17858	Rock Island, caboose, brown or red body.	2	3
	(A) Four- or eight-wheel version.	2	3
	(B) Eight-wheel deluxe, bay window, antenna, metal rails and ladder, 1958-59.	16	30
18326	New York Central, caboose.		
	(A) White or yellow body, four-wheel.	12	20
	(B) Brown or red body, four- or eight-wheel.	2	5
	(C) Black body, four-wheel.	10	15
18326	Penn Central, eight-wheel caboose, green.	5	10
18918	Great Northern, deluxe eight-wheel boxcar, brown.	25	35
20053	Seaboard, deluxe eight-wheel boxcar, dark red or tuscan, 1957, 1959.	35	50
20309	L & N, deluxe eight-wheel gondola, 1959-61.		
	(A) Brown body, seven cardboard pipes.	50	75
	(B) Yellow body, no load.	35	50
21429	Lehigh Valley, deluxe eight-wheel hopper cars, 1965- 76.	7	12
21913	LV, four- or eight-wheel hopper, various colors, 1965- 74.	3	6
34178	Great Northern, eight-wheel boxcar, green, 1961, 1975.	3	6
39520	SP, deluxe eight-wheel flatcar, two yellow cable reels, 1958.	25	35
43461	Pacific Fruit Express, deluxe eight-wheel refrigrator, white, 1955.	4	8
44535	SAL, deluxe eight-wheel flatcar, gray, black pipe.	25	35
51100	"SOU.", deluxe eight-wheel flatcar, automobile carrier, various colors, 1955-73.	15	20
51170	Erie, deluxe eight-wheel gondola, drop ends, various colors, 1952-70.	8	12
54099	Missouri Pacific, deluxe eight-wheel stock car, 1956-57, 1960, 1974. Note: Operating version has cow that slides out when door opens, loading ramp, and platform.		
	(A) Red body, operating.	5	10
	(B) Red body, non-operating.	5	10
	(C) Green body, operating.	25	35
	(D) Green body, non-operating.	5	10
	(E) Orange body, non-operating.	100	125
	(F) Yellow body, brown door, non-operating.	75	100
74563	ACL, deluxe eight-wheel flatcar, red, lumber load, 1961.	20	45
77003	B & M, deluxe eight-wheel boxcar, turqoise or blue, 1952, 1955, 1957.	10	15
147815	Rock Island, deluxe eight-wheel boxcar, 1952-59.		
	(A) Red body.	10	15
	(B) Tuscan body.	20	30
176893	NYC, deluxe eight-wheel boxcar, green.	7	12

Gd   **Exc**

147815 Rock Island boxcar.

186028	Union Pacific, deluxe eight-wheel boxcar, tuscan, 1955.	20	30
249319	Marlines, deluxe eight-wheel boxcar, red or white, 1955, 1959.	12	18
259199	Canadian Pacific, deluxe eight-wheel boxcar, tuscan.	50	90
339234	Canadian Pacific, deluxe eight-wheel gondola, black or tuscan, 1965- 76.	15	25
347100	Pennsylvania, eight-wheel gondola, gray, orange, or red, 1952-73.	2	4
715100	NYC, eight-wheel gondola, green, 1973.	3	6
95050	Lehigh Valley, four-wheel caboose, red body, 1974.	2	5
131000	Seaboard Coast Line, four-wheel gondola, blue or yellow body, 1973.	2	4
161755	New York Central, four-wheel boxcar, yellow body.	7	12
174479	New York Central, four-wheel boxcar, green.	7	12
347100	Pennsylvania, four- or eight-wheel gondola, various colors, 1952-73.	2	4
467110	Baltimore & Ohio, four- or eight-wheel boxcar, various body colors.	3	5
715100	New York Central, four- or eight-wheel gondola, blue, red, or green.	3	6

Highlights of Ives History

Although founded in 1868 the Ives Company was, in a sense, reborn after a devastating fire swept the factory in 1900. Because the assets had been properly insured, Ives was able to design a new toy line that would reflect the innovations of the newest toy products.

The first trains produced by Ives in the twentieth century (1901) helped satisfy a common Christmas wish expressed by boys and girls — the desire for a train on a track. Until the 1890s virtually all clockwork trains ran on the floor without the benefit of track, but German imports soon filled this gap. Now, with a fresh start, Ives introduced a line of O Gauge clockwork trains with track. These were produced in great quantity and in multitudinous variations until 1930. From 1901 through 1906 Ives offered two types of O Gauge clockwork locomotives — stamped-steel and cast-iron. After 1906 the company offered only the cast-iron versions of steam locomotives. Electric-outline locomotives were made of stamped-steel.

Ives also chose to build 1 Gauge clockwork trains that ran on track (as opposed to clockwork floor toys) and followed the approach of European companies who made sectional track, which was easier for both children and adults to assemble than the ribbon steel track offered by Carlisle & Finch and also in Lionel's early line. Ives first 1 Gauge locomotive was the clockwork No. 40 steam locomotive, which was introduced in 1904.

Ives did not produce electrically-powered O Gauge trains until 1910. The line included steam and electric-outline locomotives, as well as passenger and freight cars. At the time, the company faced competition from Howard, Knapp, Elektoy, and, most importantly, Bing from Germany. (Bing's popularity dwindled, however, in the face of anti-German sentiment after World War I.)

The first electrically-powered 1 Gauge locomotive, the 3240, appeared in 1912. The 1 Gauge line included both passenger cars and freight cars, although Ives down-played the freight cars and promoted instead the more glamorous passenger trains. The passenger car line originally featured cars lithographed to represent wood-sided cars that had been prevalent on the real railroads, but these were supplemented in 1915 by a line of cars with the newer steel bodies that represented the newest trains on America's railroads. The range of 1 Gauge freight cars included several basic designs, plus the ever-popular red caboose.

Starting in 1915 Ives faced stiff new competition in O Gauge as Lionel entered the field. In fact, Lionel literally hammered at the reputation of Ives' trains with its aggressive advertising. In 1921 Ives abandoned 1 Gauge to build trains in the slightly larger 2-1/8" gauge that Lionel called "Standard Gauge." Ives promoted the trains with the name "Wide Gauge."

Originally, Ives' Wide Gauge electric-outline locomotives featured cast-iron frames, but they were refitted with stamped- steel frames in 1926. This change represented one of the many modifications made as Ives' attempted to meet Lionel's competition. Ives also adopted the use of brass nameplates in 1926 — these were all the rage in the toy train world, as they were considered much more elegant than the rubber stamping they replaced. The Ives Wide Gauge line included a pleasing variety of locomotives, passenger cars, and freight cars, plus track and accessories.

The early 1920s saw a dramatic increase in the number of Wide Gauge manufacturers — including American Flyer, Boucher, and Dorfan, but Ives trains competed well with their attractive proportions and innovative reversing units (introduced in 1924). The device provided a sequence of forward, neutral, reverse, neutral, and then forward again. This ingenious device was invented by H. P. Spark and B. A. Smith and licensed to Ives. Clearly, this innovation improved sales, and Lionel reacted accordingly by instructing its engineers to develop a comparable unit that would not violate Ives' patent. By 1926 Lionel achieved this goal.

At the same time (1926) Ives ran aground financially and had to seek new capital. In addition to paying debts, Ives used the money to create new models that would, hopefully, buoy the sinking company. Finally in 1928 one of Ives largest creditors, Blanchard Press, Inc., sued Ives for payment, and Ives responded by seeking relief under the United States Bankruptcy law.

On July 31, 1928 Mandel Frankel, a Lionel representative, successfully bid $73,250 for the stock, fixtures, and plant of the Ives Company. A very low price for a company with half a million to a million dollars in sales, the sum was split between Lionel and American Flyer. The two larger companies owned Ives jointly until 1929 or 1930, when Lionel bought American Flyer's share.

Lionel continued production of Ives trains for three more model years, 1930, 1931, and 1932, and then in the face of substantial losses discontinued the separate marketing of the line.

1 Gauge Trains (Clockwork and Electric)

Note: Restored models bring prices slightly below those indicated for "good" original models. In some cases, restorations bring much less.

The elegant proportions of Ives trains, such as this No. 40 steam locomotive, have won the favor of many collectors.

		Gd	Exc
40	Steam locomotive, 4-4-0, clockwork, cast-iron boiler, colored trim.		
	(A) Red and yellow cab roof trim, 11-1/2" long, 1904-09.	2500	4000
	(B) Red and gold headlight, 12" long, 1910- 11.	2000	3500
	(C) Painted trim, 13-1/2" long, 1912-15.	1500	3000
41	Steam locomotive, 0-4-0, clockwork, cast-iron boiler, red and yellow cab roof, 10" long, 1908-11.	3000	4000
70	Twentieth Century Limited Express, baggage car, lithographed steel, yellow, 11" long, 1904-09.	600	1000

		Gd	Exc
70	New York and Chicago, baggage car, lithographed steel, white, 12" long, 1910-14.	250	500
71	Twentieth Century Limited Express, buffet car, lithographed steel, 11" long, 1904-09.		
	(A) Yellow sides.	200	500
	(B) Dark red sides.	700	1500
	(C) White sides.	600	1200
	(D) Brown sides.	200	500
71	New York and Chicago, buffet car, lithographed steel, brown sides, 12" long, 1914-20.	250	450
72	Twentieth Century Limited Express, parlor car, lithographed steel, 11" long.		
	(A) Yellow sides.	500	1000
	(B) Brown sides.	250	500
72	New York and Chicago, parlor car, lithographed steel, brown sides, 12" long, 1914-20.	200	400
73	Merchandise car (boxcar), lithographed steel, 11-5/8" long, 1905-14.		
	(A) Cream and yellow, red trim, gray roof.	400	900
	(B) Green, black trim, light green roof.	400	900
73	Observation car, lithographed steel, brown sides, 12" long, 1915-20.	300	700
74	Stock car, lithographed steel, 11-5/8" long, 1905-14.		
	(A) Cream and yellow, red trim, gray roof.	400	1000
	(B) Green, black trim, light green roof.	400	1000
75	Caboose, lithographed steel, 11-5/8" long, 1905-14.		
	(A) Cream and yellow, red trim, gray roof.	400	1000
	(B) Green, black trim, light green roof.	400	1000
76	Gravel car, lithographed steel, 11-5/8" long, 1905-14.		
	(A) Cream and yellow, red trim, gray roof.	400	1000
	(B) Green, black trim, light green roof.	400	1000
77	Lumber car, lithographed steel, gray or black frame, red stakes, 11-5/8" long, 1909-14.	150	400
181	Buffet car, embossed steel, 1912-20.		
	(A) Dark green, lettered "NEW YORK CENTRAL LINES".	225	475
	(B) Dark green, lettered "THE IVES RAILWAY LINES".	150	300
	(C) Light green sides.	225	350
182	Parlor car, embossed steel, 1912-20.		
	(A) Dark green, lettered "NEW YORK CENTRAL LINES".	225	475
	(B) Dark green, lettered "THE IVES RAILWAY LINES".	150	300
	(C) Light green sides.	175	350
183	Observation car, embossed steel, dark or light green, lettered "THE IVES RAILWAY LINES", 1912-20.	150	350
1129	Electric-outline locomotive, 2-4-2, electric-powered, cast-iron, black, 1915-20.	1050	1800

		Gd	Exc
3239	NYC-style electric-outline locomotive, 0-4-4-0, cast-iron, painted black, gray or olive green, 13" long, 1913-20.	450	1000
3240	NYC-style electric-outline locomotive, 0-4-4-0, electric-powered, cast-iron, painted black, 1912-20. Should have original steel roof for these values.	450	1000
7345	SFRD, merchandise car (boxcar), embossed steel, yellow sides, 11-1/2" long, 1915-20.	200	500
7446	PRR, stock car, embossed steel, 11-1/2" long, 1915-20.	75	175
7546	Caboose, steel, red, 11-1/2" long, 1915-20.		
	(A) Brown roof, red cupola, silver lettering.	125	300
	(B) Brown roof and cupola, white lettering.	100	200
7648	"PENNA. COAL & COKE CO." hopper car, steel, black, 11-1/2", 1915-20.	75	175
7849	Texas Oil, tank car, embossed steel, 11" long, 1915-20.	250	300
7950	Coke car, steel, brown, 11-1/2" long, 1915-20.	125	300

Wide Gauge Trains

These models ride on 2-1/8" gauge track. Wide Gauge models were mostly made of heavily tinned, relatively thin steel. The surface worked well for soldering, put paint often flaked. All of the locomotives are electric-powered.

Between 1921 and 1930, the Ives freight car line underwent many changes. These included refinements in Ives' manufacturing processes, as well as the major changes under American Flyer and Lionel management. The listings here are greatly simplified, as very detailed study is necessary to distinguish the variations. Some variations do have significant premiums.

Because of the possibility that a common piece may be repainted in the colors of a less common variation, restored examples of rare variations bring only the price of common cars.

		Gd	Exc
10/10E	Electric-outline locomotive, 12" long, peacock blue, 1931-32. The "E" version has remote-control reverse.	125	300
20-190	Tank car, blue or orange tank made by American Flyer, 1928.	425	975
20-192	Merchandise car (boxcar), stamped-steel, 14" long, 1928-29.		
	(A) Pea green body, dark red roof.	175	425
	(B) Yellow body, blue-green roof.	150	300
20-192-C	Circus equipment car (boxcar), yellow, two rubber-stamped barred windows on each side, stamped-steel, "20-192" on plates, 1929.		
	(A) "THE IVES RAILWAY LINES".	900	1800
	(B) "THE IVES RAILWAY CIRCUS".	375	900
20-193-C	Circus animal car, American Flyer body, brown sides, lettered "THE IVES RAILWAY LINES" twice on each side, and "20-193", 1929.	775	1400
20-194	Gravel car (gondola), American Flyer body, black, brass nameplates, 14" long.	90	175
20-195	Caboose, American Flyer body, six windows on side, 14" long, 1928-29.		

		Gd	Exc
	(A) Dark red, maroon roof.	120	225
	(B) All light green.	250	600
20-198	Gravel car (gondola), American Flyer body, black, brass nameplates, 14" long.	75	150
170	Buffet car, green or tan, lighted, 13-1/4" long, 1925-27.	90	175
171	Parlor car, green or tan, lighted, 13-1/4" long, 1925-27.	90	150
172	Observation, green or tan, lighted, 13-1/4" long, 1925-26.	90	150
173	Observation, green, lighted, 13-1/4" long, 1924.	90	150
173-3	Observation, green, lighted, 13-1/4" long, 1924.	90	150
180	Buffet car, 17" long, 1925-28.		
	(A) Rubber-stamped lettering, red or orange body.	90	150
	(B) Brass plates, orange or light green body.	120	225
	(C) Brass plates, maroon body.	175	350
	(D) Brass plates, dark olive green body.	225	475
181	Parlor car, 17" long, 1925-28.		
	(A) Rubber-stamped lettering, red or orange body.	90	150
	(B) Brass plates; orange, maroon or light green body.	175	350
	(C) Brass plates, dark olive green.	225	475
182	Observation, 17" long, 1925-28.		
	(A) Rubber-stamped lettering, red or orange body.	90	150
	(B) Brass plates; orange, maroon or light green body.	175	350
	(C) Brass plates, dark olive green.	225	475
183	Gemini club car, dark blue, 13-1/4" long, 1922-24.	90	150
184	Buffet car, various colors, 13-1/4" long, 1921-25.	35	75
184	Club car, various colors, 13-1/4" long, 1926-1930.	50	95
185	Parlor car, various colors, 13-1/4" long, 1921-30.	35	75
186	Observation, various colors, 13-1/4" long, 1922-30.	35	75
187	Buffet car, red or orange body, 17" long, 1921-30.	90	150
187-1	Buffet car, 1922-24.		
	(A) White body, gold rubber-stamped lettering.	700	1500
	(B) Red or orange body, black lettering.	90	150
188	Parlor car, various colors, 17" long, 1921-28.	90	150
188-1	Parlor car, 17" long, 1922-24.		
	(A) White body, gold rubber-stamped lettering.	700	1500
	(B) Red or orange body, black lettering.	90	150
189	Observation, various colors, 17" long, 1921-28.	90	150
189-1	Observation, 17" long, 1922-24.		
	(A) White body, gold rubber-stamped lettering.	700	1500
	(B) Red or orange body, black lettering.	90	150
190	Tank car, 1921-30.		
	(A) "TEXAS OIL", various colors.	90	150
	(B) "Wanamaker Railway Lines" script, maroon, 1922-24.	425	900
	(C) "DOMINION OIL", orange, 1923-25.	150	300

Gd   **Exc**

The Ives 195 caboose has a very distinctive feature —a cupola that looks like it has been squashed! R. Bartelt photograph.

		Gd	Exc
	(D) "IVES", yellow, tank made by Lionel, 1929-30.	300	725
191	Coke car, stamped-steel, 1921-30.		
	(A) Brown, regular issue.	75	175
	(B) Maroon, "Wanamaker Railway Lines" script, 1922-24.	425	900
192	Merchandise car (boxcar), stamped-steel, 1921-28, 1930.		
	(A) Ives body, various colors, regular issue, 1921-28.	90	175
	(B) Ives body, maroon, "Wanamaker Railway Lines", 1922-24.	350	950
	(C) Lionel body, yellow, blue-green roof, 12-1/2" long, 1930.	525	1000
192-C	"THE IVES RAILWAY CIRCUS" boxcar, yellow, light red roof, 1928.	775	1450
193	Stock car, stamped-steel, 1921-28, 1930.		
	(A) Ives body, various colors, regular issue, 1921- 28.	150	275
	(B) Ives body, maroon, "Wanamaker Railway Lines", 1922-24.	425	950
	(C) Lionel body, orange, dark red roof, 12-1/2" long.	725	1450
193-C	Stock car, American Flyer body, 14" long, 1928-29.		
	(A) Pea green body, red roof.	175	350
	(B) Orange body, dark red roof.	150	300
194	Coal car, 1921-30.		
	(A) Green, gray, or black; regular issue.	150	275
	(B) Maroon, lettered "Wanamaker Railway Lines", 1922-24.	425	950
195	Caboose, 1921-30.		
	(A) Ives body, five windows on side, red or maroon, 11-1/2" long, 1921-27.	150	300
	(B) Ives body, two windows on side, red, 11-1/2" long, 1928.	525	1000
	(C) Lionel body, two windows on side, red, maroon roof, 12-1/2" long, 1930.	120	250
196	Flatcar, stamped-steel, 11-1/2" long, 1922-28.		
	(A) Regular issue, dark green, stamped lettering, 1921-25.	75	125
	(B) Maroon, lettered "Wanamaker Railway Lines", 1922-24.	350	725
	(C) Olive green, Harmony Creamery special with milk tanks.	600	900
	(D) Regular issue, orange, stamped lettering, 1926- 28.	45	75
	(E) Regular issue, orange, decal lettering, 1930.	90	175

		Gd	Exc
196-C	Circus flatcar, yellow, two circus wagons, 11-1/2" long, 1928. Note: deduct $400-500 if wagons are not present.		
	(A) Lettered "THE IVES RAILWAY CIRCUS".	775	1200
	(B) Lettered "THE IVES RAILWAY SHOW".	900	1325
197	Lumber car, four stakes on each side.		
	(A) Ives body, six-piece lumber load, orange or light green, 11-1/2" long, 1928-29.	120	225
	(B) Lionel body, one-piece lumber load, green, 12-1/2" long.	300	475
198	Gravel car, Lionel body, black or maroon, 12-1/2" long, 1930.	120	225
199	Derrick car, Lionel body, peacock blue; dark green trim, 12- 1/2" long, 1929.		
	(A) "199" on brass plate.	450	800
	(B) "199" rubber stamped below each window.	825	1425
241	Club car, top of the line model, twelve wheels, 19" long, 1928-29. Note: reproductions have been made; they bring significantly lower prices.		
	(A) Black body, red roof and trucks.	775	1800
	(B) Green body and roof, black trucks.	1200	2500
	(C) Copper-plated body, nickel roof and trucks.	1425	2950
	(D) Orange body, black roof and trucks.	1050	2400
242	Parlor car, top of the line model, twelve wheels, 19" long, 1928-29. Note: reproductions have been made; they bring significantly lower prices.		
	(A) Black body, red roof and trucks.	775	1800
	(B) Green body and roof, black trucks.	1200	2600
	(C) Copper-plated body, nickel roof, and trucks.	1425	2950
	(D) Orange body, black roof and trucks.	1050	2400
243	Observation, top of the line model, twelve wheels, 19" long, 1928-29. Note: reproductions have been made; they bring significantly lower prices.		
	(A) Black body, red roof and trucks.	775	1800
	(B) Green body and roof, black trucks.	1200	2600
	(C) Copper-plated body, nickel roof, and trucks.	1425	2900
	(D) Orange body, black roof and trucks.	1050	2400
244	Baggage car, light green, eight wheels, 19" long, 1929.	650	1500
245	Pullman, light green, eight wheels, 19" long, 1929.	650	1500
246	Dining car, Lionel body, detailed interior, 18-1/4" long, 1930.		
	(A) Blue body, red roof and trucks.	1200	2400
	(B) Orange body, black roof and trucks.	2400	4800
	(C) Black body, red roof and trucks.	2400	4200
247	Club car, Lionel body, detailed interior, 18-1/4" long, 1930.		
	(A) Blue body, red roof and trucks.	175	350
	(B) Orange body, black roof and trucks.	175	350
	(C) Black body, red roof and trucks.	200	400
248	Chair car, Lionel body, detailed interior, 18-1/4" long, 1930.		
	(A) Blue body, red roof and trucks.	1200	2400

		Gd	Exc

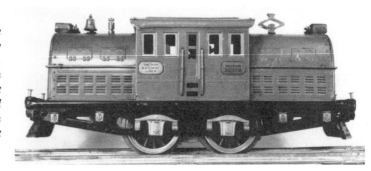

Another example of the elegant designs produced by Ives, the 3237R locomotive. This design is described as an "electric-outline" because it follows the design of a real locomotive that operated on electricity. R. Bartelt photograph.

		Gd	Exc
	(B) Orange body, black roof and trucks.	1300	2900
	(C) Black body, red roof and trucks.	1300	2400
249	Observation, Lionel body, detailed interior, 17-1/2" long, 1930.		
	(A) Blue body, red roof and trucks.	1200	2400
	(B) Orange body, black roof and trucks.	1300	2900
	(C) Black body, red roof and trucks.	1300	2400
332	Baggage car, peacock blue, dark green roof, 12" long, 1931-32.	50	120
339	Pullman car, peacock blue, dark green roof, 12" long, 1931-32.	50	120
341	Observation, peacock blue, dark green roof, 12" long, 1931-32.	50	120
418	Pullman car, green body and roof, 18-1/4" long, 1931.	425	725
419	Club car, green body and roof, 18-1/4" long, 1931.	425	725
431	Club car, green body and roof, 18-1/4" long, 1931.	600	1200
490	Observation, green body and roof, 17-5/8" long, 1931.	425	725
1132	Steam locomotive, cast-iron, 0-4-0, hand reverse, stamped-steel number 40 tender, 1921-26.		
	(A) Black finish.	350	800
	(B) Tan finish.	750	1500
	(C) White finish.	1000	2500
	(D) Black finish, special "John Wanamaker" script lettering.	2000	5000
1132R	Steam locomotive, same as 1132, but automatic sequence reverse, 1924-26.		
	(A) Black finish.	350	800
	(B) Tan finish.	750	1500
	(C) White finish.	1000	2500
1132	Steam locomotive, cast-iron, 4-4-0, black, engineer in cab window, stamped-steel 40 tender, 1928.	1000	2500
1134/1134R	Steam locomotive, cast-iron, 4-4-0, 40 tender, 1927. "R" version has sequence reverse.		
	(A) Olive green, stamped-steel tender.	1000	2000
	(B) Olive green, die-cast tender.	1500	2700
	(C) Black, stamped-steel tender.	1500	2700
	(D) Black, die-cast tender.	1500	2700

		Gd	Exc
1134/1134R	Steam locomotive, die-cast, 4-4-2, die-cast 40 tender, 1928-29. Copper- and nickel-plated versions must have original castings to bring the full price.		
	(A) Black.	1000	2200
	(B) Copper- or nickel-plated.	2000	5500
	(C) Green.	1200	2700
1134/1134R	Steam locomotive, die-cast, 4-4-2, concealed headlight, removable boiler front, 1930.		
	(A) Black.	1000	2500
	(B) Red.	1700	4500
1760/1760E	Steam locomotive, 2-4-0, black, brass nameplates, 1931. The "E" version has remote-control reversing.	800	2000
1764	Electric-outline locomotive, 4-4-4, terra cotta sides, maroon frame. Reproductions sell for $150-300.	1500	2500
1766	Pullman, terra cotta color, maroon roof, 15" long, 1932. Reproductions have been made.	350	750
1767	Baggage car, terra cotta color, maroon roof, 15" long, 1932. Reproductions have been made.	350	750
1768	Observation car, terra cotta color, maroon roof, 15" long, 1932. Reproductions have been made.	350	750
1770/1770E	Steam locomotive, 2-4-2, black, brass nameplates, 1932. The "E" version has remote-control reversing.	600	1000
1771	Lumber car, black, eight stakes, one-piece lumber load, 11-1/2" long, 1931-32.	50	100
1772	Gondola, peacock blue, brass plates, 1931-32.	60	100
1773	Cattle car, green sides, orange roof, 1931-32.	80	150
1774	Boxcar, yellow, orange roof, brass plates, 1931-32.	80	150
1775	Oil car, white tank, brass plates, 1931-32.	100	200
1776	Coal car, red, brass plates, 1931-32.	100	250
1777	Caboose, green, brass plates, 1931-32.	75	150
1778	Refrigerator car, white, blue-green roof, 11-1/2" long, 1931-32.	200	450
1779	Derrick car, made by Lionel, 1931.	—	1000
3235/3235R	Electric-outline locomotive, brass nameplates, 1925-27. The "R" version has remote-control reversing.		
	(A) Various colors, regular issue.	80	150
	(B) Maroon, "Wanamaker Railway Lines".	1000	1500
3236/3236R	Electric-outline locomotive, various colors, brass nameplates, 1925-26. The "R" version has remote-control reversing.		
	(A) Cast-iron frame, 1924-27.	80	160
	(B) Steel frame, 1928.	80	160
	(C) Lionel #8 body on Ives steel frame, 1929-30.	80	160
3237/3237R	Electric-outline locomotive, stamped-steel, brass nameplates, 1926-30.		
	(A) Olive green, regular issue.	650	1500
	(B) Cadet blue, "TRANSCONTINENTAL LIMITED".		NRS
	(C) Cadet blue, "SOUTHERN PACIFIC".		NRS
3240	Electric-outline locomotive, cast-iron, 0-4-4-0, black, 14-1/2", 1921.	725	2000

		Gd	Exc
3241/3241R	Electric-outline locomotive, cast-iron, 0-4-0, 1921-25; may be found with cast-iron or steel frame; rubber-stamped lettering or brass plates. The "R" version has remote-control reversing.		
	(A) Various colors, regular issue.	200	300
	(B) Maroon, "Wanamaker Railway Lines" script.	900	1500
3242/3242R	Electric-outline locomotive, stamped-steel, 1921-30; may be found with cast-iron or steel frame; rubber-stamped lettering or brass plates. The "R" version has remote-control reversing.		
	(A) Various colors, regular issue.	130	275
	(B) Maroon, "Wanamaker Railway Lines" script.	400	900
3243/3243R	Electric-outline locomotive, stamped-steel, 4-4-4, 1921-28. The "R" version has remote-control reversing.		
	(A) Orange, red, or olive green.	350	650
	(B) White, gold lettering.	1500	4000
3245/3245R	Electric-outline locomotive, stamped-steel, 1928-30. The "R" version has remote-control reversing. Reproductions sell for $400-500.	1500	3200

O Gauge Mechanical (Clockwork) Locomotives

This is one of the most difficult areas of Ives to properly describe, as it was undoubtedly their most prolific. In thirty years of production, the company made many, many changes in the product line — ranging from subtle variations in the body castings to distinct changes in the colors or wheel arrangements. Both tinplate (1901-1906) and cast-iron bodies (1901-1930) were used. Advanced collectors will note that competitive models produced by American Miniature Railway Company were often similar.

The listings presented here provide an introduction to the topic and an excellent guide line for estimating value. Some of the earlier variations of the items listed bring appreciably higher prices, however careful analysis is required to make a positive identification. If one encounters a substantial collection of these trains, or if one develops a particular interest in them, it would be very wise to consult *Greenberg's Guide to Ives Trains, Volume II* for further details.

No. 1	Stamped-steel or cast-iron body, four-wheel tender.		
	(A) Stamped-steel, 2-2-0, red "IMC" below cab window, 1903-04.	150	300
	(B) Stamped-steel, 2-2-0, gold "No. 1" below cab window, 1905-06.	150	300
	(C) Cast-iron, 2-2-0, lithographed plate below cab window, 1907-10.	125	250
	(D) Cast-iron, 0-4-0, two square cab windows, no lettering, 1917-25.	40	75
	(E) Cast-iron, 0-4-0, white rubber-stamped lettering below cab window, 1926-29.	60	100
No. 2	Stamped-steel or cast-iron body, four-wheel tender.		
	(A) Stamped-steel, 2-2-0.	200	300
	(B) Cast-iron, 0-4-0.	200	300
No. 3	Stamped-steel or cast-iron body, four-wheel tender.		

		Gd	Exc
	(A) Stamped-steel, 2-2-0, gold lithographed lettering below cab window, 1902-06.	225	400
	(B) Similar to (A), but lithographed red numberboard with gold lettering below cab window, 1907-09.	200	300
	(C) Stamped-steel, 0-2-2, gold lettering below window, 1907-10.	200	300
	(D) Cast-iron, 0-2-2, white lettering on red numberboard, 1911.	200	300
No. 4	Cast-iron, 2-2-0, white lettering on red numberboard, 1912.	200	300
No. 5	Cast-iron, 0-4-0, black, 1917-22.	40	75
No. 6	Cast-iron, 0-4-0, black, 1917-28.	40	75
No. 7	Cast-iron, black, limited information available.		NRS
No. 9	Cast-iron, 0-4-0, rubber-stamped lettering below cab window, 1915-16.	140	250
No. 11	Cast-iron.		
	(A) 2-2-0, black, gold trim, 1901.		NRS
	(B) 0-4-0, black, red plate painted below cab window, no lettering, 1906.	140	250
	(C) 0-4-0, black, lithographed red plate with gold lettering, 1909.	140	250
	(D) 0-4-0, black, lithographed black plate with white lettering, 1910.	125	225
	(E) 0-4-0, black, white rubber-stamped lettering below cab window, 1915-16.	75	125
No. 17	Cast-iron, 0-4-0, black.	85	185
No. 21	Electric-outline engine, dark red.	200	350
No. 30	Electric-outline engine, red and green.	175	300
No. 31	Electric-outline engine, red and green.	175	300
No. 32	Electric-outline engine, red and green.	200	375
No. 176	Cast-iron, 0-4-0, black, rubber-stamped number, four-wheel tender with decal, circa 1930.	150	285

O Gauge Equipment

This section includes passenger cars, freight cars, and electrically-powered locomotives. Mechanical (clockwork) locomotives are listed separately in the preceding section.

		Gd	Exc
50	Baggage car, four-wheel, 1902-30; cars have solid wheels unless noted.		
	(A) Spoked wheels, hand-painted green body and frame.	200	400
	(B) Lithographed, black and white sides.	150	300
	(C) Lithographed, yellow/red or red/yellow.	20	40
	(D) Lithographed, green.	20	40
	(E) Lithographed, orange.	30	60
51	Passenger car, four-wheel, 1901-30; cars have solid wheels unless noted.		
	(A) Spoked wheels, hand-painted green or red body, Gothic arch windows.	300	600
	(B) Spoked wheels, hand-painted green or red body, rectangular windows.	200	400

		Gd	Exc

The 60 Limited Vestibule Express car is from the shorter 60 series. Toy manufacturers often made several different series at a time so that customers could chose their price level.

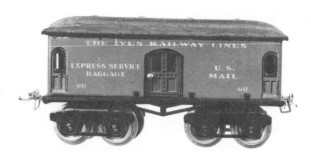

		Gd	Exc
	(C) Lithographed, red or yellow, Gothic arch windows.	200	400
	(D) Lithographed, yellow, "LIMITED VESTIBULE EXPRESS" above windows.	200	400
	(E) Lithographed, green, "LIMITED VESTIBULE EXPRESS" above windows.	75	150
	(F) Lithographed, yellow and brown, "PENNSYLVANIA" above windows.	30	60
	(F) Lithographed, various colors, "THE IVES RAILWAY LINES" above windows.	20	40
52	Passenger car, four-wheel, lithographed, 1908-30.		
	(A) White and black, "LIMITED VESTIBULE EXPRESS".	60	120
	(B) Yellow and brown, "PENNSYLVANIA LINES".	50	100
	(C) Various colors, "IVES RAILWAY LINES".	20	40
53	Merchandise car (boxcar), lithographed, four-wheel 1908-30. Note: car has open doorway but no door.		
	(A) Yellow sides, 4-1/2" long, 1908-09.	100	200
	(B) White, orange, or red sides, 5-1/2" long, 1910-14.	20	40
54	Gravel car, four-wheel, 1901-30.		
	(A) Hand-painted (original), green; red or white stripes; cast-iron wheels, 1901-04.	100	200
	(B) Lithographed, red, black or white stripes, 1905-09.	100	200
	(C) Lithographed wood side detail, red or green car, 1910-30.	20	40
55	Stock car, lithographed, four-wheel, 1908-30.		
	(A) Yellow; black or green lettering, 4-1/2" long, 1908-09.	100	200
	(B) Orange sides, maroon trim, 5-1/2" long, 1910-14.	50	100
	(C) Gray; maroon trim, 5-1/2" long, 1915-30.	20	40
	(D) Tan; green stripes, 5-1/2" long, 1915-30.	20	40
56	Caboose, lithographed, 1908-30.		
	(A) Questionable existence, 4-1/2" long.		NRS
	(B) White sides, gray and maroon trim, 5-1/2" long.	60	120
	(C) Dark brownish-red, 5-1/2" long.	20	40
57	Lumber car, stamped-steel, lumber load, 1910-14.		

		Gd	Exc
	(A) Tan or brown frame.	30	60
	(B) Orange or green frame.	15	30
60	Baggage car, 1901-30.		
	(A) Earliest model, four-wheel, cast-iron wheels, red or green, white horizontal stripes.	250	400
	(B) Four-wheel, lithographed, various colors, "LIMITED VESTIBULE EXPRESS".	200	300
	(C) Eight-wheel, lithographed, various colors, "LIMITED VESTIBULE EXPRESS".	100	150
	(D) Eight-wheel, lithographed, various colors, "THE IVES RAILWAY LINE".	10	35
61	Passenger car, 1901-28.		
	(A) Earliest model, four-wheel, cast-iron wheels, red or green, white horizontal stripes.	275	400
	(B) Four-wheel, lithographed, various colors, "LIMITED VESTIBULE EXPRESS".	275	400
	(C) Eight-wheel, lithographed, various colors, "THE IVES RAILWAY LINE".	10	35
61	Chair car, eight-wheel, various colors, 1915-21.	10	25
62	Parlor car, 1901-30.		
	(A) Earliest model, four-wheel, red or green, white horizontal stripes.	275	400
	(B) Four-wheel, various colors, "LIMITED VESTIBULE EXPRESS".	200	300
	(C) Eight-wheel, various colors, "LIMITED VESTIBULE EXPRESS".	100	150
	(D) Eight-wheel, various colors, "THE IVES RAILWAY LINE".	10	35
63	Gravel car, four- or eight-wheel, 1902-30.		
	(A) Four-wheel, approx. 5-1/2", hand-painted, vertical stripes.	150	300
	(B) Four-wheel, approx. 5-1/2", lithographed, vertical stripes, blue/gray or tan/brown.	125	250
	(C) Four-wheel, approx. 6-1/2", lithographed, simulated-wood, buff/brown.	75	150
	(D) Eight-wheel, lithographed, steel finish, dark green.	45	150
	(E) Eight-wheel, lithographed, steel finish, gray.	15	45

64 Series Cars

One of the many ways in which Ives won favor with its customers was the promotion of a variety of railroad logos (called heralds) on its freight cars. The 64 series includes several cars that share the design of the No. 64 boxcar; the cars in the series have various numbers, but they are generally collected as a series.

64	Merchandise car (boxcar), eight-wheel, lithographed, 1908-30.		
	(A) White body and roof, red roofwalk.	100	300
	(B) Yellow, gray roof.	75	225

	Gd	**Exc**

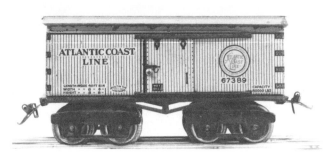

Ives used a variety of railroad heralds to enhance the realism of their toy trains. The 67389 Atlantic Coast Line boxcar is from the 64 series. R. Bartelt photograph.

64158	Lehigh Valley, merchandise car, eight-wheel, lithographed, orange sides, gray roof, 1913-30.	85	200
64159	NYC & HR, merchandise car, eight-wheel, lithographed, orange sides, gray roof, 1913-30.	85	200
64160	Pennsylvania Lines, merchandise car, eight-wheel, lithographed, orange, gray roof, 1913-30.	85	200
64385	Baltimore & Ohio, merchandise car, eight-wheel, lithographed, red, gray roof, 1913-30.	75	175
64386	NYNH & H, merchandise car, eight-wheel, lithographed, red, gray roof, 1913-30.	85	200
64387	Canadian Pacific, merchandise car, eight-wheel, lithographed, yellow, gray roof, 1913-30.	100	275
64388	Northern Pacific, merchandise car, eight-wheel, lithographed, yellow, gray roof, 1913-30.	100	275
64396	Santa Fe, merchandise car, eight-wheel, lithographed, orange, gray roof, 1913-30.	100	275
67389	Atlantic Coast Line, merchandise car, eight-wheel, lithographed, yellow, red or gray roof, scarce, 1913-30.	150	300
85829	Erie, merchandise car, eight-wheel, lithographed, red, gray or red roof, 1913-30.	100	250
118658	Chicago and North Western, merchandise car, eight-wheel, lithographed, orange, gray or red roof, 1913-30.	175	300
151370	Rock Island, merchandise car, eight-wheel, red, gray or red roof, 1913-30.	100	250
641506	Illinois Central, merchandise car, eight-wheel, yellow, gray or red roof, 1913-30.	150	300

Numerical Listing, Cont'd

65	Cattle car, stamped-steel, circa 1906-30.		
	(A) Four-wheel, dark gray lithography, brown and red trim.	80	175
	(B) Eight-wheel, white lithography, red roofwalk.	100	225
	(C) Eight-wheel, enameled body, rubber-stamped lettering.		NRS

		Gd	Exc
	(D) Eight-wheel, lithographed, yellow, gray roof.	20	40
66	Tank car, 6-1/2" long, 1910-28.		
	(A) Red tank, green or red dome, lithographed, "TANK LINE".	125	200
	(B) Black tank and dome, no lettering.	35	100
	(C) Brown tank, black dome, "66 STANDARD OIL 66" on sides.	35	100
	(D) Orange or dk. blue-gray tank, black dome, rubber-stamped lettering.	20	60
67	Caboose, eight-wheel, lithographed, 1910-30.		
	(A) White simulated wood, grayish-white roof.	75	150
	(B) Red simulated wood, gray roof.	60	100
68	Merchants Despatch, refrigerator car, eight-wheel, lithographed, 1910-26.		
	(A) White sides and roof, red roofwalk.	100	250
	(B) White sides, gray roof.	100	250
68	Observation car, eight-wheel, lithographed, green, 1925-30.	15	25
69	Lumber car, eight-wheel, lumber load, enameled, var. colors, 1910-30.	25	45
70	Baggage car, eight-wheel, lithographed, 11-5/8" long, circa 1912. Note: This is a 1 Gauge car mounted on O Gauge trucks.		
	(A) White sides.	200	400
	(B) Brown sides.	150	325
	(C) Yellow sides.	150	375
70	Baggage car, eight-wheel, lithographed, red sides, 6-1/2", 1923-25.	15	35
71	Buffet car, eight-wheel, lithographed, brown or white, 11-5/8" long, circa 1912. Note: This is a 1 Gauge car mounted on O Gauge trucks.	400	700
71	Chair car, eight-wheel, lithographed, red sides, 6-1/2", 1923-25.	15	40
72	Chicago, passenger car, eight-wheel, lithographed, brown or white, 11-5/8" long, circa 1912. Note: This is a 1 Gauge car mounted on O Gauge trucks.	400	700
72	Drawing room car, eight-wheel, lithographed, red sides, 6-1/2", 1923-25.	15	45
121	Caboose, eight-wheel, red enamel, gray roof, 9", 1929-30.	35	85
122	Tank car, eight-wheel, yellow enamel, brass dome, 9", 1929-30.	50	150
123	Lumber car, eight-wheel, enameled frame, wood load, 9", various colors, 1910-30.	15	45
124	Refrigerator, eight-wheel, lithographed, 9".		
	(A) White sides and roof.	70	150
	(B) White sides, gray roof.	40	125

125 Series Cars

One of the many ways in which Ives won favor with its customers was the promotion of a variety of railroad logos (called heralds) on its freight cars. The 125 series includes several cars that share the design of the No. 125 boxcar; the cars in the series have various numbers, but they are generally collected as a series.

125	Merchandise car, eight-wheel, lithographed, 9", 1904-30.		
	(A) Yellow sides, brown roof.	100	300

Gd   **Exc**

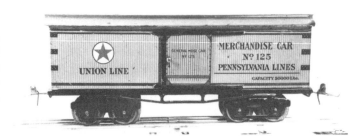

The No. 125 Union Line box-car is from the longer 125 series of boxcars. This group is a popular area of specialization for Ives collectors. R. Bartelt photograph.

		Gd	Exc
	(B) Reddish-brown sides, brown roof.	80	250
	(C) White sides, gray roof.	50	100
	(D) Off-white sides, red roof.	75	200
12578	Union Pacific, merchandise car, eight-wheel, lithographed, yellow, brown roof, 9", 1915-30.	250	500
12579	Cotton Belt Route, merchandise car, eight-wheel, lithographed, orange, black roof, 9", 1915-30.	250	700
12580	Wabash Railroad, merchandise car, eight-wheel, lithographed, gray, 9", 1915-30.	250	500
12581	MKT, merchandise car, eight-wheel, lithographed, gray, 9", 1915- 30.	250	500
12582	Frisco, merchandise car, eight-wheel, lithographed, red, 9", 1915-30.	250	500
12584	Salt Lake Route, merchandise car, eight-wheel, lithographed, red, 9", 1915-30.	250	600
12585	Chicago Great Western, merchandise car, eight-wheel, gray, black roof, 9", 1915-30.	350	800
37158	CB & Q, merchandise car, eight-wheel, lithographed, off-white, gray roof, 1913-30.	100	175

Numerical Listing, Cont'd

		Gd	Exc
126	Caboose, four-wheel, lithographed, red, 1904-09.		
	(A) Gothic-arch windows.	125	300
	(B) Flat-top windows.	100	200
127	Cattle car, eight-wheel, lithographed, 1904-30.		
	(A) Early design, yellow or gray, no diagonal bracing on sides.	100	300
	(B) Later design, yellow or gray, diagonal bracing on sides.	40	100
128	Gravel car, eight-wheel, lithographed, 1904-30.		
	(A) Early flat-bottom frame, gray, blue lettering.	75	250
	(B) Frame with truss rods, greenish-black, silver lettering.	20	60
	(C) Frame with truss rods, light gray, red lettering.	15	50
129	Parlor car, eight-wheel, lithographed to represent wood or metal sides, 1904-29.		

		Gd	Exc
	(A) Various colors, wood-side lithography, "LIMITED VESTIBULE EXPRESS", 9" long.	100	200
	(B) Forest green, wood-side lithography, "LIMITED VESTIBULE EXPRESS", 9-1/2" long.	40	75
	(C) Red, steel-side lithography, 9-1/2" long.	200	400
	(D) Olive green, "THE IVES RAILWAY LINES", steel-side lithography, 9-1/2" long.	50	100
	(E) Orange, "THE IVES RAILWAY LINES", steel-side lithography, 9-1/2" long.	30	75
130	Buffet car, eight-wheel, lithographed to represent wood or metal sides, 1904-29.		
	(A) Yellow sides, wood-side lithography, "LIMITED VESTIBULE EXPRESS", 9" long.	150	400
	(B) Various colors, wood-side lithography, "LIMITED VESTIBULE EXPRESS", 9-1/2" long.	40	75
	(C) Orange or green, steel-side lithography, "THE IVES RAILWAY LINES", 9-1/2" long.	25	75
131	Baggage car, eight-wheel, lithographed to represent wood or metal sides, 1904-30.		
	(A) Various colors, wood-side lithography, "LIMITED VESTIBULE EXPRESS", 9" long.	150	400
	(B) Forest green, wood-side lithography, "LIMITED VESTIBULE EXPRESS", 9-1/2" long.	40	100
	(C) Orange, steel-side lithography, "THE IVES RAILWAY LINES", 9-1/2" long.	50	100
132	Observation car, eight-wheel, lithographed, 1924-29.		
	(A) Orange body and roof.	30	75
	(B) Green body and roof.	50	100
133	Parlor car, brass plates, 8" long, 1928-30.		
	(A) Blue or orange body and roof.	15	30
	(B) Green body and roof.	30	60
	(C) Black, red roof.	25	50
134	Observation car, brass plates, 8" long, 1928-30.		
	(A) Solid blue or orange.	15	30
	(B) Solid green.	30	60
	(C) Orange/black roof or black/red roof.	25	60
	(D) Blue/red roof.	45	85
135	Parlor car, brass plates, 1926-30.		
	(A) Tan, orange, or blue, 8" long.	15	30
	(B) Red, 8" long.	25	50
	(C) Red, 8-3/4" long.	25	50
	(D) Blue; red roof, 8-3/4" long.	45	85
136	Observation car, brass plates, 1926-30.		
	(A) Tan, orange, blue, 8" long.	15	30
	(B) Red, 8" long.	25	50

		Gd	Exc

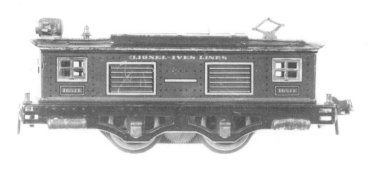

After Ives went bankrupt, Lionel used the Ives name on its own low-priced sets for a short time. The 1651E is an example of a Lionel-Ives locomotive.

		Gd	Exc
	(C) Red, 8-3/4" long.	25	50
	(D) Blue; red roof, 8-3/4" long.	25	50
141	Parlor car, brass plates, 1926-30.		
	(A) Copper plated.	500	1000
	(B) Black body, red roof and trucks.	100	200
	(C) Gray, green, orange, or olive.	60	120
142	Observation car, brass plates, 1926-30.		
	(A) Copper plated.	500	1000
	(B) Black body, red roof and trucks.	100	200
	(C) Gray, green, orange, or olive.	60	120
257	Steam locomotive, 2-4-0 with tender, stamped-steel body, black, 1931-32.	185	300
258	Steam locomotive, 2-4-0 with tender, stamped-steel body, black, 1931-32.	185	300
550	Baggage car, four-wheel, lithographed, 6-1/2", 1913-30.		
	(A) White, red or dark red.	20	40
	(B) Emerald green, black roof.	25	50
	(C) Light blue and buff two-tone.	25	50
	(D) Buff.	25	75
551	Chair car, four-wheel, lithographed, 6-1/2", 1913-30.		
	(A) White, red or dark red.	20	40
	(B) Light blue and buff two-tone.	25	50
	(C) Buff.	25	75
552	Parlor car, four-wheel, lithographed, 6-1/2", 1929-30.		
	(A) Emerald green.	20	40
	(B) Light green and buff two-tone.	25	50
558	Observation car, four-wheel, lithographed, 6-1/2", 1927-30.		
	(A) White, red roof.	25	50
	(B) Emerald green, black roof.	20	40
	(C) Green/buff or blue/buff two-tone.	20	50
	(D) Buff.	25	75
562	Caboose, four-wheel, Lionel body, red, 1930.	50	100

		Gd	Exc
563	Gravel car, four-wheel, lithographed, dark green or light gray, 1917-30.	25	50
564	Atlantic Coast Line, merchandise car, four-wheel, lithographed, 1917-28.	85	175
564	Canadian Pacific, merchandise car, four-wheel, lithographed, 1913-30.	85	175
564	Erie, merchandise car, four-wheel, lithographed, 1917-28.	50	100
564	NYNH & H, merchandise car, four-wheel, lithographed, 1929-30.	75	150
565	Stock car, four-wheel, lithographed, light yellow or orange, 1913-30.	20	40
566	Tank car, four-wheel, painted body, 1913-29.		
	(A) Rubber-stamped "STANDARD OIL Co."	30	60
	(B) Brass plates lettered "IVES".	60	125
567	Caboose, four-wheel, lithographed, dark red, 1913-30.	30	60
569	Lumber car, four-wheel, black or green, 1913-30.	15	30
610	Pullman, eight-wheel, olive or light green, 9", 1931-32.	25	60
612	Observation car, eight-wheel, olive or light green, 9", 1931-32.	25	60
1100	Steam locomotive, cast-iron, four-wheel tender.		
	(A) 2-2-0, lithographed numberboard, 1910-13.	100	200
	(B) 0-4-0, lithographed numberboard, 1914-18.	75	150
	(C) 0-4-0, rubber-stamped lettering, 1917-22.	60	100
1102	Steam locomotive, 0-4-0, cast-iron, black, red and gold trim, 1910-13.	250	500
1116	Steam locomotive, 0-4-0, cast-iron, black, gold trim, four-wheel tender, 1916-22.	80	150
1117	Steam locomotive, 0-4-0, cast-iron, lithographed numberboard, 1910-16.	65	125
1118	Steam locomotive, 0-4-0, cast-iron, four-wheel tender, 1910-25. Note: Earlier versions are worth significantly more, however the differences are very subtle and require careful study.	75	150
1120	Steam locomotive, cast-iron, two different versions.		
	(A) 0-4-0, sold without tender, 1914.	125	200
	(B) 4-4-0, eight-wheel tender, 1928.	300	500
1122	Steam locomotives, 4-4-2, die-cast boiler, brass trim, elaborate detail, 1929-30. Beware of reproductions and restorations.		
	(A) Black boiler and tender.	200	350
	(B) Copper boiler and tender.	1500	3000
	(C) Crimson red boiler and tender; original paint almost always shows some flaking or bubbling.	750	1200
1125	Steam locomotive.		
	(A) 4-4-0, black, usually with red and gold trim, 1912-17.	250	450
	(B) 0-4-0, blue boiler and tender, 1930.	125	350
	(C) 0-4-0, black boiler and tender, 1930.	250	500
1504	Pullman, four-wheel, lithographed, 5-1/2", 1931-32.	10	20
1651	Electric-outline locomotive, eight wheels, steel frame, blue or red, 1931.	60	120
1651E	Electric-outline locomotive, eight wheels, steel frame, red, 1932.	60	120
1661	Steam locomotive, 2-4-0, stamped-steel boiler, black, 1932.	75	150
1663	Steam locomotive, 2-4-2, stamped-steel boiler, black, 1931.	300	500

		Gd	Exc

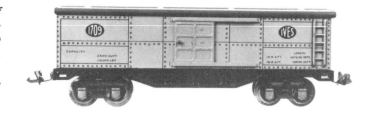

Another example of Lionel-Ives production is the lithographed 1709 boxcar of 1932. Such low-cost items were appropriate during the Great Depression.

		Gd	Exc
1677	Gondola, eight-wheel, lithographed, blue, 1931-32.	15	30
1678	Cattle car, eight-wheel, lithographed, green, 1931-32.	30	60
1679	Boxcar, eight-wheel, lithographed, yellow, blue roof, 1931- 32.	15	30
1680	Oil car, eight-wheel, aluminum finish, 1931-32.	15	30
1682	Caboose, eight-wheel, lithographed, red, 1931-32.	15	30
1690	Pullman, eight-wheel, lithographed, yellow/blue or red/brown, 7-1/2", 1931-32.	10	25
1691	Observation car, eight-wheel, lithographed, yellow/blue or red/brown, 7-1/2", 1931-32.	10	25
1694	Electric-outline locomotive, 2-D-2, beige and maroon, 1932. Note: Reproductions sell for approximately $300 in exc. condition.	1100	2200
1695	Pullman, twelve-wheel, light gray, maroon roof, 12", 1932. Note: Reproductions are available.	300	600
1696	Baggage, twelve-wheel, light gray, maroon roof, 12", 1932. Note: Reproductions are available.	300	600
1697	Observation car, twelve-wheel, light gray, maroon roof, 12", 1932. Note: Reproductions are available.	300	600
1707	Gondola, eight-wheel, lithographed, tan and burnt orange, 1932.	25	50
1708	Cattle car, eight-wheel, lithographed, light green, 1932.	30	60
1709	Boxcar, eight-wheel, lithographed, two-tone blue, 1932.	30	60
1712	Caboose, eight-wheel, lithographed, orange-red, 1931-32.	30	60
1810	Electric-outline locomotive, four-wheel, lithographed, blue, 1931-32.	60	100
1811	Pullman, four-wheel, lithographed, blue and orange, 6", 1931-32.	10	20
1812	Observation, four-wheel, lithographed, blue and orange, 6", 1931-32.	10	20
1813	Baggage, four-wheel, lithographed, blue and orange, 6", 1931-32.	10	20
1815	Steam locomotive, 0-4-0, black, 1931-32.	60	100
3200	Electric-outline locomotive, four wheels, cast-iron.		
	(A) Green, gold trim, 1910-13.	400	800
	(B) Black, gold trim, 1911-13.	250	500
	(C) Maroon, gold trim, 1911-13.	400	700
	(D) Tan, gold trim, 1911-13.	400	800
	(E) Black, red trim, 1914-16.	125	200

Gd   Exc

The 3254 Ives Railway Lines electric-outline locomotive dates from 1925-28.

		Gd	Exc
3216	Electric-outline locomotive, four wheels, cast-iron, gray or black, 1917.	125	250
3217	Electric-outline locomotive, four wheels, cast-iron.		
	(A) Maroon, gold and red trim, 1911-13.	300	600
	(B) Black, red trim 1914-16.	75	125
3218	Electric-outline locomotive, four wheels, cast-iron.		
	(A) Maroon, red and gold trim, 1911.	400	800
	(B) Red, gold trim, 1913.	300	600
	(C) Black, red and gold trim.	150	300
	(D) Black, red and gold trim, 1917.	125	200
3220	Electric-outline locomotive, eight wheels, cast-iron, black, 1916.	300	600
3238	Electric-outline locomotive, 1-D-1, cast-iron, top of the line model, black, 1910-17.		
	(A) Early model, raised lettering.	450	800
	(B) Later model, rubber-stamped lettering.	250	450
3250	Electric-outline locomotive, four wheels, stamped-steel body, cast-iron frame; various colors: forest green, brown, blue-gray, salmon-red, tan-orange, maroon, dark green; 1918-25.	50	125
3251	Electric-outline locomotive, four wheels, stamped-steel body, cast-iron frame; various colors: olive green, red, maroon, peacock blue, dark green; 1918-27.	50	125
3252	Electric-outline locomotive, four wheels, stamped-steel body, cast-iron frame; various colors: dark red, dark green, light green, black, maroon, burnt-orange, peacock blue, red; 1918-27.	50	125
3253	Electric-outline locomotive, four wheels, stamped-steel body, cast-iron frame; various colors: light brown, orange, green; 1918-25.	90	200
3254	Electric-outline locomotive, four wheels, stamped-steel body, various frame types; various colors: orange, red, maroon; 1925-28.	90	200
3255	Electric-outline locomotive, eight wheels, stamped-steel body, various frame types.		
	(A) Various colors, cast-iron frame.	125	300
	(B) Orange, black stamped-steel frame.	75	200
	(C) Black, red stamped-steel frame.	250	400
	(D) Blue, red stamped-steel frame.	300	500
3255R	Electric-outline locomotive, four wheels, stamped-steel body, cast-iron or steel frame, 1925-30.		

		Gd	Exc
	(A) Green body, cast-iron frame.	110	300
	(B) Orange body, cast-iron frame.	75	200
	(C) Blue body, cast-iron frame.	150	300
	(D) Light brown body, cast-iron frame.	200	450
	(E) Green body, black stamped-steel frame.	150	300
	(F) Orange body, black stamped-steel frame.	100	200
3257/3257R	Electric-outline locomotive, four wheels, stamped-steel body, 1926-30.		
	(A) Gray body.	175	300
	(B) Orange body.	250	400
	(C) Light green body.	250	500
3258	Electric-outline locomotive, four wheels, stamped-steel body, 1926-30.		
	(A) Green body and roof.	60	300
	(B) White body, maroon roof.	60	200
	(C) Buff (or pale yellow) body, dark green roof.	60	200
3259	Electric-outline locomotive, four wheels, stamped-steel body, white, red roof, 1927.	225	400
3260	Electric-outline locomotive, four-wheel, stamped-steel body, 1929.		
	(A) Cadet blue body and roof.	150	300
	(B) Orange body and roof.	225	400
	(C) Dark satin blue body, black roof.	300	600
3261	Electric-outline locomotive, four-wheel, stamped-steel body, black, 1929-30.	150	300
12578	See listing under "125 Series" heading.		
12579	See listing under "125 Series" heading.		
12580	See listing under "125 Series" heading.		
12581	See listing under "125 Series" heading.		
12582	See listing under "125 Series" heading.		
12584	See listing under "125 Series" heading.		
12585	See listing under "125 Series" heading.		
37158	See listing under "125 Series" heading.		
64158	See listing under "64 Series" heading.		
64159	See listing under "64 Series" heading.		
64160	See listing under "64 Series" heading.		
64385	See listing under "64 Series" heading.		
64386	See listing under "64 Series" heading.		
64387	See listing under "64 Series" heading.		
64388	See listing under "64 Series" heading.		
64389	See listing under "64 Series" heading.		

AMT (American Model Toys)

Later "Auburn Model Trains" • Produced O Gauge Three-rail and HO Trains

AMT is best known among collectors as the company that gave Lionel "a run for the money" in the early 1950s. The company was founded in 1948 by Jack Ferris, who had been involved in other train-making ventures before World War II. Ferris' son had repeatedly asked for streamline passenger cars for his layout. Ferris determined that he could produce the cars using sand-cast aluminum bodies. In the following year, AMT, now incorporated, modified production of the cars to feature extruded-aluminum bodies.

In 1952 and 1953 Lionel flooded the market with its own series of aluminum cars and thereby reasserted its strong position. Nevertheless, AMT's line grew to include a series of O Gauge plastic-body freight cars and a model of the popular EMD F-7 diesel.

AMT's rendition of the ever-popular Santa Fe war bonnet pain scheme on an F-7 diesel.

Facing Lionel's stiff competition and the realization that his business had grown faster than its capital really allowed, Ferris sold AMT to Kusan in 1954. Much of the tooling was later reused by Kusan, which is described in another section.

Additional information and listings can be found in *Greenberg's Guide to Kusan Trains* by John O. Bradshaw, which features a chapter concerning AMT history and production.

Selected O Gauge Listings

		Gd	Exc
104	Santa Fe, caboose, red, white lettering.	40	75
322	Santa Fe, F-7 diesel, powered, blue and yellow.	120	190
322	Santa Fe, F-7 diesel, non-powered (dummy), blue and yellow.	70	150
1001-1003	Pennsylvania, die-cast passenger car; value per car.	100	175
1004-1006	New York Central, die-cast passenger car; value per car.	100	175
1008	Gerber's, refrigerator car, blue and white.	25	80
3160	New York Central, RDC car, aluminum, black lettering. May be found with other names at same value.	85	160
19509	Great Northern, boxcar, tuscan, black doors.	12	40
25439	Erie, boxcar, tuscan, black doors.	12	35
51297	L & N / The Old Reliable, gondola, black.	18	60
56312	Pennsylvania Merchandise Service, boxcar, tuscan and white.	15	50
90079	Chesapeake & Ohio, caboose, red, white lettering.	60	110
174479	New York Central Pacemaker, red and gray, white lettering.	12	40

Boucher

Pronounced "Boo-shay" or "Boosh-er" • Produced Three-rail Standard Gauge Trains

An example of Boucher's handsome steam locomotives.

According to an early catalogue, the Boucher Manufacturing Company was originally organized to build scale models of yachts, freight and passenger vessels, and battleships, both for the use of naval architects and for exhibition purposes. In 1922 the company purchased the Voltamp line of 2" Gauge trains. The design was modified to match the widely-used 2-1/4" Gauge that Lionel called "Standard Gauge."

Asserting that it made "Toys that are more than just toys," Boucher emphasized the scale accuracy of its trains. Indeed, they were premium items, with the Pacific steam locomotive and tender selling for $65 in 1922.

The locomotives were made of pressed steel with enamel finishes and lacquered brass trim. In addition to locomotives and cars, Boucher's catalogue featured transformers, track, and a selection of accessories. At least a few of the accessories were manufactured by Lionel. Additionally, Boucher sold model parts for hobbyists who wished to construct their own trains.

After struggling through several years of the Great Depression, the company folded in 1934.

Selected Listings

		Gd	Exc
2100	B & O Atlantic (4-4-2) steam locomotive and tender, 14-3/4" long.	1200	2500
2105	Day coach, 18" long.	140	350
2108	B & O, boxcar, sliding door, 13-1/2" long.	60	150
2110	B & O, caboose, five windows each side, 13-1/2" long.	60	150
2140	Observation car, 18" long.	140	350
2500	B & O Pacific (4-6-2) steam locomotive and tender, 20-1/2" long.	1500	2700

Carlisle & Finch

Credited as first American manufacturer to make an electric train
Produced two-rail 1 Gauge trains

Founded in 1894, the Carlisle & Finch Company of Cincinnati, Ohio manufactured its first electric train, a four-wheel streetcar made of polished brass, in 1896. Although the first sets were made with three-rail track, Carlisle & Finch quickly switched to the two-rail system that it retained throughout production.

The company's trains were generally sold without brand identification in catalogues of large electrical supplies, such as J. Elliot Shaw & Company, Philadelphia.

For the first few years, Carlisle & Finch offered a small variety of trolley sets, but by 1901 the line had grown to include many new accessories and a greater variety of rolling stock. Carlisle & Finch addressed the high-end of the market with its elegant No. 45 locomotive, which was advertised with a shipping weight of 45 lbs. in its wooden shipping crate! A system of T-rail track and larger cars was also offered to complement the No. 45.

Carlisle & Finch steam locomotives like this 82 NYC & HR locomotive have an undisputable charm and elegance in their proportions.

It is astonishing to the contemporary collector or modeler when one realizes that these models were operated by wet-cell batteries, water-powered electric generators, and other early electrical power sources. Indeed, the electric model trains reflected the state of the art at the turn of the century.

For additional information about Carlisle & Finch, consult the upcoming *Greenberg's Guide to Other American Toy Trains, Volume II* (due out in 1991).

Selected Listings

		Gd	Exc
1	Motor car, four arched windows on side, "ELECTRIC RAILWAY" under windows, 7" long.	250	600
3	Coal mining locomotive; four-wheel steeple-top (no cab) locomotive, "ELECTRIC COAL MINING LOCOMOTIVE" on side.	220	475
4	0-4-0 locomotive with tender, "684" on cab, eight-wheel tender with "L.S. & M.S.R.R." on side, 18" combined length.	350	800
12	Boxcar, tin, eight wheels, lettered "1141 / C.B. & Q. / R R".	90	200
13	Passenger coach, lettered "ELECTRIC RAILWAY", lacquered brass, wooden floor, 12" long.	190	350
45	Atlantic (4-4-0) locomotive and tender, 27-1/2" long with tender, 1902-08.	1400	3500
46	Caboose, heavy tin, 10" long, 1908.	110	250

Dayton-Dinky

Produced a Remote-controlled 4" Gauge Train

From 1922 through (approximately) 1925, Milton and Byron Dunkelberger manufactured a unique train called the Dayton-Dinky. Advertised as a "Practical, Durable and Educational Toy," the train's novelty and claim to fame was its unique remote-control operation. Using the control box, the operator could start, stop, or reverse the locomotive, change speed, couple or uncouple, and dump the load from the cars automatically.

The locomotives were built around a simple 0-4-0 tank locomotive design (without tenders). They featured worm gear drives and electric motors. In addition to the stubby locomotive, each set featured two four-wheel cars — a flatcar and a dump car. The dump car could be remotely controlled to dump its load of coal or sand at any location.

Typical of the time, the track system consisted of wooden ties and ribbon steel rail. Atypically, the gauge was set at a rather large four inches. Perhaps the chunky size indicates Dayton-Dinky's sincerity in marketing the trains as educational toys for children.

In reflecting upon innovative items such as the Dayton-Dinky, it is not uncommon to use the phrase "ahead of its time." Within a few years of Dinky's introduction, American Flyer and Lionel introduced a number of the remote-controlled trains and accessories that are so fondly remembered today. Perhaps the phrase applies.

Selected Listings

		Gd	Exc
Locomotive	0-4-0 with remote-controlled motor, no valve gear.	500	1200
Flatcar	Four-wheel car with grooved bed.	90	200
Dump car	Four-wheel car with high-riding dump body.	90	200

Dorfan

Produced "Wide Gauge" and "Narrow Gauge" Trains
(Commonly called Standard Gauge and O Gauge)

Founded in 1924 by Milton & Julius Forchheimer, Dorfan was one of the promising train manufacturers that succumbed during the Depression. In a time when most train manufacturers promoted their products as "educational toys," Dorfan distinguished itself by making locomotives that could be readily disassembled (and reassembled) with only a screwdriver. Young enthusiasts were encouraged to disassemble their locomotives for cleaning or just to see how they work.

Dorfan also distinguished itself with its extensive use of the "Dorfan alloy," a die-casting alloy of copper and zinc. The initial strength and light weight of the alloy made it a very favorable choice initially. Unfortunately, impurities in the alloy oxidized and the metal ex-

Dorfan (cont'd)

*The 52 electric locomotive has "DORFAN LINES" in raised
letters below the windows.*

panded and cracked. Today most Dorfan castings are cracked and deteriorated. However, due to the scarcity of the items, many collectors are willing to replace defective castings with reproductions.

Dorfan is favorably remembered for its clever and thoughtful placement of passengers in the passenger cars. The die-cast cars featured highly-detailed die-cast busts that were painted as well as miniature military figures of the time. The less expensive lithographed cars featured flat lithographed figures.

Dorfan stopped production in 1934, although remaining inventory was sold for several years afterwards. Additional information about Dorfan, as well as color photographs of these interesting models, will be included in *Greenberg's Guide to Other American Toy Trains, Volume III* (due out in 1991).

Selected Listings

		Gd	Exc
52	"Take-Apart" electric locomotive, Narrow Gauge, var. colors, 6-1/2".	100	190
156	Steam locomotive, Narrow Gauge, windup, black, 11-1/4" long.	100	225
470	Dorfan Lines, coach, Narrow Gauge, lithographed, green or red.	25	45
600	CCC & St L, gondola, Narrow Gauge, lithographed, yellow/tan.	20	40
602	Union Pacific, boxcar, Narrow Gauge, lithographed, green.	20	40
606	Pennsylvania, caboose, Narrow Gauge, lithographed, red.	25	40
785	Pullman, Wide Gauge, olive green, 13-1/4" long, 1928-29.	80	150
800	New York Central, gondola, Wide Gauge, orange, 1928-30.	85	200
801	Santa Fe, boxcar, Wide Gauge, green, 1928-30.	85	190
806	Pennsylvania, caboose, Wide Gauge, brown, 1928-30.	125	225
3920	"Loco Builder" electric engine, Wide Gauge, various colors, 13" long.	350	800
3930	"Loco Builder" electric-outline engine, Wide Gauge, various colors.	550	1000

Elektoy

Produced Three-rail 1 Gauge (1-3/4") Trains

For a few years before World War I, the J. K. Osborne Manufacturing Company produced a series of nicely-detailed models using the tradename Elektoy. Some sources give the production dates of 1911-1913, while others cite 1910-1917. In any case, the Elektoy line did not reappear after the wartime limitations on raw materials were lifted.

Constructed primarily of stamped-metal parts, Elektoy's trains are described by collectors as having a certain finesse and attention to detail. They were offered to compete with 1 Gauge models then offered by Ives and German companies, such as Bing and Märklin. Sales were made through Osborne's five distributors, which serviced small hardware and electrical supply shops. Unlike the big-name trains, Elektoy models were not sold in department stores.

Many of the trim and ornamental parts of the Elektoy trains were heavily nickel plated and polished to a bright lustre. Cars were lithographed in a variety of attractive colors. Additional details, such as sliding doors and brakewheels, made the cars more realistic. The locomotives were small steam-outline 0-4-0s cleverly designed for easy servicing.

Additional information about Elektoy will be presented in *Greenberg's Guide to Other American Toy Trains, Volume II* (due out in 1991).

The 903 tank locomotive exemplifies the attractive proportions and polished nickel trim common to Elektoy trains. L. Archer, Jr. Collection.

Selected Listings

		Gd	Exc
Note: Numbers listed are catalogue numbers; the numbers on the trains may differ.			
901	Four-wheel trolley, "PUBLIC SERVICE", four-color finish.	200	500
902	Eight-wheel trolley, "PUBLIC SERVICE", four-color finish.	250	600
903	Tank locomotive (without tender), black, nickel trim.	300	750
907	Hopper car, black or maroon, 8-1/2" long.	30	75
910	Cattle car, sliding doors, various colors.	30	75
911	Boxcar, lithographed, 9-3/4" long.	30	75
912	Caboose, yellow or red, 8-1/2" long.	30	75
914	Combine, lithographed, metal trim, 10" long.	35	80
915	Pullman, lithographed, metal trim, 10" long.	35	80

Hafner

Produced Two-rail O Gauge Windup Trains • Used "Overland Flyer" Markings

In 1900 or 1901 William Hafner formed the Hafner Company to manufacture mechanical toys. Hafner continued to tinker and succeeded in fitting a clockwork motor into a cast-iron locomotive shell in 1905. In 1907 he joined with Edmonds-Metzel Manufacturing Company, which changed its name to American Flyer Manufacturing Company in 1910.

From 1907 to 1914, the company produced Hafner-designed O Gauge mechanical trains with great success. In 1914 Hafner broke away from American Flyer to form his own company. He sold his trains with "Overland Flyer" markings, which has led some train collectors to mistake them for American Flyer trains of the time.

Hafner was one of the few toy train firms to survive the Depression. In order to economize during these rough times, the company often purchased rejected tin bottle cap stock. As a result, quite a few Hafner trains will have unusual printing — describing soft drinks, juices, etc. — inside or underneath. Hafner also recycled its own reject material, so a lithographed car may have another lithographed design inside. These occurrences have little or no effect on the values of the items as collectibles.

During World War II, production was suspended. Founder William Hafner retired in 1944, leaving his son John to run the company. In 1951 John retired and sold the company to the All Metal Products Company of Wyandotte, Michigan, the maker of Wyandotte Toys. In 1956 Wyandotte filed for bankruptcy. Louis Marx & Company eventually purchased the Hafner tooling and shipped it to Mexico, where production continued for several years.

Additional information about Hafner will be presented in *Greenberg's Guide to Other American Toy Trains, Volume II* (due out in 1991).

Selected Listings

		Gd	Exc
No Number	Various windup locomotives, cast-iron, without numbers.	20	45
1010	Hafner, tank car, lithographed, silver or orange.	6	15
1110	Locomotive, lithographed, red, marked "1110".	50	110
1180	Overland Flyer, tender.	25	50
2000	Hafner Trains, locomotive, lithographed, multi-color.	8	20
4825	ATSF, refrigerator car, lithographed, cream.	6	12
31320	Overland Flyer, boxcar, lithographed.	40	80
91876	Hafner Trains, sand car, various colors.	3	8
115041	Locomotive, lithographed, yellow, blue, orange, and silver.	8	15
M-10000	Union Pacific streamline, power unit.	30	75
M-10000	Union Pacific streamline, matching cars, each:	15	35
Hafner's Streamliners	Passenger cars, various colors.	12	25
Overland Flyer	Passenger cars, various colors.	15	30
Sunshine Special	Passenger cars, several varieties.	20	40
Toy Mfgs USA	Special passenger car for American toys.	75	175

Hoge

Produced O Gauge Trains, Including "Tom Thumb" Series

The 900 streamline train is probably the most familiar of Hoge trains.

Hoge is one of the numerous non-train toy firms that ventured at least briefly into the toy train field. In 1930-1931 Hoge introduced a line of inexpensive lithographed trains sold as the "Tom Thumb Railroad." The series included an electric-outline locomotive, a passenger car, a boxcar, and a caboose — all with the same basic proportions! There was also a steam locomotive with brass details.

The company also produced a circus train with a Vanderbilt-type locomotive and animated livestock cars.

In 1938 Hoge introduced a series of larger trains, including a larger Vanderbilt steam locomotive and two different streamline trains. In the following year, Hoge discontinued its venture into the highly-competitive train field and returned to the production of its other toys.

Selected Listings

		Gd	Exc
900	U.S. Mail, streamline power unit, chrome and blue.	125	275
900	Hoge Stream Line, coach, chrome and blue, 8" long.	40	80
900	Hoge Streat Line, observation, chrome and blue, 9" long.	40	80
990	Tom Thumb Railroad, steam locomotive, 0-4-0, black.	50	125
990	Tom Thumb Railroad, four-wheel tender, black.	15	40
990	Tom Thumb Railroad, Pullman, blue-green.	15	40
990	Tom Thumb Railroad, observation car, blue-green.	15	40
1000	Vanderbilt steam locomotive with articulated tender.	40	90
1901	Tom Thumb Railroad, gondola, green, yellow, and black.	10	30
1902	Tom Thumb Railroad, boxcar, brown and yellow.	10	30
1903	Tom Thumb Railroad, tank car, pink, red, and green.	10	30

Hornby

Formerly Manufactured Tinplate Trains for American Market

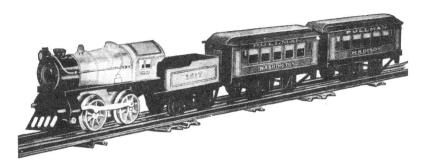

Although very successful in Britain and Europe, Hornby had only a brief span of production for the American toy market.

Hornby is the oldest British manufacturer of toy and model trains. Today it offers a line of HO/OO scale model trains, mostly of British prototype. In the 1920s and 1930s the company produced an extensive line of O Gauge mechanical trains.

Well known for its Meccano line of construction sets, Hornby established an American factory in 1913 to manufacture and distribute its products for the US market. During the height of the "roaring twenties" and the accompanying toy train craze, Hornby introduced its own American-style mechanical toy trains, which ran on O Gauge track. Unlike many competitive models, the Hornby locomotives featured lithographed steel bodies that were claimed as superior to the "breakable" cast-iron bodies used by others.

Unfortunately, Hornby never had much of a chance with its US tinplate trains. Competitors such as American Flyer, Hafner, and Marx had come too far. Hornby's limited selection and comparatively high prices could not offer much competition. Nor could Hornby face the Crash and Great Depression better than others.

Hornby's American tinplate trains were produced from 1927 through 1929. The Meccano construction series was purchased by American Flyer, while the tooling for the trains was returned to England, where it had some use. The 0-4-0 windup locomotives listed in the sets are all red and black. Both freight and passenger cars are of the four-wheel variety.

Selected Listings

		Gd	Exc
M-1	Passenger train, 0-4-0 windup locomotive, two passenger cars (green and gold).	125	275
M-2	Passenger train, 0-4-0 windup locomotive, two passenger cars (yellow and black).	150	300
M-3	Freight train, 0-4-0 windup locomotive, Pennsylvania boxcar, Union Tank car, and NYC caboose, various colors.	100	225

Howard

Produced 2" Gauge Two-rail Electric Trains with Head Lamps

A Howard eight-wheel passenger coach with open arched windows and a 4-2-0 steam locomotive; both are marked for "N.Y.C. & H.R.R.R."

From 1904 to 1907 the Howard Miniature Lamp Company produced a series of attractive and somewhat distinctive electric trains. The line included streetcars (very popular at the time), as well as steam and electric locomotives and a variety of cars. The company is credited with producing the first miniature electric locomotive with an operating headlight.

Howard's trains were sold through the catalogues of several electrical supply houses. The earliest models were produced of fairly light materials, including wooden cylinders, but the trains were quite sturdy by the time they were discontinued, with the later locomotives having cast-iron frames and heavier-gauge steel bodies.

Howard ceased production of electric trains during the recession of 1907. The company continued to make its other electrical products instead.

Selected Listings

		Gd	Exc
1	Four-wheel trolley, 7-1/2" long, body may be removed to operate as open freight car.	350	800
2	Electric Traction Line, trolley, interior seats, numbered "459", 12" long.	400	950
5	Steeple-cab 0-4-0 locomotive, numbered "897", 12" long.	450	1100
6	Steam locomotive, 0-4-0T, lettered "P.R.R.", 11" long.	350	750
8	Steam locomotive, 4-4-0, black, nickel trim, 21" with tender.	400	950
21	Pennsylvania, eight-wheel gondola, 9-3/4" long.	40	90
22	Pennsylvania, coach, 11-1/2" long.	40	90
25	Eight-wheel caboose, lettered "P.R.R.", 10-1/4" long.	40	90
26	Four-wheel dump car, lettered "P.R.R."	35	80

Katz

Produced "The Five-Fifteen Limited" O Gauge Trains

An appropriately small "TOM THUMB RAILROAD" gondola from the Tom Thumb series produced by Katz.

Henry Katz & Company produced an electric tinplate train that was offered in 1930 and perhaps for a few years thereafter. Constructed of attractive lithographed steel, the inexpensive "Five-Fifteen Limited" consisted of a boxcab electric- outline locomotive and two passenger cars. The locomotive had a cowcatcher and headlight at one end and a roof-mounted pantograph at the other end.

The set was advertised as "new" and "improved" in *Youth Companion* magazines of the 1930s, leading one to believe that the set may have been introduced a little earlier. We are uncertain.

Selected Listings

		Gd	Exc
515	Locomotive, lithographed, "FIVE-FIFTEEN LIMITED" above windows.	65	150
515	Coach, lithographed, "FIVE-FIFTEEN LIMITED" above windows.	15	40
521	Transformer, concealed in lithographed station building.	20	50

Knapp

Produced Two-rail, 2" Gauge Electric Trains

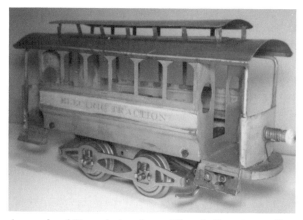

A sample of Knapp's handsome Electric Traction trolley.
L. R. Archer, Jr. Collection.

Founded in 1890, Knapp Electric & Novelty Company introduced its line of 2" Gauge trains circa 1904. Careful not to confuse the items with toys, the company's catalogue described them as "railways in miniature" for which Knapp made an entire selection of goods, including locomotives, cars, track, and transformers.

The company ceased production of its 2" Gauge trains in 1913. Later, Knapp tried the model railroad field again with a line of ready-to-run HO scale trains that was introduced in 1938. These were discontinued before or during World War II.

Selected 2" Gauge Listings

		Gd	Exc
211	Electric Traction, four-wheel trolley, 9-1/2" long.	300	750
212	Electric Traction, four-wheel trolley, dummy, 9-1/2" long.	250	600
216	Steeple cab electric locomotive, four wheels, 10-1/2" long.	400	900
232	Coal car, four-wheel design, may be lettered "N.Y.C. & H.R."	60	125
217	Steam locomotive, 0-4-0, "PENNSYLVANIA" tender, 11" long locomotive, 6" long tender.	400	900
234	Boxcar, eight-wheel design, 11" long.	60	125
236	Caboose, eight-wheel design, 11" long.	60	125

Kusan

Produced O Gauge, O27, and HO Scale Trains

In 1954 Bill McLain, president of the Kusan Corporation, purchased the tooling of AMT (described in another section) for the production of O Gauge trains. Established in the plastics business, McLain had wished to enter the toy train field and rival the likes of Lionel and American Flyer by producing low-cost train sets that he expected to sell in high volume.

Kusan designed a new AC transformer for use with the trains, as well as an innovative track system that allowed two- or three-rail operations of the O Gauge models. The company also designed a new "K-series" of trains made to be compatible with Lionel's smaller O27 trains. Kusan made its first showing at the New York Toy fair in 1955.

121834 Southern Pacific boxcar.

In the late 1950s, Kusan added novelties such as the "atomic" train to capture the imagination of its young audience. The company also added a very inexpensive four-wheel diesel to bring down the cost of its low-end sets even farther. Lionel, not really pressured by the newcomer, nevertheless responded with its own novelty trains and trains with mostly-plastic construction.

The 1960s were very difficult years for all train makers — the slot car fad and the craze for space toys (but not mere trains with rocket loads) took away the prime audience. After a consignment sale to Sears failed in 1958 (resulting in a tremendous return of unsold stock), Kusan began to dismantle its train-marketing efforts.

The year 1961 was the last year in which any of the trains would be advertised or sold. The tooling was eventually sold to Kris Model Trains of New York. For additional information, consult *Greenberg's Guide to Kusan Trains* by John O. Bradshaw.

Selected O Gauge and O27 Listings

		Gd	Exc
316	General Electric, hopper, black, white lettering.	20	50
501	C & O, four-wheel diesel switcher, blue, yellow lettering.	20	50
1500	Union Pacific, Alco diesel, yellow and dark gray, powered.	25	50
2710	Kusan, caboose, red, yellow or white lettering.	10	20
XT2716	United State Army, Alco diesel, olive drab, powered.	25	60
3206	Kusan, boxcar, red or yellow.	4	6
5066	Reading, gondola, black, white lettering.	4	6
5124	Minneapolis & St. Louis, boxcar, green, yellow lettering.	20	45
18841	Western Pacific, boxcar, tuscan, yellow and orange lettering.	60	115
121834	Southern Pacific, boxcar, silver, red and black lettering.	50	100

McCoy

Producer of Reproduction and Original Tinplate Trains

Located in Kent, Washington, McCoy Manufacturing produces Standard Gauge trains in the tinplate tradition. Originally, McCoy made reproductions of and replacement parts for Lionel trains. Later, the company introduced its own line of simple but pleasing Standard Gauge trains, which it continues to offer today.

From 1957 through 1961 McCoy offered reproductions of the desirable Lionel 2-7/8" Gauge trains. These accurately capture the proportions of the originals, while differing somewhat in the decoration. The reproductions are stamped with McCoy's name on the underside.

In 1966 McCoy introduced its own line of Standard Gauge trains with a group of freight cars featuring several colorful silk- screened designs. The cars were constructed of sturdy stamped- steel parts. Two years later, McCoy added a selection of passenger cars, including a baggage car, a combination car, and two coaches. The company also began production of its own steam and electric-outline locomotives.

In addition to its regular production, McCoy has offered a considerable number of commemorative and specialty items directed toward collectors. These include special souvenir cars for various collector conventions and attractive circus cars.

Most of the trains made by McCoy are marked in some way with the company's name. Most of the cars, for example, are either embossed or rubber stamped "McCOY MFG./KENT, WASH." Catalogue numbers are rubber stamped on the underside of many items.

Selected Listings

		Gd	Exc
1	Cascade Railroad, 4-4-0 steam locomotive, maroon, green, and red.	150	300
2	U.S. Mail, baggage car, maroon, green roof.	30	50
5	Suquamish, coach, maroon, green roof.	30	50
45	McCoy Lines, handcar, yellow, two figures.	20	40
51	Union Line, trolley, two-tone green.	50	80
250	Tin Plate Collectors, gondola, orange.	30	40
254	Knott's Berry Farm, boxcar, two-tone brown.	15	30
260	Great Northern, caboose, red.	15	30
264	Hooker Chemical, tank car, blue and black, orange logo.	15	30
285	Miller Brewing, refrigerator car, cream and red.	15	30
301	Black Diamond, log car with logs, black.	15	30

Thomas Industries

Produced O Gauge Trains During the 1950s

Jim Thomas founded Thomas Industries to produce a line of O Gauge trains that would be compatible with Lionel. Although the company never achieved great fame, Thomas did succeed in introducing an O Gauge model of the General-type steam locomotive before Lionel offered a similar model. Thus, Thomas captured the attention of numerous tinplate operators who might not have otherwise noticed the company.

Thomas produced O Gauge trains both for the scale and tinplate markets. In 1950 the company acquired the Scale-Craft & Company line of O Gauge cars. Originally located in Wenonah, New Jersey, Thomas moved to Shawnee, Michigan to expand its facilities after the Scale-Craft purchase.

If you have any of these boxes in your attic or storeroom, then you have some of the O Gauge trains made by Thomas — a little known but important manufacturer.

In addition to its General-type locomotive, Thomas distinguished itself by producing car types missing from the selection offered by Lionel, Marx, etc. For example, the big firms were usually content to place a couple of logs on a flatcar and call the combination a "log car." Thomas, however, offered an actual tinplate model of a log car, with its distinctive open framework clearly portrayed. The company's tinplate items were equipped with Lionel-compatible couplers to further enhance sales.

In 1959 Jim Thomas died suddenly of a heart attack. Several of the products were manufactured by other concerns up until 1964, when the tooling was destroyed by a fire.

Selected Listings

		Gd	Exc
Flatcar	With removable stakes, tinplate.	20	55
Frisco	Wood-type gondola, tinplate operation.	20	55
General-type	Steam locomotive, 4-4-0, dark green, gold and red trim, 1953.	150	300
Operating Crane	Tinplate for use with Lionel.	35	75
Pioneer Coach	Steel body; yellow, green, or red; "1869".	35	80
Pioneer Combine	Steel body; yellow, green, or red; "1869".	35	80
Pulpwood Car	Black, tinplate car with bulkhead ends, logs.	20	55
Wabash	Wood-type gondola, tinplate operation.	20	55

Unique Lines

Produced Lithographed O Gauge Tinplate Trains • Made the "Jewel T Circus" Trains

If you remember seeing trains advertised on NBC's Howdy Doody show, you may already be familiar with Unique trains. Produced by the established Unique Art Manufacturing Company, makers of lithographed sheet-metal

One of the two units in the Rock Island AA set.

toys, Unique trains were designed to capture a portion of the highly-competitive low-end market. In fact, Unique advertised, "Electric trains, previously a high income luxury, are now available to Mr. Average Citizen for less than a ten dollar bill."

Unfortunately, two major factors limited the life span of Unique's train line, which was produced only from 1949 through 1951. First, the stiff competition of established firms such as Louis Marx & Company. Second, the shortage of materials due to the Korean War Effort and government-imposed restrictions.

The Unique line consisted of colorful and sometimes amusing lithographed O Gauge clockwork and electric trains. Some of the stamped-metal bodies were produced from modified Dorfan diework. All of the passenger and freight cars have four wheels. After 1951 Unique discontinued its train line in favor of producing its other toys and office products.

Selected Listings

		Gd	Exc
100	Unique Lines, boxcar, marked "3905", silver and blue, 7-1/2".	15	35
101	Hopper car, no number on car, orange and red.	15	35
102	City of Joplin, Pullman, blue, silver roof, passengers in windows.	65	100
102	Garden City, passenger car, blue, silver roof, passengers in windows.	75	150
105	Unique Lines, caboose, no number, red, white trim, 7-1/2" long.		
	(A) Non-animated.	20	40
	(B) Animated version with moving brakeman.	30	80
107	Unique Lines, cattle car, no number on car, red and yellow, 7-1/2" long.	50	85
109	Jewel T Circus, boxcar with animals, no numbers, red and yellow, two different variations with animals, 7-1/2" long.	55	125
109	Circus "U", high-side gondola with animals on side, red and yellow, two variations.	75	150
742	Clockwork locomotive, steam type, gray, multi-color trim.	65	100
1950	Electrically-powered locomotive, steam type, blue, gray, black and white.	65	100
2000	Rock Island, AA diesels (two-unit set).	75	200
No number	High-side gondola, no number on car, orange and red.	60	100

Voltamp

Early Manufacturer of Two-rail, 2" Gauge Trains

The Voltamp B & O Pacific (2500) is a highly accurate model.

In 1897 Manes E. Fuld, the owner of the Voltamp Electric Manufacturing Company, constructed a model train for his son to enjoy. As these stories often go, the son was not the only one impressed by the toy, so Fuld eventually decided to put the train into production.

Around 1903, Voltamp introduced its line of electric toy trains operating on 2" Gauge track. They were contemporary to other electric train manufacturers such as Carlisle & Finch and the early Lionel, but Voltamp never gained widespread distribution of its product line. In fact, Voltamp was the fortunate beneficiary of a strong regional interest in the company's trains, which included many designs based on Baltimore-area trains and streetcars.

Among the trains were models of elegant B & O steam locomotives, B & O electric locomotives (then new on the real railroad, which used them for tunnel operation), and local street cars. The trains were constructed mostly of stamped-steel parts with cast-iron trucks and durable motors. Voltamp also made accessories such as signals, bridges, lamp posts, and trolley poles to complement the trains. Additionally, the company offered many of its component parts individually for adventurous modelers who were building or modifying their own trains.

In 1922 Voltamp sold the entire train line to Boucher (covered in another section). Boucher modified the line to match the 2-1/4" track gauge that Lionel had popularized by this time. For additional information about Voltamp, see *Greenberg's Guide to Other American Toy Trains, Volume II* (due out in 1991).

Selected Listings

		Gd	Exc
2100	B & O, 4-4-0 steam locomotive and tender, 25" long total.	1500	3500
2123	Double-truck trolley, lettered "UNITED ELECTRIC", powered.	700	1200
2125	Double-truck trolley, similar but non-powered trailer.	600	1100
2126	B & O, four-wheel gondola car, 8-1/2" long.	100	225
2127	B & O, four-wheel dump car, 7-1/2" long.	100	225
2129	B & O, four-wheel caboose, 9-3/4" long.	100	225
2130	B & O, steeple-cab electric locomotive, four wheels.	500	1100
2219	New York & Washington, coach, 10" long.	110	250
2500	B & O, 4-6-2 steam locomotive and tender.	1500	3500

Williams

Reproduction and Original Trains; Standard Gauge and O Gauge

Founded in December 1971 by Jerry Williams, Williams Reproductions Limited first introduced a series of reproduction models based on rare and/or desirable trains from the bygone years of tinplate production. Originally, Williams focused on Standard Gauge, in which it produced reproductions of the Ives 1694 electric, the Lionel 9 electric, and the Lionel 381 electric locomotives. These accurate and attractive models captured the impressive look of the originals, while bringing them within the financial reach of the average collector. None of these early reproductions included motors. However replacement and original motors have frequently been added by their owners.

As the company grew, the line of reproductions grew to include models of Lionel's everpopular O Gauge "Madison" cars (Lionel 2625, 2627, and 2628). Overwhelmed by the response, Williams created several original cars — baggage, combine, and observation — to complement the Madison cars.

Williams also produced a set of O Gauge aluminum cars that proved very popular and led to the creation of the company's original E-60 electric locomotive, which operators used as motive power for their sets. The company continued to introduce new items, and, through Andy Kriswalus, purchased some of the old Kusan dies for use in an attempt to enter the mass market.

Eventually Williams abandoned the production of its Standard Gauge reproductions, which are now made by Mike's Train House, in order to focus on its O Gauge products, including a successful line of premium, hand-crafted brass models made in the Orient. For additional information, please refer to *The Story of Williams Electric Trains*, A Greenberg Publication, by John Hubbard.

Selected Listings

		Exc	Mint
9	Lionel reproduction locomotive, Standard Gauge, steel, various colors, with motor.	250	350
381	Lionel reproduction locomotive, Standard Gauge, steel, two- tone green, with motor.	325	450
960	Amtrak, E-60 locomotive, O Gauge, silver.	85	125
1694	Lionel/Ives reproduction locomotive, O Gauge, stamped steel, maroon or silver.	190	350
2321	Lackawanna, F-M Trainmaster diesel, maroon and gray.	150	275
2621	Pennsylvania "MADISON" car, O Gauge, plastic, tuscan.	30	50

Glossary

0-4-0: this designation refers to the arrangement of wheels on a locomotive. The first numeral indicates the number of small leading wheels; second numeral indicates the number of driving wheels; third numeral indicates the number of small trailing wheels.

4-6-2: another wheel designation; in this example the locomotive has four leading wheels, six driving wheels, and two trailing wheels.

A unit: lead unit for certain diesel locomotive designs, such as F-3 diesels; has cab for crew.

AA: combination of two A unit locomotives.

AB: combination of an A and B unit.

ABA: combination of an A unit, a B unit, and a second A unit.

Alco: manufacturer of locomotives for full-size railroads; made the FA and PA units popularized in miniature by Lionel and American Flyer respectively.

articulated: adjective used to describe cars that share a common truck; for example, two articulated cars might have a total of three trucks.

B unit: trailing unit for certain diesel locomotive designs, such as F-3 diesels; has no cab or windshield.

Bakelite: synthetic resin or plastic used in the early manufacture of toy trains.

bay window caboose: caboose with no cupola, but with extended side windows.

box cab: electric-outline locomotive with a rectangular body.

boxcar: perhaps the most familiar type of freight car; rectangular body with one or more door(s) on each side.

Budd RDC: self-propelled **R**ail **D**iesel **C**ar; resembles a passenger car.

clockwork: windup models using springs, gearing, or other features of clockwork; very common in early 20th century before widespread use of electricity.

coach: basic passenger car; usually has windows along entire length of each side.

combine: car used in passenger trains with combination of uses, such as baggage-passenger combination, or baggage-Railway Post Office combination.

couplers: mechanical devices used to connect cars; made in many different variations on toy trains.

die-cast: metal cast in a die or mold; sometimes brittle.

dummy: non-powered locomotive; for example, the B units in many AB combinations sold by toy train companies were dummies.

electric-outline: locomotive model that represents an electric locomotive as used on the real railroads; term used to distinguish between the visual design, which may be steam, diesel, or electric, and the actual toy mechanism, which may be electric or clockwork.

F-3: specific type of diesel locomotive; rounded nose, no walkways.

FAOS: F. A. O. Schwarz; famous New York store for which special trains were occasionally produced by toy manufacturers.

Fairbanks-Morse (FM): Manufacturer of locomotives for the real railroads; produced the "Trainmaster" made popular in miniature by Lionel.

frame: bottom part of a car or locomotive, to which wheels or trucks are attached.

gauge: distance between the rails; specific names are used to describe the commonly used sizes, such as O Gauge, Standard Gauge, etc.

GE: abbreviation for General Electric, manufacturer of locomotives for real railroads.

GG-1: popular electric locomotive used by the Pennsylvania Railroad; created by famed industrial designer Raymond Loewy; modeled by Lionel and others.

gondola: open-top freight car used for a variety of loads.

GP-7 or GP-9: specific types of diesel locomotives; boxy, walkways around sides.

heat-stamped: process of lettering toy trains using heat; usually makes a slight impression on plastic surface.

lithographed: process of applying paint or ink to sheet metal; commonly used by early toy manufacturers and in the production of early trains; no longer in favor, but continued in usage for low-priced items.

live steam: locomotive models that actually use steam for power; usually alcohol-burning.

Magnetraction: special design element of Lionel locomotives using magnetized components to improve traction (pulling power).

NW-2: specific type of diesel switcher modeled by Lionel.

observation: passenger car usually used at the end of a train; open platform or rounded end with large windows for "observation" of scenery by passengers.

O Gauge: the size most likely remembered by those who had toy trains in the 1950s; 2-1/4" between the rails; used extensively by Lionel; used by American Flyer only before World War II.

OO Gauge: early alternative to HO scale; popularized in Britain, where it is still used.

PA: specific type of Alco diesel locomotive; twelve wheels, long body, rounded nose; popularized in miniature by American Flyer.

powered: refers to a locomotive with a mechanism; used when necessary to distinguish between an operating locomotive and a dummy.

Pullman: specific type of passenger car originally designed by George Pullman; often used as a generic term for better-grade passenger cars.

reefer: slang term for a refrigerator car, such as those used to ship meats and other perishables.

rubber-stamped: process of lettering toy trains using rubber pads.

scale: proportion of a model to its prototype; for example, an O scale model is 1/48 actual size; therefore O scale is also referred to as 1/48 or 1:48 scale.

steam-outline: locomotive model that represents a steam-powered locomotive as used on real railroads.

steeple cab: electric-outline locomotive with profile similar to that of a steeple; i.e., ends that slope upward toward a peaked or tall cab at the center of the locomotive.

stock car: commonly called a "cattle car"; used for hauling livestock.

streamlined: locomotives and other trains featuring aerodynamic designs; highly popular in the 1930s.

switcher: type of light-duty locomotive usually used in railroad yards.

tender: commonly called a "coal car" by non-railroaders; used to haul fuel for a steam locomotive.

three-rail: track system popularized by Lionel; features two outside running rails (electrically grounded) and a single rail along the center that provides the positive current.

tinplate: toys made from tin-coated steel; also used loosely to describe items that are caricatures of real trains rather than scale models.

truck: assembly that mounts the wheels beneath a railroad car.

truss rods: steel rods used on the underframes of freight and passenger cars on early railroads; once associated with hobos, who slept on the truss rods beneath the cars.

two-rail: track arrangement similar to that used on the real roads; commonly used by American Flyer (for its S Gauge models) and by most scale model railroad manufacturers.

OTHER TOPICS COVERED BY
WALLACE-HOMESTEAD

All the following books can be purchased from your local book store, antiques dealer, or can be borrowed from your public library. Books can also be purchased directly from **Chilton Book Company, Chilton Way, Radnor, PA 19089.** Include code number, title, and price when ordering. Add applicable sales tax and **$2.00** postage and handling for the first book plus $ .50 for each additional book shipped to the same address. VISA/Mastercard orders call **1-800-345-1214** and ask for Customer Service Department (AK, HI, & PA residents call **215-964-4000** and ask for Customer Service Department). Prices and availability are subject to change without notice. Please call for a current Wallace-Homestead catalog.

COLLECTOR'S GUIDE SERIES

Code	Title/Author	Price
W5339	Collector's Guide to Baseball Cards, *Troy Kirk*	$12.95
W5479	Collector's Guide to Early Photographs, *O. Henry Mace*	$16.95
W5320	Collector's Guide to American Toy Trains, *Susan & Al Bagdade*	$16.95
W5568	Collector's Guide to Autographs, *George Sanders, Helen Sanders, and Ralph Roberts*	$16.95
W5487	Collector's Guide to Comic Books, *John Hegenberger*	$12.95

COLLECTIBLES

Code	Title/Author	Price
W5258	American Clocks and Clockmakers, *Robert W. & Harriett Swedberg*	$16.95
W4529	British Royal Commemoratives with Prices, *Audrey Zeder*	$24.95
W4464	Check the Oil: Gas Station Collectibles with Prices, *Scott Anderson*	$18.95
W4723	Clock Guide Identification with Prices, *Robert W. Miller*	$14.95
W3786	Coca-Cola Collectibles, Wallace-Homestead Price Guide to, *Deborah Goldstein Hill*	$15.95
W4235	Collectible Clothing with Prices, *Sheila Malouff*	$14.95
W0175	Collecting Antique Marbles, *Paul Baumann*	$12.95
W5460	Commercial Aviation Collectibles: An Illustrated Price Guide, *Richard Wallin*	$15.95
W5177	Contemporary Fast-Food and Drinking Glass Collectibles, *Mark E. Chase & Michael Kelly*	$16.95
W4731	Dolls, Wallace-Homestead Price Guide to, *Robert W. Miller*	$16.95
W4936	Dr. Records' Original 78 RPM Pocket Price Guide, *Peter A. Soderbergh Ph.D.*	$12.95
W5118	Food and Drink Containers and Their Prices, *Al Bergevin*	$16.95
W4901	Girl Scout Collector's Guide: 75 Years of Uniforms, Insignia, Publications & Keepsakes, *Mary Degenhardt and Judy Kirsch*	$21.95
W5185	Guide to Old Radios: Pointers, Pictures, and Prices, *David & Betty Johnson*	$16.95
W5436	Herron's Price Guide to Dolls, *R. Lane Herron*	$16.95
W0060*	Illustrated Radio Premium Catalog and Price Guide, *Tom Tumbusch*	$34.95
W5371	Jigsaw Puzzles: An Illustrated History and Price Guide, *Anne D. Williams*	$24.95
W121X*	Oil Lamps: The Kerosene Era In North America, *Catherine M. V. Thuro*	$38.95
W5312*	Petretti's Coca-Cola Collectibles Price Guide, *Allan Petretti*	$29.95
W4944	Plastic Collectibles, Wallace-Homestead Price Guide to, *Lyndi Stewart McNulty*	$17.95
W5169	Presidential and Campaign Memorabilia with Prices, Second Edition, *Stan Gores*	$18.95
W541X	Psychedelic Collectibles of the 1960s and 1970s: An Illustrated Price Guide, *Susanne White*	$21.95
W5657	Space Adventure Collectibles, *T. N. Tumbusch*	$19.95
W4154	Steiff Teddy Bears, Dolls, and Toys with Prices, *Shirley Conway & Jean Wilson*	$17.95
W538X	Steiff Toys Revisited, *Jean Wilson*	$18.95
W4847*	Thimble Collector's Encyclopedia: New International Edition, *John von Hoelle*	$35.95
W1236	Thimble Treasury, *Myrtle Lundquist*	$12.95
W3972	Tins 'N' Bins, *Robert W. & Harriett Swedberg*	$16.95
W4642	Tobacco Tins and Their Prices, *Al Bergevin*	$16.95
W5584	Tomart's Illustrated Disneyana Catalog and Price Guide, Condensed Edition, *Tom Tumbusch*	$19.95
W5576	Warman's Americana & Collectibles, *Edited by Harry L. Rinker*	$14.95
W5606	Warman's Antiques and Their Prices, 24th Edition, *Edited by Harry L. Rinker*	$13.95
W0140*	Zalkin's Handbook of Thimbles & Sewing Implements, *Estelle Zalkin*	$24.95
W4383	Yesterday's Toys with Today's Prices, *Fred and Marilyn Fintel*	$14.95